THE ULTIMATE GUIDE TO INTERNSHIPS

100 Steps to Get a Great Internship and Thrive in It

Eric Woodard

ALLWORTH PRESS
NEW YORK

Allworth Press books may be purchased in bulk at special discounts for sales promotion, corporate gifts, fund-raising, or educational purposes. Special editions can also be created to specifications. For details, contact the Special Sales Department, Allworth Press, 307 West 36th Street, 11th Floor, New York, NY 10018 or info@skyhorsepublishing.com.

20 19 18 17 16 15   5 4 3 2 1

Published by Allworth Press, an imprint of Skyhorse Publishing, Inc.
307 West 36th Street, 11th Floor, New York, NY 10018.

Allworth Press® is a registered trademark of Skyhorse Publishing, Inc.®, a Delaware corporation. www.allworth.com

Cover design by Chris Ritchie

Library of Congress Cataloging-in-Publication Data is available on file.

ISBN: 978-1-62153-438-9
Ebook ISBN: 978-1-62153-456-3

Printed in the United States of America

0352

This book is dedicated to my family, whom I love so much.

INTERNSHIP: A learning experience guided by a mentor in the workplace, which supports the academic or career goals of a student not employed there professionally.

ALSO BY ERIC WOODARD

Your Last Day of School: 56 Ways You Can Be a Great Intern and Turn Your Internship into a Job
Why Internships Are Good: The Best Education Money Can't Buy
How Do I Find an Internship?

ALL MINE

Unless stated otherwise, all ideas and opinions expressed in this book are my own—they don't necessarily reflect the beliefs of any people or organizations I have worked with or for.

Contents

PART II:
How to Thrive During Your Internship   *113*

Acknowledgments

This book includes some content from previous work but also lots of new material. It is the culmination of wisdom and support I have been blessed to receive for so long from so many. Without the support of numerous friends, colleagues, and my family—this book would not be.

I am grateful to Skyhorse Publishing for finding me and working with me to publish this book. It has been the most pleasant and wonderful surprise to work with them on this project.

Additionally, I would very much like to thank the legions of interns I've had over the years. So often, regardless of whether I was a good manager or not, their excellent work demonstrated to me time after time how great interns can be a force of nature when it comes to serving others and making a positive impact in the world. Thank you, my former interns. You know who you are.

I would also like to thank First Lady/Senator/Secretary Hillary Rodham Clinton for showing me what it means to be a great leader and accepting me as one of her interns so long ago. I also want to thank all the fantastic colleagues I had the pleasure to work with over the years in Hillaryland. It is there that I started as an intern and learned how to be a pro. If you're reading this and you served with me in the

White House, the Senate, or the State Department, I'm talking about you.

It goes without saying that I am also so grateful to the many fantastic people I learn so much from every day at the Smithsonian.

This book is dedicated to my family. So much of what I know, who I am, and what I can do is a credit to my parents who I love so much, John and Dixie Woodard.

Massive appreciation goes to my sweet, smart, and beautiful daughter Piper, and my indomitable, brave, amazing sons Fletch and Deacon. The only reason I was able to work on this book with three toddlers in the house is because they are such fantastic kids.

Last, I want to acknowledge that this book would not have been possible without the encouragement, inspiration, advice, and love of my beautiful smart, fearless, fantastic wife Keri. Because of her, my life is so full, and I learn so much. I'd be her intern anytime.

Introduction

"You are about to embark upon the Great Crusade, toward which we have striven these many months. The eyes of the world are upon you."
—Dwight D. Eisenhower

Are you about to take that great leap between school and work? If so, listen up.

If you are anything like I was when I took my first steps into the working world, you are bursting at the seams to take that leap. It feels like you should be ready for this moment, but you wonder, "Am I prepared?" As you approach the academic finish line, you feel like you've done more than enough to earn the world's respect without question. But are you getting the respect you feel you deserve? As you leap into the working world, will you land on your feet?

There is a persistent meta-narrative out there that says, "Study hard, follow the rules, and you will be successful!" Until fairly recently, that might have been good advice. But, increasingly, one need only look around to recognize how such promises now ring hollow. Young professionals trying to bridge the divide between school and work cannot rely on that narrative anymore. In recent years, unemployment for those between the ages of twenty and twenty-four has had a pesky habit of running at least twice as high as unemployment among everybody else. Those numbers are pretty daunting if you're a young person headed into the workplace. Even more, if you've spent zillions of dollars to go to school and are in debt up to your eyeballs, you could be asking yourself, "OMG! Was this all worth it?!? How am I ever going to repay all this money!?"

Don't panic. It was all worth it. However, I'm afraid I have some bad news for you. *To excel in today's competitive work world, all those years in the classroom alone aren't enough. You need something more. Most young people leaping into today's job market lack two things: a niche and career capital.*

A niche is your specialty. The thing you are the best in the world at. Don't get me wrong, it's great to be well rounded so you can make all those little cross-disciplinary connections that others may miss. But you also need to have a specialty. The thing that you are known for. Thomas Huxley once said, "An educated man should know everything about something and something about everything." Nowadays lots of young professionals are pretty good at knowing something about everything, but very few know everything about something. To succeed in today's working world, you need to know everything about something. That is your niche.

Career capital is the evidence to show that you do know everything about something and that you can offer more value in a particular area than anybody else. Plenty of young professionals today focus on the passion they have in a specific area. Passion is great and can fuel lifelong devotion to a specific subject. But in the working world, passion is not enough by itself. You also need to build career capital.

How do you establish a niche and get career capital? You get an internship, and you crush it. That is what this book is all about.

Being the clueless new person on the first day of the job has a long tradition. In the past, it has been understood that most people rarely know what the hell they are doing on their first day. There was a time when employers generally assumed that a new hire's first several years on the job would be mostly on-the-job training. At that time, it was more acceptable because once hired, the trend was that most employees might remain with the same organization for their whole career.

However, those days are over. For most employers the luxury of the long on-the-job learning curve is now too expensive. Today's employers need workers who are ready to go out of the box. In this case, the box is school. Employers expect and require that new employees are ready to go with at least some career capital in a specific niche on day one. Nowadays, most on-the-job training takes the form of an internship.

But most people are behind. Well-meaning educators never received a memo to say that college was the place where students now need to define a niche and gather career capital, but that's now the situation and schools are working to catch up. Some students are understandably resentful that after so much school, they still seem unready for the working world.

But for you, my friend, this represents an amazing opportunity. I honor you for picking up this book because, in doing so, you have done what 99.9 percent of your job market competitors will not—you have decided to use an internship as a springboard into the working world in the most effective way possible. Calling something the "ultimate guide" to internships is a tall order. But that is what this book is—a ton of very practical advice and tactics that will help you accelerate your career success through an internship faster than you thought possible.

It's worth mentioning that internships have a lot of cousins. A recent study by Gardner and Bartkus identified eleven different types of work education experiences delivered in six different ways such as apprenticeships, practicums, cooperative learning, service learning, and externships, in addition to internships. While the ideas offered here are specifically aimed at how to get an internship and then thrive during it, they might apply just as well to other work-based learning experiences.

In this book I'll show you how to get the internship you want and how to be a fantastic intern once you do. I'll reveal secrets that most internship supervisors never talk about, and I'll teach you tricks about the workplace that nobody ever learns in school. The cool stuff I offer here is based on years as both an intern and an intern supervisor. This information is candid, specific, powerful, and unique; you won't find it anyplace else. The books I like to read the most are by authors who write the way they talk. I have done my best to write this book that way. My focus is not to create high literature but to give you useful, actionable information. Admittedly, I have not included a lot of references or statistics here. Rather, the tips I offer here are largely based on my own expertise and firsthand experience. These techniques worked for me and countless interns I have mentored, and they will work for you.

In 1997, I landed an internship at the White House, and within a year I was able to turn that opportunity into a full-time job. Since then I've supervised hundreds of students pursuing internships with some of the most competitive programs in the country. Through trial and error, and lots of hard work, it's taken me over fifteen years to put together many of the internship lessons I offer here; all you have to do is read this book! I sure wish I'd had access to this knowledge when I started as an intern. I am so excited you do.

Whether you're trying to find an internship, about to start your first internship, or midway through your tenth internship, I guarantee that this information will help you by leaps and bounds. Many of the ideas discussed are practical, actionable steps you can take that will not only make you stand out way above the crowd but also will earn your colleagues' respect. Let me show you a path to being a highly successful, extremely hirable intern that is easy and possible to start NOW.

As I will explain, *this book is about getting an unfair advantage.* Part I explains how you can stack the deck in your favor when trying to get an internship, and Part II explains how you can get an unfair advantage when trying to be successful during an internship. But in order to do either of those things, it will help to first understand a little bit about where I'm coming from and what internships actually are. So, that's where we will begin.

1

Some Advice about Career Advice

"When you do the common things in life in an uncommon way, you will command the attention of the world."

—George Washington Carver

In this book I'm going to offer you a bunch of career advice. But, before I do, the most important career advice I can offer is this: *anything you do with your résumé or your internship application, or how you present yourself, or your performance during your internship must be your own.* It must be genuine. Because if it's not, people will usually be able to tell and, when they do, they will tend to run away from you.

If some of the ideas I offer in this book don't match your style, you shouldn't follow my advice exactly. Instead, take the idea and convert it to the way you might do it. Make it your own.

It's also worth noting that the advice I offer here is just one person's (my own) opinion; I could be wrong. Of course, I don't think I am. If I thought I was wrong I wouldn't be writing all this stuff. However, you should decide for yourself. As you proceed in your career it can never hurt to get lots of advice from lots of people. But again, the advice you choose to follow in the end must be your choice.

2

A Brief History of Internships

"History will be kind to me for I intend to write it."

—Winston Churchill

A 2013 study by internships.com found that over two-thirds of U.S. college undergraduates completed at least one internship before graduating. This means that in the United States, over one million college students are doing an internship every year—and that doesn't even include high school, vocational, and graduate students and those not enrolled in school who do internships every year too. In their modern form, internships are as big as they have ever been.

But the roots of what we recognize as an internship today go way back. My friend Michael True of Messiah College pointed out to me that one of the earliest references to internships can be actually be found in the Code of Hammurabi from ancient Babylon, which stated that "if an artisan take a son for adoption and teach him his handicraft, one may not bring claim for him." By the eleventh and twelfth centuries, master craftsmen belonging to the European trade guilds took on apprentices who became journeymen and, in time, master craftsmen themselves. These traditions were carried to America by European settlers such that by 1776, many signers of the Declaration of Independence—including

Franklin, Washington, Jefferson, and Adams—had started their careers by doing apprenticeships.

By the beginning of the twentieth century, apprenticeships in the United States continued to thrive as a way to transfer occupational skills and knowledge from one generation to the next. In 1911 Wisconsin became the first state to pass legislation that created an organized system of apprenticeships, and in 1939 the U.S. Congress passed a National Apprenticeship Act. During this period, American Pragmatists like John Dewey and Eduard Lindeman wrote about the importance of informal education outside the classroom for both life and work. It was also around this time that the word *intern* first started to be used in the United States to describe a medical physician who had received a medical degree but did not yet have enough practical experience or a license to practice medicine. Since that time, the concept of the internship has grown beyond just the medical context into the ubiquitous multidisciplinary American institution it is today: an informal learning experience in the workplace, which supports the academic or career goals of students not employed there professionally but guided by staff mentors who are.

3

Internships Today

"CNN had 25,000 applicants for five intern jobs."

—Larry King

Though different stakeholders offer a variety of definitions, *modern internships represent a crossroads between students, educators, and employers.* A 2011 study by the U.S. Department of Labor found that employers increasingly perceived a decline in soft skills—the ability to work and get along with others—among potential new hires. In this same vein, a 2014 survey by Los Angeles found that 55 percent of Fortune 500 hiring managers felt that being able to work well with others was essential for new hires, while only 6 percent believed new hires having strong technical skills like math and statistics were important. While employers want their new hires to have soft skills, recruiting young professionals who have these skills is increasingly more difficult to do. Hosting interns is one way employers can both screen for and cultivate soft skills among potential new employees.

However, these soft skills are often difficult to cultivate in a formal classroom environment. So, colleges and universities have increasingly pushed their students to seek out high-quality mentor-based internships because research shows that such experiences strengthen students' overall education and ultimate employability.

SOFT SKILLS

One of the most important things you will develop and/or hone during your internship are soft skills.

What are soft skills? They are a little hard to define, but when I say *soft skills* I basically mean interpersonal skills, leadership skills, empathy. *Soft skills have to do with one of the most important pieces of advice I have ever received: that one should always deal with people where they are and not where you want them to be.*

You, of course, already have these skills from the time you have spent on this earth before an internship. However, there is perhaps no more important place to wield soft skills than the workplace. If an internship is your first foray into a workplace, it may be your first opportunity to really focus on soft skills.

As you interact with staff and other interns, be mindful about how your soft skills are getting better. During your internship, you will learn nothing that is more important.

Meanwhile, students are interested in internships for a variety of reasons related to both their own professional development and their developing a better understanding about how the working world works. They may dive into an internship as a way to explore career possibilities or simply to build up work experience on their résumé. In some cases, especially where a student has already identified a career path, internships may also allow one access to specific networks or communities of practice relevant to their professional aspirations.

But for all three—employers, educators, and students—*the main purpose of internships is related to education.* In recent years, especially during economically challenging times, this perspective on internships as a means of education has sometimes been lost. Instead of focusing on internships as a vehicle for education, some view internships as just another form of employment—criticizing internships as an economic issue rather than viewing it as an educational one. I fear this mind-set is very limiting for young professionals who are convinced by it because those who dismiss internships as just a form of unpaid or low-paid work may miss out on vital learning opportunities.

4

Paid or Unpaid?

"An investment in knowledge pays the best interest."
—Benjamin Franklin

This can be a controversial topic, so I might as well share my take on it so you can decide whether I'm crazy or not and if you want to keep reading this book. Like I said before, for me, internships are all about education.

Some internships come with a scholarship paid in the form of a stipend, some do not. According to the IRS (see Publication 970), by definition, scholarship payments are meant to help defray living expenses during tenure of study, not as salaried compensation. Internships that offer funds to help support an intern engaged in learning during an internship are great. For some students, stipends make the difference between whether a student can accept an internship opportunity or not. No doubt, just like we need more funding for education across the board, we also need more funds out there to support internships.

On the other hand, *if an intern receives payment as compensation, tax-wise they become a salaried employee just like every other salaried employee.* In such cases there isn't necessarily any educational component involved.

As a result, some positions labeled as *internships* are really just short-term jobs that don't necessarily have anything to do with learning. In my opinion, this is too bad, because the thing that makes internships special is that they should be all about learning.

When students hand in papers to teachers, they are not paid for the schoolwork they do. When a professor starts assigning too many assignments, there are no union representatives that step in to mediate. There is no collective bargaining in the classroom because school is about education, not labor; *just because internships take place in the workplace does not mean they have anything less to do with education.*

As so many have experienced firsthand, a real internship is a learning experience guided by a mentor where a young professional has an opportunity to pick up knowledge and skills that can only be accessed in the working world. *Are some internships exploitative? Sure. However, the issue has little to do with pay, and exploitation is certainly not exclusive to the world of internships.* In such cases, educators must continue to make strides to ensure that all internships represent great learning experiences. Where there is no mentorship, an intern receiving pay learns just as little as an intern receiving no pay. The minimum wage an intern may or may not receive during and internship is secondary compared to the educational benefits an intern can receive during a good internship.

How do I know this to be true? As they do every year, I see thousands of summer interns descend on Washington, DC. Some will be paid, some will not. But yet they all come, from a diversity of communities across the nation and around the world, because their teachers, their parents, and the incoming interns themselves know that through these internships they will have a chance to learn lessons they are not taught in school. Contrary to what some critics claim, these interns are not displacing any employees. Every summer interns come and go, and Washington keeps on humming without any massive layoffs or hiring sprees to compensate. While they are here, Washington interns do not perform jobs or displace workers: they learn.

Some critics protest internships because they say it is much easier for students with means to take advantage of unpaid internships while disadvantaged students are left out. While this may be true, it is certainly not unique to internships. Underserved students face extra challenges at many places along the path to college. The only difference with internships is that, while many schools charge tuition, most internships do not.

Moreover, there are numerous internship programs that are specifically designed to reach out to underrepresented and underserved students. In fact, the U.S. Office of Personnel Management actually cites internships as a way federal agencies can promote diversity and inclusion through the unique access these programs provide.

Those who fight against inequality and advocate for the vital importance of people receiving a full living wage understand that maintaining a vibrant middle class truly hinges on access to education (see Robert Reich's great documentary *Inequality for All*) not the minimum wage that interns may or may not receive during the relatively short duration of an internship. Requiring employers who offer high-quality mentorship-based internships to pay interns (or threatening them with lawsuits if they do not) could lead to the chilling possibility that employers will just stop offering these life-changing educational opportunities.

That would be a real shame. If internships started to disappear because of focus on pay over education, so many students from all walks of life would learn less and miss out. The internship I did taught me so much and changed my life for the better. I take great satisfaction in knowing an abundance of these opportunities, paid or not, remain open for so many young people starting out today. *Internships are about education, not pay, because some lessons are priceless.*

On the other hand, I feel very happy for those young professionals who approach internships as learning experiences and have seen the benefits that come from this mind-set firsthand. Are there some internships that wind up not being great learning experiences? Of course, and we will get into how to handle situations like that a little further on. But if you focus on an internship as a learning opportunity (presumably, if you're still reading this, you do) rather than a form of unavoidable, indentured student servitude, it may wind up being a great opportunity for you. Moreover, you can take satisfaction in knowing that for every one of your peers who dismisses internships, there is one less competitor out there for you.

5

Understand That They Don't Teach You Everything in School

"Ready are you? What know you of ready?"

—Yoda

When it comes to the working world, you don't have a clue. Sorry, I know that sounds harsh—but if you're currently in school or just out of school, it's true. Why are you clueless? Because *they don't teach you everything in school.*

The thing that drives me crazy is that even though the rules of the working world are actually pretty straightforward, young professionals making the transition between work and school just seem to have damn few opportunities to learn about these rules. I think this may have at least a little bit to do with the fact that those who care the most about students' education—their teachers—are often, by nature, oriented toward theory and academics such that they themselves are not up to speed on the latest dynamics of the working world. On the other hand, the people who have the working world knowledge that students need—seasoned professionals—tend not see educating young people as their responsibility.

There are many seasoned professionals who maintain a sense that they paid their dues in the working world when they were young and now you should too. This is a very old-fashioned attitude, but it's there. On the other hand, the good news is that there are other seasoned professionals who remember that people helped them when they were young, and now they feel an obligation to pay it forward. These are the kinds of mentors you should look for.

As a young professional entering the working world, it is important for you to understand this dynamic: that there are some pros out there who can be fantastic mentors and some who cannot.

Not only has your formal education not offered you everything you need to succeed in the working world, but more than that, some professionals you encounter in the working world are intentionally not going to help you fill the gap. However, if you (1) keep a lookout for the other kind of mentor—the sort that is interested in helping—and (2) learn how to manage the more old-fashioned colleagues and supervisors you encounter at work, you can master the universe.

On your first day of school, before you got into the heavy stuff (counting, right hand/left hand, nap time, etc.), I bet your teacher spent some time teaching you how to learn, right? I know that's how it was for me. My first day of kindergarten was a little scary, but Mrs. Guy took the time to make sure everybody knew where to go, what the rules were, and that everybody in the class was special. All through that first year I learned how to keep my stuff together, how to treat my classmates, and countless other things about how to thrive in the classroom. All that stuff worked great for about the next sixteen years. But then, something happened to me and, if it hasn't already, it will happen to you too. I left the classroom. Oops.

It is unbelievable to me how much time, money, and care we put into educating young people so they will be prepared for the real world. But then, we spend almost NO time teaching students about real life work. *Dtow!* It feels like I should have had a V8. Most who walk down the commencement aisle (high school, and especially college) feel ready to take on the world! Did you feel that way? I know I did. But during school, how many courses were you required to take called "how to find work" or "how to choose a profession"? How many lectures did you attend regarding what you should expect or how to act in the workplace? My guess: not too many.

That's a tragedy because students entering the workplace today are some of the most skilled, energetic, and talented in history. Newly minted "grown-ups" today have more opportunities to reach their full potential than ever before!

Kate is a promising young woman I know who, after four years of tremendous dedication and hard work, is about to graduate from college. Once she takes that final exam and turns in that final paper, she's not sure exactly what she'll do. But she has over $75,000 in student debt and even though her parents are incredibly supportive, she feels a lot of pressure to find a job. In fact to her, almost any job would do.

After all that time in school, Kate is just bursting to be a full-fledged grown-up, to be independent, to meet expectations, and to be respected. Kate knows all her hard work is supposed to pay off somehow—people have been assuring her of this her whole life—but she's just not sure how and nobody has really explained it to her. I know so many students who are in the exact same boat as Kate.

Have you ever known somebody who was a professional student? It's understandable why some take refuge in school. After all the time the average student spends in school, it's comfortable, it's known— most of us get to be pretty good at school.

To be fair, I'm not the only one to recognize the need for students to know more about the workplace before they leave the classroom. Plenty of schools encourage their students to get internships—which is great! But they get the transition all wrong.

6

My Internship Story

"Not all who wander are lost."

—J. R. R. Tolkien

When I emerged from the classroom, I was pretty much a poster child for somebody that didn't really have a clue about how the working world worked. During the early days of my career I was pretty clueless and followed an especially random path.

I grew up as an expatriate kid in Bangkok, Thailand. My dad did community development training for the Thai government, and my mom taught at the International School of Bangkok, where I went to school. Bangkok was an *awesome* place to grow up, and my closest friends in the world are still the ones I made there.

By the time I graduated from high school I knew a lot about the world, but not much about the working world, and not very much about living in the States. I looked and sounded American, but I'd never really lived in the United States. American slang sometimes got the better of me.

I remember my first summer back in the United States—in Missouri—I got a part-time lifeguard job at a local swimming pool. Before reporting to work on the first day, I asked the pool supervisor over the phone if there was anything special I might need for the first day of work. She replied, "Just your swim trunks and plenty of elbow grease."

Assuming that "elbow grease" was some kind of special suntan lotion for lifeguards, I proceeded directly to the nearest Walmart where I searched relentlessly up and down the aisles until finally a sales associate asked, "Young man, can I help you?" When I told her I was searching for elbow grease she looked at me like I was a mental patient. I was a little bit lost, to say the least.

As I headed off to my freshman year of college, my disorientation continued from there. Over the next four and a half years, I transferred colleges *seven times*. I wound up attending schools in Illinois, Missouri, Oklahoma, Hawaii, and Guam. Finding a college where I could fit in was a real struggle for me. I had moved around so much; it was really hard to know where I belonged.

After all that, I was frazzled. I felt like I needed to get away from it all. So, I packed up my gear and headed back to Guam to be a scuba instructor. This was about as far away from the typical office setting as you can imagine. In fact, I remember when flying into Guam, a flight attendant remarked to me how beautiful the water looked from the air. I explained to her with a smile, "I know. That's my office." I went from school, to a school of fish.

I wound up diving on Guam for the next three years. My hair grew out into this giant sun bleached crown of curls, and I rarely wore shoes. I literally spent thousands of hours underwater with the fish and the octopuses and the puffer fish and the turtles. It wound up being thousands of hours of therapy.

By the time I was twenty-four, I started to get my bearings. Getting through college had been so hard for me, I felt like I needed to do something to show for it. Spending hours under the sea was fun, but I was restless to use my brain. So, I thought to myself, "Where would be the most prestigious, respectable place I could work?" My answer: the White House.

I had always loved politics and public service. But, as a salty dog on the sea, I had no idea how I might get to the White House. It was literally on the other side of the earth. This was in the mid-'90s, when the Internet was just starting to get off the ground. Information online was still scarce and Guam was far, far way.

So, I sat down and wrote a letter. Something along the lines of, "Dear White House, how can I come help out?" I slapped a stamp on it, drove my beat-up green Suzuki Samurai to the Guam post office, put it in the mail, and figured I'd never hear back. But I was starting to get inspired. So, I sent off a bunch more letters to graduate schools asking for their application info. I figured that maybe something would come through.

Over the next couple of months, I started to get catalogs and application forms from all sorts of graduate schools. To my great shock, I also heard back from the White House. They sent me an official White House internship application in an official White House envelope. At that point, I had never really heard of such a thing as an internship, but it sounded pretty good to me.

Having transferred colleges so many times, one thing I did become very good at was filling out applications. So, still in my scuba-fied state, I started filling out a ton of applications to graduate schools and, on

---

LANDING IN A NEW PLACE TO DO YOUR INTERNSHIP

You may be in a situation where, in order to do an internship, you will need to travel to a new place. Sometimes, the work and extra costs associated with setting up shop in a new place discourage students from pursuing an internship in the first place. Do not let this happen to you.

Instead, realize that as a student intern, you don't need very many creature comforts to get by. Go into your internship like a Spartan. Maintain a mind-set that you will be able to get by on very little. Plan to spend a lot of time at your internship—don't worry if the place you're staying isn't the most ideal. All you need is a place to sleep and a place to get ready in the morning. Maybe some place to do laundry if you're lucky. Don't fret about not having a car—get by on public transportation if you can.

Be lean during your internship. Eliminate distractions. Focus on the internship.

a whim, even sent in the application to the White House. I figured if nothing else came of it, I could still keep the cool White House envelope.

That spring, to my great surprise, I received an acceptance letter from the International Affairs program at George Washington University in Washington, DC. My first thought was, "I'm going to have to start wearing shoes again." After making some quick arrangements, a few short weeks later I landed in DC with a single backpack and the hope that being a grad student would be easier than being an undergraduate.

To my great relief, getting set up in DC wasn't nearly as hard as I thought it might be. There were a few incidents of dumpster diving for needed furniture, but after a few days of class I quickly made a bunch of great new friends. I started running around the monuments on the National Mall almost every morning. It was during one of these runs, as I went past the White House that I thought, "I should call those guys. They never even sent me a rejection letter." So I did.

I managed to get ahold of the White House internship coordinator. She asked, "Is this Eric Woodard?"

"Yes," I said. "I was just wondering what happened with my application."

"Eric from Guam?"

"Yes, from Guam, but I'm in DC now"

"Eric!" she said. "We've been trying to get in touch with you! Can you start your internship next week?"

I couldn't believe it.

So, one week later, there I was: an intern in the White House, assigned to the Office of the First Lady Hillary Rodham Clinton. I was more than wet behind the ears; I was a fish out of water.

How did I manage to land that internship? I didn't have any real political connections and wasn't a particularly accomplished student. By any conventional measure, there is no way I should have been able to pull it off.

I didn't realize it at the time, but I stumbled my way into the White House by doing a lot of things right without even knowing it. To be honest, I just got lucky—it really shouldn't have happened. Was it fair that I got so lucky? Absolutely not.

Which brings me to a very important point that almost nobody tells young professionals making the transition from work to school: *the working world is not fair.*

Because of this, *you need an unfair advantage.*

This is one of the more important pieces of advice I can offer you. Over the years I've noticed that when some young professionals discover this truth, they react by dwelling on the moral judgment that the working world should be fair. But I'm not sure this serves anyone well.

Alternatively, those who embrace the unfairness and quickly move on to mastering their ability to overcome it seem much more able to serve themselves and others. I believe the best place for young professionals to learn how to navigate the working world and get an unfair advantage for the purpose of saving the universe is through an internship.

7

Getting an Unfair Advantage

"There is always inequality in life. Some men are killed in a war and some men are wounded and some men never leave the country. Life is unfair."

—John F. Kennedy

*T*he working world is unfair. It's rigged. Unfortunately, as most students move from school to work in pursuit of career success, nobody explains this to them. But if you can accept the unfairness, and quickly move on to learning how to overcome it, you can turn working world unfairness into your advantage.

Does the word "unfair" make you uncomfortable? Get over it.

If you are in school, or if you've just left school, I can understand why the notion of the working world being "unfair" might make you nervous. School, for the most part, is based on fairness. Teachers (in theory, at least) are supposed to grade tests and papers objectively. Students generally have equal access to information. If somebody has a special need, schools and teachers do what they can to level the field.

But remember, getting an internship is not a fair process. If you expect that it is, you will be disappointed. If you dwell on the notion that finding an internship should be fair, let me humbly suggest that you are wasting your time and missing the point.

Has the process for getting an internship ever been fair? I don't think so. One need only look back through history to realize that apprentices, squires, ladies-in-waiting, aide-de-camps—pretty much every version of what we would now call an internship has never been a completely equal employment opportunity.

Depending on where you live, various laws (and let's hope in most cases just basic human decency) prohibit discrimination based on things like gender, race, sexual orientation, religion, etc. But let's be honest, anyone who has faced discrimination based on one of these factors will tell you that the system is still not fair—and may never be. So, as you enter the working world stop working on the assumption that things are fair and learn how to get an unfair advantage.

There are plenty of factors that internship hosts and employers use to discriminate between applicants. Some of these factors may be merit based, like your grades or test scores or awards you've received. Other factors may not be merit based, like schools you attended or because you come from a certain place. Some of these factors may seem legitimate, some may not. But regardless, it is really important that you develop a fine-tuned understanding about what these factors are, and then use this understanding to gain an advantage over your competitors. For goodness sake, *don't become resentful of the system because it is unfair; just get your own unfair advantage.*

I see it so often—students who do amazingly well in school have a really hard time finding their way in the workplace because they've never been taught about the differences between work and school. Techniques you used as a student that led to success—getting into certain colleges, landing a part in the play, or making a spot on the team— probably won't work very well during the internship hunt. Why? They won't work because the working world is not fair.

Realize right now that if you're going to be competitive in the working world, you can't play fair. Now, don't get me wrong, I'm not talking about cheating or stealing your co-workers' lunch money, or being a bully, or being somehow malicious. *If you use your unfair advantage for dark purposes, it won't work.* The unfair advantage I'm talking about only works if it comes from a place of authenticity and ultimately, service to others. In the long term, the unfair advantage tactics I'm going to teach you in this book will only work for positive, constructive purposes. If you attempt to use the unfair advantage for malicious purposes, it will backfire.

But I am saying that you should forget about playing by the rules you've been taught. If you want to get a great internship, you should drop a lot of the assumptions you have about what will make an employer want to mentor you as an intern. In order to land that perfect internship, you need to get your own unfair advantage.

Having this unfair advantage will show potential employers that you are mature beyond the years of your professional experience. Having this unfair advantage will make you stand out from the crowd. Those who get this unfair advantage will stand out like a blinking bright light to potential employers. Those who have this unfair advantage will make reviewers of internship applications stop, sit back, take a drink of Diet Coke, and say, "Dear Lord, finally, at long last, thank you for putting this application in my hands." Those who have this unfair advantage will have an adamantium edge when it comes to getting a great internship. If you want to get a great internship and do well in it, you need to get an unfair advantage.

Ninety-nine percent of students applying to internships today will go about getting an internship kind of haphazardly, without a plan. The internships a lot of these students wind up doing will likely reflect this lackluster strategy. But by possessing this book, you already have an unfair advantage because the rest of this text will focus on two things. First, it will explain to you how you can use an unfair advantage to get an internship. Second, it will explain to you how to use an unfair advantage to thrive during your internship.

PART I:

How to Get an Internship

8

You Know

"Every child is an artist. The problem is how to remain an artist once we grow up."

—Pablo Picasso

Do you know want to be when you grow up?

Maybe you already know. Maybe you already know what internship you want to do. Maybe you already know what kind of internship will let you rub shoulders with experts in a specific field and help you learn what you need to know.

If so, congratulations! But if that's not you, why not?

Is it because you are still trying to "find your passion" because you've heard that if you just follow your passion and do what you love, work will never seem like work?

If so, let me let you in on a few secrets. You're never going to feel like a grown-up, much less know what you want to do when that mythical day arrives. Also, *it's called "work" for a reason—because it's work.*

You should also know that nobody has just one passion; passions change through life. In his book *So Good They Can't Ignore You,* Cal Newport offers a really great argument to illustrate that the trendy career advice of "follow your passion" is actually really counter-productive.

I have seen students, convinced they have some undiscovered passion that is just waiting to be discovered, drive themselves bonkers trying to find it. This quest sometimes leads to a student doing fifteen different internships, all in different subjects, which doesn't serve anybody.

A better strategy, I believe, is to develop what Newport calls "career capital." That is, evidence that you can present to a potential employer or internship host that that you can offer value—or at the very least, are focused on a career path. Now you may ask, "But I have lots of interests, how can I choose just one, and which one do I choose?!?" First off, realize that just because you pursue one interest for a career doesn't mean you need to give up the others. This can be incredibly liberating. You don't have to choose one passion—you can do all of them—you just have to choose one for a career.

But is one interest just as good as another? Which one do you choose for a career?

Choose one that people are paying for—*pursue an interest that is rare and valuable, and that people are hiring others and paying them well to do.* How do you find out which one is in demand? Go to a job board and take a look. Talk to professionals in your fields of interest and ask them questions like, "Hello, what positions are the most difficult to fill in your area?" Or, "What skills will be in short supply five years from now?"

Then, start to build career capital in that area. What counts as career capital? Take courses, get certifications, start clubs, write books, start blogs, attend conferences, publish papers, reach out to the experts in the field and get to know them—build a war chest of career capital that says, "The other people may be passionate about this topic, but I've got skin in the game, and I already have a lot of expertise in it—I'm all in."

Especially for a would-be internship mentor, who do you think they are more likely to choose as an intern? The applicant who professes that they have tons of passion in a subject, but not quite enough passion to have taken any initiative toward gaining any experience in it? Or, are they going to choose the applicant who has acted on their passion and already has demonstrated that they are committed to that career path?

The word "decision" comes from the Latin root "caedere," which means "to cut." It might be worth your while to do some deciding, to do some cutting. You might feel tempted to believe you can wait, that you still have time to do some exploring. That may be true, but let me caution you that while you ponder whether you want to pursue a career in Ancient Babylonian cabinet making or Ethiopian sign language, somewhere in the world there is a nine-year-old who has already decided they are going to be the world's greatest Ancient Babylonian cabinet maker. That nine-year-old is your future job competition, and unless you are eight, that nine-year-old is just going to have more time than you to master Ancient Babylonian cabinets (or whatever field you choose may be). No pressure or anything.

If you need some convincing that mastering almost anything is just a matter of the quantity and quality of time we devote to mastering it, check out Geoff Colvin's book *Talent is Overrated*. Colvin makes the argument that it's really easy for anybody to become better than about 90 percent of everybody else at anything. But to get to the top 1 percent—that takes a lot of time. Because of this, those who are at the top 1 percent of any discipline often are in the greatest demand. That is where you want to be, the top 1 percent, one of the best in the world. But that takes time. Don't wait. Choose.

Sometimes young professionals think they have made a choice, but their chosen career path winds up being incredibly broad or vague: "I want to do public service" or "I want to study history." You've got to be more specific. Again, cut away your options. It might be very difficult to become the world's expert in history—but if you decided you wanted to be the world's expert in the history of Russian comic books—well now that might be possible.

Again, let the job market guide you—don't just guess. Are there employers out there looking for Russian comic book experts? I have no idea. Wherever your interests lie, do some research. If you have an interest related to something that is in high demand but not a lot of others are doing, that is where I'd pursue an internship. Even if that field is not the area that you feel most passionate about, by developing skills that are rare and valuable, you will be in a much better position to pursue all those other passions you have—not because you have to for a paycheck, but because you truly want to and have the flexibility to do so.

9

But You Want to Explore

"I've been lucky. Opportunities don't often come along. So, when they do, you have to grab them."

—Audrey Hepburn

Do you want to use an internship to explore your career options?

Stop.

Go back and read the chapter just before this one. *Is there any way you can narrow your options before attempting to choose an internship?* Have you interviewed some people in the fields that are your top contenders? Have you spoken to a good career counselor about the competing options?

If so, and if you're truly at an impasse, know that using an internship as a way to get exposure to a new career is legit—but it's not as good an option as going into an internship knowing what you want to do.

Have I made you feel guilty enough about not knowing what you want to do with the rest of your life? Sorry. It's just that I don't want you to waste time if you don't need to.

Let me let you in on another secret. *It is very rare that one is ever completely convinced they are fulfilling their life's purpose professionally.* Some people say they are completely sure, but it's rare. When you're thirty, you're probably still going to wonder. When you're forty, you'll likely still wonder. When you're fifty you'll still wonder. It may sound crazy, but if you have a list of options that all seem possible, consider flipping a coin.

In her essay "Wear Sunscreen" (popularized in song by Baz Luhrmann), Mary Schmich writes,

> Don't feel guilty if you don't know what you want to do with your life. The most interesting people I know didn't know at twenty-two what they wanted to do with their lives; some of the most interesting forty-year-olds I know still don't. Your choices are half chance, so are everybody else's.

If you must, it's okay to use an internship to explore a possible career. Just don't mess around too long—make narrowing down your options a constant goal. The sooner you do, the faster you'll find a professional purpose that is truly fulfilling. Perhaps even more importantly, the faster you discover a fulfilling professional course, the faster you will master it, become the world's expert at it, and become incredibly in demand for it.

10

The Long Interview

"Judge a man by his questions rather than his answers."

—Voltaire

If and when you have some clarity about your professional future, you may look to do an internship with an organization because you want to find a job there. Is this a good reason to do an internship? You bet it is.

Let me ask you a question. If you are somebody responsible for hiring others, are you going to hire somebody who has already been interning for you, who already knows the work, and who has been doing a tremendous job? Or, are you going to hire somebody who is a relative unknown?

One way to think of an internship is to think of it as an "extended job interview."

If you're doing an internship and your host is just dangling a job prospect in front of you to keep you around, you should leave immediately. However, if you're interning at a place where expectations are clear and you've been given an honest appraisal about the likelihood of your being hired, where you still feel it's in your interest to stay—then you should stick with it. Stick around and be such a great intern that they'll bend over backward to hire you, if they can.

11

When You Should Say No

"Learn to say 'no' to the good so you can say 'yes' to the best."
—John C. Maxwell

There are plenty of reasons to do an internship. But sometimes, there are also plenty of reasons not to do an internship.

If you have clarity about where you want your future career to lead, and you have an opportunity to do an internship in an unrelated field, should you take it just because you can? I don't think so.

Once you've committed to a particular career path, there can be plenty of distractions to dilute your resolve, including internships. Don't let these opportunities distract you, even if they are great opportunities in another field. Instead, stick to your guns and cut away other options. You may know the story about Cortes when he reached the New World. When the conquistador landed in America, many on his crew became restless and wanted to head back to Spain. Cortes scuttled his ships so that his men only had one path open to them: forward. *When you are committed to a career path, burn your ships.* Decide that you will not accept any opportunities, internship or otherwise, except those that build the sort of career capital that you seek.

Likewise, if you are offered an internship and it just doesn't feel right—don't take it. The purpose of an internship is to strengthen your education and enhance your professional development—only pursue and/or accept those opportunities you believe will do that.

12

Making Ends Meet

"The foundation of a financial fresh start actually has nothing to do with money or specific financial dos and don'ts."

—Suze Orman

In a perfect world, education would be free.

In a perfect world there would be no such thing as tuition, and teachers would be among the highest paid professionals in our society. Of course, we do not live in a perfect world.

Nevertheless, some forms of education come pretty close to free. In the United States, taxpayer-funded public schools offer education to everyone at no charge. We have a range of student loan and scholarship programs available to help make college a real possibility for almost anyone who wants to go. But maybe the purest form of free education are internships where an employer says, "Spend some time in our workplace and we'll teach you."

As much as you can, you shouldn't let the question of pay factor into what internship you're trying to get. You may be in a tough financial situation. You may be in a situation where you can't afford to do an internship full-time. If that's you, I sympathize—I've been there.

So, treat the situation just as you would if you needed to be a part-time student. Go find the highest-paying job you can, doing whatever part time, so you can afford to do an internship with the rest of your time. Look for grants and scholarships that might be available to help you fund your internship. Be creative: use things like Kickstarter, busk on the curb, do what you have to do.

If you're a young professional and you want to get an internship, this is not the time to be faint of heart. Cut every bit of extra fat out of your living expenses. Live lean. Living lean means living for free with friends or relatives when you can, it means public transportation, it means living off peanut butter and jelly. It means no video games or shopping for fancy shoes, no frills.

Think that is too tough? Are you unwilling to take such drastic measures? If not, rest assured, your competition will. How far are you willing to go to overcome financial challenges in order to get a great internship? It's your choice.

Early in your career is a time when you can live lean. During this time, chances are that you don't have a mortgage, or a car payment, or a family to support. Later in life, your lifestyle may cost more.

When I did my first internship, I woke up at 3:15 AM daily so I could report to a job from 4 AM to 10 AM so I could do my internship from 10 AM to 6 PM, and then attend classes from 6 PM to 9 PM.

Was I tired? I was totally tired. Was it worth it in the end? It was absolutely worth it, and I would do it again. If I did it, you can too.

Don't let money stand in the way of your education any more than it has to. As much as you can, don't let financial challenges effect what internship you choose any more than you must.

13

Take Refuge

"College is a refuge from hasty judgment."

—Robert Frost

There is one more really good reason to do an internship. That reason is: you just need to take refuge for a while. If you've made it through the gauntlet of higher education and are now crossing what seems to be a desert of unemployment, getting an internship might be the oasis you need.

It is often said that finding a job is much easier when you have a job. I think this is absolutely true. But of course, when you don't have a job in the first place, that's a real catch–22, isn't it?

If you think getting an internship will force you to get out of a rut, to get over some horrible break-up, to wake up at a certain time in the morning and actually go to the trouble of bathing, you might be right. If you think going to an internship and just doing something productive with your day might give you the energy you need to traverse the unemployment desert you're currently trying to cross, you might be onto something.

Because you're reading this book and you've actually made it this far, I suspect you are a person that has some kind of work ethic. I believe you are the sort of person who takes pride in doing things that are useful with your time.

When one goes from having a crazy class schedule to exams to nothing, and all of their social networks from college have dispersed, well, that can be shocking. This transition can knock the tar out of pretty much anybody.

If you need a refuge where you can regroup, an internship might give you the structure you need. But treat it as a temporary refuge, not a permanent one.

14

Internship Sites

"To find out what one is fitted to do, and to secure an opportunity to do it, is the key to happiness."

—John Dewey

In this day and age, the obvious place to look for internships is online.

But often the easiest places to look aren't always the best places to look. Especially if you're hoping to avoid competition against the bazillions of other students trying to find an internship the exact same way, you might want to consider trying to find an internship via alternative routes. One great technique is to use online listings to get ideas about where you might like to do an internship, but then pursue those ideas offline. Do not let yourself get lost in a sea of online inquiries that an internship host receives. Stand out.

However, there are a ton of online resources to help students find internships. There are plenty of places worth a look; here are some of the main ones.

Disclaimer: not all internship sites are created equal. As with anything online, you should use your good judgment when giving out personal information or paying somebody money to help you get an internship.

That being said, I think these sites are some of the best places to start an internship search:

THE BIG FREE ONES

Indeed (http://indeed.com)

In my opinion this is the grand poobah of internship and job-searching sites. It aggregates listings from a ton of places. A great place to start. It's free.

Craigslist (http://craigslist.com)

This is perhaps the *most* overlooked place to find great internships, especially local internships and internships with small organizations. If you want to find internships that a lot of people don't know about, this is the place to go online.

Internships.com (http://internships.com)

This is another heavy hitter in the internship world. Lots of internships to be found here. It's free, though they also offer a premium service that you pay for.

USAJobs (http://usajobs.gov)

If you're looking to find an internship for the federal government, this is the place to look. It's a massive directory, but it often lists internships right along with other federal job opportunities.

ALSO REALLY GOOD FREE GENERAL SITES

These three are all big job listing aggregators, but they often list a bunch of internships; they are similar to Indeed:

Idealist (http://idealist.org)
Experience.com (http://experience.com)
Simplyhired (http://simplyhired.com)
Career Sushi (http://careersushi.com)

GREAT FREE SITES THAT FOCUS ON JUST INTERNSHIPS

Youtern (http://youtern.com)

Full disclosure, I work closely with these guys and I think they are awesome. Their site lists plenty of unique internship opportunities you might not find anyplace else, especially with small start-up companies.

Intern Match (http://internmatch.com)

Great service that focuses on listing just internship opportunities.

The Intern Queen (http://internqueen.com)

Lauren Berger has a huge following—and she lists lots of internships that you may not see elsewhere. Definitely worth checking out.

SOME PAY SITES

Intern Qube (http://internqube.com)

This site has a minimal subscription fee and was created by Michael True, one of the most respected internship experts in the nation.

The Internship Series (http://www.internships-usa.com)

Check to see if your school subscribes to this service; if it does, the Internship Series online lists a bunch of opportunities.

Dream Careers (http://summerinternships.com)

This site encourages students to apply and then offers internship placement for a hefty fee. Dream Careers' business model has received criticism, but some students are happy with the service, so I list it here.

INTERNSHIPS IN WASHINGTON, DC

Capitol Hill
(http://www.senate.gov/employment/po/positions.htm)
(http://www.house.gov/content/jobs)

The House and Senate employ a ton of interns, you can find out about some of these opportunities through their respective employment bulletins.

Brad Traverse (http://bradtraverse.com)

This former Hill Staffer charges a small monthly fee to see his daily DC job and internship listings.

Tom Manatos (http://tommanatos.com)

This former Hill guy does the same.

DC Public Affairs & Communications Jobs Blog (http://publicaffairsjobs.blogspot.com)

Gordon Barnes runs an awesome blog that has plenty of DC internship listings. It's free.

The Washington Center (http://twc.edu)

This nonprofit places students in internships for a tuition fee. It's been around forever and has placed thousands upon thousands of students over the years.

The Washington Internship Institute (http://www.wiidc.org)

Another nonprofit that charges tuition fees to place students with internships in Washington, DC.

INTERNSHIPS OUTSIDE THE USA

Intern Abroad (http://internabroad.com)

Part of a larger study abroad site, this web page offers listings about internship opportunities overseas.

Smart Intern China (http://smartinternchina.com)

They place interns in China.

Of course, in addition to all these sites, individual organizations often list information about internship programs on their own websites. The big intern directories are great, but a better strategy is to find the random listing in the less-trodden virtual place that everybody else is going to miss.

15

Unlisted Numbers

"If it's the Psychic Network why do they need a phone number?"
—Robin Williams

I don't think there will ever be a way to prove it, but it's often said that *75 percent of jobs are never listed*. As in, the only way you find out about these jobs is by talking to people. I'm not sure if it's actually 75 percent, but I do believe there are a ton of internships available that are never actually listed. You should never hesitate to go after these.

So, how do you do that? You talk to people. You let people know that you are looking for an internship!

When you're in internship-hunting mode, go out of your way to meet new people and when you do, make sure you say explicitly, "I'm looking for an internship right now." Your status on Twitter and Facebook should be, "I'm looking for an internship right now."

I can't stress this enough. So often I see students who kind of beat around the bush. They reach out and "want to have coffee." By the way, I actually don't drink coffee. But even if I did—does having "coffee" mean that we could just sit there and drink without talking? It might get weird, but at least we'd have coffee.

No!

If you want somebody's help finding an internship, say, "I'd be grateful for any help you can give me with my internship search." Or, "Do you know of anyone looking for an intern? Because, I'm looking for an XYZ type of internship."

Suppose you are fortunate enough to be one that knows what kind of internship you want to do. If that's you, make a list of the four or five places where you would like to intern. Then, check them out. If you don't see information about an internship program, give them a call and ask, "Do you have an internship program?"

I've actually worked with an organization that purposely does not list information about their internship programs online because they only want to consider applicants who are interested enough to take initiative and call. *Just because you don't see information about an internship opportunity doesn't mean it isn't there.*

16

Career Centers

"A career is born in public, talent in privacy."
—Marilyn Monroe

Believe it or not, if you're in school, there is a really good chance that your school has a career center that you can go to. Did you know that?

I must admit, when I was in college, I never visited a career center. What's worse, having transferred seven times between five schools over the course of my college career, I missed *five* different career centers.

Have you visited your school's career center? If you have, good for you! If you haven't, you should. I never visited a career center in school because as a student, I just never thought it was relevant. Maybe if I had visited a career center, I would have had more of a clue about internships and jobs before stumbling into the working world.

If you're looking for an internship, go to your school's career center. There is a good chance that your school has an established relationship with organizations that might interest you.

Think about it, students come and go—but schools and employers tend to stay. If a student from your school was a great intern last year, that employer might really like the idea of taking another intern from your school (you) this year without needing to go through all the trouble of advertising an open internship position.

It's a little old school, but the perfect internship position for you might be on a flier on the bulletin board of your college career center right now. But, if not, your school's career center can also tell you about any structured internship program opportunities that are available.

17

Semester in . . .

"I spent a college semester in a small town in Italy—and that is
where I truly tasted food for the first time."

—Alton Brown

If you are in college, your school may already have a number of
"semester in wherever" internship programs that they have developed and maintain. These tend to be among the most structured
internships out there—but that is not necessarily a bad thing. If the
internship is already tied into your academic course of study, such
programs can actually work really well.

A possible downside to these programs, though, is that they basically
just export your school experience to a different place for a semester.
Instead of interacting with new people in a new environment and
truly getting a sense about what it feels like to be on your own in the
working world, you wind up taking shelter among familiar people and
things. This isn't always true, but it's something to watch out for.

If you are going to go to the trouble of doing an internship, make
sure it's a real internship that gets you outside your comfort zone. An
internship that still feels a lot like being in school is probably just that.

18

Make Your Own Way

"Have it your way."

—Burger King

Even though it seems like internships should be everywhere, many organizations don't have internship programs. Why?

They don't know how to set them up.

They don't know how to put together an internship application or how to get students to apply. They don't feel confident that they can manage interns or they worry about the legal ramifications of hosting an intern.

Here's the thing: running an internship program really isn't that hard. As long as an employer is acting as a mentor and a student is learning a ton, they're pretty much good to go.

So, if you would like to do an internship someplace, but that place doesn't offer an internship program, let them know that one of your first projects as their first intern will be to set up an internship program for them.

Does approaching an employer and suggesting you act as their intern even when they don't have an internship program sound too forward to you? If it does, get over it. Let other young professionals stand down while you step up.

You might be amazed by the number of organizations that would be incredibly receptive to being approached by an eager young professional (you) who takes the initiative.

What do you have to lose?

19

Virtual Internships

"We all live every day in virtual environments, defined by our ideas."
—Michael Crichton

I f you are not in a position to travel across the country and temporarily relocate in order to do an internship in a new place physically, virtual internships are becoming increasingly common and may be a great option for you.

What is a virtual internship? Think of it as the internship version of teleworking. Instead of interacting with a mentor in a workplace, you do it virtually.

Some projects work really well for virtual internships and some don't. Editing, managing social media, translating, graphic design, curating digital records, video editing, and publishing digital newsletters are the kinds of projects that work well as a basis for a virtual internship. Other projects, like event planning or lab work, don't work so well virtually because, well, you sort of have to be there.

Is a virtual internship as effective a learning experience as a physical internship? In my experience, no. A lot of learning that occurs during an internship happens tacitly by just being there. However, is a virtual internship better than no internship at all? Absolutely.

Even if you are not able to be involved with an internship in person, especially if it's an organization that is *the* place you want to intern, a virtual internship can be a really great option. Most organizations don't even know about virtual internships. If the place you want to intern doesn't seem to have a virtual internship program, ask them if they would like you to be their very first virtual intern.

20

Results in Advance

"For it is in giving that we receive."

—St. Francis of Assisi

What if your first contact with a possible internship host had nothing to do with your asking for an internship? What if, instead, it revolved around your showing results in advance?

"Results in advance? What's that?!"

Results in advance means you do a little homework to find out what an employer is interested in, or where they need help. This is way easier than it sounds.

Let's say you decide that you want to be the world's expert on synthetic worm fish lures, and because they are some of the best in the world when it comes to fake worms, you want to intern with Bob's Tackle Shop.

First, find out what Bob needs. Go to his website—what sorts of things are Bob and the other folks at the shop talking about? What problems do they have?

Is there anything that they are missing?

You may be thinking, "But what if Bob doesn't even have a website?"

Well, then your work is easy—help Bob establish a website!

Radical thought: reach out to Bob and let him know you are interested in starting a career that revolves around fake worms. Ask him if he wouldn't mind meeting with you.

People are flattered when you seek their advice. Ninety-nine percent of the time the Bobs of the world are going to welcome meeting with anybody to talk about their business and their career.

When you meet with Bob, ask him what might make his business better. Ask him what he's tried that hasn't worked. When you leave, say "Thank you very much."

Then you follow up. Take some steps that might help Bob solve some of his problems. Suppose Bob said one of his issues has to do with displaying all the fake worms to customers. What would happen if you wrote up a plan or diagram about how the fake worms might be displayed in a better way and then you sent that plan to Bob with a nice note? What if you did some research about how other stores display their fake worms and wrote up a summary for Bob? Do you think Bob would like this? You bet he would.

Do this a couple of times. Stay in touch with Bob and ask for nothing in return.

When the time comes to approach him about doing an internship, do you think Bob will be receptive? Absolutely.

Why? Because you've already showed Bob that (1) you care about his business and (2) you are capable of adding value to his business.

The best foundation for anyone applying to be an intern is to show results in advance.

Give first and you shall receive.

Disclaimer: your warming up to a potential internship employer can't be fake; it's got to be genuine. In other words, if you really don't care about a potential employer or their work and you're just trying to get close to put an internship on your résumé, it won't work. They'll know.

On the other hand, if you are genuinely interested in what a potential employer is doing, then offering results in advance of your internship will be easy.

Second disclaimer: does this sound like a lot of extra work? It is.

Are you unwilling to take this extra step? That's okay, just don't be surprised if/when you don't get the internship.

ALL'S FAIR IN LOVE, WAR, AND INTERNSHIPS

During the internship application process, some students get all hung up on inconsiderate behavior by a potential employer.

The thinking starts to follow this pattern: I'm jumping through all these hoops to show them what a fantastic intern I would be, and they won't even return my calls! Screw 'em. Or, it's something like, I'm amazingly talented, if they don't recognize how amazing I am and aren't begging me to be their intern, screw 'em! Yes, it's a lot like dating.

That line of reasoning isn't necessarily wrong, but if your purpose is to get the internship and access to the people and skills that come with it, I'm not sure how far your focusing on the unfairness of the process will get you.

Fairness is one of those things that most students don't learn enough about when they are in school. In school, things are always supposed to be fair. In the working world, sorry to be the one to tell you but as I've said before, things are very rarely fair.

Is it fair that you may have to jump through a bunch of hoops just to be considered for an internship? Nope. Is it reality? Yes. The sooner you understand that things in the working world aren't always fair, the sooner you'll be able to thrive in that world. You don't have to perpetuate unfairness, but you need to understand it.

Will "results in advance" always work? No. But it will help your chances a ton if you're willing to do it.

Third disclaimer: what if you just can't figure out how to make contact with the "Bob" where you want to do an internship? With a little work, it's almost always fairly easy to find somebody's telephone and email address. At the very least you can find their mailing address. Here are some tricks:

When it comes to email addresses, sometimes a simple Google search will do it. If that doesn't work, try Googling their name with their organization's @domain name. For example, you could search for "Bob Smith" + "@btackleshp.com"

Often, companies will use the same naming conventions for email addresses. So, if you see that Suzie Jones at the tackle shop is SJones@btackleshp.com, then BSmith@btackleshp.com is worth a try for Bob.

This is a situation where something like LinkedIn can be helpful. Look to see if you know somebody who knows Bob and might be willing to introduce you.

Ask around to family, friends, and relatives to see if anybody is in a position to introduce you.

Lastly, a simple phone call to Bob's office might do the trick. Even if you're only able to reach Bob's assistant, chances are that he or she will be willing to give you Bob's email address or, at the very least, convey your message to Bob.

21

All-Access Pass

"We must open the doors of opportunity. But we must also equip our people to walk through those doors."

—L. B. J.

You might think that you are not worthy of getting an internship, that only "those other people" can get an internship, but not you. But you are wrong.

Do some students and young professionals get internships because of family and/or political connections? Yep. Is that how things generally work in the working world? Sometimes. Is that fair? Nope.

This is why you need an unfair advantage.

Let's suppose you have some kind of disadvantaged or unusual background—as in, you don't summer in the Hamptons at the country club with Todd and Margie. If you apply to an internship and somebody rejects you because of your ethnicity, sexual orientation, religion, age, economic status, or whatever—let me be clear, they suck.

First, they're most likely breaking the law. But, more important than that—they're probably not somebody you will learn very much from during an internship.

But the good news is, in real life, most internships aren't like that. In fact, I've seen plenty of cases where employers actually use internship programs to help diversify their workplace both in the internship program itself and for interns that kick butt, as a recruitment tool for staff positions.

In this way, an internship can provide an avenue for people to access organizations, no matter who they are. *If you feel like you're being held back because of where you come from or who you are, doing an internship might unlock more doors than you imagine.*

In some cases, if your background represents an underrepresented demographic, you may be able to use this to your advantage. Is this a politically correct idea? No. It is fair? No. But remember, this isn't about fair, this is about getting an unfair advantage.

It may not work in every scenario but say, for example, that you are a Pacific Islander and an organization currently has zero Pacific Islanders. Depending on the situation, this same argument could work if you are a man, a woman, a Hindu, over sixty—pretty much anything—but for argument's sake, let's say Pacific Islander. You are probably not going to get hired because you are a Pacific Islander (because that would be discrimination, which is illegal). However, the fact that you represent a different community and an organization might increase its diversity by accepting you as an intern will certainly not hurt your application. So, don't hide who you are. *When trying to get an internship be yourself, be authentic, be proud of your story and don't be afraid to tell people about it.*

This means that if there are things you have done that are relevant to an internship opportunity at hand, don't hide them. For example, if you are Mormon and spent a year doing mission work, don't hide it. This means that if you graduated from high school a long time ago and are afraid to list it on your résumé because it will show how old you are, don't hide it. This means that if you are active in an African American sorority, don't hide it. This means that if you founded an LGBT group, put it on there. All of these things are part of your story, show you are authentic, and make you interesting. This is what will make you stand out from the rest.

Guess who tend to not be very good interns? Students who are not proud of who they are. Organizations who host interns know this and tend not to select applicants who are not proud of who they are. Be proud of who you are and show it off.

22

Stereotypes

"For whatever reason, I didn't succumb to the stereotype that science wasn't for girls."

—Sally Ride

*B*e genuine; don't hide who you are. On the other hand, we all hold *stereotypes.* You probably know lots of them.

Millennials work well in groups and are great with technology, but they can work independently and carry a sense of entitlement.

Asian students are smart, but all they do is study.

French people are sophisticated and stylish, but rude.

Engineers are great at solving technical problems, but they have no social skills.

Of course, none of these stereotypes are true. But as you work toward getting an internship (or pitching yourself for anything, for that matter) *you can counteract any stereotypes that others may see in you to get an unfair advantage* by contradicting any subconscious stereotypes, right out of the gate.

For example, generally, a lot of people over forty think people under twenty have a disproportionate sense of entitlement. If I'm a twenty-something trying to convince a forty-something to choose me for an internship, I might contradict that stereotype right out of the gate by relaying something like, "I know there are so many long-time staffers at your organization who have put in many years and have so much to offer, especially for somebody like myself who is just starting out." Most people who hire interns have never heard a young person say something like that. But if they did, it would get their attention.

But contradicting stereotypes goes way beyond generational stuff. Let's say you went to Harvard, you might need to overcome the stereotype that you are privileged and have never done a hard day's work in your life. If you went to a public school, you might need to overcome the stereotype that you are not as well educated. Let me be clear, none of these stereotypes are true, but be mindful of any that people might see in you and then turn them to your advantage.

23

Stand Out Like a Sore Thumb

"Two roads diverged in a wood, and I—I took the one less traveled by, and that has made all the difference."

—Robert Frost

It wasn't my intention, but when I applied for my first internship at the White House I was such a weirdo at the time, I couldn't help but stand out from the crowd. A place like the White House receives hundreds of applications for its internship program, and they all look pretty much alike.

Basically, the average applicant is a college sophomore or junior attending a very prestigious if not Ivy League school. Chances are, they are attending a school someplace between North Carolina and Maine—there might be a few Californians or Michiganders in there—but most applicants are from the East Coast. As a dude who had transferred colleges seven times, and then was in Guam, I was about as far away from the mold as possible.

It never ceases to amaze me how so many internship applicants will try to hide that they are different. If you represent a minority group (ethnic, geographic, sexual orientation, whatever), let that come through on your résumé. Don't hide it! Beat the reviewer over the head with it. Most programs are always on the look for diversity, and if they're not, you don't want to intern there anyway. Being unique makes you scarce, and being scarce makes you valuable.

Often students will try to "stand out from the rest of the crowd" by seeming more accomplished than the rest. Surrounded by a group of highly qualified and motivated competitors, this is really hard to do. Being super amazing isn't that much better than being really amazing. Instead of trying to be more amazing than the rest, just be different and be very specific and explicit in describing how you are exactly what the person reviewing your application is looking for.

Suppose you are reviewing a stack of internship applications. Going through the stack, you would likely be on the lookout for one or two specific factors to help you decide whether the application in hand should go in the "yes" pile or the "no" pile. This is exactly what most who review applications do.

As an applicant, your job is to figure out what those one or two factors a potential internship host or employer is looking for might be. Once you do, everything you present in your application should hit them between the eyes with those factors.

As a bleary-eyed reviewer going through a stack of a zillion applications, you are looking for some specific factors, but you are desperate to find something that is just different than the rest. As a reviewer of applications, I've actually caught myself shouting out loud, "Good lord! Please, just say something, anything that is different!" because all the applications look the same. If you can, make the actual physical application different. Print it out on some crazy colored paper or print it sideways—anything that is different.

Many who dwell in the working world see the same things day after day, year after year. I believe the boredom level of the average American worker would be hard to overestimate. Help them overcome that boredom, send them a surprise that gets their attention. Don't be like everybody else.

24

Tell a Story, Be a Human

"Don't try to be perfect; just be an excellent example of being human."

—Tony Robbins

My White House internship application required essay answers to two questions. I recall my answer to the first question addressed my philosophy about the role of government, the second talked about my story under the ocean all the way out in Guam. I guarantee that the second essay was the one that helped me get accepted.

I can't tell you how many times I've looked at a stack of applications from a group of similar applicants and have needed to do a double take regarding the essays they've submitted because they were all the same. Not too long ago, I was reviewing answers to the question, "What has been your greatest learning experience?" Ninety percent of the applicants talked about graduate school as being their most important learning experience. Is there anything wrong with that answer? No. Is it possible that happens to be the truth for those people who answered that way? Sure. Is it particularly attention grabbing? No.

Among that group. I remember one applicant who stood out by describing the bike ride he took that morning. It was different and way more interesting, partly because he told me a story. His was the one I pulled from the pile. I just needed an excuse to pull one application and that essay was all I needed.

Maggie was an intern who worked for me years ago who I remember very well not only because she was a terrific intern, but also because her intern application told a crazy story. You may not have a story like Maggie's—but if you do—use it! I can't remember what the question was, but Maggie's essay described how she had been in a terrible car accident that resulted in her arm being "severed." Think that application stood out? You're damn right it did. Maggie got accepted in about two microseconds.

The thing was, when Maggie showed up for her first day of her internship, she had two arms! When I asked her what happened, she explained that her arm had actually been only partially severed, and that doctors had been able to re-attach it so she had almost full use of her arm. I knew she was telling the truth because she still sported a big bandage. I was glad Maggie kept her arm; she had a great story and turned out to be a spectacular intern.

Now you might be saying, "But I don't have a story that makes me look good." If that's true for you, then it is all the better. In fact, I think you're much better off telling a story that describes a failure. Why? Because everybody can relate to struggle, everybody can relate to failing. When somebody writes about all the great success they've had, it's not so interesting. Do you have a story about how you've failed, messed up, were arrested, been beaten down, but are still standing? If so, you may have a blockbuster on your hands.

I remember one occasion where I was left with two candidates to fill one internship slot. It was a really close call. I re-read both applications and noticed that Tom listed how he played trumpet, the other candidate did not. Tom seemed more human, so he got the internship. He turned out to be a heck of a nice guy, and I still remember him as one of the best interns I've ever worked with.

SO YOU'RE A RECOVERING DRUG ADDICT WHO SPENT TIME IN JAIL FOR CLUBBING BABY SEALS?

Have some crazy failure or lapse in judgment in your past that you're embarrassed about? Are you worried that failure will keep you from getting an internship? Feel like you need to hide it? Don't.

Instead, embrace that crazy thing from your past. In fact, bring it up yourself. Put it out there all raw and human for the reviewer of your internship application to see. Is it possible that your checkered past will scare the reviewer off? It's possible.

However, I think the greater danger is that a reviewer will dismiss you because you're boring. If your internship application stands out because you're willing to show your flaws, warts and all—at least it's going to be interesting. More than that, telling the ugly truth conveys to the reviewer that you learn from mistakes and have some real life experience. It will show the reviewer that you're not afraid to tell the truth and that more than anything, you're not afraid to show who you are—that you are authentic.

As you put together your application, if you can't bring yourself to reveal your life's struggles, at least make sure you reveal that you are a human. If you're a runner, make sure it shows up someplace in your application. If you do scrap-booking, talk about it! You never know, the person reading your application may be a scrap-booker too. Unless you're applying to a very exotic internship program, you are almost guaranteed that the application reviewer is human, so make sure it comes across that you are too.

The people deciding whether or not to accept you as an intern are interested in knowing whether you are the sort of person they can tolerate in the workplace. *Staffers want reassurance that they can survive co-existence with you and ideally, might even enjoy hanging out with you. A lot of things about the workplace are inhuman enough already, make sure you don't come across as a droid through your internship application.*

25

Video Killed the Radio Star

"Everything makes me nervous—except making films."
—Elizabeth Taylor

If you really want to stand out from the crowd in your search to get a great internship, you probably need to be using more video. Actually, I think everybody should be using more video to spread ideas and information, generally (look at how popular TED talks have become). For convincing an internship host that you are the intern for them, there is almost nothing more powerful than video.

Over the years, I've been involved with a number of internship application review committees and as a reviewer, I can tell you firsthand that even the most mediocre credentials described on video can look better than the best credentials on paper. Why? I think it probably has something to do with the fact that everybody is conditioned to associate video with fun. Most of the time when we watch video in our lives it is on TV or at the movies, when we're relaxing in our homes or with friends doing something fun. Many people, including those who are apt to review your internship application, have an association between video and happiness. You should use this to your advantage.

In the materials you send to a potential internship host, include links to videos of yourself or others talking or demonstrating how awesome you are. Make sure the video you do aligns with the narrative you are building to represent yourself in front of a particular organization or person. As part of your internship application. a video can be funny or serious—the most important thing is that it correlates with the story you are telling as part of your pitch.

26

Research Bleesearch

"Success depends upon previous preparation, and without such preparation there is sure to be failure."

—Confucius

If you're going to make the material in your internship application war chest the best it can be, then you're going to need to do a little research.

You don't need to spend a ton of time doing it, even ten minutes of focused time might be enough. You want to look for things that an organization has chosen to highlight prominently. Chances are, those are the things that are central to their mission and, to the people involved with deciding to hire you as an intern, really important.

When you see issues displayed prominently by an organization, those are your clues. Those are the things to focus on. Ask yourself: "How could I help this organization reach its goals? How could I add value to this organization?" Make sure your answers come through in your application.

27

Break Rules

"The young man knows the rules, but the old man knows the exceptions."

—Oliver Wendell Holmes

*A*s you approach your quest to find an internship, commit now to break the rules. When your application instructions suggest you should only submit two essays, why not submit three? The internship description doesn't ask you to reach out and introduce yourself to people at the host organization, but you will.

Do you run the risk that the evaluator of your application will ding you for not following rules to the letter? It's possible. But, I think it's more likely that by not following the rules to the letter, you'll just stand out as being extra awesome.

For example, if an application requires you to send a résumé, send a cover letter too. If the application asks for information from you, why not send it as a poem, or a video, or a collage.

Is this approach a little risky? Yes. But, that's why it's probably worth doing.

Of course, you've got to walk a fine line here. You don't want to get so far outside the parameters of what your potential internship employer is looking for that you get too far afield.

But, if you can walk that line and break the rules just a little bit, you'll benefit in at least two ways.

First, breaking the rules will allow you to send more. You can send more examples of your work that demonstrate that you are awesome. Use as much of that internship application campaign war chest of materials as you can.

Second, by sending stuff that others don't, you stand out. I may have a stack of resumes with cover letters stapled in front. But, if I catch a glimpse of something neon yellow in the pile (the thing you were brave enough to send)—chances are I'm going to pull that one from the pile first just to see what the hell it is.

Break the rules and be different. Just because internship application instructions don't explicitly say you can do something doesn't mean you can't.

28

Your Campaign

"We shall find a way, or make one."
—Hannibal of Carthage

*A*s you compete to get an internship, you should adopt a multilayered *strategy*. Many will do one or two layers, but you are going to do all of them, and this is what will give you a truly unfair advantage.

What will the layers include? Here is a good list:

- Cover Letter
- Résumé
- Application (if there is one)
- Testimonial/Reference sheet
- Creative Résumé/One Sheet
- Social Media Footprint
- Online Portfolio
- Recommendation Letters
- Interview
- Thank-you Note
- Third Party Follow-Up Calls

THEY ALREADY KNOW YOUR STORY

In his book *The Seven Basic Plots: Why We Tell Stories*, Christopher Booker argued that human beings really only tell seven different stories in our books, our movies, our myths, etc. The stories that make up your personal history likely fit into the mold of a story that anyone reviewing your application will recognize, even if only subconsciously. When pitching yourself for a possible internship, if you emphasize the universal aspects of your story, those evaluating your application may feel like they relate to you without knowing why. If they do, there is a better chance that they will choose you over your competitors.

What are universal stories? Let me offer a few examples—you should recognize them just by their titles: everybody told me I couldn't but I did, I stumbled into an opportunity, David vs. Goliath, hometown girl makes good. Any stories from your personal history that demonstrate a time you encountered difficulty can be especially powerful because everybody, including an internship application reviewer, can relate to a time of difficulty.

Based on your career past, don't be afraid to weave universal stories of difficulty into your internship application. A cover letter is a great place to do this.

Do you need *all* of this stuff to get an internship? No. But the more you have, the greater the chance you get the internship you want.

Let's take each of these pieces in turn.

29

Cover Me

"More than kisses, letters mingle souls."
—John Donne

*I*nclude a cover letter with your application, even if they don't ask for one. When you do, it communicates a bunch of messages to your application reviewer. It indicates that you are willing to do extra work. It says you care enough about this opportunity to do extra. Including a cover letter suggests you have initiative and are prone to over-deliver. An unsolicited cover letter indicates that you are polished and take pride in your work. Including a cover letter when one isn't required indicates that you are able to think outside the box—that you can think beyond simple instructions. When you have a cover letter and most other applications don't, you will stand out.

As Alison Green writes in her *Ask a Manager* blog, there are "two reasons your cover letter sucks: (1) It doesn't exist. You just send your résumé. Adding a three-sentence note in the mail doesn't count. (2) It exists, but it might as well not, because it just repeats the same info that's on your résumé." Don't let your cover letter suck.

The other thing that internship applicants often miss when it comes to cover letters is that they write letters that are all about themselves. This is understandable, but *as you make the transition from school to work, it's important to understand why your letter should be oriented toward the employer, not yourself.*

While one is in school, what is their primary professional responsibility? To learn, right?

But, when one moves to the working world, what is the primary responsibility now? Results, right?

So, even if it happens to be true, you don't want to send in a cover letter on an internship application that has the theme of, "Dear Ms. Employer, your internship would be really great for me because I would learn a lot." Ms. Employer will probably be very glad to get that letter, and even if she is prepared to be a good mentor that cares about your education, she is still going to be asking herself, "What's in it for me?"

Instead, write your cover letter along the lines of, "Dear Ms. Employer, I know all about your organization (because you've researched the crud out of it, right?), I understand your goals and current activities, here are the five ways I can add value to you." See the difference?

Take the time to format the letter correctly. Look up the recipient's address and put it in the right place. Make sure the letter has a salutation and a close. Sweat the little details. If you do, it communicates to the person reading it that (1) you care, (2) you are a professional, and (3) you have the skills to pay attention to detail.

30

Résumé

"I'm kind of a big deal."

—Ron Burgundy, *Anchorman*

Everybody has a different opinion about résumé. But without getting too far into the weeds, let me give you some of my best suggestions.

The most important advice I can offer about a résumé is that, in the end, it must be your own. Whatever your résumé looks like, it needs to be something that you are proud of and that authentically represents you. If it's not, anyone reading it will be able to tell, and they will run away from you. If some of the ideas I offer here don't fit your personality, that's okay; do the version that fits your personality.

A résumé tells a story, so be mindful about the story your résumé is telling. Whether something strengthens your résumé or weakens it very much depends on the story you are trying to convey at a given time. Depending on the opportunity at hand, that story will change.

Bear in mind that *a résumé is not a transcript, it does not need to list every single thing you've ever done in your career.* Rather, a résumé should be customized for every purpose. *A résumé is not fact, it is perception.* You shouldn't put anything untrue on a résumé, but you also don't need to include every single thing. If something is not relevant or does not contribute to the narrative you are building to convince someone to accept you as an intern, then leave it off.

The purpose of a résumé is just to get to the next step, which is usually an interview. A reviewer will probably only look at your résumé for ten to fifteen seconds, and then if it catches their attention, they will spend longer on it. A résumé is just a marketing piece—it's just to get a reviewer's attention. *A résumé is an extended business card. Write your résumé that way.*

AN EXCEPTION TO THE RÉSUMÉ ATTENTION-GRABBER RULE

In most cases, you should consider a résumé as just an attention grabber. However, there are some exceptions. If you are submitting your work history through a system that is designed to simply quantify how much experience you have to meet some standard, like USAJobs.gov or similar systems, less is not more. If the first review of your résumé is just to clear a certain bar before it gets to a more critical review, then don't try to be strategic about the work experience you list. Instead, pile it on; list everything.

Later, after you've passed the litmus test step, get strategic.

Because it is just an attention grabber, I believe there is no reason for a résumé to be more than one page, though some disagree with that. It is true that, for certain disciplines or for very academic resumes that need to list publications, multiple pages are necessary. But in general, shoot for one page. Think you can't fit all your stuff on one page? See all that white space around the outside of your résumé? Fill it in.

When you send a résumé electronically (as most résumé now travel), make sure it is one file and that the file is your name (i.e., EricWoodard.doc, EricWoodard.pdf). In other words, you want to avoid file names like EricResume#15.doc. Send it as a Word or Adobe file. If you are sending your résumé with other documents as part of an application, send it all as one file. Scan it and send as an Adobe file if you need to. Send it whichever way is going to make it easiest for the receiver to handle it, open it, read it, and share it.

Sometimes an electronic application system requires that you enter your résumé information in a pre-set system, you can't send a résumé in your format. In these cases, go ahead and use the system the application asks for, but if you think it will help your cause, go ahead and send in your résumé and all the other stuff, as you have it (more about this later).

If you're just starting out and aren't sure where to start with a résumé, do this. Put your name and contact information at the top. Then, create three sections going down the page in this order: Education, Experience, Other. Then fill each of those sections to the hilt. Unless you're applying to do an internship at a graphic design company, your résumé doesn't have to look pretty, it just needs to be readable. Skip old-fashioned things like "Objectives" or "References Available upon Request." You don't need them.

WANT MY REFERENCES? GO TO HELL

In the name of Pete and all that is holy, *please* don't put "references available upon request' at the bottom of your résumé. Let me ask you, if you're applying for an internship, and the application reviewer calls and says, "Hey, I really like your application but let me ask you, do you have any references I might contact?' Are you going to reply, "Oh my God! I can't believe you asked me that! Although you've made the request, there is no way I'm going to give you my references. Screw you man!!"

Never send in the same résumé for the same opportunity ever again. You are better off sending a highly tuned résumé off to one opportunity than you are sending a generic résumé off to twenty. A great strategy is to go ahead and flesh out an extensive, multipage résumé that lists everything you might put on a résumé. But then, every time you use it, you distill that über résumé down to just one page of the most relevant stuff for a particular opportunity at hand. Though be careful when you do this, because with every version you run the risk of incorporating some little syntax or spelling mistake.

On a résumé, even little mistakes and inconsistencies matter a lot. A reviewer is going to assume that your résumé represents your very best work. So, if one hyphen is a different size than another or if one place you use state abbreviations and in another, you write out the state name—the reviewer will assume that you don't pay attention to detail. Don't give them any excuse to put your résumé in the "no" pile.

Instead, consider the factors that a reviewer might be looking for, and make sure that everything on your résumé speaks directly to those factors. Even if something you did was not principally related to something you highlight on your résumé, if you can build a connection without saying something untrue, that is what you want to do. Remember, a résumé is just a tool to get a reviewer's attention.

Make sure your résumé is explicit in the way it says "here is why you should put me in the 'yes' pile." Let your résumé reach out and bash the reviewer over the head with that message.

If you speak Spanish, you don't need to specify that you have "moderate ability" in Spanish. Just put down Spanish and if the reviewer wants to know how well you speak Spanish, make them call you in for an interview.

Be mindful about the address you put on a résumé. If a position is located in Denver, CO, and you have any address you can conceivably put down in Denver (even the address of the hotel you might stay at were they to ask you for an interview) use that address. Don't give a reviewer the excuse of not calling you because they don't want to make you fly across the country. Put the Denver address. If they call you for an interview, then it will be up to you if you want to pay to fly there for the interview, or not. But at least the decision is yours.

Bear in mind the message that your address conveys. If you list a "school" address and a "home" address, that really screams "college student." If you're applying for an internship in New York City but you list a

Newark address, it raises the question, "Is this person available? Are they going to try and commute?" On the other hand, if you're applying to work for a member of Congress from Montana—you'd better list a Montana address if there is any way you truthfully can.

Put an email address on there that isn't crazy. In high school I did a lot of really cool bird and duck imitations (which are still awesome). For that longest time I sported the email address bird12@. In hindsight, that probably didn't make me seem too professional, but back then email was still kind of a newfangled thing anyway, so maybe it was okay. But it's definitely not okay today. If you don't already have one, get a professional sounding email address that is some version of your name. Pick one you like because as soon as you start giving it out, that will be the address you use to start building your professional network.

List organizations where you have experience on your résumé first, not titles. You might have had the same title five times in a row, but that is not what will interest a reviewer—though the places you've been will.

Some people say you shouldn't put your high school on a résumé, but I think they are wrong—isn't that part of your story? What if you put your high school on a résumé and the reviewer (or their wife or their cousin or their father) went to the same high school? Think that might give you an in? I think it would.

Put your social media links on that résumé. Anybody giving serious attention to your résumé is going to Google your name. So, make it easy for them. Show them you have nothing to hide. Put your links to Facebook, Twitter, and LinkedIn right on there. Don't have a presence on any of those places? We'll talk more about that later.

Finally, and this is the big one that everybody always seems to forget. *Use hyperlinks in your résumé.* It's possible that somebody will be looking at it printed out, but chances are better that a reviewer will be looking at your résumé on a screen. So, if you were the project coordinator at the Kansas City Chapter of the Ancient Babylonian Cabinet Making Club—then be sure to hyperlink the name of the club to that website. This way your résumé becomes four dimensional. Not only does it show a potential intern mentor that you are good at using technology, it also expands the information you can offer on that one sheet limitlessly.

31

Application Matters

"Apply yourself. Get all the education you can, but then, by God, do something. Don't just stand there, make it happen."

—Lee Iacocca

L et me paint a picture for you about the life of a typical internship hiring manager.

After putting out a call for internship applicants, an internship coordinator is accustomed to hearing *nothing* for the longest time.

Then, maybe a day or two before the application deadline, there is this tsunami of internship applications. At the same time, the coordinator can expect to start getting a ton of calls from applicants with questions about the application.

In addition, there will likely be more than one applicant that calls to find out if there is any way they can send their application in after the deadline because of a variety of excuses.

What if an internship hiring manager received your application a day or two after they sent out a call for applicants?

What if between the time you sent in your application and the deadline, you sent the internship coordinator or host organization something that might help them (remember chapter 15)?

Do you think your early application, along with your willingness to show results in advance, would make the internship coordinator think that you were highly organized and helpful? I think it would.

Here's another angle: if that internship coordinator is just looking for a reason to choose one application over another, is the fact that your application was the first she received give her a reason to choose your application over another? It totally does.

When your internship application is the first one an organization receives, way ahead of all the rest, it's going to get noticed and either consciously or unconsciously the person evaluating that application is going to give you a bump for being first.

When you're gunning for an internship, be aware that the supply of interns in the universe often varies. Typically, your competition for a summer internship is going to be way more intense than fall or spring. So if you're applying for a dream internship, and you have the option—definitely stay away from summer.

Along those same lines, organizations are often strapped for help between the traditional times student interns are available—usually August and May. So if you let a potential internship host know that you are willing and able to serve when most other students can't or won't, your chances of getting into that internship you want are much, much greater.

Bear in mind that employers often looking for interns who can best fulfill their needs at times when they can offer the greatest learning experiences. This means that the greater flexibility you can offer in terms of your availability, the more attractive an applicant you will be.

When putting together an internship application, put down as much flexibility on your schedule as you can honestly and conceivably imagine. Realize when you do that you're not making any commitments about your time yet by simply listing your availability. Rather, you're just indicating times you might be available to work if you are accepted. When you are accepted to the internship, you can work out your work schedule then. Understand that on the application, you want to remain honest, but you also don't want to pass up any opportunity to make yourself appear as the best candidate possible.

In terms of submitting an application, sometimes electronic systems can be your worst enemy. Most people will follow the rules and submit an application that way, and so will you. But, that's not all you will do. Don't be afraid to also send in a hard copy of your application, and when you do, send it in a Priority Mail envelope so it stands out. Avoid FedEx or UPS; that can result in somebody having to make a trip downstairs to get your application from a courier—not good. Stick a note in there with an explanation about why you're sending a hard copy. Something like, "I'm sending you a hard copy because I know you already have enough of these to print out and wanted to save you the trouble of printing mine." Or, "I'm sending you a hard copy because I wanted to include this (portfolio, recording, DVD, awesome thing that makes you look good, etc.).

Even better, if there is somebody, anybody, who might have a connection with anybody else at the organization, have them send in a copy of your application too. Third-party emails mentioning internship candidates have a way of getting noticed. *Remember, all an intern manager needs is a reason to pull your application out from the rest. Give them every reason you can to pull yours.*

It's a little sneaky, but if you're in a position to do it, you could even ask a professor or other third-party person who is in your corner to forward your application cold. Even if the intern hiring manager doesn't know or recognize the sender, you will still benefit from the social proof of a third person flagging your stuff. When you watch a commercial, do you know the person claiming that Mentos make life better? No. But nevertheless, those strangers still make you consider that Mentos might make life better, don't they?

32

Testimonial/Reference Sheet

"Can I get a witness?"

—Marvin Gaye

A great testimonial/reference sheet is another vital secret weapon you can employ during your internship search to give yourself an unfair advantage.

What the heck is a testimonial/reference sheet? It's easy. Whenever somebody says something nice about you, write it down. Then, just write down those quotes on a piece of paper. If you haven't been collecting quotes like that, start now. Meanwhile, in the near term, reach out to some of your teachers, friends, and past employers and ask them to send you a quick quote. Put them all down on a piece of paper and you'll be amazed how great it makes you look. On the same piece of paper, put down the names and contact information (name, title, organization, telephone, email) for three to five people who have agreed to serve as a reference for you. Can some of the people you list as a reference be the same people you quote? Of course.

Note about letters of reference: some internship programs will ask you for a certain number of letters of recommendation, which we'll discuss in a little bit. If you don't have a good file of such letters already built up, start now. Instead of asking for a simple quote, ask some of your allies for a full letter. Then quote from it or use the full letter as you need to. When you can, always get letters of references written generically to "Whom it May Concern" and get a copy for yourself. That way, you can use them over and over and over as you need to.

Testimonies on paper are great, but you know what is better? Video.

If somebody is willing to say something nice about you, ask them to say it into that little rectangular box you carry around all the time (your cell phone). Then, put together a video of a bunch of people saying how awesome you are, and send it everywhere you apply. If a picture is worth a thousand words, when it comes to social proof, a testimonial video is worth a thousand more.

33

Creative Resumes and One-Sheets

"Everybody born comes from the Creator trailing wisps of glory. We come from the Creator with creativity."

—Maya Angelou

D o me a favor, sit down in front of a computer and Google the term "creative resumes."

See what I mean? Do you suddenly feel boring?

If you're not in front of a computer and are wondering what the heck I'm talking about, creative résumés are essentially résumés that don't look like a résumé at all. Quilt a résumé, do it as a poem, make it look like a Facebook page—those are creative resumes.

If you were going through a stack of resumes and ran into a hand-painted résumé, do you think it would get your attention? You bet it would. Would you be impressed/want to talk to that candidate?

It depends. But studies are increasingly showing that creative résumés work. I know that when I encounter something creative, I almost always want to at least talk to that person. People greatly underestimate the level of boredom in the working world and how much employers are interested in finding something new.

Why do creative résumés work? They're risky, which makes them rare. Because they're rare, they seem valuable. When your résumé seems valuable, so do you.

Will creative résumés work in every situation? Probably not. If you're applying for an internship with "Stuffy Gray Suit Banker Inc.," maybe you hold the creative version back. Or, if you're doing battle with some kind of online application form that won't take a creative résumé—you don't really have too much of a choice (unless you want to really take initiative and get that creative résumé to the employer by somehow bypassing the system, hint, hint).

So, maybe you maintain two versions of your résumé, the more traditional one and the creative one. But by all means, free your thinking about whether your résumé looks "formal" enough.

Another option is to include a one-sheet with a traditional résumé. Hollywood has a long tradition of pitching movie ideas to producers and ultimately moviegoers through "one-sheets" (Google it). Think mini movie poster. You should consider using a one-sheet to pitch yourself to a potential internship employer.

What is a one-sheet? In the movie business it's basically one sheet of paper that summarizes a product for publicity and sales. The movie ones are often big; you can do yours on a regular sheet of paper.

Be creative, use pictures, create a small poster that is going to grab the attention of the reviewer and suggest all the amazing things you can do for their organization if they choose you as an intern.

You might ask, "But doesn't my résumé give all the relevant information I need to give out about myself?"

You're right, it does. But different people absorb different information in different ways, and your internship campaign is all about making yourself stand out.

34

Social Media Footprint

"Open the kimono."

—Tim Ferriss

Author Tim Ferriss writes about "opening the kimono": I'd like to take this opportunity to steal that line.

What do I mean by "opening the kimono" in terms of your social media profile? Well, it means that you should listen to all those people who are telling you to take all the questionable photos off of Facebook and that you shouldn't say anything blatantly political on Twitter.

You should listen to them, and then completely ignore them.

If a potential employer is going to search around for you online and choose to enter your personal world, then they do so at their own risk. If they are any sort of worthwhile human being, they will understand that everybody is human and the fact that you are too only means you're going to be a better intern.

Everybody puts their shorts on one leg at a time.

So I say: don't clean up a thing. *Be authentic, let all your competitors in the application process sanitize their social media stuff so you can stand out.*

Let me ask you this. In cleaning up your social media footprint so you look good for potential employers, isn't that kind of lying? The hard part about lying is, once you do it, maintaining the lie becomes exhausting. If you conceal something about who you are to a potential employer, how soon will it be before they discover the truth and when they do, what will happen?

If you had fun on spring break, leave those photos up there.

The only thing worse than having a cleaned-up social media profile is not having one at all.

These days, not having a social media presence is almost more suspicious than any drunken photos that might wind up online. Having a social media presence is quickly becoming as important as cover letters, resumes, all of it. If you're behind on your social media skills and/or establishing an online presence, then start now.

35

Online Portfolio

"When I go to my blog, my Facebook page, my Twitter account, I talk to different people from all over the world."

—Paulo Coelho

Building an online portfolio is similar to establishing a social media presence, but by "online portfolio" I mean something more specific.

Start a space; it can be a fancy webpage like yourname.com, but it doesn't have to be. There are a ton of online tools that can help you do this (WordPress, about.me, Blogger, Tumblr, etc.) Build a place online where you can display your best work: writing, photos, movies, art—all of it.

By creating this reservoir of your genius, it gives you a place of reference that can be used for all your internship campaign materials. Instead of mentioning something you did, hyperlink that mention to a movie that shows it. Rather than simply describing a project you led, hyperlink to pictures that show it.

This is also a great place to build career capital. It's fine to use this space to talk about how passionate you are about something, but it's much better to use this space to display your expertise in a subject. If you are going to be the world's expert in Himalayan tectonics, then this is a place where you can write about Himalayan tectonics, display pictures of Himalayan tectonics, show videos about Himalayan tectonics, and post testimonials from other people saying that you are the world's expert on Himalayan tectonics.

36

Recommendation Letters

"You don't carry in your countenance a letter of recommendation."
—Charles Dickens

A lot of people treat letters of recommendation like they are state secrets and this drives me absolutely nuts.

Before computers were mainstream and email was so groovy, when I applied to college I had to ask people to seal letters in an envelope and sign the back—like the signature was some sort of unbreakable seal. Some folks still rely on this medieval requirement.

It would be easier to get a Somali pirate to write a fake letter of recommendation, stick it in an envelope with their signature across the back, and mail it anywhere in the world than it would be to get a bona fide academic teacher to provide a real letter. I don't know where people get the signature across the back thing. Is it to make the letter author feel like they can write candidly?

I've got to tell you, if somebody doesn't have the backbone to tell a student what they really think about the student's performance, they're probably not a very good teacher and therefore, their judgment forming the basis of their letter probably isn't worth much.

As you go through school or as you have bosses or internship supervisors you think would speak highly of you, ask them for a generic letter of recommendation addressed, "To Whom It May Concern." If you need to, offer to draft a letter for them. Also (this is important) ask for these letters while you're still seeing them on an everyday basis. Teachers and internship supervisors see a lot of students. You want them to write the letter for you while you are still front and center in their mind.

Once you have a collection of these letters you'll never need to worry about asking for a letter from the biology professor you had six years ago. If you're applying someplace that requires a letter writer to send the letter directly, just print out a copy and send it to the letter author with an addressed stamped envelope and a nice note requesting that they seal the letter and drop it in the mail.

Increasingly, some people write letters formatted as emails. Whenever you can, ask the people who write your letters of recommendation to stick their words on letterhead, so you can send them as an attachment (normally a pdf) to an email. People, especially those who review internship applications, are conditioned to scan email. If your letter of recommendation comes formatted just as an email, it might not get the attention it deserves just because it looks like an email.

37

Meet the Intern

"I sometimes find that in interviews you learn more about yourself
than the person learned about you."

— William Shatner

If your application has found its way into the right pile, you might
get a letter straight away saying the internship is yours. But chances
are pretty good that, if you're still in the running, an intern host
will reach out and ask you to do an interview instead.

It might be a phone interview, it might be a video interview, it
might be an interview in person, and it might be a combination. Whichever way things go down, you want to be prepared. Most importantly,
remember that any interviewer puts on their shorts one leg at a time
just like everybody else. There is no reason for you to be intimidated
or lack confidence.

When you apply for an internship and a potential internship
host reaches back out to arrange an interview, you've got to decide
how much of a priority that particular internship opportunity is for
you. This may sound a little hard core, but I think it's a pretty black
and white sort of thing. That is, either you don't care at all about this
internship or it's a really big deal for you. If you don't care, politely let

the host know that you appreciate their reaching out, but you're not interested. By the time you reach the interview stage, either bail or go all in—no half measures.

If getting this internship is a big deal for you, then you should treat it as such. What does this mean? It means when they ask when you might be available to do an interview, your answer back to them is "at your convenience." That's right—if you need to, you skip class, skip work—you do whatever you need to do to convey that this internship is a priority for you and you're willing to move mountains to make the potential internship host's life easier. Now, I suppose there might be a few exceptions—a sick loved one, major exam that can't be rescheduled, etc. But, for the most part, you frame the interview so it's at the interviewer's convenience.

Next, if it's a phone interview, you do the interview on the best-sounding line in the quietest place you can. This is a bigger deal than you might suppose. Cell phones and Skype are so ubiquitous nowadays that you might think they are okay for an interview, but they're not. You want to sound crystal clear to an interviewer. Do anything you can to do that interview call from a hard line. If the interviewer is planning to call you, this might take some planning on your part to figure out where you'll be, and when.

If it's a video interview, make sure all your technology is good to go. Test out everything—sound and picture—way beforehand. There still could be a glitch, but as long as the glitch is on the interviewer's end, you'll be fine. It may actually help you because the interviewer could feel bad that their technology failed on you. Just don't let your video technology fail on them. Regardless, have a contingency plan for what you will do if some technology fails during the interview.

Also for a video interview, be mindful about what is behind you and around you. You don't necessarily need to sanitize the area so it's completely bland. Instead, make sure it aligns with the overall message you're trying to send to a potential host about the value you can bring to an internship and why they would be smart to invest in your learning. If it fits your personality, you can even be creative. What if the background to your video screen had a big sign that said, "Subliminal message: you should accept me into your internship program!" Sure, it's corny, but at least it would show you care, and you put in some effort to prepare.

What to wear for a video interview can be a little tricky. Putting on a full suit in your house could look weird. Instead, focus on something that makes you look good and professional on camera. A suit may not be it.

But if interviewing in person, wear a suit. Unless you're interviewing to intern at a fashion outlet or some offbeat place, don't worry about getting creative. Your goal is to look professional. You may be overdressed, that's okay. Carry pen and paper, you're going to be taking notes during the interview. Most students new to the workplace don't know to do this—but it's hugely important. Some might ask, "Why should I take notes, I don't even intern here yet." With that mind-set you never will. On the other hand, if I'm interviewing you, and you think what I have to say is important enough to take notes on *before* you even intern for me, then I'm going to want to see what you can do after you're interning for real.

Turn all your electronics off. No cell phones going off during the interview. Carry several copies of your résumé with you so if your interviewer asks, "Do you have a copy of your résumé with you?" you will.

For an in-person interview, get to your interview spot about thirty minutes ahead of time, but walk on by, don't go in. Find a place nearby to look over your notes one last time, get a drink, cool off, check your look—whatever you want to do. Then, time it so you walk into the interview spot about five minutes before your start time. Never, ever, ever be late for an interview.

If, when you arrive, the interviewer seems rushed or suggests you speak while she goes to get lunch, or if you get the sense the that the interviewer isn't showing you very much respect, just very politely ask if there would be a better time for you to come back to do the interview. Some interviewers will use this technique to rattle you—they make you do the interview in the lunch line, etc. Don't fall for it. If you push back just a bit, you'll beat the interviewer at this game.

Now, this is important—*when you're being interviewed, for goodness sake, please do not fall into the trap of trying to answer an interviewers questions!* Wait, what did I just say?

If you've ever watched any of the political pundit spin shows you may notice that the talking heads tend to be really good at delivering certain talking points, regardless of what question is asked. Within reason, this should be your strategy during an interview. Before your interview, think of three or four messages that you want to deliver to your interviewer. The messages can be simple, like "I'm a great manager" or "I'm very detail-oriented." Come up with some scripts and stories that will permit you to deliver those talking points in response to a variety of questions.

During the interview, don't worry so much about answering the questions. Instead, use the questions as an excuse to deliver the exact message you want to. Often, an interviewer is really just trying to solicit some kind of response from you. They are likely not really interested in the answer to the specific question they give but rather just want you to respond to something so they can get a sense about you. There may be a few specific questions that they are actually looking for you to answer like, "Where are you from?" or "Do you know how to use Microsoft Access?" But, *for the most part, during an interview, the sounds coming out of an interviewer's mouth are just to get you to make sounds from your mouth.*

Don't be afraid to let the interviewer do a lot of talking, but if the conversation gets too far off, politely steer it back to why you would be the best intern this organization could ever hope to have. You've come to this interview for a reason, it's your opportunity to deliver a specific message that meets an internship hosts' goals. Don't pass up the opportunity to steer the conversation in a way that is advantageous to you.

Be prepared with a question or two for the interviewer—because they will probably ask you if you have any questions. When they do, you should be ready. Make sure you ask about something that you couldn't just as easily look up on your own. Some of the best questions are ones that assume you've already gotten the internship. For example, you could ask, "What is the first thing I could do when I start my internship that would be the most valuable to you?" This will force the interviewer to imagine you as their intern, which is exactly what you want them to do.

Another great tactic is to ask questions that will set you up to offer results-in-advance later when you email the interviewer to thank them. For example, ask an interviewer questions like the following:

- "What would it take to double your organization's success?"
- "Where do you hope your organization will be one year from now?
- "What has your organization tried that didn't work?"

Based on those answers, you'll hopefully have something to offer the interviewer as a follow-up.

A really great way to get good at doing an interview is to interview a few people yourself. Find some friends and do a mock interview with each other. Or even better, do a pretend job interview with someone you do not know well. You will be amazed at what an educational experience this can be. Chances are, you'll think, "Wow, this person's answers are way better than mine." Or, you'll think, "These are exactly the same answers I tend to give and wow, they sound really terrible."

Just like your cover letter, your résumé, your application, your references, and your stuff online, the interview you give should not be accidental, but built around a specific message aimed at persuading a prospective internship host that you are the intern they should pick.

38

Thank You

"Develop an attitude of gratitude, and give thanks for everything that happens to you, knowing that every step forward is a step toward achieving something bigger and better than your current situation."

—Brian Tracy

I used to think that sending handwritten notes following an interview was the best way to go because it might make one really stand out. I still think something handwritten is a nice touch. But nowadays, in most situations, that's just too slow.

Either later in the day or the next day following an interview, email a thank-you note to your interviewer and anybody else you might conceivably need to thank. It doesn't have to be long, it doesn't even really need to reiterate why you would be the best person for their internship position. More than anything, it just needs to be genuine.

You might use the thank you as a way to follow up on something you mentioned during the interview. If you have something new that you can offer to further show the value you could offer during an internship, send that with the thank you. Another angle: if, during the interview the interviewer mentioned a problem they have or information they lack, you could use the thank you to offer the interviewer results-in-advance by sending information that helps solve their problem.

Let the interviewer know that you are grateful for the opportunity to meet them and for their consideration. If there was anything you found particularly interesting or enjoyable about the interview, let them know. Offer to provide any more info that would be helpful.

39

Because You're Worth It

"To be in *Vogue* has to mean something. It's an endorsement. It's a validation."

—Anna Wintour

This may be something you already lined up when you first applied for the internship. But, if not, it's something you need to do before an interview or very soon after an interview: line up your references.

Get into the habit of keeping a current list of supervisors, peers, and if you have them, subordinates who can speak about how awesome you are. Sometime around the interview stage, potential internship hosts may ask you for the names and contact info of people you've worked with who can vouch for you as a good human being. Have this list ready. Beyond just names and contact info—put a little blurb next to each about how you know each person.

Give each of these people a heads-up whenever you think it's possible a potential internship employer might reach out to them. Not only is this a polite thing to do for your references, but it will very likely equip them to say just the right thing about you, depending on the opportunity at hand.

Don't be afraid to use your references proactively. If this is an internship you really want (It is right? This is all or nothing, right?) and you have references that might be in a particularly good position to do so, ask them to reach out to the potential employer proactively and sing your praises.

If a potential internship host gets several emails and calls voicing the particular merits of a particular candidate, they are going to be more likely to at least look at that candidate. Is this a little heavy handed? Yes. Is it a little aggressive? You bet. Will it give you an unfair advantage? Absolutely.

40

But I Don't Know How to Do All That

"I don't even have any good skills. You know, like nun-chuck skills,
bow hunting skills, computer hacking skills."
—Napoleon Dynamite, *Napoleon Dynamite*

Now after reading about all the layers of stuff you should do to get a great internship, you may be thinking, "But I don't know how to put up a website! I don't know how to edit video! I don't know how to design a creative résumé!" This is where most people don't follow through, but don't let this be you.

If you don't know how to do fancy graphic design, hire somebody to help you. You can go on http://elance.com and hire somebody to do just about anything.

If you're not in a position to hire somebody, do you have a friend with skills who might be able to help you? Why not trade what you've learned in this book for what they know about graphic design or video editing, and you'll both get great internships?

If you don't have any friends with skills, well, it may be time to learn how to do some graphic design and video editing. There are tons of free resources online and in libraries that can offer you the basics.

If you can afford it or your school has a subscription to it, check out http://lynda.com, which can teach more than one could learn in a hundred lifetimes.

Object to having to learn new skills to apply for an internship? Well—it may be that you don't have the career capital you need to apply. Gaining skills is what I mean by building career capital. Before you can convince someone else to invest in your education by mentoring you in an internship, you had better be willing to invest in yourself. Does that make sense?

41

You Have Nothing to Lose

"Never pick a fight with an ugly person, they've got nothing to lose."
—Robin Williams

So you've gone all in. You've found the right internship, you've sent in awesome materials with your application, you did everything just right with the interview, and now—nothing. You haven't heard squat.

Take satisfaction in knowing that you're in good company. This is a story that is incredibly common. What does it mean when you don't hear back?

Is it possible that they've hired somebody else? Is it possible that they've decided not hire anybody? Is it possible that a key decision maker is out sick? Is it possible that you offended them horribly? Is it possible they sent you an email and it just didn't go through?

Yep.

If the time period when a potential internship host committed to get back to you has come and gone, there's only one thing you can do: follow up with them. Now, don't get me wrong, I'm not talking about a situation where you interviewed on Monday and you're just anxious so you reach out to them on Wednesday. Rather, if it's been a couple of weeks and/or several days past the time they promised they would get back to you—reach out to them. You have nothing to lose.

Don't be shy; call them. There are hundreds of reasons you might not have heard from a perspective internship supervisor. Maybe they lost your number, maybe your acceptance letter got stuck in the mail, maybe your dog ate it, maybe their server is funky and their message went in your spam folder, maybe they are just busy and need you to call so they can just offer you the position on the spot. I often think, when I applied to the White House, what if I'd never called to follow up? What an opportunity I would have missed!

If, after all this, you get word that your application has been rejected, you're still not finished. Most people miss this next step. *Reach out to whoever reviewed your application and ask them for feedback.* Ask them specifically how your application could be improved and what turned them off. You may find that your application was awesome—that there were just other circumstances at play. Or, you may get some really valuable feedback that will help you next time round.

Even after you've received the rejection—if it's an internship you really want—follow up with the intern coordinator one last item. Send them one more thing, a piece of writing, an article, something you've created, with a short note along the lines of, "Dear intern coordinator, I just wanted to thank you again for reviewing my application. On the off chance that you've had a slot open up, I just wanted to share this [insert thing that makes you look awesome] so you can see that I would be really qualified to fill your opening."

Do you think this is overkill? Tam didn't. Tam applied to a summer internship program I managed many years ago for Senator Clinton. I really wanted to accept Tam. But, for various reasons, I just didn't have the slot to offer him. While rejection letters started to go out, I even made up a fake "waitlist" category for Tam in the hope that I might find a solution. In the end however, I had to call Tam and explain we just couldn't take him. At that point, most students might have thrown in the towel, but not Tam.

A few days later, the front office called to let me know that someone had dropped off an envelope for me. It turned out to be a thank-you note from Tam with just one more writing sample to show how awesome he was. I decided that we needed to accept Tam on the spot. A few months later, Tam was hired as a full-time staffer. Several years later, Tam became Sen. Clinton's intern coordinator. Besides being awesome, Tam never gave up, and it really paid off.

IF YOU NEED TO, GUILT THEM INTO IT

Suppose you hit the end of the road. The internship supervisor has given you a final "no." Short of becoming a stalker, there are three more things you can do. First, give the reviewer one final thank you. Second, let them know that if they wind up losing an intern mid-term you stand ready to step in. Third, let them know that you fully intend to apply for the next internship session.

If you're lucky, the internship supervisor will get your earnest message right around the time some of the interns that were chosen are acting particularly entitled and goofy. When the internship supervisor compares your attitude with the attitude of other students who were accepted, they may feel so guilty that they will just tell you to come in.

42

Don't Make Them Sorry They Chose You

"Don't feel entitled to anything you didn't sweat and struggle for."
—Marian Wright Edelman

Something terrific happens. You get the call/email/letter from the organization of your dreams saying, "YES! We want you to come be our intern!"

Good for you! Now you can relax, kick back, have a Diet Tab, and let it all hang out, right? No way.

I've seen plenty of examples where internship applicants undergo a radical transformation when they get accepted into an internship program. Before getting accepted, they seem awesome but after getting accepted, they turn into dorks.

Don't be a dork when you land the internship of your dreams. If you do start acting like a dork, is there anything to prevent an organization from retracting their internship offer? In most cases, there isn't. Internships aren't like getting into college in the sense that once you're in, you're in.

In fact, in the vast majority of internships, an organization can dismiss you with very little cause. FYI, this is true in a lot of jobs too.

Welcome to the working world and congratulations on encountering another lesson internships can provide: job interviews really never end.

What does this mean for you? It means that once you land that dream internship, pat yourself on the back for about five minutes. Then move forward on the premise that you're going to have to work every day to keep it.

PART II:

How to Thrive During Your Internship

43

Learn the Basics Before You Begin

"Our species needs and deserves a citizenry with minds awake and a basic understanding of how the world works."

—Carl Sagan

Several years ago, Nick was assigned to be my intern. Nick had just completed his sophomore year at an Ivy League school, and I could tell from the beginning that he was incredibly smart (definitely smarter than me) and superbly well intentioned. However, he didn't have a clue about work, and it showed.

SOME PEOPLE WON'T LIKE THIS VERY MUCH

In my experience, there is almost always an inversely proportional relationship between an arriving intern's practical skills and the level of prestige associated with the school they attend. In other words, a lot of time the student from the University of Michigan arrives at an internship better equipped for the workplace than the student from Harvard.

Now, this is a generalization. Have I had fantastic interns from Harvard and sucky interns from Michigan? You bet. But, I've had more good ones from Michigan. The point: when it comes to internships, don't fret about whether you attended a well-known school. A lot of internship supervisors are actually a little bit biased against the fancy schools.

If you're an Ivy Leaguer, well—I bet you're smart enough to figure out how to overcome those biases on your own.

In part as a warm-up, and also because I needed it, I asked Nick if he would please make a single copy of a one-page document. After forty-five minutes, poor Nick returned, head down, with my single page original now slightly crumpled in his hand.

I asked, "Nick! What's the matter?"

Nick said, "I couldn't do it."

"Couldn't do what?" I asked.

He replied, "I couldn't make the copy."

This story might sound crazy—but when was the last time you used a photocopier? Would you recognize the buttons, know how to clear a paper jam, or refill paper on an unfamiliar machine?

Now, you might be saying, "I don't need to know how to make copies; I'm way more advanced than that!" Well, speaking from personal experience, the only thing I can say to you my friend is that when there is nobody else around and your big boss turns to you and says, "Would you mind please making four copies of this double sided and stapled?" you damn well better know how to do it—accurately and *fast*. While you're at it, don't let the bead of sweat dripping off your brow hit the paper.

Nick studied Shakespeare, organic chemistry, calculus, and had 3.9 GPA. But he became paralyzed by a photocopier because he didn't know a few simple things. He was a product of state-of-the-art education, but nobody had taken the time to teach him even the most basic things about the workplace.

At this point you might be saying, "But isn't that what an internship is for? Isn't an internship *supposed* to be the place where you learn basic office skills?"

That might be true. You could spend your *entire* internship learning about basic workplace skills through osmosis. But I think you can do better than that. I can guarantee that the people you're competing against for that one full-time staff opening plan to do better than that.

If you're spending your entire internship learning basic office skills, you're not going to have much time to focus on the unique skills, people, or opportunities you should. So don't. Get a handle on the basic stuff ahead of time. *Make the most of your internship time by going in with the basics already mastered, so you can learn the more advanced stuff.*

THINK THAT STINT AT MCDONALD'S TAUGHT YOU NOTHING?

Think again. A lot of times the most menial, seemingly meaningless jobs you take as a student can teach you a lot skills that you'll use later in the workplace. When a restaurant manager tells you to refill the soda machine and there is a crowd of thirsty people who want a drink, you somehow figure it out. Because, if you don't, that thirsty mob might just kill you.

Don't seek out a job that makes you empty trashcans. But, if that's what you wind up with when you're starting out, realize it may not be a total loss. Pick up what skills you can doing grunt work and you'll have an edge over your peers who have no experience getting their hands dirty in the real world.

44

Be Great on Day One

"I need a hero."

—Bonnie Tyler

Let me put it this way: if you show up on day one of your internship and you already have the basic stuff down, you're going to have a *huge* advantage over your peers. Make no mistake, when it comes to internships, first impressions are a big deal. When a staffer knows they are going to have to work with an intern for the next however many months, they are just looking for any clue they can find to figure out who the best interns might be.

That first impression will likely determine where you'll work, when you'll work, who you'll be working with, what you'll be doing, and how you'll be doing it. Remember when you got picked for a reading or math group in school and how that kind of tracked you for the rest of your days? That first impression you give during your internship is a little bit like that.

Once, I recall a time when a new group of interns arrived on a day when I happened to be out of the office. When the new group walked around to meet everybody in the office, I missed it. The next day one of these new interns, Michelle, took it upon herself to come find me so she could introduce herself. Bravo—great initiative. Way to stand out from the crowd!

Except in Michelle's case, she wound up shuffling in my office slurping on an iced coffee through a straw. She didn't have a pen, she didn't have paper—she didn't have a card, just the coffee through a straw. Not a good first impression.

Imagine instead if Michelle has stepped forward with pen and paper in hand, ready to take notes about any cool projects I happened to need help with. What if she had her contact info all ready to hand over? What if she had given off the vibe that she was ready to work rather than, I'm sipping Starbucks?

DOES SOMEBODY HAVE THE WRONG IMPRESSION?

If, for whatever reason, you wind up working with somebody (another intern, a staffer) during your internship that has the wrong impression about you, change it. If they take an action or make a comment that implies something about you that is untrue, call them on it.

For example, suppose somebody has the impression that you are antisocial and they invite everybody but you to an after work thing that you would actually like to be a part of. Simply ask them in a nice way, "Why do you think I wouldn't like to come?' Interrupt their assumptions about you. Don't wait to do it, do it early on. The longer false assumptions remain unchallenged, the deeper they sink in.

I've seen it countless times. A new group of interns arrives, but there are some who stand out on the first day because they are more focused, more confident. Over the years I've mentored hundreds of interns. Some I remember, some I don't. A lot of the ones I remember are now colleagues, because they got hired.

Are you worried that you've already started out on the wrong foot? Don't worry. Just like the reading or math group in school, it's possible to jump onto a better track—it just takes a little more work. Take steps to correct any false first impressions colleagues might have adopted about you.

45

Don't Get Rattled by the GLARE

"Son, I've lived a life of reading people's faces, knowing what the cards are by the way they've held their eyes. Now if you don't mind me saying, I can see you're out of aces. For a taste of your whiskey, I'll give you some advice."

—Kenny Rogers

For whatever reason, nobody tells bright-eyed, world-changing young professionals such as you the truth. Which is: as a young person in the workplace, especially as an intern, you have to watch out for the GLARE!

What is the GLARE? It's the silent look a battle-hardened twenty-year workplace veteran gives a first-day intern when the intern says something that shows their youth and professional inexperience. The GLARE is a look that says, "My God child, you are so naïve and clueless." The GLARE says, "Young man/lady, you are going to have to *earn* every ounce of respect you get from me." The GLARE says, "Grrrrrrrrrrrrrr." Sound harsh? It is.

I'm sorry to be the one to have to tell you about the GLARE. It's a secret that everybody has been keeping from you. We keep it from all the young people. After enough scrapes and bruises in the workplace, most people learn about the GLARE the hard way, on their own. Believe it or not, I consider myself a glass-is-half-full personality—an optimist—and it's hard for me to be such a downer. I just want you to understand that the work world is a very different place from the school world.

However, the good news is that if you understand some of the differences between work and school going in, you will be ready to avoid the GLARE or handle it when it happens. If you know what to expect from your internship, if you have the right skills, have the right attitude, and know how to communicate effectively, you can jump across many workplace pitfalls like an intern ninja.

46

Putting Out a Contract on Yourself

"It's a very sobering feeling to be up in space and realize that one's safety factor was determined by the lowest bidder on a government contract."

—Alan Shepard

If you doing an internship as part of an academic course, your school has probably already asked you to write down internship learning objectives, and for your internship mentor to write down objectives they have. But regardless of whether you are in school, if this hasn't happened, it might be a really good idea for you to do on your own.

What are learning objectives? Basically, pretty simple—it's what it sounds like. You write down what you want to learn through the internship. You might be thinking, "Oh yes, I have those, they are in my head." Not good enough—actually write them down. Put them someplace where you can refer to them regularly.

Along those same lines, talk with your internship mentor—ideally, at the beginning of your internship—about what they expect you will learn during the experience. If your mentor is willing to also write these things down, that's great. But if need be, you should write down what your mentor says for them.

It's a little formal, but I'm a huge fan of both mentor and intern actually signing a copy of both the intern's learning objectives and the mentor's mentorship objectives. When they do, it offers a symbolic way for both intern and mentor to demonstrate that they are committed to making sure the internship is a great learning experience.

47

Reflect It

"Follow effective action with quiet reflection. From the quiet reflection will come even more effective action."

—Peter Drucker

From just about everything research tells us, reflection is a really important part of learning. In other words: it's great to have new experiences, but unless there is an opportunity to reflect about what those experiences mean, learning is stifled. Especially in the busy working world where an intern dwells, not having an opportunity to reflect on what is being learned can be a limitation.

So, to make sure you learn a ton during your internship, just make sure you give yourself an opportunity to reflect about the experience and make sense of the lessons you are learning. It has never worked well for me, but some find it helpful to do learning journals and that sort of thing. Others find talking with others the most effective way to process new information.

Whatever works best for you, just make sure you give yourself time to do it.

48

Learn Deliberately

"I am still learning."

—Michaelangelo

O nce they enter the working world and make the switch between work and school, many modern professionals have a tendency to rely exclusively on informal learning. For sure, lots of informal learning happens at work and in life after school. Indeed, that is huge part of the reason why people learn in internships. Informal, lifelong learning is hugely important.

However, I believe that a lot of professionals today miss the boat because, once they enter the working world, they tend to stop all forms of formal learning. Some employers strive to counteract this by mandating that workers have so many hours of formal training every year, but that can sometimes be more symbolic than anything.

I would encourage you to avoid this trap. Right away when you first enter the working world through your internship, make it your habit to continue your formal education deliberately. When I refer to *formal education,* I don't necessarily mean sitting in a classroom, but I do mean deliberately going after new skills. For example, you might work on a new language by listening to Rosetta Stone for twenty minutes a day, you might work on learning the words to all the verses in the "Star-Spangled Banner", you might spend twenty minutes learning keyboard shortcuts in Microsoft Word. It doesn't really matter so much what you learn as much as you make it a habit to learn at work deliberately as well as experientially.

If you do, you will quickly find that the little skills you pick up through this habit will greatly amplify the career capital you can bring to bear during your internship and later as a staffer.

49

Know the Bright Line

"I was a loner as a child. I had an imaginary friend—I didn't bother
with him."

—George Carlin

ristotle said, "Man is a social animal." I agree. In school, if your
experience was anything like mine, there were a few loners,
bullies, introverts, etc., but generally, it's safe to assume that
most people are out to make friends of one kind or another. However,
it's important to understand that at work, this isn't always the case.

Typically, a new intern fresh out of the classroom approaches work
with the logical assumption that everybody is interested in being
friends: other interns, staff, their boss, etc. This might be true, but not
always.

Modern workers often spend more time with their coworkers than
their family members. Understand that some office dwellers draw a
very specific line between their work relationships and their personal
relationships because they want to make sure that the former never
threaten the latter.

Is this okay? You bet it is. People are paid to be at work to do work,
not make friends. Do people work better with each other when they

are friendly with each other? Yes, they do. But it's not necessarily a prerequisite.

THE HALLWAY

I don't know if you'll experience this, but I remember when I first started out as an intern, the experience of passing people in the hallway was a little surreal.

When I just started out as an intern, I noticed that the way people passed each other in an office hallway is very different than a school hallway. Specifically, there seems to be a lot less smiling, nodding, and in general acknowledgement of other human beings in the workplace hallway.

If close coworkers encounter each other in the office hallway, or people who have something to discuss bump into each other—things tend to be friendly. But otherwise, a lot of people maintain that thousand-yard stare when they are on the move at work.

People at work tend to be focused, they tend to have things on their mind, they tend to have things to do. As a new intern, if you feel like people are looking straight through you, don't worry. It's them, not you.

If you're a newbie in the workplace, it's important to understand that this has nothing to do with you—it's nothing personal. If somebody you work with doesn't show interest in being your friend, don't be offended.

In fact if, as a new intern, you encounter a staffer (especially a supervisor) who seems overly friendly (especially compared to the behavior of others), you might want to exert just a bit of caution. I've seen situations where staffers who have trouble getting along with colleagues decide they will build their social circle around each new group of interns. It goes without saying that this phenomenon can cause all sorts of trouble for an intern.

Be aware that any office you enter already has its own tangled web of personalities and internal politics. As an intern, you're there to learn and get access—the best way to do this is to stay above the fray. Especially when you first start out, don't worry about making close friendships with coworkers. Instead, focus on building a reputation for being a good worker. After you've been in the trenches long enough with colleagues, friendships will come through respect for your work. When you're first starting out, those are the kind of relationships you want at work.

In the workplace, people with a good sense of professionalism are reluctant to befriend people they are charged with supervising, especially when they haven't known each other for very long. After all, it is difficult to reprimand a friend. The best staff will often maintain a certain professional distance with more junior staff. Since, as an intern you will likely be the lowest person on the totem pole, be prepared for some cold shoulders when it comes to making friends at the office. Even if a boss or supervisor really wants to let their hair down and reach out, understand they might have reasons to hold back.

It's always fascinating to me to watch a boss's behavior on an employee's last day; I've seen this so many times. When it's time for the final goodbye, the boss who has been a little stiff and buttoned up for years with an employee will suddenly melt. You'll see smiles, hugs, effusive praise, even tears. The boss doesn't have to worry about managing that staffer any more. A supervisor who may have repressed a natural inclination toward friendliness for a long time is suddenly free to show their true feelings to their subordinate.

They don't teach this stuff in school. Most new interns haven't considered the aspect of making friends at work, but you should.

50

You're the FNG

When I was in Guam, I often worked with Clubmates. These were young men and women from the U.S. mainland, mostly just out of college, who would rotate on and off the island for a six-month stint working at a resort. During my years diving in Guam I saw several generations of Clubmates come and go. It was a little like reality TV and always interesting to watch people getting acclimated to island life between their first day and their last. New arrivals to the island were often lovingly referred to as "FNGs" (aka F$%^#$★ New Guys) by the veterans.

When I came to Washington, seeing groups of interns come and go completely reminded me of my experience with FNGs on Guam. The term "FNG" actually originated out of the Vietnam War, stemming from the U.S. rotation policy with soldiers. When new recruits arrived as FNGs, more veteran soldiers already partway through their tour would have to show them the ropes.

Remember, as a new intern, you are a FNG.

This is part of the reason for the GLARE, and it's also part of the explanation behind the slow friendship phenomenon. Understand that staffers have likely invested a full semester training your intern predecessor, and now you've arrived all bright eyed and bushy tailed but clueless, so now they have to train you. Staff are glad you've arrived and need your help, but they also dread the learning curve.

Another aspect of the FNG phenomenon is that, as a new person, you haven't really earned your spurs yet, so to speak. Resident office workers may have worked in the trenches together for years. Until you've spent some time there too, you will be regarded as an outsider.

If your new office is one where internship terms overlap such that some interns have been there longer than others, you may find that veteran interns tend to treat the new ones like FNGs. Does this sound a lot like rushing a fraternity or sorority? It is.

You may not be into the Greek thing, but as a new intern, don't be surprised if you have to play that game just a little bit. Remember, your purpose is professional. You're interning to get access, you're interning to learn.

51

Tune In

"So a prudent man should always follow in the footsteps of great men and imitate those who have been outstanding."

—Niccolo Machiavelli

In school, it's logical to expect that you will follow a regular schedule. Certain classes meet at certain times; lunch happens at a certain time; you go home at a certain time. Schools even have bells that go off to signal a change from one time to another.

In the U.S. Senate they have little bells that go off to alert Senators whenever a vote is being called, and of course on Wall Street they open and close with a bell. But that's about as close as most workplaces get to having bells. In most offices, the signal to switch modes is much more subtle and in my experience, new interns miss it all the time.

If you walk into an office and things are dead quiet, with people working heads down at their desk, you should adopt the same posture. You might walk into your office and find people shouting and running around urgently. This is not the time to try and ask questions that can wait or engage in idle chitchat. On the other hand, people are kicking back, laughing—talking about stuff that isn't really work related—means you can relax too. *The point is: read the signs.*

So many times when I've been in a situation that was pretty much verging on crisis—people running around, phones going crazy, smoke coming out of peoples' ears—an intern has chosen that opportune time to ask about something that could wait or, even worse, tried to start up some small talk. I think what happens sometimes is that interns know something is going on, and they either (1) want to help or (2) want to be involved, but they're not sure how to do either because they don't really understand what is happening. So, they default to small talk. Don't be one of these interns.

If you walk into a situation that is clearly a crisis and you're not exactly sure what is going on or how you can help, the best thing to do is stay out of the way. Is it okay to stand to the side so you are available to help if called on? Absolutely. That is actually a good idea. However, be careful not to be a distraction. An intern in this situation should be like Hippocrates: "Do no harm."

ALL AHEAD FLANK SPEED

Have you seen the movie *The Hunt for Red October*? In the film there is a scene where rogue Soviet submarine captain Ramius (played by Sean Connery) suddenly asks his crew to increase speed as they're going through a particularly tricky spot near the ocean floor. The crew has to re-plot their course on the fly to avoid smashing into an underwater mountain. Captain Ramius is making his crew sweat on purpose.

You may encounter supervisors during your internship that intentionally chose the most inopportune times to request that you do the most mundane things. They will ask in a way and during a time that makes it almost seem like they are testing you. It will feel that way because they are.

So be ready for this. When you're in the heat of some hectic crisis, be prepared for a supervisor to come up with something extra at the worst time. If and when they do, don't bat an eyelid. Take the request in stride. If you show constant cool under pressure, that is something that will make you stand out as a super duper intern.

Whether they know it or not, people tend to like and trust others who look and act like themselves. So, if your intern supervisor is focused like a laser, you should be too. If your supervisor is relaxed, you should be too. Being a mimic will give you increased access and opportunities to learn.

52

Show Your ID

"I carry a badge."

—Joe Friday, *Dragnet*

When you start your internship, chances are you're going to be issued some kind of ID badge. In fact, going off to get your ID badge may be one of the first things you're asked to do as in intern. Don't be surprised if you spend at least part of the first day of your internship going to some hard-to-find office where you wind up waiting to get a picture taken (think student ID office).

Some badges are fancier than others. At the low end, you may receive something that looks like it's not much more than a business card. You might look at it once, put it in a drawer, and never think about it again. More than likely, though, your badge will have a few more bells and whistles than that. In our increasingly security conscious world, badges are becoming a bigger deal.

Generally, badges consist of some kind of laminated credential that includes your photo, an expiration date, and sometimes your title/office. At the high end, a badge displays your security clearance and contains some kind of magnetic device required to access your workplace.

In very secure workplaces I've seen situations where one is required to show a badge to an officer, then scan the badge, then enter a pin number, then walk through a metal detector. Then, you need the same badge to use the elevator, and eventually get through your office door. These are the sorts of places where badges must be displayed at all times.

Depending on your particular workplace, people may take the security badge stuff very seriously or not seriously at all. Whatever the case, somewhere at your workplace somebody has probably written down what the policy is regarding badges. Chances are that whoever that person is, they believe it is their life's purpose to enforce the policy. Beware: interns are easy prey.

So, the thing to do is (1) know policy regarding security badges and be ready to comply with it if somebody gives you grief but (2) behave the way established staffers behave when it comes to badges.

Why not follow the badge policy to the letter? Well, this may sound crazy, but if you are too much of an eager beaver when it comes to wearing your badge, you can get judged for it. As in, "Look at the new intern so proud of their shiny new badge—they are so young . . . "

Is there anything wrong with being proud of your ID badge? Nope. Let me confess, I've got a drawer full of old ID badges from over the years. They are trophies of experience. However, flaunting a work ID is an intern tell. You don't want people to be distracted by how you're wearing your badge, you want people to respect you and focus on how awesome you are.

Believe it or not, during the summertime in Washington, DC, interns can sometimes be seen flaunting their intern badges out in public like a status symbol. I've seen young men and women wearing their badges in the grocery store . . . on a Saturday (and no, it didn't look like they had been working overtime, they just liked their badge).

I've even seen interns try to use their ID badges to try to get into bars and restaurants. This is wrong on so many levels: (1) it won't work, because the bouncer doesn't care that you work for Congressman Flung-a-dung, (2) any time you produce a work ID, it implies you are representing your employer, (3) if word got back to your employer that you were using a work ID to ask for special privileges in public they would definitely think you were a dork, would likely be really pissed, and might fire you (not to mention that using a public position for private gain like that is also very illegal).

People wear badges in different ways. Sometimes badges come with little clips or pins that can be attached to a pocket or lapel. Workplace culture permitting, a cooler way to wear a badge is on a lanyard around your neck. You can buy lanyards like this online—they're often made from metal chains or cloth straps. Whatever they are made from, make sure the lanyard you have isn't going to break and cause you to lose your badge.

If you wear an ID around the neck, make sure it rests around the outside of your collar, otherwise it looks weird coming up around the sides of your neck. Also, when you're not at work, take off your badge or at least slip it into a shirt pocket while still around your neck.

A work ID may seem new to you, but consider that staffers may have had one of these things around their neck for fifteen or thirty years. Don't be surprised if you see colleagues on staff twirling their badge or playing with it. Make no mistake, in the workplace, an ID badge can affect a person's identity in more ways than one. Even if only subconsciously, your colleagues are going to be hyper-aware of how you wear and otherwise handle your ID badge. Treat it like something you've been wearing for thirty years and people may give you the same respect they would have for someone who has worn an ID for that long.

53

Shield Your Magnetic Personality

"They had to replace my metal plate in my head with a plastic one."
—Cousin Eddie, *National Lampoon's Christmas Vacation*

In the summer, Washington, DC, can get hot. Not just regular hot, but swampy Degobah, Yoda-like hot. I grew up in the tropics and understand humidity. But the thing about the tropics is most folks don't make you wear a suit there. If you're working in a muggy American city, work clothes can be a bit of drag.

There is almost nothing worse than walking around outside, in your work clothes, in DC, in the summer except when you reach the entrance to your air-conditioned destination only to find the entry way blocked by an intern fishing for loose coins, trying to get through a metal detector.

Damn.

Want to engender goodwill among your colleagues? *Don't be the new intern who holds things up at the metal detector.*

This might sound like a simple thing, but getting through the metal detector actually takes a little forethought. If the entrance to your workplace is guarded by a metal detector, make sure you can produce and then later retrieve all magnetic contraband (phones, Blackberry, coins) for the X-ray machine in one motion.

Remember, at the same time you do this, you'll also likely need to display your ID badge too.

On the first day of your internship, decide where you're going to make a habit of keeping all your metallic stuff; before long going through the metal detector will become automatic. Ladies, keep the shiny jewelry in your bag till you've passed through the magnetometers, and dudes, forget about wearing any kind of shoes with steel in them. Remember, during the day you may be called on to enter/exit the building on short notice. If your supervisor says "Come with me" and winds up taking you through a metal detector, don't be the intern that requires your boss to slow down while you get your act together. More than likely your supervisor will assume that, like interns she's worked with in the past, you will require extra time to go through the metal detector. Surprise her.

54

Find a Place to Dwell

"A ream of fresh paper lies on my desk waiting for the next book."
—Pearl S. Buck

When you find out that you've been accepted into an internship program, it seems logical to assume that during your internship, somebody will point to a desk and say, "Welcome! This is your desk!"

It seems like you would be right to expect something like that. Except that, if I agreed with you, we'd both be wrong.

You might have the fortunate situation where your office assigns you a desk that is meant for just you for the duration of your internship. But, more than likely—you will be lucky to have a place to work (desk, chair, computer, phone) on any given day, much less a permanent set-up devoted just to you.

In today's cost-cutting, mobile, start-up world, it's not unusual to see permanent staffers fighting it out for workspace. As an intern who is even lower in the food chain, available workspace for you may sometimes be slim pickings.

So what should you do? How can you do your work if you don't have a place to work? Well my friend, if you're going to be a stellar intern, it's time to get creative. First of all, you've got to be bold. That means if there is physically an empty space available to do your work, assume it's up for grabs unless somebody tells you otherwise. Don't ask for permission, ask for forgiveness.

WHO WORE IT BEST?

Pretend you are a big huge gigantic boss walking around an office, the sort that can decide to hire, or not hire, new interns as staff.

You see two interns: the first one is just kind of standing there, or maybe talking to somebody else. When you ask them what they are doing the intern replies, "I'm waiting for a desk because I don't have a place to work."

The second intern you see is sitting on the floor working on something furiously. When you ask what they are doing, the intern says, "I'm working on this important project because it needs to get done."

Which intern do you think the big boss is going to have more sympathy, admiration, and gratitude for? Which intern will that boss remember when it comes time to hire?

Obviously, the less senior person's space you can hijack, the better. When faced with a shortage of workspace, most interns will do a 180 degree turn back to their supervisor and say, "I need a place to work." Instead of solving the problem on their own, the intern hands their problem over to their supervisor.

Be different, look for desks that aren't being used because somebody is out sick or at a long meeting or on vacation or whatever. Do everything you can to avoid messing up their space, and be ready to vacate the space at a moment's notice. But don't stand around with work to do because you're afraid to use an empty workspace.

If this philosophy makes you uncomfortable, think of it this way. The workplace where you are interning has invested tons of resources to establish an office and, presumably, the work you have been tasked to do is important. An unused desk and an idle intern are wasted resources.

Be bold, sit down, and do your work. If somebody more senior shows up, vacate immediately. In the meantime, do your thing.

When you can't find a place to work in the office (or if staffers have kicked you out), think about what you might be able to do without a desk, or by sharing a desk. If part of your work involves just phone calls, find a phone, any phone (a courtesy phone, a cell phone, etc.). If you need web access, bring your laptop from home if you've got one—march yourself down to the nearest coffee shop that has free Wi-Fi. Sometimes organizations have rules about working off site or with using personal equipment. But unless somebody tells you not to do it, do it—and for God's sake, don't ask permission. Chances are, if you don't raise the question, no one else will. This is especially true if the work you are doing is important and you are finding a way to get it done, overcoming any barriers you encounter on your own.

When Hillary Clinton was sworn into the U.S. Senate in January of 2001, I helped move her office from the White House to a very small, cramped transition office in the basement of the Dirksen Senate Building. As Senator Clinton's office quickly accumulated new staff in order to serve the constituents of New York, we had to get creative in terms of office space.

By March of that year we literally had built a peninsula of desks pushed end to end. In order to get to their desks, some staffers had to traverse an area we called the Cape of Good Hope—all the way past everybody else's desk—to get to their desk. At that time, we were especially slammed with people wanting to meet with the new Senator's office. So, we took meetings in the cafeteria down the hall or, if need be, standing in the hallway. Until we received access to our permanent office, the interns we hosted that first spring literally didn't have a place to sit, ever. They were busy and did all their work on foot, usually standing outside in the hall.

If you find yourself in a situation like that with your internship and it bothers you, consider this: I could be wrong, but my sense is that the best internships are often ones that place an intern in a little bit of chaos like this. Why? Because if an organization is really vital and active and flying close to the edge in terms of what they do, chances are they won't be stable enough to field enough desks for everybody. When you are interning for an organization that is truly growing and making a difference in the world, sometimes there are more important things than having a desk, much less one of your own.

55

Show Up and Be Present

"Concentrate all your thoughts upon the work at hand. The sun's rays do not burn until brought to a focus."

—Alexander Graham Bell

"Show up and be present" is advice that can be found on lots of "tips for success" lists—but it has special meaning for those wishing to achieve intern awesomeness.

It might not feel like it sometimes, but as an intern, one advantage you may have over more veteran staffers is that you are fresh. Sure, older, more established workers might have access to greater resources, but they also likely have a lot more responsibilities, baggage, and frankly, are much more singed with signs of burn-out. You, on the other hand, can be much more present.

For example, established staffers in the office may be dealing with mortgages, lawns to mow, kids, aging parents, etc. If you're like most interns, your biggest worry may be, "Where should I order pizza from tonight?" Don't get me wrong, I love pizza too. My point here is that you have the ability to be present a lot more at work than most people, and you can use this to your advantage. Yes, I know you have schoolwork to do—but trust me, you've still got fewer demands on your time than most of the people you work with.

Chances are, compared to the veterans in your office, you are younger, have more energy, are in better shape, have fewer personal obligations and have much greater flexibility in your schedule than others in your office. Use this to your advantage.

Not too long after my internship at the White House when I had been hired as a permanent staffer, King Hassan II of Morocco died. The news came late in the afternoon. Within a few hours, the decision was made that President Clinton and the First Lady along with several of the former presidents and a bunch of really important people, would attend the funeral. Following Islamic tradition, the funeral was going to happen fast. This meant that the Presidential Advance team would need to leave immediately.

Following my usual practice of staying later than most, that evening I was summarily recruited from my desk to be the deputy lead of that advance team. Within hours I was on a C-130 bound for Rabat and one of the best adventures I've ever had. I could go on a trip like that with almost no notice because I was young, had no real obligations, and was crazy enough to do it. As an intern, you should be too. During your internship, be present, and be ready to take advantage of opportunities.

Be the first one at the office and the last one to leave. It sounds twisted, but there is nothing more impressive to an intern supervisor than arriving at work and seeing an intern standing in the hallway because that intern got there so early that they arrived before the doors were unlocked. Obviously this isn't a trick you need to do every day—but it's an excellent way to show your dedication and for you to stand out from the crowd.

If your supervisors are ordering you to leave, then leave. But otherwise, hang around. In my experience, the biggest crises (aka opportunities) often break after hours when there are just a few people around. If you are one of those few people, you're going to be able to offer tons of value to the staffers who are there. You might even save the day without realizing it.

When you leave your office, there is no need to talk about office stuff outside the office. Now, don't get me wrong, if your parents or your faculty advisor ask you about your internship—tell them about it. But, there is no need to blabber on about work in public places (busses, parks, Facebook, etc.).

I was once in line at a store behind two young women who, wearing their work IDs out for all to see, I quickly identified as interns from a particular organization; I couldn't help but overhear their conversation. They were going on and on about this event they were helping to put together and how their organization was going to list Senator Clinton as a confirmed speaker on the invitation, regardless of whether she could come or not, just so they would get a good turnout. They had no idea that Hillary Clinton's scheduler was standing right behind them. Let me assure you—that organization got an earful from me the next day. Remember, when it comes to work stuff, you never know who is listening.

The same thing goes with paper. If you've got documents or records or flash drives you're working on at work, leave them at work—unless there is a real reason you need to have them outside of work. The rationale is: if you aren't carrying stuff around, you can't lose it. Shortly before I started interning at the White House, an intern got in huge trouble because they decided it would be cool to take home a copy of the president's schedule to show their friends. Unfortunately, on their way home, they managed to leave the schedule on a park bench seat. Somebody else found it and turned it in to the Secret Service.

When you are at work, be present at work. Beyond getting there early and staying late, make sure that you're around. If other interns are going for long lunches, be the one intern who stays behind and is always *there*. Time bathroom breaks so they happen when you'll least likely be needed. Bring lunch from home so you won't have to spend time going to get lunch (we'll talk more about this later). This may sound extreme, but trust me—it's worth it. By being around as much as you can, especially while others are away someplace else, you greatly increase your chances of standing out above the crowd.

I'll talk about this more later, but during your internship make sure you get into the habit of having your cell phone always charged and close by, so you are reachable. More than that, make sure your supervisors and especially the people who are doing the cool work you'd like to be more involved in know how to reach you if they ever need to. Make sure everybody knows that you are available to help them if they need it.

About a month into my White House internship I remember one of the big bosses on the First Lady's staff asking me out of the blue, "Eric, what time will you get here tomorrow?" My immediate response was "Whatever time you tell me!" It turned out that they wanted me to be there the next morning at 4 AM to help prepare for an early morning interview the First Lady was doing for the *Today Show*. I was there at 3:45 AM, and it was one of the coolest things I got to do during my internship. If I hadn't been right there when they were looking for somebody to help or if I'd balked at the idea of such an early morning, I would have missed out big time.

Some interns are hard workers, but they forget to be present because they are so focused on the future. For example, I've seen interns who were great for a couple of weeks, but then they clearly started to become distracted with thoughts about the future. Instead of laserlike focus on "this is what I need to do now" they started to worry about "how long will I need to intern here before they hire me?" This is a common mistake. During your internship, *be present* and the rest will follow. As Yoda admonishes Luke in *The Empire Strikes Back*,

A Jedi must have the deepest commitment. Hm? The most serious mind! This one a long time have I watched. All his life has he looked away, to the future. To the horizon. Never his mind on where he was! Hm? What he was doing! Huh. Adventure. Eh! Excitement. Eh! A Jedi craves not these things. You are reckless!

When you first start your internship, your supervisor will likely ask you to commit to a particular schedule. If they don't ask you to do this, then you should commit a certain schedule to yourself and then share what that schedule will be with your supervisor. Either way, once you make that commitment, stick to it.

This means no "I'm sorry I was late" or "I would have been here on time, but there was so much traffic." Stick to your commitment. If you do, it will create an incredible contrast between you and many of your intern colleagues.

Now, if something comes up (an exam, an important paper, a cool opportunity, whatever)—you *ask* your supervisor whether you can do something different from the schedule you have committed to. That's fine. What most interns do is *tell* their supervisor that they are making a change, or worse, they just do it without asking or telling anybody.

Here's another tip about being present that even a lot of seasoned staffers get wrong. If you get this right as an intern, you'll go far. *Either be at work, or don't—but don't try and be in between.* If you are feeling bad and decide you are too sick to work, then call in sick, and let that be that. Don't call in sick and then still try and work a little bit from your deathbed. If you are too sick to work, then you are obliged to give up your responsibilities to somebody who is well. Let go, get better, then come back when you are well.

This idea is more important than some people realize. When workers are sick, they will often do one of two things. Sometimes, people will come into the office even though they are sick and risk making everybody else sick—but then they do kind of a half-ass job of working because, after all, they are sick! Other times, people will call in sick but then dictate that nobody can do their work but them—so the whole operation becomes bottlenecked because of one person.

If you come into the office to do your internship, be present and be at 100 percent. If you are indeed not feeling well, then go home and get better. Be present or go away; you can't do both at the same time.

56

Prevent, Predict, Problem-Solve

"You can always amend a big plan, but you can never expand a little one. I don't believe in little plans. I believe in plans big enough to meet a situation which we can't possibly foresee now."
—Harry S. Truman

When I was training to be a scuba instructor, one of the things I learned was the importance of preventing situations where problems might occur, predicting when problems might occur, and managing problems when they did occur.

During my internship, I never ceased to be amazed by how often I used this same philosophy in the office. Likewise, of the hundreds of interns I've supervised over the years, the best interns are always able to prevent, predict, and problem-solve. During your internship, you should focus on this too.

One skill that is often not taught in school, but that I've found useful in the workplace both as a staffer and an intern, is the art of contingency planning. It is second nature to me now, but I remember when I was fresh out of school—I never put as much emphasis on contingency planning as I do now.

What do I mean by contingency planning? Contingency planning is the habit of always having plan B, plan C, and even a plan D up your sleeve for pretty much everything you do. For example, let's say somebody asks you to make five copies of a single-page document. How many contingencies can you come up with?

In that situation, this is the sequence that would happen in my mind right off the bat: photocopy, five copies. What if I forget the instruction? How could I handle that? Where is the nearest copier? Where are the two nearest after that? What if the first copier is out of paper? Where is the paper? What if it has a paper jam from the last person who used it? How easy is that copier to clear? What if that copier is out of toner? Where is the extra toner? Do I know how to change the toner? If I'm not sure about one of these questions, who might know the answers? If they're not around, who else might know? How can I reach them? If all else fails, what is my holy s#$@ plan?

Chances are, you or I would walk up to that first copier, hit a button, and everything would be fine. But—if the universe throws a curveball at you—you'll be way better off if you've spent even a moment thinking about contingencies.

How was Scotty always able to give Kirk Warp 6 when, just a little earlier, the engineer swore to the captain that the *Enterprise* could only go Warp 5? Scotty was an excellent contingency planner, and he made a habit of always holding a little extra in reserve.

How can you become a great contingency planner during your internship? A good first step is to learn the landscape of your workplace. Snoop around. Look in cabinets, notice where the First Aid kit is, notice who has what kind of cell phone charger, pay attention.

Run exercises in your mind. Make a habit of asking yourself things like, "How would I help my boss if a pen exploded in his shirt pocket?" Ask things like, "how bad would it be if the hard drive with that important project failed? What could I do to mitigate against a disaster like that?"

The idea is not to become obsessed with every possible calamity but rather, as the Scouts say, "Be Prepared." If you've done just a little thinking about how you would handle big disasters, then you'll be more than ready to handle everyday challenges. That is the mark of a great intern.

Here is another benefit to contingency planning: you will get to the point where you can anticipate tasks before people ask you to do them. There is almost nothing more satisfying than when a boss, especially a demanding boss, asks you to do something or even complains about why you haven't done something and you can reply, "Already did it."

Most interns don't take the time to study their workplace or the people in it. If you do, even just a little, you can be a psychic intern. Let me tell you, nobody messes with a psychic intern. Psychic interns get respect.

WALK A MILE IN YOUR BOSS'S SHOES

Everybody has particular preferences and when it comes right down to it, nobody can predict what another person will like or dislike all the time. However, if you get into the habit of giving just a little bit of extra thought about how you can add value to your internship organization, it can make a huge difference.

For example, suppose you are preparing a binder full of documents for a supervisor. Before you hand off your work, stop, take a breath, and pretend for a moment that you are your boss in the exact situation your boss will be when they need that binder. Is there any way your work could be better? Are the tabs arranged in a useful, legible way? Are the materials in the binder organized in a way that is the most useful? Is the binder labeled in such a way that it isn't likely to be mistaken for another? Is there too much info in the binder? Is there not enough?

Nobody's work is ever perfect. Work product can always be better. However, a habit that will set you apart from other interns is the practice of always thinking about how your work might be improved and then doing one or two little things to make it better every time. When you do work in an office, especially when you're under the magnifying glass of an internship, try and improve your work just a little bit every day—then repeat.

57

Manage Your Manager

"I have eight different bosses right now."
—Peter Gibbons, *Office Space*

The whole concept of the classroom is pretty much built around the idea "follow the teacher's instructions, do what the teacher says." Most students who take on internships make the natural leap in logic that when they enter the workplace, their boss assumes a role similar to that of a teacher.

Sorry, that answer is incorrect. That's a chip up the nose, I'm afraid.

In the workplace, management and leadership is often more of a two-way street. That is, as much as bosses manage their subordinates, sometimes it's the other way around. In the modern workplace, management is less about vertical leadership and more about shared leadership.

During your internship, you should be prepared to take a step forward. When the situation calls for it, be ready to take initiative and manage your supervisor. This sometimes takes some subtle maneuvering and savvy, but if you're able to master this skill, you'll go far.

I once heard a story about a well-known political operative. This particular person is incredibly smart and influential but also has a legendary temper and some find difficult to work under him. Three weeks into a particular campaign, he had gone through three interns—nobody was making him happy. In a fourth attempt, the campaign intern coordinator paired him up with April. On April's first day, before she'd really even met her new boss, he was inside his office ranting and raving, "God damn those sons-of-bitches! Damn it!" Then he called out, "Get those sons-of-bitches on the phone right now!"

Having no idea what or who the boss was talking about, April called back, "Which sons-of-bitches would you like to get on the phone, sir?" She was a success in that job for the rest of the campaign.

It's not always true, but in my experience, in the workplace there is often a direct correlation between seniority and a boss's need to be managed from below. In the office, everybody can use some help sometimes with getting organized, setting boundaries, and talking through ideas. The big bosses are lonely up there on top; they can use management from below. Interns are often in a great position to do this because they don't pose any threat of upsetting office politics.

If you are assigned to a big boss during your internship, don't be a shrinking violet. Step forward. Chances are, the bigger the boss, the more help they'll need. If you see a messy desk—get in there and help them get organized. Take care not to mess up their business, but push the envelope little by little. If you cross a boundary (e.g., where did that piece of paper go?!?), you'll know soon enough. Most likely, however, they'll be pleasantly surprised by your initiative and will encourage it. Help your boss solve problems they don't even know they have.

Pay attention. If your supervisor likes a certain drink, help them find a way to always have that on hand. If they like to write with a certain pen, make sure you have a supply. Look for things that need to get done that have been sitting around for months—take initiative there. If the boss hasn't been able to take action on something that has been sitting around for that long, chances are they aren't going to mind if you take a stab at it. Don't overstep your limits right out of the gate, take baby steps.

We'll get into this a bit later, but often interns run into situations where they have nothing to do because they don't spend any time looking for things they can do. If you wait for your boss to give you every assignment, you'll most likely be bored. Instead, look for assignments you can give yourself. If your boss isn't being a good supervisor, start assigning tasks to yourself—I promise this will get their attention.

58

Slay Dragons

"The great defense against the air menace is to attack the enemy's aircraft as near as possible to their point of departure."
—Winston Churchill

*T*he notion of managing your manager pre-supposes, of course, that your boss is a relatively decent human being, that as a mentor they have an interest in your education, and that they want to see you succeed.

Some bosses are hard, but it doesn't necessarily mean they are bad. In fact, some of the best bosses I've had have been incredibly demanding with unbelievably high expectations. Like a tough coach, a tough boss can be great because they are able to get you to do things you never thought you could do.

However, there is a big difference between bosses like this, and Dragons.

Dragons are bosses in the workplace who, for whatever reason, are just mean. The hallmark of a dragon is disrespect. A boss can be tough, even yell about things. But, if their concerns remain focused on the work and they remain respectful of you as a person, that's legit.

On the other hand, if you are faced with a supervisor who is just a bully, someone who directs their criticism towards your worth as a human being, then you've got to slay them—fast. The very moment you're sure they've crossed the line, you've got to respond. How do you know you're sure? As a great intern you've thought it through, because you do contingency planning, right?

If you're having a difficult time with your boss, do some thinking about where your red line lies. Do the mental exercise where you determine what kind of criticism is acceptable, and what is not.

Prepared in this way, you won't have to think about whether your supervisor has crossed the line during the heat of battle, you'll just know. If/when a supervisor does cross that line, you've got to push back right away. I once had a boss who pretty much told me I didn't listen and was stupid—she wasn't referring to my work, she was criticizing my value as a person. So, I let her have it. I shed any air of subordination and explained in no uncertain terms that I required her never to speak like that to me ever again, because it negatively affected the work I was trying to accomplish for her. Did she fire me? Nope. Did she yell back at me? Nope. She backed the hell off. That's what bullies do when you push back.

REMEMBER, YOU'RE NOT THEIR FIRST

If you're dealing with an internship supervisor who is a true bully, chances are you're not their first victim. In fact, most likely the issue of that supervisor's ability to manage subordinates has come up before with that supervisor's supervisor. Bullies in the workplace are usually sensitive to people accusing them of being a bully because they have a history of being a bully.

As an intern faced with a bully supervisor you may feel that your word won't count for anything against a supervisor. But remember, chances are you're not the first person to cry wolf. If you're right about your supervisor being a bully, there is likely a thick personnel file someplace with similar complaints. Bullies don't want that file to get any thicker.

When someone who is your supervisor acts or speaks to you appropriately, they step out of their role as your boss. When this happens, you can likewise step out of your role as their subordinate with a professionally clean conscious.

On another occasion, I had a boss who was just badgering me verbally about the tasks she had wanted me to do, repeatedly asking me the same questions over and over not to get the answer, or to make sure I understood the assignment or to motivate me. Her goal was clearly just to harass me—I was sure. So, I slew the Dragon. I changed modes and asked her, "Have you forgotten my response when I answered these same questions just a few moments ago? Do you remember the conversation we just had about this? I feel like you are asking these questions just to badger me? Is that true? If so, then why?" She didn't expect that, and she stopped.

In truth, bosses may be bad managers or incompetent, but you will rarely find one that is openly disrespectful to subordinates. In my career, I've only run into two or three. However, if you run into a boss who disrespectful (verbally, physically, whatever) don't be shy about explicitly telling them to stop. If they don't stop, tell their boss or tell your H.R. department—then keep moving up the chain until somebody responds to your concerns.

In the workplace, you should expect people to be tough as nails about the work, but if they are ever disrespectful to you as a person, don't tolerate it for a second. Slay any dragons you meet right away and don't look back.

59

Lead and Shun the Herd

"We herd sheep, we drive cattle, we lead people. Lead me, follow me,
or get out of my way."

—George Patton

On your first day of elementary school, high school, or college—you might not have realized it at the time—the
people you happened to make friends with first likely had
a huge impact on your social life for years to come. When you are in
a situation where everybody is new, your best friend may become the
person you just happen to sit next to at lunch, etc. The same is often
true on the first day of an internship.

On the first day of an internship, like the first day of school, it's a
little nerve-racking. Everybody is in a new place with new people, the
urge to find some sort of group, to quickly find a place to belong, can
be overwhelming.

But remember—there is a reason you've worked so hard to land
this internship. Your first priority is not to make friends. I know this
sounds harsh, but you can find friends lots of other places. Your internship is the place to focus on learning new skills, and getting access to
people who can help with your professional goals.

So on that first day of your internship you may see lots of other interns acting like it's the first day of school, banding together, relating with each other. There will be gossip, people hooking up—all the normal stuff. That's fine, but I don't want you to follow that herd. Take the path less traveled. Be the intern who stands out because they are focused more on work, less on the social scene. By doing this you will come across to everybody, both staff and other interns, as way more mature—and everybody will respect you more for it.

Don't get me wrong, you don't have to be a snob or a cold fish—just be the intern who is focused like a laser. In fact, with this strategy you can quickly become a leader among other interns.

During your internship, put yourself in the position where other interns are coming to you for help. Whenever they do, go out of your way to help them. People on staff will notice this more than you know. After all, a great way to show that you're ready to graduate from intern to staffer—that you're ready to be hired—is to naturally be the intern that winds up supervising and helping other interns.

Sometimes interns wind up being incredibly competitive with other interns—you want to avoid this path. Dwight Eisenhower once said, "You can get a lot done if you don't worry about who gets the credit." Go out of your way to make others in your office, both other interns and staffers, look good. If a boss praises you for work that someone else had a part in, make sure you receive the praise by recognizing whoever else deserves credit.

Even if you are a brand-new intern, come in with the mind-set that your job is to help staffers and other interns. Constantly look for opportunities to do this.

60

The Last Suit You'll Ever Wear

"You're going to like the way you look."
—George Zimmer (Men's Wearhouse dude)

Adolescence can be kind of tricky—all these weird things happen to your body. It takes a while to learn how to deal with all those physical changes. Believe it or not—and this is something most interns never understand going into their first internship—maintaining yourself as a professional takes some adjustment, too!

If you're interning in a place that requires daily professional dress, you've got to develop some habits you may never have needed before. First off, you've got to have the right clothes—they don't necessarily need to be super expensive—but you've got to have the right duds. If you're not sure what the right clothes are, do a little research. Find some professional pictures of the most important men and women who work at the organization where you will be interning—you need to dress pretty close to them.

Most professional clothes require maintenance, and a little planning. Before your internship starts, figure out what dry cleaner you are going to use and how often you need to get to them. Especially if you only have a few sets of work clothes, make sure the dry cleaner's hours and turn-around time are going to work for you. You'll need a plan for keeping your shoes shined and in good shape. Make sure you have easy, regular access to an iron and an ironing board. Learn how to use it. Dudes, do you know how to tie a tie?

One time there was an intern walking around the halls of the White House—this guy was wearing a shirt that was crazy wrinkled along with a tie that had a bunch of golf clubs on it. A senior staffer approached this intern and said, "Young man! Do you own an iron?"

This poor kid was so clueless, he thought she was talking about a golf iron, so he replied, "Yes! I own a full set of clubs." Yeah—that guy got sent home that day. Get an iron.

If you have never had to wear office clothing everyday, it takes a while to get used to and is way easier to mess up during the day than the sturdier threads you are probably used to wearing. If you have a place to stash it, keep some extra stuff at work, just in case you forget your socks or tie, or pants, etc.

During my first internship I had the good fortune of living just a few blocks from the White House. Knowing this, an intern colleague of mine once begged me to let him go borrow an extra shirt from my place. He had gotten sunburned at the beach that weekend, and he now had blisters popping all over his back and through his dress shirt—really, really nasty. At the time, I only owned three shirts—just enough to have a clean one every day. So, I told that guy he was on his own (yeah, it was really gross—poor bastard).

Ladies, this is outside my area, but be smart about how much skin you show. Don't hold back, be a fashionista and glam it up. But be a distraction because how awesome your work is, not because of how low your neckline goes. If you're not sure where the line lies, ask another woman in the office you respect.

Shoes are another area where I've seen interns have trouble. New interns tend to run a lot of errands and may not have an actual chair to sit down—they tend to be on their feet a lot. If your feet aren't used to wearing dress shoes or you're trying to get by in shoes that don't fit really well, you're toast.

A trick I learned from Secret Service agents (they get to stand all day long) is to get shoes that are a little loose—feet tend to swell throughout the day. Ladies, if you're going to wear heels, make sure they are the type you can do battle in. If you need to, wear sneakers to and from work—change when you arrive. Gents, I don't know about you, but I look for the thickest soles I can find. Old government buildings tend to have granite floors that like to eat shoes.

61

Everybody is Human

"Humanity's fate has been sealed. You will be destroyed."
—Q, *Star Trek*

*T*he *Matrix, The Terminator, Battlestar Galactica*—how many movies have you seen where machines decide they need to rid the world of humanity because people are just too damn messy?

Believe it or not (red pill or blue pill), but you should expect that your internship will be a little bit like the Matrix. Yes, you will have super powers. Yes, you can create your own reality. But more importantly for our discussion here, you are the messy human, surrounded by machines, being judged.

In today's office world we are all increasingly surrounded by and dependent on technology. As a result, for better or worse (probably for worse), most people in the office are expected to perform with machine-like efficiency and sterility. It may not be right, but in the office world—especially as an intern—keep your biological impact to a minimum.

This means: don't be the intern with horrible breath. Don't be the sweaty intern or the intern that smells terrible. Get it?

I once had an intern who had a habit of sneezing incredibly loudly—such that every time he sneezed (and he sneezed a lot) it brought the office to a standstill. If it was a medical problem, people might have understood—but this wasn't the case with this intern. Rather, this kid just liked to sneeze really loudly—he didn't make any effort to tone it down. This intern could have been the greatest worker in the world and it wouldn't have mattered. The only thing people associated with this intern was that he sneezed really loudly. Don't be like this.

Make extra effort to do the simple things—preferably in a private place before you appear in the office. Blow your nose, brush your teeth, pop a mint, brush your hair—whatever you have to do in order to get yourself together. My wife once worked with a person who had a habit of combing his beard during office meetings. Intern: do not do this!

People in close office quarters have all sorts of pet peeves. As the intern, people are going to tolerate your biological leavings less than anybody. So, don't chew gum. If you're going to sneeze, cough, hiccup, burp, or God knows what else, step outside the office if you can.

In the movie *The Shawshank Redemption*, Morgan Freeman plays a man recently paroled from jail who has found work at a grocery store. Having been under lock and key for so long, Freeman's character keeps asking the grocery store manager if it is alright to go to the bathroom. The manager corrects him, "You don't have to ask every time to go to the bathroom, just go, okay?"

You are a grown up. Not only that, but an office is not the same as jail. So, as an intern, don't feel like you have to ask every time you need to excuse yourself. If you act like a grown up, people will give you the benefit of the doubt that when you excuse yourself, there must be a good reason.

SLEEP IT OFF

This is something you actually *should* have learned in school, but just in case you didn't:

If you want to be sharp during your internship, you've got to get some sleep. It also helps to do the other stuff (eat right, drink water, exercise), but if you just get enough sleep, you'll do well.

I've actually had interns that drew my attention at work during the middle of the day because they were snoring. I have no problem with somebody catching a nap during a break at work, but these snoring interns weren't really on break—they just conked out because they were hungover from partying to all hours the night before. Don't be one of these interns.

If you're thinking, "I don't need somebody to tell me this, I'm not a child"—that's good. Then you already know.

If you are thoughtful about your personal space and the effect your presence has on the office environment, you will be showing wisdom beyond most interns' years. This means, keep your cell phone on buzz, and don't leave it behind when you leave your seat. Avoid bringing smelly food into the office for lunch. If you play sound from your computer, keep it really low or use head phones.

You may find that others in the office, especially more senior staffers, aren't so considerate. As an intern wanting to get ahead, your best play in the short term is to tolerate it. Just remember though—when you are the boss, be more considerate.

If more senior people in the office like the office dark, don't turn the lights on. When the high-ranking staffer in an office likes the office at sixty-eight degrees, then don't mess with the thermostat. You can, however, bring a small lamp. You can, however, wear a sweater. If the big kahuna in the office plays annoying music, pop on some head phones. Get it? Go out of your way to avoid polluting the office, and find ways to mitigate the effect of supervisors messing up your space. Later in your career when you're working with peers or subordinates, you'll be able to tell them to be quiet, turn on the lights, turn up the thermostat and get rid of their smelly food.

I've seen so many interns, who were awesome workers, completely undermine their track record by not carrying themselves appropriately in the office. The modern-day persecution of smoking has no respite in the office world. If you're a smoker, hide it and—if you can—don't let the habit be the reason you're in the office less.

In an office, people have an unconscious respect for colleagues that bring their lunch. Brown bagging it signals that you have your act together enough to plan lunch ahead and that you are smart enough to save money by bringing lunch to work. So, if you can do it, bring your lunch to work. While everybody else is off spending money to buy lunch, you'll be ready to catch that opportunity, which everyone else is going to miss.

It's okay to make/take personal calls from the office—just don't do it a lot at the beginning of your internship, and don't make it a regular thing. Do it only when you need to do it. It goes back to the idea that, if you act like a grown-up, that's how people will treat you.

When you're out of the office, maintain the professional habit of keeping your cell phone very charged. Be the intern that is always reachable, who almost always answers the phone. This is a habit I learned when cell phones were just coming into vogue during my time as an intern in Hillary Clinton's First Lady Office.

Years later, when I served as her scheduler on Capitol Hill, Senator Clinton would occasionally call during off hours to inquire about something on her schedule. On one of these occasions, she called and noticed that I was particularly out of breath. When Senator Clinton asked why I was so winded, I explained that at that particular moment I was running mile eighteen of a marathon. I'm not sure how many points that particular instance of being so reachable got me with the boss, but she shouted "Go Eric!" and reassured me that I shouldn't worry about her question just then. It was enough of a boost to get me to the finish line, that's for sure.

62

Stand Out in Time

"How did it get so late so soon?"

—Dr. Seuss

On any "tips for young professionals" list, being on time is one of the most common items. Being on time is one of the easiest ways to stand out from the crowd, but it's also something that most people fail to do.

Three words: BE ON TIME. Always—not sometimes. Always.

If you're supposed to get to work at 8 AM, be there at 8 AM with whatever morning drink you need in hand, with breakfast in your belly. Be ready to go. The typical new intern is on time their first couple of days, but then it quickly goes downhill when they see the example of others in the workplace. In most offices, people aren't on time. When they do arrive, the first part of the day is kind of a warm up. They get coffee, they get breakfast, they surf news on the web.

Do not follow this example. Be the intern who is on time. As I stated earlier, if you can make a good impression by getting to work early then definitely be there early. If you can manage it, be the intern that arrives before your boss and departs after your boss. Be the intern who is the first in, the first to have their computer booted up, the first to be ready to go.

If someone calls a meeting or schedules a conference call for 2:00 PM, show up or call in at 2:00 PM. Chances are, by being on time, you'll be the first to arrive other than the meeting organizer. This means you get one-on-one time with whoever that is. Before the meeting time, think about whom the meeting organizer is and what questions you would like to ask them. That person will greatly appreciate your being on time and be more than willing to chat for a moment while others are dragging themselves in.

Staffers and even your boss might be late or even completely forget about meetings, but that doesn't mean you should. Stand out in your office by being the only intern—and likely the only person—who is consistently on time.

63

Keep Your Desk Insanely Neat

"If a cluttered desk is a sign of a cluttered mind, of what, then, is an empty desk a sign?"

—Albert Einstein

This is another part of office life where the vast majority of people fall down on the job. You can tell a tremendous amount about somebody by how they keep their desk.

Over the years, I've walked into hundreds of offices—the state of one's desk says as much about someone as just about anything else. Most people maintain piles of paper all over the place—this is not good. As an intern, if you maintain the habit of keeping your desk extremely neat, people will notice.

At the beginning of your internship, assuming you actually get your own desk, there is a good chance that it will be messed up. Knowing that they are just going to be there temporarily, prior generations of interns may have neglected to make the investment to clean things up.

One of your first tasks as a new intern, no matter what shape your workspace is in, should be to clean it up and get it organized. It's a good bet that most of the things in or on your desk can be gotten rid of. But, if you're worried about getting rid of something important, get yourself an empty photocopier paper box and chuck anything that might be important in there temporarily. If after a month or two into your internship nothing has been needed—kill everything in that box.

Even if the duration of your internship is short, act as if you're going to be at that desk for the next twenty years. Obviously, if you are sharing that desk space with other interns, talk to your intern colleagues about how you can effectively share the space. Whatever you particular case may be, remedying a messy desk situation is really important for two reasons. First, if your desk is messy, you're not going to be able to work in an organized, efficient, clear manner. Second, if you have a messy workspace, others will assume it's your mess, and they'll judge you accordingly.

Consider it from a staffer's point of view. If I'm a staffer with a really important project that I need help with, am I going to choose the intern who has a really messy desk? More likely, I'm going to ask for help from the intern who has a desk that says, "I have my act together and I'm not going to lose anything you give me."

In fact, if you display a knack for being organized and keeping a neat workspace, don't be surprised if others in the office, including big bosses, ask you to help them organize their workspace. If a senior person in your office asks if you would be willing to help them get organized, the correct answer is "Yes." More than that—keep an eye out for people in the office you'd like to work with who happen to have a messy desk. Ask if you can help them organize their workspace—you never know, they might really welcome the offer.

THE CLUTTER OF YOUR MIND

You may not realize it, but the state of your surroundings has a huge effect on your ability to be creative and productive as an intern. When you are surrounded by clutter, your mind is also filled with clutter.

As an intern, you may not have a lot of control over your office surroundings, but take measures to enhance the aesthetic of your workspace as far as you can. It's a small thing, but it will give you an edge.

64

Become a Filing Ninja

"If you file your waste-paper basket for fifty years, you have a public library."

—Tony Benn

The big reason so many interns and people in an office have messy workspaces is because they have never learned the correct way to file paper. As a result, random piles of paper accumulate over weeks, months, and years.

With the onset of digital information, the paper problem is lessening somewhat, but there are still plenty of traditional office packrats out there. Here are my rules about filing. Follow these rules, and help others in your office to follow these rules, and you'll be seen as an intern who is wise beyond their years.

When you can, file by date. Most people make the mistake of filing paper by project names in alphabetical order. In some cases, when one is filing materials related to a subject that is truly ongoing, this makes sense. However, for most information, it's better to file things chronologically by date. Time is the only real standard measure we have—this is why newspapers and magazines and blogs are always indexed by date. The other advantage of filing by date is that it's easier to get rid of the oldest stuff when it becomes obsolete.

Don't file anything that is mass produced or available online. Every time you're about to file something, ask, "If I didn't have this particular piece of paper, could I find it easier elsewhere?" If the answer is yes, you don't need to keep it.

Don't keep multiple copies: This seems obvious, but sometimes people are lazy and, rather than pull out one example from a pile of copies, they will save time by just filing a pile with fifty copies of the same document.

Don't file a hard copy of something you have digitally—if you have a document on the computer, there is usually no need to file a hard copy also. Sometimes there is an exception to this rule when it comes to documents with handwritten notes or signatures. But generally, if you have something digitally, get rid of the hard copy.

Of course, these days filing is more than just paper and file cabinets—maintaining digital files is often hugely overlooked, too. Perhaps because digital files don't create piles of actual paper, people have a tendency to name files by all sorts of different systems and then store them pretty randomly. Computer search functions makes organizing digital files slightly less of an issue. However, there are a lot of good reasons to be just as organized with digital files as you are with paper files.

When your digital files are organized, finding information is faster and backing up digital information is easier. Chances are, when you arrive at your internship nobody in the history of that office will have thought too much about organizing digital files. Especially if you don't have a lot to do right off the bat, ask your supervisor if you can help organize their digital files. When you're new, there is no better way to get to know an organization and the people there than by organizing their files.

If your office has the right supplies, use hanging folders in drawers to file paper; hanging files tend not to bend under their own weight like other file systems. If your office is like most, you'll notice many files are labeled with tabs handwritten out in chicken scratch. Be a pro—get into the habit of printing out file tabs. You don't even need to have the fancy perforated kind with the specific computer template—just take a couple of guesses with fonts until you find a size that works when you cut it out.

The other good alternative to hanging file folders are three-ring binders placed on a shelf. Binders are especially good for filing materials on a subject that has a finite beginning and end, but must be referenced frequently. If you're filing something in a three-ring binder, the most important thing is to get a three-ring hold punch that works and is set correctly. If you're not sure where the holes are going to punch, practice first on a scratch piece of paper.

Most interns don't take the extra step of printing out a cool-looking cover for a three-ring binder—or figuring out how to print a cool label for the binder spine—but you can. Take a little time and make your work look good. Again, print out tabs for the divider labels within the binder. Small details like these may seem unimportant, and that's why most interns don't think to do them, but you can. When you do, you will stand out from the intern pack.

Filing is an art unto itself (just ask a librarian). But if you master a few basic good habits when it comes to filing, those habits will carry you well through your internship and beyond.

65

The Mighty Pen

"He listens well who takes notes."

—Dante

Want to stand out as being the most amazing intern in the world? Here's a clue: *carry a pen and paper AT ALL TIMES.*

This is one of those things that becomes second nature to most folks in the work world after a while, but isn't something most people learn in school.

When you go to a meeting, take a pen. When you're walking down the hallway and your boss stops you to describe a task she needs you to do, take out your pen. When you're talking to somebody and they mention a resource you don't know about, write it down. When you have a great idea on your way to work—take out a pen and write it down.

If you're like most new interns, or most people for that matter, you trust your mind. Don't do it. Your mind can play tricks on you. If your boss asks you to complete project blue by Thursday, chances are your mind will remember it as: complete project green by Wednesday. Even if you remember correctly, your boss may not.

But, if you are a super intern who carries the mighty pen, you can win by writing things down. If there is ever a discrepancy between what somebody else says and what you remember, you can win by taking out your notes.

HANDWRITING

You need a pen. Paper is nice, but you can get by without it. How? Write on your hand.

Sound stupid? Maybe it is. But writing on your hand is better than not writing down things at all and it can make you seem a little extreme. As in, "I'm so dedicated as an intern I'm willing to write on myself to get the job done."

The truth is it's not that extreme. All that ink washes off pretty easily. But when it comes time for your internship supervisors to consider whether you were truly dedicated, their memory of you writing on your hand in a pinch might actually make you look good.

If nothing else, the simple act of writing down information will help you remember things correctly. Subconsciously, when you write things down your mind starts to work on solutions.

At the very least, writing things down during a meeting gives you something to do. When someone is speaking and you write things down, it is a sign of respect to the person who is thinking. By writing things down, you display that not only are you present, but you care about what the speaker is saying and you find their words valuable.

Any supervisor with high standards will demand that their staff write things down. If you are the one intern who is constantly writing things down, they will notice and you will gain their confidence more quickly.

Have you ever given your order at a restaurant and your server just memorized the order without writing things down? How did you feel about that? Research actually shows that servers who write down orders and repeat them back seem more competent and tend to get bigger tips.

You may not get many tips as an intern, but the concept still holds true. When a supervisor gives you a task, get into the habit of writing it down and then briefly restating the task as you understand it from your notes. This is a mark of a master intern.

66

Party Like Your Career Depends on It

"Here's a good thing to do if you go to a party and you don't know anybody: first take out the garbage. Then go around and collect any extra garbage that people might have, like a crumpled napkin, and take that out too. Pretty soon people will want to meet the busy garbage guy."

—Jack Handey

Unless your office is a real sweatshop, at some point fairly soon into your internship, you will likely be involved with some sort of office party. Chances are, you might actually be tasked with going out to get stuff for said party. But either way, in the end, it's a good bet that you will be standing shoulder to shoulder with most of the office in a social situation before you know it.

First off—and this is something I wish I'd mastered sooner during my internship and career—accept every social invitation you possibly can. Sure, you have lots of work to do. Sure, you're tired. Sure, you may not know anybody. Sure, it could be awkward. But psych yourself into going all the same.

Why? You will stand out.

Most interns are intimidated as hell by office parties, so you should do the opposite. When the awkward conference room birthday party convenes—show up. First of all, the person having the birthday will notice, and appreciate it. Second, the person or people who worked to throw the party together will notice too.

On the TV show *The Office,* the Party Planning Committee was a hotbed of competition and political intrigue. The show didn't have this completely wrong. Office parties are a weird thing—definitely not something you learn about in school. Office parties are kind of an artificial environment where you're expected to socialize with people who aren't necessarily your friends, but you know them well.

Take the opportunity at office parties to (1) get free food and drinks but also (2) get to know people in the office you otherwise might never have contact with. Honestly, some of the biggest career moves I've made in my life have been the result of conversations that started at parties. As an intern, the office party is the one place where it's okay to network, to be a little forward about where your interests lie.

You may have the opportunity to witness intern colleagues approach staffers or bosses during the workday to inquire about when it might be possible to talk about career development. This isn't necessarily a bad thing to do—but the savvier intern will take the opportunity to raise questions like this during the office party.

In truth, office relationships are often based on work. When colleagues get together for a party, they don't want to be lame and talk about work—but then, they really don't have much to talk about. The office party is a perfect occasion for you to get to know staff better and for them to get to know you and your goals.

67

Let's Meet

"A meeting is an event where minutes are taken and hours wasted."
—Captain Kirk, *Star Trek*

During your career, you will likely never get more out of meetings than you will as an intern.

Some may disagree, but in my humble opinion, most office meetings are too long and kind of a waste of time in terms of accomplishing work. If one adds up all the salaries of people attending a meeting and then multiplies that by the length of a meeting, the cost of a meeting can be pretty staggering.

That being said, as an intern—even if you're not accomplishing work by being in a meeting, you're at least learning about office life through osmosis.

Especially when you're new, you may not be invited to many meetings. But, if/when you are included in a meeting, you might not know some things that you'll want to know.

As I explained earlier, for the love of Pete, bring something to write with and be prepared to take notes. Also, as I explained earlier, be on time—even if you are the first person to arrive.

Whether people are actually conscious of it or not, when it comes to meetings, there is a pecking order to who sits where. If you're in a new place or a new situation and you're not sure where to sit, just stand until somebody gives you a hint about where you ought to sit. If you are shunned to the far end of the room, don't take offense. As an intern, especially as a new intern, people assume you will likely have the least to contribute; they will seat you accordingly.

This goes back a little bit to the FNG thing. Where you sit in a meeting is an indication of status. Status is a function of whether you've earned your spurs. Be respectful by not presuming that you are entitled to sit in the middle of things, and people will think better of you for your lack of being presumptuous.

Once you find a place to sit or stand or whatever, unless you're expecting a call from the president or something really important, put your cell phone on buzz. If the room is boiling hot, don't sit there sweating like a dork, take off your jacket. If other people have drinks, it's fine for you to have a drink too.

If you find yourself in a long, long meeting, excuse yourself if you need to. If you find yourself falling asleep, it's better to excuse yourself and leave rather than risk falling asleep during a meeting. Come up with a fake reason if you need to.

The good thing about attending meetings as an intern is that you can learn a lot. The bad thing is, until you wind up being more involved, you may need to be a fly on the wall for a little while.

WHEN MEETINGS GO WRONG

If you're in an endless meeting and you don't feel like you're learning anything or adding anything valuable and you have a ton of other work to get done, don't hesitate to get the hell out of there. Just because you are an intern doesn't mean your time isn't valuable.

How do you escape from an endless meeting? Just stand up and walk out. As far as anybody in the room knows you might have another commitment, or you might be going to the bathroom, or you might be about to barf. If you're truly not adding value to the meeting, people won't worry too much about it and chances are they will be jealous because they're not having much fun in that meeting either.

68

I Can't Do It! She's Breakin' Apart!

"Why does it say paper jam when there is no paper jam? I swear to God, one of these days, I'm going to just kick this piece of shit out the window."

—Samir Nagheenanajar, *Office Space*

A s an intern, one device you may have the opportunity to become very well acquainted with is: the photocopier.

It's not an environmentally friendly creature, it's not particularly cooperative, but as a new intern, you should try and make friends with this beast.

The photocopier has some relatives—they're called "printer," the very old but wise "fax machine," and the newer "scanner." The smart intern makes friends with all of them.

One way you can make photocopier, printer, and fax machine like you (and make others in the office like you too) is to feed them every day. Most people forget to feed these machines—don't be like other people. Photocopier, printer, and fax want paper every morning—so fill them up. Don't overfill them with paper, because that will cause them to jam. Give them just enough to fill their drawers.

The best way to learn about office machines is to work with them. As a new intern—try to learn everything you can about making office machines work. The main problem most modern printers, fax machines, and copiers face revolve around paper jams. Get familiar with all the doors and latches that open these machines up to the world—you'll be surprised at where paper jams can hide.

If this all sounds weird or too complicated, don't get freaked out. Getting paper out of a machine is actually pretty easy, but most interns are intimidated by it. Realize that you're not going to break these machines, so open them up wide and see if you can fix things.

Standard operation procedure for most interns facing a paper jam is: this photo copier isn't working—so I'll go find another one. Don't be like this—be a problem solver. Be the intern who notices a copier is jammed and fixes it, even though you weren't the one who caused the problem.

Printers and fax machines run out of toner. If you're working with a printer that is out of ink, open it up and shake the hell out of the toner cartridge. This will likely get the printer through another couple of hundred pages (be careful though—don't get ink on yourself messing with the toner cartridge).

During your internship, find out where new toner cartridges are kept and help your office stay on top of whether they need to order more.

DOES IT SCAN?

If you're lucky, your office will have an easily accessible scanner. But if you don't have access to a scanner, and really need to email a document that you have only on paper, consider retyping it into the computer. It's not a particularly efficient use of time, but sometimes it's the easiest thing to do if you need to convey a message about information you only have on paper.

If you type at a reasonable speed, you can knock out a couple of pages in less time than you might imagine.

Know how to swap out old toner cartridges for new ones. FYI—most new cartridges require that you pull out a paper tab before they will work.

Find out what your office does with old toner cartridges. Often there is some kind of recycle procedure that involves more than just tossing them in the trash.

In my experience, there is something about office machines that are like intern kryptonite. Interns who run into trouble with copiers and printers give up way too soon. If an office machine is giving you trouble, tangle with it. Be the intern who is a tenacious problem solver and people will notice.

69

Your "Back to Internship" List

"An architect's most useful tools are an eraser at the drafting board, and a wrecking ball at the site."

—Frank Lloyd Wright

Most students, especially in elementary school, know about having a "back to school list." This is a list of school supplies they will need to bring on their first day of school. In high school and college, the list focuses more on textbooks than school supplies—but the list is still there.

When you start out as an intern, there are certain office supplies you will need. I suppose if you're working in some specialized field, this list might not apply. But for survival as a general office dweller, the list below describes all the things you will need.

Get this stuff however you can—from the office supply cabinet, from stuff lying around, wherever. Once you get it, make sure folks know that you have dibs on it (label it if you need to). If your office doesn't provide this stuff, make a trip to Target or get it from home.

Here is the list:

- An in/out box. This is a must for personal organization at the office and most folks miss it. Sit it on your desk and make sure the "in" part is clearly labeled and separated from the "out" part. Real pros have an in/out box like this and you should too. Especially as an intern you may not use the out box much (you don't have anybody working for you yet who will check it), but put it on your desk anyway.
- A three-hole punch that works. This is one of the most elusive pieces of office equipment. Get a three-hole punch and practice with it on scrap paper so you know the correct settings for getting the holes just right.
- A highlighter
- Scotch tape and dispenser
- Good stapler and staples
- Small container of paperclips and binder clips
- White out
- Scissors
- Ruler
- Notebook or pad of paper
- Three pens that work that you like
- One pencil and a way to sharpen it
- One black sharpie
- Post–its
- Thumb drive

70

Don't Be Bored

"Are you bored with life? Then throw yourself into some work you believe in with all your heart, live for it, die for it, and you will find happiness that you had thought could never be yours."

—Dale Carnegie

One of the biggest frustrations, and unexpected situation, most new interns experience during their internship is the circumstance of being bored and/or not having enough to do.

First off, let me just say, this is going to happen sometimes. Even the busiest person in the world with the most hectic schedule can have periods of lull where they're a little idle. However, there is a difference between the occasional slow day and feeling like you're spending your whole internship sitting around.

Whether you know it or not—there is ALWAYS SOMETHING TO DO. The trick is figuring out what that is. As an intern, there are plenty of regular, valuable tasks that need doing. From the first day of your internship—make a list of these. They may not be the most glamorous tasks, but somebody has to get credit for doing them, and it might as well be you. These might include: adding paper to the machines, watering the plants, making sure the voicemail has been checked, orga-nizing the supply cabinet, cleaning the office refrigerator, organizing your boss's desk, fluffing couch pillows, organizing files on the office shared drive, etc. You see, there is always something to do. It may not be stuff you necessarily want to do, but don't fool yourself, it's there.

The thing is, if you are the intern that is constantly doing stuff that nobody seems able to identify or willing to do, more substantive work will certainly come your way soon. More senior staff will want to reward you for doing the unglamorous stuff and they will recognize your can-do attitude.

In the end, if you've truly hit your bottom in terms of struggling to find stuff to do, do some learning. Find ten articles related to the organization where you are interning and read them. Memorize the lyrics to a song you'd like to know. Memorize the presidents of the United States in order. Get into the habit of bringing a book to work (or nowadays, just load one onto your phone). The point of an intern-ship is to get access and learn new skills. If you're sitting at your desk and there is no access to be had right then, focus on learning—even if it's not necessarily related to your internship.

The worst (or maybe the best) thing that could happen would be for a supervisor to walk by and notice you're doing something unre-lated to work. This would be an opportunity for you to remind that person that you don't have enough to do just then related to work, and you're ready to help with whatever needs doing, but you don't want to waste time.

Honestly, if you are extremely idle during your internship, this is a failure of your internship program. If you suspect that a good intern-ship program is one where interns are so busy they don't have time to see straight, you're right. However, not all internship supervisors are skilled enough to manage interns this way—you may find yourself in a situation where you are a bit idle.

If this becomes a persistent problem, you may be in a situation where your intern program is not living up to their end of the bargain. In such a case, spend some of that idle time looking for another internship where your talent might be put to better use.

71

Speak Up

"Ten people who speak make more noise than ten thousand who are silent."

—Napoleon

Most interns make the mistake of chattering on about things that don't advance the work, but then when they know something of true value, they don't speak up.

If you're an intern who knows something, speak up! This means of course that you *know* something (not think something—we'll get into this later). Most interns, however, get intimidated. They have good ideas, but they are afraid that somebody will think they are stupid.

Here's the thing about which I'm convinced: deep down *everybody* thinks their ideas might be stupid. The difference between the average intern and the great intern (or the average/great anybody) is that the great person faces the fear and speaks their mind anyway. When you have an idea, say it.

All through school we are taught to address our teachers as: "Mrs. Smith," "Mr. Johnson," "Dr. Brown," etc. But remember, the office is not school. One of the biggest tells interns have is the way they address colleagues. It comes from a good place; it comes from trying to have manners and show respect.

However, here's a little secret that nobody ever teaches in school: in the office, there are very few people that need to be addressed as Mr. or Mrs. or Dr. The choice is actually up to you whether you want to put the title in. For me, I tend to use titles for elected officials, ambassadors, religious leaders, and sometimes people who are much older than me who I greatly respect. You should make your own choice. However, I would caution you about using Mr. or Ms. on too many people.

Call colleagues by their first name—it may feel weird at first, but just do it. Calling adults by their first name makes you a grown-up too. In the end, you must realize that everybody puts their shorts on one leg at a time. If somebody's first name was good enough for their momma when they had their diapers changed, it's probably good enough for you too.

Sometimes it can be hard for new interns to know when they should respond to their supervisor verbally or whether they should respond to their boss some other way. Here's a trick: if your boss asks you a question verbally, respond verbally. If your supervisor asks you a question in writing, respond in writing, if by email, respond by email. Get it? You can assume that if your boss attributed enough importance to an issue to raise it verbally with you, it's important enough to respond verbally too.

As a new intern, it's also sometimes unclear to whom you should respond about an issue. If you're unsure, respond to the person who asked the question. Especially when you have hot info, it's tempting to broadcast to a wider group. Don't do it. You may not understand the full context of the question you've been asked. Respond to the person who raised the issue with you—then you'll be on safe ground.

For example, suppose Deputy Director Bob asks you to do some research that Director Sally needs. You do the research and find some excellent stuff. If you were to take it directly to Sally, you put Bob in a tough position. Maybe Bob has some more information to add or maybe he wants to present it to Sally in a particular way. When you circumvent Bob, you put him in a position where he is responsible for a result over which he had no control. If you have any interest in doing work for Bob in the future, don't put him in this position.

You may be under the impression that people in an office don't curse. This would be incorrect. Some of the most respected, powerful, admired people in the world curse like bandits. Should you curse in the office as an intern? It depends on the culture of your office and of course, your own personality. But in general, I think you should.

When you curse it shows several things: (1) you're being genuine, (2) you have passion, and (3) you're not too afraid about what other people think. To somebody supervising you, these are all pretty good qualities to display.

Now, don't get me wrong—you may not want to use every expletive in the book when you're trying to impress a customer or constituent on behalf of your internship employer. However, don't feel like you need to whitewash your personality in order to score points during your internship. Be passionate and be real, and people will want to work with you.

When it comes to the spoken word in the office, there is one other important issue to consider. Among your friends, you may be in the habit of referring to others with terms of affection: "sweetie," "honey," etc. Realize that this is a no-no in the office, especially when dealing with members of the opposite gender. Even if you mean these terms in a completely harmless way, people can interpret them as being disrespectful—don't use them. "Buddy," "friend," "comrade," words like that are totally fine—just avoid the amorous stuff.

Along those lines, be careful about commenting about colleagues' appearance—especially those of the opposite gender. You might think this is predominately an issue of men speaking about women, but trust me, it goes both ways. It's fine to tell somebody they look nice, or maybe even that you like a certain aspect of their outfit—but unless you know somebody really well, just avoid this area, especially as an intern.

If somebody looks like they've gained weight, are pregnant, wearing a wig, has a lazy eye—don't say a damn thing about it, at least not in the office!

72

Secret Language

"One if by land, two if by sea."

—Paul Revere

People in an office, or pretty much any organization for that matter, tend to naturally form a tribe. As such, they tend to develop their own secret language.

Slang, acronyms, abbreviations, etc. are all ways that people in an organization can distinguish themselves from those outside an organization. Being at work is sometimes like being a member of a secret club. As a new intern, you are the FNG, the new inductee of the club. If you want to make progress, you better get hip to office lingo.

Every office is different, and the cool lingo changes over time. But here are some phrases you can use that will make you sound cool. Even if these terms aren't used in your particular office, people will recognize them as cool office-talk that must come from someplace. If you speak more like an office pro and less like an intern, people will treat you more like an office pro.

PUSH BACK

Meaning: to resist an idea or action. "Alice felt very strongly that we should make the offer now, but I pushed back."

PULL THE TRIGGER

Meaning: to launch. "Are we ready to pull the trigger on this program or not?"

PULL THE PLUG

Meaning: to end. "This initiative sucks, let's pull the plug on it."

CRASHING

Meaning: very busy. "I can't talk right now, I'm crashing."

OFFLINE

Meaning: away from the group. "Rather than take up everybody's time on this conference call, let's take this issue offline."

NEEDS MORE WORK

Meaning: not ready yet. "This idea is good, but the proposal needs more work."

THE PAPER

Meaning: document, any written material. "Do you have the paper about next week's event?"

RADIOACTIVE

Meaning: something that is messed up or somebody who messed up such that they are now untouchable. "Fred stole money from the company to support his gambling habit and he was caught being mean to puppies, he's radioactive now."

HAND-HOLDING

Meaning: reassurance. "I've never pulled off an event this big before, I need a little hand-holding."

BREAKUP

Meaning: no longer willing to deal with/engage, "They've called me five times with five different answers, I'm breaking up with them."

HEAVY LIFT

Meaning: a difficult task. "Most of the work has already been done so it shouldn't be too much of a heavy lift."

LOW-HANGING FRUIT

Meaning: easy tasks that are high impact. "Before we make this heavy lift, let's go after the low-hanging fruit."

NOT THERE YET

Meaning: not ready. "I think we should have a conversation eventually, but we're just not there yet."

73

You've Got Mail

"I get mail; therefore I am."

—Scott Adams

One could devote an entire book to the art of office email etiquette—but for sanity's sake, let me put forth the most important things you should know about email in the workplace. These are things that most interns don't know.

Chances are, as a new intern, you're likely coming from a younger and more e-savvy generation than most of your work counterparts. As such, you are probably wired to be more casual about email than you should be, at least at work.

When somebody emails you at work with a question, you should email them back—preferably sooner rather than later. Ideally, you email back with an answer to their question. Avoid responding with an "I'll check that" answer unless you know it will take too long to get the actual answer. In other words, don't email an "I'll check that" response, and then five minutes later send the answer. Just send the actual answer.

If somebody challenges you on email, but you believe you are right, respond. No response implies that you yield. However, don't ever email anything that you wouldn't want seen by everyone. Heated discussions about work over email are fine, just so long as you don't get personal. Never email somebody in anger and avoid getting in fights over email. If you get angry over email, you lose.

Some in the workplace treat their inbox like a river where they catch some things that go by but are resigned to miss others. Don't be like this. Even in settings where you might get hundreds of emails per day, be on top of everything and delete anything you don't need immediately. Shoot to get your email down to one screen. In other words, no more than twenty or twenty-five emails pending.

If you're becoming overwhelmed by email, take the time to unsubscribe or block stuff you don't want. When you need to cut down the number of messages in your inbox, use the sort by subject function to lop off all but the newest version of every email string. Sometimes it can be helpful to print out an email as a reminder to take action on it, and then delete that message in your inbox.

When you're out of the office, some people make a big deal about posting an automated out-of-office message. It's fine to turn on your out-of-office notice, unless of course you're going to have access to your email while you are away anyway. When I email somebody and get their out-of-office message, I assume they are away. Then, if I get a message from them—well, it's just kind of a dorkish thing to do.

Especially among eager-beaver young professionals (read: interns), there isn't a good sense about when to send emails. With smart phone technology, emails aren't nearly the passive form of communication they used to be. Nowadays, if I receive an email at 9 PM on a Saturday, I feel a little pressured to reply right then. So, avoid sending non-important, non-urgent emails after hours. If you need to, go ahead and write the email, but then use the delayed send function to send it.

Another piece of emailing that a lot folks new to office life neglect is their signature line. Use that signature line to put your name, title, and contact info. If you want to be really groovy, stick a URL in there that makes you look cool (LinkedIn page, even a Facebook page if it fits the context, etc.). Avoid random quotes or weird calligraphic fonts in your signature line.

Bonus tip: as an intern, be mindful about the title you list in your email signature line. (You set up your email signature in your new internship email account, right?) You don't need to hide the fact that you are an intern. But at the same time, in some contexts, especially when working with people outside your office, you don't necessarily need to advertise it either. Consider listing your title as "Assistant"— it's not untruthful, you are acting as an assistant in your office. But, it also prevents people from the outside world dismissing you as "just an intern." Titles can sometimes be touchy things. You don't want to lie about your title, but on the other hand, you don't need to go out of your way to handicap yourself in your email signature line either.

THE POWER OF THE P.S.

What happened to the P.S.? Back in the olden days (read: before email), adding a P.S. after a signature of a letter was more common. Perhaps because it's so easy to change text with a computer now (as opposed to how difficult it was when people wrote letters by hand), the P.S. has fallen out of favor.

However, when you send email during your internship, you can use the P.S. to your advantage. For whatever reason, people will skim through the text of an email, but they tend to read the P.S.—just because it's something they don't see that often. So, when you send emails during your internship, put some really important stuff in the P.S.

When you do, it will make your communication more effective and will make you a more effective intern.

P.S. Remember to use a P.S.

I don't know about you, but when I get an email with a neon background and yellow letters, it makes me want to take anti-seizure medication. Keep a white background and use a standard font like Times New Roman or Arial—if you want to be really nifty use Verdana. Some people in the office have bad eyes—use a reasonable font.

If you're emailing somebody who sends you a message in large font, especially an older person, do them a favor and email them back in the same font. They're not trying to shout at you on email, they are writing in a font they can see. Respond the same way.

Another aspect of email that people in the office often get wrong is "reply all." If somebody in the office emails a whole list about who can attend Bob's birthday party, you don't need to reply all back to let everybody know that you can't make it because you're getting a wart removed. Let the original sender know that you won't be able to attend, and leave it at that.

When one replies to an email with an attachment, most email programs default to dropping the attachment. Just be aware that when you reply, take the fifteen seconds to copy that original attachment back into your reply. You'll be saving any future recipients the time it would take to go back through their email to find the original attachment.

74

Reach Out and Touch Someone

"I have gone on the air and announced my telephone number at the
Washington Post."

—Bob Woodward

C an you believe there was a time before email when people
had to rely on just phones and mail? Actually, there was a
time before phones and mail too—but that is too medieval
to even think about, so we'll just consider phones for now.

With email now more than mainstream in the workplace, phone
etiquette is definitely becoming a lost art. During the fifteen years of my
career, I've seen the ways in which folks operate on the phone steadily
decline. For the new intern in the office, not much is expected in terms
of phone skills—if you show even the slightest ability for handling
yourself on the phone, you'll stand out like a sore dialing finger.

When you answer a phone at work, come up with standard way
of doing it that sounds professional. If you've ever seen the reality TV
show *Flipping Out*, Jeff Lewis makes all his workers answer the phone
by saying, "Hello! It's a great morning/afternoon/evening at Jeff Lewis's Office!" Jeff Lewis has the right idea.

Unless you live under a box completely off the grid of civilization,
you don't need me to convince you how phone skills are at an all-time

low. In my experience, it's not unusual that I need to ask somebody to repeat themselves when they answer the phone in order for me to figure out what the hell they just said.

When I was an intern in the First Lady's Office, I was taught and later taught others to answer every call clearly with "Office of the First Lady." Individual staffers would answer by saying, "This is (say your first name)."

"This is Eric" is actually how I still answer my phone today.

Come up with a standard professional way of answering your phone from the very first call you receive. When others hear you answering your phone like a professional, they will start treating you like one.

If you get somebody on the line and you need to put them on hold, ask them if they can hold (note, ask them—don't tell them to hold), then use the hold button to put them on hold! Most new interns totally get this wrong—and it's a true tell that they are newbies. When I say put a caller on hold, it doesn't mean hold the phone to your chest or whisper to your coworker, "What do I do?" It means press down the hold button.

Make this a habit, if you're not sure how to use the hold button—practice with somebody between two phones in the office on your first day until you can do it in your sleep.

If a second or third call comes in while you are already on the phone, again, ask your current caller if they can hold. If they can, put them on hold. Then, answer the incoming call and ask (don't tell them, ask them) if they can hold.

When I was an intern in the First Lady's Office I once asked a second caller if they could hold and they clearly said, "Yes, I can hold." I finished the first call in just a moment and then came back to the second call. The second caller said, "Hi Eric, this is Hillary—can you bring over a copy of today's press clips?" I had just put the First Lady on hold—but, it was okay, because I'd asked, and she was very cool.

In the office, some folks just let incoming calls go to voicemail. However, I would encourage you to get into the habit of trying to catch all calls when they come in live, even if that means you have to ask your callers to hold sometimes. First, it's more efficient (because you don't have to call the person back and/or run the risk of playing phone-message tag with them). Second, if somebody is calling you, they probably want to talk to you right then—chances are they will be okay with holding a bit in order to get you. Third, if somebody is calling you, you never know when it might be urgent; voicemail might be not be good enough.

Make a habit of being reachable and you will be a more valuable asset in the workplace during your internship and beyond.

If you find yourself on the phone in a situation where you need to take a message from somebody, there is certain information you need to take down. Sometimes offices will have little message pads that you can fill out. But whether your office uses a certain phone message form or not, make sure to write down the time and date of the call. Write down the caller's name, organization, and telephone number.

Ask the caller if they want to say why they are calling. If they answer with an issue that you can resolve, help the caller yourself (this is the mark of a truly excellent intern). If they don't want to say or it's something that can't address, write that down. Once you have that information, depending on the protocol of your particular office, either put it on the recipient's chair or email it to them.

If you're in an office, invariably you'll get a caller that should be transferred to somebody else. The transfer always trips up new interns. Again, if you're not sure how to transfer a call on the phones in your office, do some practice runs with phones in your office. Generally, to transfer a call on most phones you (1) hit transfer (2) dial the new number and (3) hit transfer again. Then, the call disappears from your phone because it has been forwarded to the other phone.

Transferring itself takes some skills that most new interns don't think about. First, when you're in your new office, find out how to dial internal calls, local calls, and long distance calls. You can be a genius at using the phone, but if you don't know how to dial the numbers, you're sunk. Next, get a current phone list of staffers in the office and put it in a place that is readily available. Otherwise, when the prime minister of Kerblakistan calls and asks to be transferred, you're going to be shuffling around looking for the right number, and the prime minister is going to know that you're a goof.

When a really savvy intern transfers a call, they will ask the caller something along the lines of, "If Bob isn't available, would you like their voicemail?" Depending on their answer, you can either let the call go into Bob's voicemail or, if Bob isn't available (he's not there or doesn't want to take the call) you can come back to the caller and let them know.

By the way, if somebody calls for a staffer who isn't there, doesn't want to talk right then, is doing interpretive dance, whatever, the correct way to describe their situation to the caller is to say that they are "unavailable." A professional intern never says, "Beatrice isn't here" or "Beatrice is on another call right now"—it's always "Beatrice is not available right now."

I don't know what it is, but sometimes interns wind up changing the pitch of their voice on the phone. My theory is that they do this unconsciously to sound less intimidating, but whatever the case, it doesn't sound good. When you are on the phone, especially if you don't have a lot of experience on the phone or you're freaked out by being on the phone in a professional setting, focus on using a grown-up voice. Speak from your chest, be fearless, sound bold.

When you call someone and get their voicemail, be very succinct with your message. The formula should be, "Hello, this is (insert your name) with (insert your organization). I'm calling about (insert subject—not the whole story, two or three words at most). If you would, please call me back at (insert your number, say it slowly). Again that number is (insert your number, say it slowly). Thank you very much." Click.

A good message shouldn't be longer than fifteen or twenty seconds. When most people leave a voicemail they try and tell their life story and then end by saying their telephone number so it sounds like, "please call me back at brreeessssssssssh" and you can't understand their number because they say it so quickly. When it comes to voicemail, don't be a dork.

PHONE LIKE A LAND LUBBER

If, during your internship, you ever need to make or receive a very important call, do everything you can to do it from a landline. Cell phone technology is amazing, but calls made through cell phones are not as clear as calls involving at least one landline.

75

Don't Be Sloppy

"Sloppy thinking gets worse over time."
—Jenny Holzer

In school, you probably got tons of experience with writing papers. When most students become interns however, for some reason, all this experience kind of goes out the window.

Maybe it's an issue of context. Whatever the case may be, during your internship you should be very careful when it comes to the written word. Don't be sloppy.

Starting with the application you fill out, the résumé you turn in, and the cover letter on top—make extra sure that you don't have any typos or spelling mistakes. Think you're good to go? Stop, look again. Challenge yourself to find the errors.

If your intern manager is a good one, they may have a habit of giving you instructions that are written down. They might hand you something with a note like this:

10/1/11: Hi Tom, please make the following edits and return to me. Thanks, Wilma

If you're the Tom in this situation you should make the edits carefully (again, carefully). Then print out the new version.

Before you even think about taking the paper back to Wilma, compare the marked-up version with the edited version. Look at each change edit by edit to make sure you've got them all. If/when you find a mistake, shred the version you just printed, make the change, and start again. Once you're double sure that every edit has been made, look at the new version as a whole—is the formatting still right? Does it look right in general?

Then, and only then, you should paper clip Wilma's marked-up version to the new version. Next to Wilma's original instructions, you write something like this.

5/4/11: Hi Wilma, edits have been made. Please let me know if you need any more changes. Thanks, Tom

If you've done a good job, Wilma should be good to go with the version you've printed. It's possible that Wilma will make some more edits and hand it back to you. If she does, that's fine. It's possible that Wilma will find an error that you missed and hand it back to you. If she does, it isn't great—but use the occasion as an excuse to make yourself be more careful next time.

When I was an intern, I had the great fortune of having a supervisor who was very patient with me. Even though I made mistakes sometimes, she didn't make a big deal about it. When you make edits for a supervisor, motivate yourself to get the edits done in one take. Can you do it? *Everybody makes silly mistakes at work sometimes—the difference is how one handles those mistakes.*

When I make silly mistakes at work like typos or reversing numbers, I get really angry at myself because there is no excuse for it. Sometimes I even think about it for a few days. I can only hope that my boss knows that I'm harder on myself about silly mistakes than they could ever be. If you can maintain a similar mind-set during your internship, you will make fewer mistakes.

Here's another tip when it comes to editing paper for your boss. Definitely include a marked-up version with the edited version of anything you edit for someone else. If that marked-up version comes back to you in the end, be sure to hang on to it, at least for a little while. You don't have to store it in some fancy file storage system—just put it someplace where you could get it again if you need to. You don't want to be in a position where your boss asks you to reference something they wrote down, but you've already discarded the thing they wrote on.

Again, if your boss puts written instructions on your chair, return the paper face down on their chair (unless of course they're sitting in it, in which case you should just hand it to them). If the boss hands you something, hand it back. If the boss puts something in your inbox, return it to their inbox.

Avoid handing paper to people as they go by just because it is convenient for you. You never know where your supervisor is headed. They might be going to lunch, they might be going to a meeting, or they might be going to the bathroom. Wherever they are going, it may not be ideal for them to carry extra paper around.

76

Walk Tall

"The body never lies."

—Martha Graham

Most folks spend so much time focusing on what they say that they neglect to think about how they're saying it. It has been estimated that 50 percent of all communication is non-verbal, and another 35 percent on top of that relates more to how you speak rather than what you say.

As a new intern in the office, people are looking for clues about you—spoken or otherwise. So, be aware of your body language. Stand tall, move confidently. Over the years I've seen plenty of interns who were supremely capable—but folks dismissed them because they kind of snuck around like they were afraid to bother anybody.

DON'T APOLOGIZE FOR BEING THERE

Especially if you wind up interning in a particularly intimidating place, you may feel like you're in a situation where you should be neither seen nor heard. Sometimes twisted staffers on a power trip will do things to make interns feel like this. They won't acknowledge an intern when they walk into the room, they will make an intern stand there and wait while they are doing something else truly trivial—these are all mind games.

As an intern, you may be in situations where you have to put up with this stuff—but don't ever get yourself in a mind-set where you feel you need to minimize your footprint or apologize for being present. Indeed, that path only leads into a downward spiral giving office bullies encouragement to engage in mind games with you even more.

Instead, focus all your energy on being an awesome intern. If you run into somebody who starts playing games to make you feel small, ignore them.

Unless you're interning at a chicken farm, don't walk on eggshells.

Pay attention to how you look—do whatever you can to look like a real pro. Instead of carrying around loose paper, carry some kind of fancy-looking folder thing (doesn't have to be expensive, almost anything looks better than loose paper). As an intern, especially during an office crisis, sometimes you need to run. But don't get rattled. Don't run just because you're rattled. Stay focused, don't panic.

Not too long after I moved from intern to staffer, I was charged with coordinating a short stop in Europe during one of the First Lady's foreign trips. I'd never been in charge of something like this before, and I was a bit out of my depth. Deep down, I was nervous about the whole thing, and it showed.

In an attempt to stay ahead of everything, during the visit I kept rushing around. I didn't realize it at the time, but my rushing made everybody else kind of nervous too. In the end, in my rush, I managed to close a car door on one of our translator's hands. It cut her hand to the bone. Rather than help with the rest of the visit, I was summarily dispatched to help get the poor injured woman to a doctor. Her hand wound up being fine, but I felt terrible and less importantly, I looked like a goof. Lesson learned: don't rush, don't panic—be steady.

If you move with confidence, people will assume that you are confident and in the end, you'll be confident. Confident interns succeed.

77

The Discard Drawer

"No Disassemble!"

—Johnny Five, *Short Circuit*

*I*n an office, one of your biggest challenges may be how to manage paper. Inevitably, you will often find yourself looking at a document and wondering, "Can I get rid of this or am I going to need it later?" Your solution is the discard drawer.

This is a drawer, preferably in your desk, where you stick documents that you might need later, but probably won't. When the drawer fills up, you pull stuff from the bottom of the stack to make more room. Depending on your paper output and the depth of the drawer, this method provides a reprieve of at least a couple of weeks for all your dubiously valuable papers.

If the rare case occurs where you actually need something that you discarded, you just dive into the drawer and find it. Because you're tossing documents in there in reverse chronological order, the deeper you go in the pile, the farther back in time you can search.

This technique is a great way to keep your desk neat while hedging against the chance that you're getting rid of something you need.

78

Start a Rolodex

"It's all about who you know."

—*Step Brothers*

O nce upon a time, keeping track of people was hard. Most folks kept an address book, with names and contact info written in pencil. If a contact moved, or changed jobs, you had to erase their old info and add the new stuff. If you lost your address book, you were cooked.

No longer.

With stuff like Microsoft Outlook and Google contacts and Facebook and all the rest, there is no excuse not to start building off a contact list from the get go. You should start this from day one of your internship.

Some people are lazy. They get a person's cell phone number or email or business card, and they don't take the thirty seconds to enter that person's info into whatever database they maintain. This is a huge mistake.

Some of the best contacts you make are in school or very early in your career—make absolutely sure that you take the time to enter the contact info for people you meet.

If for no other reason, you might need a particular person's contact info handy during some unforeseen future crisis. With smart phones now being what they are, there is no excuse not to have all your contact info in one.

WHERE DO YOUR CONTACTS LIVE?

Where should you keep all your contact info? This may not seem like an important question at the outset of your internship, but remember—whatever system you adopt now will likely evolve into a version of whatever system you use your entire professional life.

For keeping contacts, I've seen interns devise their own Excel spreadsheet systems, I've seen interns tape business cards into address books, I've seen them throw business cards into a shoe box. But the question of where and how to keep business contacts is one where technology is now our friend. If I were a new intern starting out now, I would definitely keep my contacts online using one of the free services designed to do just that. Gmail, Yahoo, Plaxo—all that stuff is pretty good. Gmail is my favorite (Gmail's tagging function is awesome) but you may have your own.

The reason I mention these online programs specifically is that they all are set up to import/export contacts through a variety of different files. Being online, these systems are accessible everywhere, and you don't have to worry about backing them up. As technology changes, the ability to import/export raw data to and from new systems is key. Moreover, all these tools have places to make notes about people you meet.

If you keep your contacts in Outlook on a hard drive, or just on a portable phone – you're sunk if either those are lost. Having your contact info online lets you access it/update it pretty much wherever you go whenever you want.

79

Build a Portfolio

"How's your portfolio?"
"I'd say strong to quite strong."

—*Meet the Parents*

Many interns are motivated to pursue an internship because they feel they don't have any professional experience. If this applies to you, it only follows that during your internship, you should document examples of your professional experience! This means you need to build a portfolio.

Clearly, you don't want to be making copies of sensitive or proprietary items at work in order to cart them out of the office (ask your intern host if you're not sure whether something is okay to snag). But during your internship, keep an eye out for samples of your work that might be suitable examples for a portfolio. If you need to, mark out any sensitive data; potential future employers can often get a sense about your work product without actually needing to see names/numbers, etc.

Keep a special eye out for any examples of your work that can be conveyed through various forms of media. Make sure to get copies of any publications you helped produce, snag examples of pictures or videos that highlight your work. During your internship, have the presence of mind to think about this stuff, and it will serve you well.

80

Candy Bowl

"All the candy corn that was ever made was made in 1911."
—Lewis Black

In an office there are many ways to gain popularity and curry favor with others. Keeping a candy bowl on your desk is one of the best.

What is a candy bowl? It's just like it sounds. Put a bowl of candy on your desk, and keep it supplied. Folks in the office who are trying to diet may avoid you, but everybody else will come like mosquitoes to a zapper. If you want senior people in the office to learn your name and know who you are, set up a candy bowl.

Warning: when people are coming by your desk, this leads to the possibility that more people are going to wind up distracting you with idle chit-chat. This is fine, unless you're on task at that particular moment.

If you've got things to do, just let people know that they're welcome to take some candy—but you're crashing right then. They'll get the idea pretty quick.

A word about the candy: get the good stuff. It'll cost you some bucks, but if you can afford it, buy the good stuff. My friend Josh Kirshner actually has a technique for his candy bowl. He keeps one filled just at the bottom—so folks are more apt to take a single piece rather than clean out what's left in the bowl.

Keep a candy bowl and you will instantly be popular in the office. Just don't pig out too much with all that candy staring you in the face all day.

81

Be a Mime

"..."

—Marcel Marceau

During your internship you can really pull off some Jedi mind
tricks, if you act like a mime.

Whether they admit it or not, a ton of research shows
that people tend to admire other people who are like them. Ask yourself, who are your biggest heroes in life? Chances are, a good number
of them are your same gender, race, and age, they likely have a similar
background to you and have similar goals.

So as an intern, if you're trying to get the attention of somebody in
the office, be a mimic. If they hold their pen a certain way, do the same.
If their posture is a certain way, do the same.

Some would call a technique like this "sucking up." Well, maybe it
is and maybe it isn't. But whatever the case, it works.

If you're a new intern who is trying to stand out above the crowd,
a little technique like this can be very effective. In the end, it's pretty
harmless and nobody will probably even notice what you're doing, at
least consciously.

82

Find a Niche

"We will now discuss in a little more detail the Struggle for Existence."

—Charles Darwin

Among my advanced internship techniques, this is one of the most important. It's important both for being a successful intern, and for being successful after your internship. The technique is this: *from the get go, you need to find a niche.*

This is advice that I wished somebody would have emphasized more when I was first starting out. However, if you are starting out now, especially as an intern, I'm glad to share it with you.

As you think about your future goals and career path, decide what you want to do better than anybody else in the world.

This idea flies in the face of a lot of advice students receive during a standard liberal arts education, which encourages students to be well rounded, to be Renaissance people, to be generalists.

Things have changed. Today, the world is so interconnected that being a generalist doesn't have a lot of value. The much smarter play is to be an extreme specialist in one thing.

It doesn't really matter what you choose. You could be the world's expert in ancient Babylonian cabinet making or Himalayan tectonics or Ethiopian sign language. The important thing is you identify a niche.

So, as your internship begins, and as you are picking up general office skills, never stop looking for a niche. Don't stop seeking an area where you could really see yourself going deep. Instead of molding yourself as the intern who is good at everything, strive to be the intern that is the best at one thing.

DELIBERATE PRACTICE

Sometimes people make the mistake of confusing experiential learning with deliberate practice (check out Geoff Colvin's *Talent is Overrated*).

You can improve your knowledge and skills in a certain area by doing work related to that area. This is called "experiential learning" and is the main reason that internships are valuable and beneficial for students. However, there is a second part to becoming a world-class expert in any subject that interns, and frankly most professionals, overlook. They forget to improve their knowledge and skills by deliberate practice.

For example, let us say you want to get better at using Adobe Photoshop. Using Photoshop for a project would be experiential learning; reading the manual would be deliberate practice. Suppose you want to become a better public speaker. Going out and giving lots of speeches would be experiential learning; working with a speaking coach would be deliberate practice.

During your internship you will likely be doing mostly experiential learning. But, as you dive into a specific niche, be sure to supplement that experiential learning with deliberate practice.

Experiential learning and deliberate practice amplify each other. The more you do one, the more you'll learn from the other and the faster you'll become the world's best in a specific area you decide to dominate.

83

Move Your Ass

"Speed kills."

—James Carville

During the 1992 campaign for president of the United States, Bill Clinton did something really smart. He set up a campaign operation in Little Rock, Arkansas, which quickly became known as "The War Room."

This intrepid effort was led by the "Ragin' Cajun" James Carville who drove home the message that if the Clinton campaign just moved more quickly than their opponents, they would win.

In 1992 the cable news era was just coming of age. The folks in the War Room figured out that they could influence the news by providing the press with responses to opponents before their opponents had hardly finished delivering the charge. On top of that, with some foresight the Clinton folks would issue counter counter-responses before their opponents were able to even deliver their counter-response in the first place.

As an intern, if you have a choice between doing something quickly and doing something slowly, do it quickly.

During my internship in the White House, I was once asked to transcribe the audio recording of an interview the First Lady had just finished. Nobody said that it was urgent, but I didn't have anything else going on, so I sat down and got to work. The task was given to me around 10:30 AM. I cranked for ninety minutes and handed the transcript to the press secretary by 12 PM.

A few minutes later, Mrs. Clinton arrived for a meeting that was about to convene in the room next to where I was working. As she arrived, the First Lady mentioned to her press secretary in passing that she would like to have the transcript of the interview she'd done that morning as soon as it was ready. Because I'd just finished it, the press secretary nonchalantly handed it to her right then.

When she asked how the work had been completed so quickly, I got the credit. Mrs. Clinton asked that I be pulled in from the room next door so she could thank me personally. She said, "Eric! You must run on caffeine. We need people like you!" A few months later I was hired on staff.

Whether your internship fuel is yoga or veganism or caffeine or whatever, unless you have a good reason to do otherwise, go fast!

84

Responsibility vs. Control

"Do what you can, with what you have, where you are."
—Teddy Roosevelt

During your internship, if somebody asks you to do something, make sure that you have the authority to get it done. In other words, don't ever let yourself be put in the position where somebody asks you to be responsible for something over which you have no control.

This is a lesson that even some of the most seasoned professionals don't really understand. Over the years in the workplace, I've often encountered people in positions of responsibility for which they have no control.

For example, suppose your intern supervisor asks you to be responsible for organizing a meeting, except that they want Bob to be the one to send out all the invites. You might diligently reserve the room, put together the agendas, and print out materials for participants. As the date for the meeting approaches however, you realize that invites still haven't gone out. You ask Bob if you can help, but he says no, he'll send out the invites. Finally, the day before the meeting, Bob sends out the invites. But it's too late, it's too short notice—nobody shows up. The meeting fails.

The meeting was your responsibility, so your boss calls you in to berate you about why it failed. You accepted responsibility for the meeting, even though you didn't have control over putting it together. Don't let yourself be put in this position.

Whenever somebody asks to you to take responsibility for something, but they won't give you the authority you need to accomplish the task successfully, let them know that you will be happy to take responsibility for the task, if they give you the control you need. Otherwise, you can't accept responsibility for completing the task. It's nothing personal, it's not being insubordinate; it's being honest, it's being professional.

It's called being an awesome intern. Whether your supervisor appreciates your stance at the time or not, rest assured, they likely will later. Either way, a great deal of your sanity will be preserved.

85

Win File

"You will never win if you never begin."
—Helen Rowland

You know that you are awesome. Other people know that you are awesome. You know other people know you are awesome because they tell you.

But, what about people who don't know you? How do you convince those people that you are awesome? Answer: you start a win file.

Anytime somebody says something particularly nice about your work, write it down with the date they said it. Whenever you get an email from somebody praising you and/or your work, paste the text of that email into you win file.

Especially during an internship when you're just starting out, be active when it comes to collecting testimonials. If you have a supervisor who you know thinks highly of you, don't be shy about asking them to write a letter of recommendation for you. Even offer to do a first draft for them if that is helpful.

If you have the technology available, ask a supervisor to talk about your great work on video.

When an intern supervisor truly thinks highly of you, they are going to be grateful to you and for the work you've done. They will be more than happy to give you whatever evidence you need to document your great abilities.

Once you part ways from a supervisor, it's very difficult to get the same level of testimonial. Memories fade, people move on. Get this stuff when/as it happens. Build a win file. The next time you are applying for a program or job or needing stuff to validate your skills online, or examples to list on an employee evaluation, use material from the win file. Start collecting this information now.

86

Don't Think

"Raise your hand if you're sure!"

—Sure deodorant

I can't tell you how many disasters have happened in human history because of the words "I think." I do know of at least several hundred disasters that have occurred because of those words uttered by interns.

Linda asks Dave, "Dave, did that fax go through?"

Dave: "I think so."

BEEP! Wrong answer. Either Dave knows the fax went through or he doesn't—there is nothing in between.

When somebody asks you a question and you don't know the answer, there is only one correct answer. That answer is, "I don't know."

Its fine to follow this up with, "But I'm happy to find out." Regardless, answering a question in the workplace with "I think" is generally a recipe for disaster.

Some people, especially young interns trying to make a good impression, are afraid to say the words "I don't know." But, let's take a closer look at how this is kind of silly.

First off, is there anybody in the world that knows everything? No. Is there anybody in the world that knows, let's say, half of everything? No way.

In fact, I bet the average person knows far less than 1 percent of all knowledge. This goes back to what I was saying about finding a niche. This is why specialists can always add more value than generalists. But, I digress.

When somebody asks you a question and you don't know the answer, say "I don't know." You might have a pretty good guess about something, and if you want to offer that information as an assumption or guess or bet, that's fine. But stipulate clearly that you don't know for sure.

On the other hand, if you do know the answer to something, don't be afraid to say it boldly. When you do, people will notice the lack of edge in your voice and might even ask, "Are you sure?" If you're sure, say so.

87

How to Apologize

"Never ruin an apology with an excuse."

—Kimberly Johnson

During your internship, you're going to make mistakes. They might even be huge, catastrophic mistakes. But here's the thing: everybody is human, everybody makes mistakes. So don't sweat it too much.

When you make a mistake, make sure you say, "I'm sorry." Say it once. Mean it. Then, move on.

The mistake probably isn't as big a deal as you think it is, so there is no reason to dwell on it. If it truly is a huge deal, your best bet is to move on, do what you can to make it better, and learn from the error so it never happens again.

Some interns feel such pressure to perform well in the workplace that when they mess up, they have a tendency to apologize over and over. Don't be like this. Apologize once, and be done with it.

When you mess up, take responsibility. Don't whine. Don't come up with excuses. Own it. Let each mistake you make be a lesson on how to do better next time, acknowledge it, move on.

FAILURE IS NO MISTAKE

Sometimes people confuse mistakes with failure. As an intern, you shouldn't.

A mistake is a situation where you goof. You said you were going to do something and you forgot. You said the work was ready but page twenty was missing. You spelled the Icelandic ambassador's name incorrectly. Those are mistakes. You should apologize when you make mistakes, once.

Failure is a situation where you attempt to achieve something and it doesn't work.

After 10,000 failed attempts at perfecting the electric light bulb, Thomas Edison was asked how he could keep going. Edison is famous for saying, "I have not failed 10,000 times, I have found 10,000 ways not to make a light bulb."

Failure means you had the guts to try something risky, to try something new, that you tried to innovate. I think people, especially interns, should try to fail more often.

When you fail during your internship, don't apologize. Be proud when you fail. If somebody gives you a hard time when you fail, give them that Edison quotation.

Of course, make sure you know the difference between failing and making a mistake.

88

Power Phrases

"I'm hip, I'm with it."

—Dr. Evil, *Austin Powers*

Here are some power phrases that have been helpful to me over the years in the workplace. If you use them as an intern, you'll make people's head spin.

"I REJECT THAT."

This is a good phrase to use when somebody is suggesting something you don't agree with or don't want to do. Rather than get into a debate about the question at hand, you simply say "Sorry, I reject that." The other person in the conversation won't expect this response, and they will be stunned for just a moment.

Use that moment to direct the conversation in another direction. If the subject turns back to the issue you don't want to address, just remind them that you've "rejected that" and deflect the dialogue in another direction.

"IF I AGREED WITH YOU, WE'D BOTH BE WRONG."

This is a variation on "I reject that." It's a somewhat passive-aggressive way of disagreeing with somebody openly in a way that can throw the other party off balance. It can create an opening for you to make a counter point before your opponent has time to regroup.

"THAT SOUNDS LIKE A PERSONAL ISSUE."

This is a good phrase to use with somebody in the workplace that is going on and on about something that is not work related such that it's becoming a distraction.

For example, let's say Tom went camping over the weekend and he got a bunch of chigger bites. Every time you try to talk to Tom he starts talking about the weekend, how he got all the chigger bites, how he hates chiggers, how he needs a better tent.

If you find this discourse on chiggers interesting or amusing, and it's not affecting your work, go with it. However, if all this chigger talk is distracting, you can shut Tom down by simply saying, "Tom, that sounds like a personal issue."

"REMEMBER WHEN—?"

This is the phrase to use in the office with a bully.

I once had a supervisor who was pretty tough (she actually had a lot of personal issues, and liked to talk about them a lot). But she also had a tendency to pick on me just because she could.

On one occasion we were on a conference call together and there was some kind of background noise. She asked me, "Eric, are you making that noise?" I told her I was not.

A short while later, she tore into me again by saying, "Eric, is that you making that noise? I think that noise must be coming from you! Is that you?" On this occasion, I'd had enough; I invoked the "Do you remember" technique.

I said, "No, I'm not making the noise. But do you remember the conversation we had just like three minutes ago when you asked me if I was making the noise and I said that I wasn't making the noise? I'm thinking you must have forgotten the conversation we had because here you are asking the very same question again. Do you remember the conversation we had or are you just asking me the same question again for no reason?" Even when she backed down I kept this up for a few more moments to make the point.

Obviously, this is a pretty aggressive technique. But if somebody is bullying you in the office for no reason and you want them to stop, this will work.

"MY FRIEND"

Sticking "my friend" or "our friends" before a subject you're about to criticize is a way to show respect, even though you are leveling criticism. It softens the critic.

For example, you might say something like, "If our friend Bob hadn't knocked over the lantern, the barn might not have caught on fire." You're still pointing out that Bob started fire, but it's a way of saying you're still friends nonetheless.

"SORRY, I'M NOT IN A POSITION TO. "

This is basically a nice way of saying "no" without having to use that actual word. Its one thing if you tell somebody "no." It's something else if you explain the situation as one where you are just not in a position to say "yes."

89

Alpha, Bravo, Charlie

"Negative Ghostrider, the pattern is full."

—*Top Gun*

Here's one of the most useful things you can learn that not many people take the time to do—learn the correct NATO phonetic alphabet so when you've got a bad phone connection and you are giving out a flight confirmation code or making sure you have an email address right, you sound cool.

Military folks know how to use "alpha, bravo, charlie, delta, echo, foxtrot, golf, hotel, India, Juliet, kilo, Lima, Michael, November, Oscar, papa, Quebec, Romeo, sierra, tango, uncle, victor, whiskey, x-ray, yankee, Zulu." So should you.

90

Top Things Most Needed in an Office

"Be prepared."

—The Boy Scouts

O ver the years I've worked in a lot of different offices. In all those offices, there are certain items that, for whatever reason, are impossible to find.

I have no idea why these items are so elusive, but they are. If you keep some of this stuff handy during your internship, I can almost guarantee that you will be the intern who saves the day at least once.

The top things most needed in an office are:.

A KNIFE

Now please be careful with this one—don't go strolling through a metal detector or anything with a bowie knife. However, a bigger knife is something every office always needs (usually to cut cake). Don't get yourself in a security situation, but if your office is one where getting a knife in isn't problematic, having a larger sized knife can save the day.

MATCHES

Again—going on the birthday theme. Offices always seem to have a dearth of healthy pyromaniacs. There was a day when so many people smoked that acquiring fire was not a challenge. I'm glad smokers have become fewer and fewer—but that still leaves the issue of finding fire in short order just before the office birthday party. Keep a box of matches handy and you could be a hero.

PLASTIC SPOON, FORKS, KNIFE, AND NAPKINS.

People eat lunch at their desks—but they tend to run out of stuff to eat with. The starving officemate desperate for a spoon to eat her yogurt at 7:30 AM is a familiar sight. Keep a stash of plastic spoons, forks, knives in your desk—and people will think you rule. Maintain a cache of napkins, salt, pepper, ketchup, and mustard—and you will truly be an intern bound for greatness. Of course the good part about all this is that you can get all this stuff for free.

BAND-AIDS

In an office people handle paper (at least for now they still do). Where hands touch paper, there are paper cuts. Unfortunately, nobody ever has Band-Aids. People at work also have a tendency to wear shoes that shred their feet too. Again, no band aids. Keep this rudimentary first aid supply at the ready and you will become an intern that is literally a life saver.

TYLENOL

. . . Or whatever analgesic you prefer. People in offices work hard, consume tons of caffeine and sugar, and don't get enough fresh air or exercise. They get headaches. The ironic thing is, almost nobody ever has headache medicine. If you keep some handy, you'll quickly become the intern who is everybody's friend.

SAFETY PINS

One particularly busy day during my internship in the White House, I was running around like a crazy man. Things were going pretty well until I happened to catch my pants pocket on part of door latch going through a doorway. RIIIIIIIIIPPPPPPPP! I tore a gaping hole in my pants. There I was, standing in the White House, with my boxer shorts hanging out. Luckily, one of the staffers had a whole drawer full of safety pins. Thanks to her, I was able to patch myself together fairly well and continue the day. Ever since then, I've always made sure that I've had a good supply of safety pins—for myself, and others.

UMBRELLA

People in offices are busy—they don't usually pay attention to the weather as much as they should. Often, the busiest staffers are the same ones that happen to go outside a lot. These are also the same folks who never have an umbrella handy when it's raining out. I can't promise that you'll always get umbrellas returned to you—but if you're the intern who always has one handy for a colleague headed out into the rain, you will likely have their gratitude.

BLANK ENVELOPES

Offices tend to have lots of envelopes—but they are almost always ones with the organization's seal on them. When someone in the office has reason to mail something not related to the organization, they need a blank envelope. Unfortunately, these can sometimes be hard to find.

Keep a stack of blank envelopes handy and people will be amazed that you actually have some you're willing to part with.

A HAMMER

It usually goes against some kind of rule, but people in offices wind up tapping little nails into the wall so they can hang pictures or whatever they want to hang. While people can usually scrounge up little nails, they almost never have a hammer. Again, don't create a security issue, but if you're able to keep a small hammer handy in the office, people will think you are some kind of intern prophet for your foresight.

PLASTIC SACKS/SHOPPING BAGS

Of the items on this list, plastic bags are probably the least uncommon (people sometimes have these)—but still, there are never enough of them around. If you are the intern who has a stash of shopping bags/ plastic bags (especially around the holidays when people are carting around gifts and treats all the time)—it will serve your cause.

91

Read News Clips

"The reports of my death are greatly exaggerated."
—Mark Twain

Some people argue that the media is messed up and that reading the news can only make you feel limited and depressed. I get the argument. To some degree, folks who believe this have a point.

On the other hand, if you're trying to make your way in this world as an intern, there are plenty of reasons why you should keep up with the news. First, knowing the news makes you better at conversation. When you're standing shoulder-to-shoulder with the big boss (the one who has the power to hire you) at the next awkward office party, being aware about the latest news in the world will give you tons to talk about.

More importantly, knowing the news will let you make little connections at work that someone less informed might miss. The time will come when you are part of a conversation where a question comes up that you can answer because you stay well informed.

Especially in very busy offices, interns sometimes feel like they don't have time to read news clips or scan the web for news stories. However, the smart intern considers it part of their job to stay up-to-speed on the news. You should too.

92

Give Cards

"When you care enough to send the very best."
—Hallmark

In this age of Facebook page likes, forwarded tweets, and quick emails, the old fashioned thank-you note is becoming a rare thing indeed. As an intern from a generation who uses old fashioned notes with decreasing frequency, you can use this to your advantage.

Before your internship even begins, get yourself a big stack of blank note cards. They don't have to be fancy—just something that looks decent and that you can stick in an envelope. From the first day of your internship, look for excuses to give thank you notes. Thank staffers, thank other interns, thank clients—anybody who helps you along the way.

Now, you might be saying to yourself, "Eric! Isn't that sucking up?" Well, it IS sucking up if that's what you do with these notes. But that's not what I want you to do.

Send some thank-you notes when you *really* mean it. If somebody takes you to lunch, or takes the time to give you advice or helps you with a project, just write out a simple thank-you note. If you mean it, the note will be accepted with gratitude.

You *definitely* want to hand out a bunch of thank–you notes if/ when your internship comes to a close—or if somebody on staff leaves the office before you do. Make sure your contact information is included—you just never know when you might run into somebody again.

> **MEAN IT**
>
> Want to write a thank-you note that will really show you appreciate the internship experience you've had and that stresses how much you would value being offered a full-time position? Keep a "thank-you file" right alongside the "win file" I mentioned earlier.
>
> During your internship there will be plenty of instances where you will have reasons to feel grateful toward the people you interact with. But trust me; by the end of your internship you won't remember everything. That is, unless you make a practice of writing these instances down in a thank-you file. It can be just a simple sheet of paper, or even better, keep it as a Google Doc.

93

Teach Other Interns

"Teaching is the highest form of understanding."
—Aristotle

O
ne of my favorite analogies about teaching others revolves around a staircase. When you teach something to someone else, it is like you are bringing them up to the stair on which you stand. However when you do this, there is no room left for you on that stair. So, you must then step up onto a higher stair.

When you teach other interns, at least three things happen.

First, when you teach skills to your fellow intern, you reinforce those skills within yourself. When you teach knowledge you become a master of that knowledge.

Second, by teaching other interns and thereby mastering the information you teach, you prepare yourself to learn more advanced information.

Third, when you teach a fellow intern you are building a bridge to that other intern. If you are known as the intern in the office who is willing to teach others, you will stand out not only to the other interns, but also to the staff charged with supervising them.

The willingness and ability to teach others is the true mark of a master intern.

94

Don't Give up

"Stay alive no matter what occurs! I will find you. No matter how long it takes, no matter how far, I will find you."

—Hawkeye, *The Last of the Mohicans*

Whether it's true or not, young folks today get pegged with the bad rap that they give up too easily. I think this comes from at least two things.

First, there was a huge increased focus on safety since the mid-1990s. Seat belts, car seats, bicycle helmets, rubberized playground equipment, etc. all really took off when most of today's college-age students were growing up.

Second, the information age took off about the same time. Among older staffers there is a sense that with the Internet, digital music, Windows, cell phones, movies on demand, etc., that today's younger set had an easier time of things.

As a new intern, older colleagues likely already have the preconceived notion that you are going to be prone to giving up on things too easily. Don't let yourself play into this preconception.

When you are given a task, make a point to adopt the attitude that your ability to complete the task is not based on a question of "if" but rather "how."

Make sure that, before you concede defeat on any project, you exhaust every possible alternative route to success.

If you truly reach the point where you can't think of what to do next, go back to your intern supervisor and let them know all the things you've tried and ask them if they have any more ideas you might try. Returning to your supervisor with this attitude is so much better than going back and just saying, "I couldn't do it."

I may be biased, but I do think a lot of young people these days do give up on things too easily. Maybe it's because they never had to tape songs on the radio or use the Dewey Decimal System, I'm not sure.

But, whatever the case, if you are the one intern in the office who gets a reputation for not giving up, you will stick out like a sore thumb. For the future prospects of a hard working intern, standing out like a sore thumb is a very good thing.

95

Roadblocks

"Come senators, congressmen please heed the call. Don't stand in the doorway, don't block up the hall—for he that gets hurt will be he who has stalled."

—Bob Dylan

I f you've read this far, I can say with complete certainty that you now know more than 99.9999 percent of the population about how to be a great intern. Congratulations!

It took me about fifteen years to synthesize all these strategies into the formula you see here. Which means, if you implement them, you'll be about fifteen years ahead of any other intern (and quite a few staffers) you encounter at work.

Here are some potential pitfalls to watch out for. Avoid these or run the risk of not being as successful during your internship as you could be:

YOU DON'T CARE

There are some interns who just honest-to-God don't care.

You might ask then, "Why are they interning?" It could be they wanted an excuse to live away from home for the summer or they were pressured into a program by teachers or parents. Whatever the case, since you've presumably read this far into the book, I doubt this category applies to you.

If it does, sorry—I don't really have an answer for you. If you don't care about your internship, go find something you care about.

YOU'RE AFRAID

Have you ever seen one squirrel chasing another? I bet you have. If you are like me, I bet you've also noticed that there is no real reason for one squirrel to be chasing another. In fact, when the squirrel being chased decides to stand his ground or reverse the chase, a lot of times that is exactly what happens!

In other words, most squirrels are the same. The only reason one squirrel chases another is often that the chaser has just a little bit more confidence than the runner. Even when one squirrel is much bigger than the other, it really boils down to boldness and confidence. I would humbly suggest that this same phenomenon takes place among people—especially people in an office.

Don't be afraid to let these strategies work. Don't be afraid to use them.

Think you might look stupid by standing out? You might. But here is the secret: everybody is afraid they're going to look stupid. The only difference between people who step out and those who don't is the degree to which one can overcome that fear of looking stupid.

Let me make a suggestion: take all the energy that you might otherwise spend on fear and put it into focusing on the right attitude, perfecting your office skills, fine-tuning your ability to communicate, and mastering special skills.

Have extreme confidence in yourself. Here is the fun part: the more you engage in these rules, the more confidence you will have in yourself. Step into these strategies without fear and you'll find yourself in a confidence-building feedback loop that will make you stand out. People won't see you as an intern; they'll see you as a professional.

YOU THINK YOU ARE ABOVE CERTAIN TYPES OF WORK

This is a common one. You may make the decision that you are only going to do certain types of work during your internship because some work is beneath you.

That's fine, you can think that way—but let me warn you, I don't think that is a very good strategy. Here's why.

Let's suppose you're in a room and it's you and your boss. Your boss needs two things: (1) a cup of coffee and (2) somebody to send an email about the Penske account. In this scenario, chances are that your boss could do the email or get the coffee, but in the allotted time, the only value you can add is to get coffee. By you going to get the coffee, resources are optimized. Results are achieved.

Now don't get me wrong—if you're not picking up useful skills along the way and/or growing professionally, that's a different story. What I'm saying here is this: Focus on adding value, and you will thrive in your internship. Grab any opportunity to add value in every situation—whether that means getting coffee or making copies or hanging out with movie stars. Focus on adding value, and you can take satisfaction in knowing that the work you're doing as an intern truly matters.

YOU ONLY WANT TO DO "POLICY"

This is a common one too. Some interns, somewhere along the way, get this meme inserted into their minds that all they want to do is "policy."

What is "policy"? Beats the hell out of me. I think people often confuse the word "policy" with "substance" to the point where they conclude that unless they are writing down thoughts on paper, the work isn't worthy.

Let me let you in on a little secret. Results achieved by pretty much any organization can be boiled down to (1) what and (2) how. In my experience the how is often more important than the what.

Say, for example, that Charlie has a great new idea that will save an organization's clients $1,000/week. But in order for the clients to save this money, they need to understand a five-step process. If Charlie can't find a way to communicate to the clients that there is an opportunity to save money, much less convince people that it's worth their while to learn the five-step process, his great idea will go nowhere. The great idea is the what, the method for publicizing the idea and teaching people how to make it work is the how.

So during your internship, if somebody asks you to stuff envelopes or check people into an event or anything else that isn't strictly writing your ideas down, don't underestimate the value you can add in such situations.

YOU DON'T HAVE ANY FRIENDS

For some, doing an internship is the first time a student has done something on their own outside of school or, at the very least, apart from peers. Some students get thrown off when they realize they are the youngest person in the office, and they really have nobody they can relate to/befriend. My advice: get over it.

I go back to the beginning of this book about the purpose of an internship, which is to gain access to special knowledge and people. Remember, if you make friends during an internship, that is fine—but that is not the purpose of an internship. If you want to make friends, go to a party. Don't let lack of socializing throw you off during your internship. Get to work.

YOU AREN'T HAVING FUN

Again, if this is your hang-up, you've got the wrong focus. As Larry Winget argues in his book with the same title, "It's called work for a reason!"

If you want to have fun, go to the circus. If you want to learn and get access to people who might be able to promote your professional development, buckle down.

Bonus: if you truly challenge yourself and dig deep with an internship, chances are you will start to have fun. Being proud of the work you do is really fun.

Conclusion

"Damn the torpedoes, full speed ahead!"

—Admiral Farragut

I f you've made it this far, you should take great satisfaction in knowing that your commitment to your education and your interest in doing an internship is going to put you leaps and bounds ahead, especially if you employ the techniques you've read about here.

But an internship, after all, is really just a step to the next thing, right? You don't want to be an intern forever. Everything I have outlined here has been designed to help you get to and through the internship step successfully. But once you've done that, how do you get to the next thing after an internship? Let me conclude this by offering some things to think about after you've found a great internship, thrived in it, and presumably are moving toward the job hunt.

96

Bask in Your Inexperience

"Optimism is the faith that leads to achievement."
—Helen Keller

Believe it or not, during a job hunt, your lack of experience and degrees can be a huge advantage.

First, a potential employer doesn't have to worry about correcting any bad professional habits you have—because, in theory, you don't have any. Second (this is good news and bad news for you) you are an attractive potential hire because, without limited experience, they can get away with paying you less. Third, as a younger, inexperienced type, they can hire you without worrying too much that you are overqualified for tasks that need to be done—that more experienced workers might think are beneath them.

Once you have an internship or two under your belt and you start applying for jobs, you can use many of the same techniques I described about how to get an internship in your search for a job. But when you do, it is important to adjust your narrative accordingly. As a job applicant you may want to come across as very experienced and accomplished. Or, it may be more advantageous to build a narrative that casts you as less experienced, but highly capable. The point it, during a job hunt, don't always assume that more experience and more credentials is better. I believe job applicants are turned away because they are overqualified as often or more often as they are turned away because they are underqualified.

As someone who has just finished an internship and is just starting out in their career, you have the great advantage of being at the less qualified end of the spectrum. Do not be afraid to use that to your advantage. When looking at candidates to fill a position, employers worry about things like, "How long will this person stay in the job?" and "How long will it be before this person is no longer challenged and outgrows this job?" As a relatively inexperienced professional, you can build a narrative that overcomes these possible objections when an employer considers hiring you.

97

Defining Yourself

"Do you know who you are? Don't ask. Act! Action will delineate and define you."

—Thomas Jefferson

You've either finished or are about to finish college, you have a major. It may feel like you are pretty well defined.

You've finished a few internships all related to a particular subject—that probably defines you, right?

You're in your mid-twenties or even pushing thirty—surely the things you have done professionally define you, right?

Trust me. Especially starting out, even after several internships you are not nearly as well defined professionally as you probably think you are. As you get older, I suspect you will realize that the five or even ten years of professional experience you now list on your résumé are all relative.

In other words, just because you majored in biology and did an internship in engineering and now want to study art doesn't mean you can't study art. Would it have been better professionally if you'd majored in art and done the internship in art? Yes. *But early in your career, especially after you've just finished an internship, you are still professionally plastic.* During a job hunt you can use this to your advantage as an early professional.

Just to be clear, I am not suggesting you should let opportunities available completely drive the choice of jobs you accept. However, as someone just starting out, realize you definitely have more flexibility in the range of jobs you select.

For example, you may really want a position in the financial department of a particular organization. However, it turns out that the only job available is a position in the administrative department of that organization. It may make sense to go for the job that is available, just to get your foot in the door. Later, when that financial position opens up, you will be in a very good position to get it. Or, you may surprise yourself and find that you actually love the administrative position. The point is, this is flexibility that you have early in your career, which you will not have as you take more and more senior positions. Don't waste this leeway while you have it.

A WORD ABOUT REINVENTING YOURSELF LATER IN YOUR CAREER

Suppose, however, you are not early in your career. Suppose that you have had a career but decided it's time for a change and have completed an internship to help you do that. College was long ago and in a way, you feel like you're starting over professionally.

Here is some really good advice: lose the mind-set that you are starting over. If you have years of experience, that represents tons of career capital you probably can't afford to just throw away. Instead, find a way to pivot your past experience to the new thing. For example, if you were a teacher for twenty years and now you want to be a zoologist, focus on teaching zoology. Or say you were an accountant for twenty years and now you want to do gardening, focus on keeping inventory of a garden.

Chances are, if you've done an internship as part of a mid-career change, you're going to have a tendency to apply for positions that you are way over-qualified for. Don't look at it a mid-career change as a reinvention but rather as just a pivot. You don't need to give up your entire identity to make a change, just tweak it a little.

98

The Post-Internship Job Quest

"It's just a job. Grass grows, birds fly, waves pound the sand.
I beat people up."

—Muhammad Ali

Mechanically, a lot of the techniques you use to find an internship can be used to find a job after an internship. If prospects are slim at the place where you did your internship, one of your best courses is to ask your current mentors for advice and help in finding a full-time position elsewhere.

First off, the people who mentored you during your internship are going to be motivated to help you because they have a huge investment in you and naturally should want to see you succeed. Furthermore, if your most recent mentors are not in a position to hire you themselves, they are going to feel some responsibility in making sure you find a job somewhere. *Make your current internship hosts your allies in the job quest.*

Don't beat around the bush when enlisting help from recent intern mentors in your job quest. Especially right at the end of your internship, you will likely know nobody better equipped, more motivated, and with as many networks as them to help you find a job. Be explicit when asking these allies for help, don't be vague. Ask questions like,

"Do you know of any organizations that might have open positions?" Or, "Is there anyone you know who might be interested in seeing my résumé?" Or, "I'm applying to XYZ organization, would you mind please taking a look at the application I'm about to send in and tell me what you think?" Or, "I'm applying to XYZ organization, do you know anybody there?"

As I've stated before, it always tends to be easier to find a job when you have a job. So, even if they can't hire you, it may be worth asking your current internship host if you can continue to come in, even if it's just part time and even if you will be using some of your time in the office to pursue the job hunt. Your internship host may be really open to that idea, especially if a new cohort of interns has already arrived, since by being around, you will be in a position to help answer questions as a mentor to those new interns. The great advantage of remaining around an office is that you will maintain a connection to all the resources and networks that office represents. If you leave your internship site completely and the right job comes along a month later, it's not so good. On the other hand, if you've got nowhere else to be, stick around your internship site if you can and if a job comes along a month after your originally scheduled departure, you'll be in a better position to snag it.

99

Job Boards after Your Internship

"We wait. We are bored."

—*Waiting for Godot*

Posting your résumé in a résumé bank hoping an internship host might reach out to you with an internship is often a little hopeless. Posting your résumé in a résumé bank hoping someone will reach out to you with a job offer, I fear, is even more hopeless. During a post-internship job hunt, I don't think this is necessarily a very good use of your valuable time.

Looking at job boards and submitting resumes to opportunities listed as available is a little better technique, but given the number of competitors who are likely doing the exact same thing, the odds are still against you. It is tempting to make this the main focus of your job search just because it is convenient and, when you send off an application to an opportunity that is listed, it at least gives you a sense of getting something done, of making some kind of progress. However, be aware that this too might not be the most effective use of your job-hunting time.

When looking for a job after an internship, the best strategy is likely to focus on just talking to lots of different people. Ironically, though it is often the most effective tactic, this strategy actually takes a lot less time and effort than spending hours on the computer. But to do it successfully, you will need to employ your best social skills. If you are really serious about your job hunt, commit to talking to one new person every day about career stuff. This means actively scheduling one meeting a day with someone new for an informational interview. These meetings don't need to be long and you shouldn't go into them with any agenda other than to get advice and introduce yourself to someone new as a young professional on the job hunt.

Consider this: setting up meetings like this isn't necessarily something you need to wait to do after your internship is over. What if you started to do meetings like this, even if it was just one per week, during your internship? At the end of a twelve-week internship that would mean that you'd have met and gotten advice from twelve different people. Think one of those twelve might hear about some kind of job position that you'd be perfect for at some point during that time? I bet they would. Especially if you stayed in touch with each of those twelve during that time, think they might pass the opportunity your way? I think they would.

It partly depends on how great the economy is at any given time, but once one enters the working world—especially once he or she has a lot of contacts within a particular industry—people start to receive emails along the lines of, "Hey, does anybody know of something who might be good for this position?" These are the sorts of jobs that employers never advertise and hope to fill on a fast track with a candidate referred to them by someone they already know and trust. Colleagues like to respond to these messages because if they wind up referring a candidate that is ultimately accepted, they'll have done a favor for both the job applicant and their colleague or another organization simultaneously. Moreover, because they were the one who referred the young professional to the new position, they now have a permanent friendly contact in the other organization.

This is a dynamic that you absolutely need to take advantage of as a young professional on the job hunt following an internship.

100

The Power of Starting

"You don't have to be great to start, but you have to start to be great."
—Zig Ziglar

No matter what stage you are at professionally, if you seek an opportunity to learn through workplace experience and build a portfolio of career capital to demonstrate that you have, an internship might be just the thing for you.

This book has described how to get an internship and how to thrive at an internship once you have one. After doing an internship you can use many of the same techniques you used to get an internship and thrive as an intern to land a job. But as in many aspects of life, all that has been described here will only work if you start.

In my experience, starting is almost always the hardest part. Whether it's applying for a new job or taking a chance on a new opportunity, the first step is always the hardest. One of my favorite authors, Seth Godin, writes about starting as "shipping." He writes that we should, "Ship often. Ship lousy stuff, but ship. Ship constantly."

When I find myself stuck on starting a project or taking a risk, I think about "shipping." I repeat a mantra to myself, "Just ship, ship it, ship it now, SHIP IT!"

If you want to move forward to the next step through an internship and you find that you are stuck, that you are having trouble getting started. I recommend this mantra to you. Don't think about it much, just start. Figure out the first thing you would need to do to get started and do that thing now. Not later now. Don't wait. Ship.

If the first step for you now is to work on your résumé, the first step to do that might be to find your old one. Do that. If the first step for you now is to visit your career center to find an internship, look up where it is and plan when you're going to go there. If the first step for you now is to get a letter of reference from your internship mentor, draft an email to them to ask for that right now. When it comes to being a great intern, don't wait. Ship now.

I very much hope the information in this book serves you well, and I honor you for the commitment you have made toward your career development and success in reading it. It's been a pleasure for me to share this information with you, and someday I hope to hear about how it helped you.

Everyone, sometime in their lives (most likely many times), is the newbie who must learn in a new situation. Moving to a new town is an internship. Meeting new friends at summer camp is an internship. Going on a first date is an internship. Everyone at one time or another is an intern. Be a great one.

What did you think of this book? Did you like it? Did you hate it? Please let me know by posting a review on Amazon. I really appreciate every single one.

About the Author

Eric Woodard is the author of several books about internships, including *Your Last Day of School: 56 Ways You Can Be a Great Intern and Turn Your Internship into a Job* and *Why Internships Are Good*. Eric emphasizes practical steps students can implement immediately to find and thrive during an internship. He focuses on the topics students often don't learn in school but are assumed to possess as interns.

Eric knows firsthand how tricky the path from school to internship to work can be. After growing up in Thailand and moving to the United States to attend college, he transferred schools seven times. After graduating from college, Eric wound up working for several years as a scuba instructor in Guam.

Using many of the lessons he now teaches, Eric managed to land an internship at the White House in Washington, DC. Eric excelled during his internship and was eventually hired on to the White House staff. Over the last fifteen years he has organized internship programs up and down scary halls of power in our nation's capital where he's had the opportunity to mentor hundreds of student interns to success.

Eric has created and managed internship programs at the White House, U.S. Senate, and the State Department. He holds a doctorate ABD in Human and Organizational Learning from George Washington University and currently serves as Director of Internships and Fellowships at the Smithsonian.

Eric lives in Alexandria, Virginia, with his beautiful, smart wife and their three genius little children.

Index

Books from Allworth Press

Allworth Press is an imprint of Skyhorse Publishing, Inc. Selected titles are listed below.

Brand Thinking and Other Noble Pursuits
by Debbie Millman (6 x 9, 320 pages, paperback, $19.95)

Career Solutions for Creative People
by Dr. Ronda Ormont (6 x 9, 320 pages, paperback, $27.50)

Corporate Creativity: Developing an Innovative Organization
by Thomas Lockwood and Thomas Walton (6 x 9, 256 pages, paperback, $24.95)

The Business of Being an Artist, Fifth Edition
by Daniel Grant (6 x 9, 336, paperback, $19.99)

Effective Leadership for Nonprofit Organizations
by Thomas Wolf (6 x 9, 192 pages, paperback, $16.95)

From Idea to Exit: The Entrepreneurial Journey
by Jeffrey Weber (6 x 9, 272 pages, paperback, $19.95)

Infectious: How to Connect Deeply and Unleash the Energetic Leader Within
by Achim Nowak (6 x 9, 256 pages, paperback, $19.95)

Intentional Leadership: 12 Lenses for Focusing Strengths, Managing Weaknesses, and Achieving Your Purpose
by Jane A. G. Kise (7 x 10, 200 pages, paperback, $19.95)

Millennial Rules: How to Sell, Serve, Surprise & Stand Out in a Digital World
by T. Scott Gross (6 x 9, 208 pages, paperback, $16.95)

Peak Business Performance Under Pressure
by Bill Driscoll (6 x 9, 224 pages, paperback, $19.95)

The Pocket Small Business Owner's Guide to Building Your Business
by Kevin Devine (5 ¼ x 8 ¼, 256 pages, paperback, $14.95)

Rebuilding the Brand: How Harley-Davidson Became King of the Road
by Clyde Fessler (6 x 9, 128 pages, paperback, $14.95)

Starting Your Career as a Graphic Designer
by Michael Fleishman (6 x 9, 384 pages, paperback, $19.95)

To see our complete catalog or to order online, please visit *www.allworth.com*.

DEJA REVIEW™
Pediatrics

DEJA REVIEW™
Pediatrics

Second Edition

Brooke T. Davey, MD

Fellow, Pediatric Cardiology
University of Pennsylvania
The Children's Hospital of Philadelphia
Philadelphia, Pennsylvania

 **Medical**

New York   Chicago   San Francisco   Lisbon   London   Madrid   Mexico City
Milan   New Delhi   San Juan   Seoul   Singapore   Sydney   Toronto

Deja Review™: Pediatrics, Second Edition

3 4 5 6 7 8 9 0   DOC/DOC   15 14 13

ISBN 978-0-07-171514-0
MHID 0-07-171514-2

This book was set in Palatino by Cenveo Publisher Services.

The editors were Kirsten Funk and Cindy Yoo.

The production supervisor was Catherine Saggese.

Project management was provided by Sapna Rastogi, Cenveo Publisher Services.

RR Donnelley was printer and binder.

This book is printed on acid-free paper.

Library of Congress Cataloging-in-Publication Data

Davey, Brooke T.
     Deja review. Pediatrics / Brooke Davey.—2nd ed.
          p. ; cm.—(Deja review)
     Pediatrics
     ISBN 978-0-07-171514-0 (pbk.)
     1. Pediatrics—Examinations, questions, etc.   I. Title.   II. Title: Pediatrics.
   III. Series: Deja review.
     [DNLM: 1. Pediatrics—Examination Questions.   WS 18.2]
     RJ48.2.D42 2011
     618.92—dc22
                                                                    2011016013

I dedicate this book to doctors in training whose hard work, sacrifice, and excitement to learn keep the medical profession moving forward.

Thank you to my family and friends for your unending support and encouragement

Contents

Contributors

John Babineau, MD
Fellow, Pediatric Emergency Medicine
Morgan Stanley Children's Hospital of
  New York
New York Presbyterian Hospital
Columbia University Medical Center
New York, New York
Genetic Disease

Marisol Betensky, MD, MPH
Resident, General Pediatrics
Children's Hospital of Philadelphia
Philadelphia, Pennsylvania
Pulmonology

Brooke T. Davey, MD
Fellow, Pediatric Cardiology
University of Pennsylvania
The Children's Hospital of Philadelphia
Philadelphia, Pennsylvania
Cardiology
Neurology

Jessica Durst, DO
Resident, Department of Pediatrics
New York Presbyterian Chidren's Hospital of
  New York
Columbia Unviersity Medical Center
New York, New York
Psychiatry
Immunology and Rheumatology
Screening and Prevention

Emily Kott Eida, MD
Resident, Department of Pediatrics
Morgan Stanley Children's Hospital of
  New York
New York Presbyterian Hospital
Columbia University Medical Center
New York, New York
Musculoskeletal Disease
Metabolic Disorders

Janienne Kondrich, MD
Fellow, Department of Pediatric Emergency
  Medicine
New York University Langone Medical Center
Bellevue Hospital
New York, New York
Dermatology
Pediatric Emergencies and Trauma

Jennifer Louis-Jacques, MD, MPH
Resident, Department of Pediatrics
Morgan Stanley Children's Hospital of
  New York
New York Presbyterian Hospital
Columbia University Medical Center
New York, New York
Adolescent Medicine
Endocrinology

Mahbod Mohazzebi, MD, FAAP
Pediatrician, Medical Director
Advocare Kressville Pediatrics
Cherry Hill, New Jersey
Nephrology and Urology
ENT and Ophthalmology

Neha Dinesh Patel, MD
Resident, Department of Pediatrics
Morgan Stanley Children's Hospital of
  New York,
New York Presbyterian Hospital
Columbia University Medical Center
New York, New York
Gastroenterology

Nefthi Sandeep, MD
Resident, Department of Pediatrics
Morgan Stanley Children's Hospital of
  New York,
New York Presbyterian Hospital
Columbia University Medical Center
New York, New York
Birth and Prematurity
Hematology and Oncology

Aarti Sheth, MD
General Pediatrician
New York, New York
Infectious Disease
Growth, Development, and Nutrition

Faculty Reviewers

Fred Bomback, MD
Clinical Professor of Pediatrics
Columbia University
College of Physicians and Surgeons
New York, New York

Marina Catallozzi, MD
Assistant Professor of Pediatrics
Department of Population and Family Health
Columbia University College of Physicians
and Surgeons
Mailman School of Public Health
New York, New York

Wendy Chung, PhD, MD
Director of Clinical Genetics
Department of Pediatrics - Molecular
Genetics
Columbia University Medical Center
New York, New York

Mary Anne Jackson, MD
Chief, Section of Pediatric Infectious Diseases
Children's Mercy Hospital and Clinics
Professor of Pediatrics
University of Missouri-Kansas City
School of Medicine
Kansas City, Missouri

Beth Kaufman, MD
Medical Director, Cardiomyopathy Program
Children's Hospital of Philadelphia
Assistant Professor of Pediatrics
University of Pennsylvania School of
Medicine
Philadelphia, Pennsylvania

Connie Kostacos, MD
Assistant Clinical Professor
Department of Pediatrics—General Pediatrics
New York Presbyterian Hospital
Columbia University Medical Center
New York, New York

Michael E. McCormick, MD
Department of Otolaryngology—Head and
Neck Surgery
Wayne State University School of Medicine
Detroit, Michigan

Nadia Ovchinsky, MD, MBA
Assistant Professor of Clinical Pediatrics
Department of Pediatric Gastroenterology
Morgan Stanley Children's Hospital of
New York
New York Presbyterian Hospital
Columbia University Medical Center
New York, New York

Sameer J. Patel, MD
Assistant Professor of Pediatrics
Department of Pediatric Infectious Diseases
Columbia University
New York, New York

David Resnick, MD
New York Presbyterian Hospital
Allergy Division
New York, New York

Rakesh Sahni, MD
Columbia University
College of Physicians and Surgeons
New York, New York

Sujit Sheth, MD
Associate Professor of Pediatrics
Columbia University Medical Center
New York, New York

Nasreen Talib, MD, MPH
Medical Student Coordinator
Department of Pediatrics
University of Missouri-Kansas City
School of Medicine
Kansas City, Missouri

David Teng, MD
Morgan Stanley Children's Hospital of
New York
New York Presbyterian Hospital
Columbia University Medical Center
New York, New York

Jeffrey J. Tomaszewski, MD
Department of Urologic Surgery
University of Pittsburgh Medical Center
Pittsburgh, Pennsylvania
Morgan Stanley Children's Hospital of
New York
New York Presbyterian Hospital
Columbia University Medical Center
New York, New York

Student Reviewers

Stacy Cooper
SUNY Upstate College of Medicine
Class of 2008
Fourth Year Medical Student

Ilana Harwayne-Gidansky
SUNY Downstate College of Medicine
Class of 2009
Fourth Year Medical Student

Rebecca Lambert
Weill Cornell Medical College
Class of 2010
Third Year Medical Student

Alison Santopolo
Weill Cornell Medical College
Class of 2010
Third Year Medical Student

Preface

Pediatrics is a broad and complex, yet exciting field, with a diverse and ever-evolving patient population. Deja Review: Pediatrics, Second Edition is written by pediatric residents and fellows for medical students. The most frequently tested pediatric subjects on those exams are covered in this book by new doctors in training and graduating medical students who have recently taken the boards. It is an effective study guide that may be used to study for Steps 1, 2, and 3 of the boards and the pediatric shelf exam. The topics addressed will reinforce a broad base of pediatric knowledge with clinical pearls that apply to the subspecialties within the field.

ORGANIZATION

The Deja Review series is a unique resource that has been designed to allow you to review the essential facts and determine your level of knowledge on the subjects tested on your clerkship shelf exams, as well as the United States Medical Licensing Examination (USMLE) Steps. All concepts are presented in a question and answer format that covers key facts on commonly tested topics during the clerkship.

This question and answer format has several important advantages:

- It provides a rapid, straightforward way for you to assess your strengths and weaknesses.
- Prepares you for "pimping" on the wards.
- It allows you to efficiently review and commit to memory a large body of information.
- It serves as a quick, last-minute review of high-yield facts.
- Compact, condensed design of the book is conducive to studying on the go.

At the end of the book, you will find clinical vignettes. These vignettes are meant to be representative of the types of questions tested on national licensing exams to help you further evaluate your understanding of the material.

HOW TO USE THIS BOOK

This book is intended to serve as a tool during your pediatric clerkship, as well as pediatric subspecialty rotations. Remember, this text is not intended to replace comprehensive textbooks, course packs, or lectures. It is simply intended to serve as a supplement to your studies. This text was thoroughly reviewed by a number of medical students and interns to represent the core topics tested on shelf examinations.

For this reason, we encourage you to begin using this book early in your clinical years to reinforce topics you encounter while on the wards. You may use the book to quiz yourself or classmates on topics covered in recent lectures and clinical case discussions. A bookmark is included so that you can easily cover up the answers as you work through each chapter. The compact, condensed design of the book is conducive to studying on the go. Carry it in your white coat pocket, so that you can access during any downtime throughout your busy day.

We hope this review book brings medical facts to life and is not only informative, but also entertaining and interesting. Good luck studying!

Brooke Davey, MD

Acknowledgments

Thank you all the medical students, residents, and attendings who worked so hard to complete this book. Your contributions were made while pursuing and practicing the art of medicine. Thank you for donating your time and keeping your commitment to the next generation of physicians.

The author would also like to recognize the faculty and staff at New York University School of Medicine, Morgan Stanley Children's Hospital of New York, and The Children's Hospital of Philadelphia. Thank you to Kirsten Funk, Cindy Yoo, Sapna Rastogi, and Midge Haramis at McGraw-Hill for their help in the process.

Finally, the author would like to acknowledge the following contributors and faculty reviewers for their work on the first edition:

CONTRIBUTORS

Kristy Ahrlich, MD
John Babineau, MD
Emily P. Greenstein, MD
Catherine Lau, MD
Mahbod Mohazzebi, MD
Joni Rabiner, MD
Aarti Sheth, MD
Melanie Sisti, MD

FACULTY REVIEWERS

Fredric Bomback, MD
Wendy K. Chung, MD, PhD
Joseph Haddad, Jr., MD
Daphne T. Hsu, MD
Anupam Kharbanda, MD
Elvira Parravicini, MD
Prantik Saha, MD, MPH
Nan R. Salamon, MD
David Teng, MD

CHAPTER 1

Birth and Prematurity

PRENATAL AND NEONATAL HEALTH

Define the perinatal period, the neonatal period, and the postnatal period.

The perinatal period starts at 22 completed weeks' gestational age (GA) and ends 7 days after birth. The neonatal period lies between birth and 28 days of life and the postnatal period is from birth to 6 weeks of life.

Why do babies born greater than 42 weeks GA typically have a normal height and head circumference for their GA but decreased weight?

These "post-mature" infants have grown normally throughout pregnancy but then experienced placental insufficiency late in the pregnancy and their nutritional needs were not met, slowing weight gain.

An infant is born weighing less than the 10th percentile for GA, and the weight, height, and head circumference are proportional. How is this baby classified?

This baby is small for gestational age (SGA) and most likely had symmetric intrauterine growth restriction (IUGR). Risk factors for symmetric IUGR are intrauterine infection, chromosomal abnormalities, dysmorphic syndromes, and intrauterine toxins. In an infant with asymmetric IUGR the head growth will be normal for gestational age and risk factors are maternal medical conditions such as chronic hypertension, preeclampsia, and uterine anomalies.

If labor is going to be induced prematurely, what medicine should be given to the mother to promote fetal lung maturity?

Steroids should be used prior to delivery to promote fetal lung maturity in premature infants. A lecithin to sphingomyelin ratio greater than 2 in the amniotic fluid is an indication that fetal lung maturity has been achieved.

How are infants who are large for gestational age (LGA) defined?

Infants with excessive fetal growth are defined as large for gestational age (LGA) or macrosomic. Their weight is above the 90th percentile, which usually corresponds to a birth weight greater than 4000 g. Neonatal complications include increased birth traumas, such as shoulder dystocia, brachial nerve palsy, and perinatal asphyxia.

A diabetic mother gives birth to her LGA daughter. What blood test is important in the management of this newborn and why?

Plasma glucose levels by means of dextrose stick should be obtained to check for hypoglycemia. This is because the baby may have been exposed to high glucose levels in utero, which results in increased insulin production by the pancreatic beta-cells. At birth, after the cord clamping, glucose levels drop but the insulin levels remain high, causing hypoglycemia.

Impaired swallowing in the fetus causes what condition that can lead to premature labor?

Impaired swallowing of a fetus may lead to polyhydramnios, which is an excessive amount of amniotic fluid over 2 L.

A fetus has bilateral renal agenesis. What additional deformities would you expect in this patient?

Bilateral renal agenesis causes oligohydramnios resulting in Potter sequence. Decreased amniotic fluid causes compression of the fetus by the uterine wall resulting in features such as club feet, compressed facial features, and pulmonary hypoplasia.

What are other common causes of oligohydramnios?

Other causes include post-maturity, intrauterine growth retardation, amniotic fluid leak, twin-to-twin transfusion syndrome, uteroplacental insufficiency, placental abruption, maternal preeclampsia, and idiopathic causes.

INFECTIONS

What pathogens are the most common causes of congenital infections?

Toxoplasmosis, *Treponema pallidum* (syphilis*)*

Others, including hepatitis B, Epstein-Barr virus (EBV), and Parvovirus B19

Rubella

Cytomegalovirus (CMV)

Herpes, HIV

A baby is born with microcephaly and chorioretinitis. Soon after birth she has a seizure. CT scan shows intracranial calcifications and hydrocephalus. What anticipatory guidance should have been given to the mother during pregnancy to avoid this infection?

This baby likely has toxoplasmosis. Pregnant women should avoid changing kitty litter as cat feces may be a source of exposure to the toxoplasma oocysts of this protozoal parasite. These mothers are often asymptomatic during the initial infection.

What is the recommended treatment for a baby with stable or rising antibodies to toxoplasmosis?

Treatment consists of a synergistic combination of sulfadiazine and pyrimethamine. If a baby has falling levels of IgG antibodies to toxoplasmosis during the first year of life, this likely represents the mother's transplacental antibodies rather than a congenital infection.

A newborn whose mother did not undergo prenatal testing develops a fever, maculopapular rash on the chest, palms and soles, rhinitis, and hepatosplenomegaly. The nasal secretions are placed under darkfield microscopy and *T pallidum* is visualized. What is the next step in treatment?

This patient has syphilis and should be treated with IV penicillin G for 10 days. In addition, the mother should be treated as the infection is most likely transmitted transplacentally.

What is the adequate treatment of syphilis in pregnancy?

Pregnant women with early acquired syphilis should receive two doses of penicillin G benzathine given 1 week apart.

In addition to a rapid plasma reagin (RPR) or Veneral Disease Research Laboratory (VDRL) and a confirmatory fluorescent treponemal antibody absorption test (FTA-ABS), what additional tests are typically performed on babies with suspected congenital syphilis?

Long bone radiographs should be obtained to rule out osteochondritis, in addition to a complete blood cell and platelet count, chest radiograph, and liver function tests.

A baby is born with cataracts, sensorineural hearing loss, a patent ductus arteriosus (PDA), meningoencephalitis, microcephaly, and mental retardation. The baby has a +IgM rubella antibody in his blood. At what stage of pregnancy did this child acquire this congenital infection?

A first trimester infection of rubella often results in neurological impairments as well as visual, auditory, and cardiac defects.

What are the clinical manifestations in an infant with a congenital rubella infection?

A baby with congenital rubella can present with classic "blueberry muffin spots," liver dysfunction, bone disease, and growth retardation. Congenital rubella has decreased dramatically in incidence due to widespread use of the vaccine.

How does the syndrome of CMV infection compare to that of toxoplasmosis?

Both congenital infections cause similar lesions, including chorioretinitis, intrauterine growth retardation, liver dysfunction, microcephaly, and intracerebral calcifications. On CT scans, the intracranial calcifications of CMV are located periventricularly, while in toxoplasmosis, they are found in the basal ganglia or in other locations in the brain. (Mnemonic: CMV calcifications circle the ventricles, Toxo calcifications traverse the cortex)

A neonate with suspected CMV is placed in isolation. If protective gowns and gloves are worn, is it acceptable for a pregnant resident to care for the baby?

Babies with congenital CMV continue to shed the virus after birth, so despite the protective measures, pregnant nurses, doctors, and other health care workers should not be exposed to this patient.

Is herpes simplex virus (HSV) typically transmitted congenitally or perinatally?

HSV is usually transmitted as the baby is exposed to active lesions during vaginal delivery. Therefore, perinatal transmission is most common. It is important to remember that lesions may not be visible at birth for the virus to be transmitted.

A mother who is 34 weeks pregnant states that she has had genital herpes in the past but on examination you see no genital lesions. How should she be managed for the rest of her pregnancy?

Given her history of herpes, she should take oral acyclovir/valacyclovir during the last 4 weeks of gestation to prevent the recurrence of genital lesions and hence the need for cesarean delivery. If there are genital lesions at the time of delivery she should deliver via cesarean, otherwise she may deliver vaginally.

An infant of a mother with active genital herpes is delivered via cesarean section. Is the infant's risk of perinatal HSV completely eliminated?

A mother with active genital herpes should always deliver via cesarean section. This infant's risk of HSV infection is reduced but not *completely* eliminated by cesarean delivery.

A 2-week-old newborn develops chorioretinitis, conjunctivitis, and vesicular lesions on the mouth and skin. The mother had some new vaginal lesions prior to delivery. Should treatment be delayed until the results of the laboratory tests come back?

No. This baby should be treated empirically with acyclovir as he or she likely has skin, eye, and mouth (SEM) disease of HSV. Treatment should start immediately as this baby is at risk for HSV meningitis or disseminated HSV.

How do patients with HSV meningitis typically present?

These patients often present with classic symptoms of meningitis including fever, irritability, lethargy, and poor feeding. Additional symptoms seen in HSV meningitis include focal or generalized seizures; subsequent disseminated disease causes liver dysfunction and disseminated intravascular coagulation (DIC).

A mother develops chicken pox 3 days prior to the birth of her baby. What is the appropriate treatment for a baby that does not show signs of infection?

This baby should receive varicella-zoster immune globulin (VZIg) at birth. Any infant whose mother develops varicella 5 days prior to birth to 2 days after birth should receive VZIg within 4 days of life.

A baby is born with many cutaneous scars and central nervous system (CNS) abnormalities as well as limb hypoplasia and growth retardation. Congenital varicella is the suspected culprit. Should this baby be placed in isolation after birth?

No. This congenital infection likely occurred in the first trimester of pregnancy, so the baby is no longer actively shedding varicella-zoster virus.

A 6-month-old infant born to a known drug user presents to clinic with persistent thrush. She has frequent diarrhea, multiple infections, failure to thrive, and has not hit her developmental milestones. She subsequently tests positive for HIV. How could this illness have been prevented?

Vertical transmission of HIV from mother to child is decreased by treating the mother with antiretroviral medications in the third trimester, performing a C-section, avoiding breastfeeding, and treating the baby with antiretroviral medications.

What treatment regimen is appropriate for a patient with congenital HIV?

These patients should receive multidrug antiretroviral therapy, trimethoprim-sulfamethoxazole for *Pneumocystic carinii* pneumonia (PCP) prophylaxis, as well as nutritional supplementation and treatment for frequent bacterial and viral infections.

Why is erythromycin ophthalmic ointment given to neonates after birth?

This ointment is used primarily as prophylaxis to prevent ocular gonorrhea infection in neonates.

BIRTH TRAUMA

A newborn was delivered using a vacuum and now has a soft collection of blood under the scalp that does not cross suture lines and does not discolor the overlying skin. What birth trauma did it undergo?

The patient has a cephalohematoma caused by a bleed that occurs under the periosteum.

How does a cephalohematoma differ from a caput succedaneum?

Unlike a cephalohematoma, a caput succedaneum causes discoloration of the overlying skin and crosses suture lines. Molding of the skull during vaginal delivery is associated with caput succedaneum. No treatment is necessary for either of these conditions.

A mother calls the office because she noted that her 2-week-old newborn daughter, who was LGA and delivered vaginally, has a bump on her clavicle. What is the next step in treatment?

This patient likely has a clavicular fracture. No further diagnostic studies or treatment are necessary.

A baby is born with a "waiter's tip." What cranial nerves were damaged during birth?

This baby has Erb palsy and cranial nerves V and VI were likely stretched and damaged from traction of the neck during delivery. This results in an extended, internally rotated arm with flexion of the wrist.

PREMATURITY

An infant is born at 28 weeks GA and is found to be grunting and retracting. Respiratory distress syndrome is suspected. If continuous positive airways pressure (CPAP) is able to provide adequate respiratory support, why is it a better option than intubation and mechanical ventilation?

Intubation and mechanical ventilation exposes a baby to high pressures, with subsequent lung barotraumas that can lead to chronic conditions such as bronchopulmonary dysplasia. CPAP allows for more gentle O_2 and pressure administration.

A 3-month-old premature infant who was born at 24 weeks GA and required mechanical ventilation for a month after birth is found to have retinal detachment and blindness. What is the pathophysiology of this disorder?

Retinopathy of prematurity is caused by abnormal growth and excessive proliferation of the immature vessels of the retina after exposure to high oxygen tensions.

A premature, low birth weight infant is not tolerating feeds and her abdomen becomes distended. Her stool is bloody and an abdominal x-ray shows gas within the bowel wall known as pneumatosis intestinalis. What is the next step in treatment?

This baby has necrotizing enterocolitis (NEC) and should be made nothing by mouth (NPO) and supported with IV fluids. A nasogastric (NG) tube should be placed for decompression and antibiotics should be started. Serial abdominal x-rays are needed to evaluate for perforation.

What additional radiographic finding is worrisome in an infant with pneumatosis intestinalis and why?

The presence of fixed dilated loops of bowel (ie, dilated bowel loops whose position is always the same on serial x-rays) is worrisome as it suggests the development of full-thickness necrosis of the bowel wall. The damage is so severe that the affected bowel can no longer undergo peristalsis and hence stays fixed in its position. This finding may precede clinical deterioration including signs of peritonitis.

What are the signs of perforation in an infant with NEC?

Air in the peritoneal cavity indicates perforation and surgical management is warranted.

Why is NEC more likely to be seen in premature infants?

Premature infants are at increased risk for hypoxia, hypoperfusion of the intestine, and sepsis, all of which can lead to necrosis of the bowel.

When beginning to feed a premature infant, what can one do to help prevent NEC?

NEC is much less common in infants exclusively fed with human breast milk. Aggressive enteral feeding may increase the risk of NEC, whereas initiation of minimal enteral feeds with gradual volume advancement may decrease the risk.

A premature female infant has no respiratory effort or chest wall movement for 25 seconds. Does she have central or obstructive apnea?

She likely has central apnea as there is no effort to make respirations. In obstructive apnea there is chest rise and efforts to breath but no air exchange.

The premature infant who has been apneic for 25 seconds turns pale and limp and is unresponsive to your touch. What is the next step in treatment?

Bag-mask ventilation is a fast and easily accessible way to provide air exchange at this time.

DELIVERY COMPLICATIONS

You are at the delivery of a term infant and note that the amniotic fluid is meconium stained. The baby is crying and has good muscular tone. How should this infant be resuscitated?

Upon delivery, all babies should be immediately warmed, dried, stimulated, and suctioned. The presence of meconium is concerning, however, this baby is vigorous (strong respiratory effort indicated by crying and good tone) and requires only routine suctioning of the mouth and nose (with bulb syringe or suction catheter). The mouth should always be suctioned before the nose to ensure there is nothing for the newborn to aspirate if he or she should gasp when the nose is suctioned.

You are at the delivery of a term infant and note that the amniotic fluid is meconium stained. The baby has poor respiratory effort and feels limp in your hands. How should this infant be resuscitated?

In the presence of meconium with a baby that is not vigorous (poor/absent respiratory effort and with poor muscle tone), immediate intubation and suctioning of his trachea should be performed before anything else is done. Once an endotracheal tube is placed, it is connected to a meconium aspirator with suction source and then slowly withdrawn. This is repeated until little additional meconium is recovered from the trachea.

A fetus with meconium aspiration at birth is born with a persistent PDA and patent foramen ovale (PFO) and appears cyanotic. How does oxygen administration help resolve cyanosis in this patient?

The chronic and/or acute hypoxia experienced by this patient can cause persistent fetal circulation and pulmonary hypertension with right-to-left shunting through the PFO and PDA. Oxygen promotes dilation of the pulmonary vasculature and closure of the PDA.

In addition to assisted ventilation, what additional treatment methods may benefit a premature infant with an apneic episode?

Additional treatment includes supplementary oxygen to maintain appropriate oxygenation, positioning and tactile stimulation, chest PT and suctioning of secretions, and a proper incubator environment to maintain a stable body temperature. Treatment with respiratory stimulants may also benefit infants with frequent, severe apneic episodes.

A premature, low birth weight infant develops a high-pitched cry and has a poor suck reflex. A head ultrasound of the fontanelle shows an intraventricular hemorrhage (IVH) in the germinal matrix and blood in the ventricles, but no dilation of the ventricles or parenchymal damage. What grade is the IVH?

This patient has a grade II IVH. Grade I is a bleed confined to the germinal matrix, where the vasculature is immature, grade II involves blood within the ventricle, grade III consists of a large intraventricular bleed that leads to dilation of the ventricle, and grade IV is an intraventricular bleed complicated with parenchymal bleeding.

A patient with a grade IV IVH develops a bulging fontanelle and a down-looking gaze several days after the insult. What will a CT scan likely show?

One of the complications of an intraventricular bleed is hydrocephalus, which this infant likely has. A ventriculoperitoneal shunt may be placed if the hydrocephalus does not stabilize, but worsens.

What infants should be screened for IVH?

Premature babies that are more than 1500 g should be screened for IVH with a head ultrasound within the first week of birth, because about 15% to 20% of them are found to have an IVH. Among all premature infants found with IVH, only 5% of them develop bleeding after the fifth day of life.

ABDOMINAL WALL DEFECTS

On a 30-week prenatal ultrasound, a fetus is observed to have a herniation of the abdominal viscera through the abdominal wall that is covered by peritoneal and amniotic membranes. What syndrome has been associated with this defect?

This patient has an omphalocele. Ten percent of children with Beckwith-Wiedemann syndrome are born with this defect.

This patient with the omphalocele is born via C-section and an NG tube is placed to decompress the abdomen. The membranes and viscera are wrapped in gauze and sterile bandages to protect the gut and prevent temperature instability. What is the definitive treatment?

Staged surgical compression of the bowel and eventual closure of the abdominal wall is the definitive treatment. The surgery must be staged to prevent compartment syndrome that could occur if the entire bowel is compressed too quickly within the abdomen.

How do infants with gastroschisis differ from those with omphalocele?

The infants with gastroschisis have no sack covering the herniated gut, while infants with omphalocele have herniated viscera through the umbilicus and within the umbilical cord. In gastroschisis the herniation happens through a wall defect typically lateral to the umbilicus. These infants are more prone to infection and dehydration due to the lack of membrane covering the viscera.

DRUG EXPOSURE

An SGA fetus is delivered and becomes irritable, tremulous, and is not feeding well. The mother tested positive for cocaine on a prenatal urine toxicology. What types of short- and long-term effects may be seen in this baby?

Cocaine has vasoconstrictive effects on the placenta that decrease blood flow to the fetus, causing IUGR and sometimes birth defects or cerebral infarcts. After birth, 10% to 30% of the infants exhibit signs of cocaine intoxication. Long-term consequences are increased incidence of learning disabilities and attention-deficit hyperactivity disorder (ADHD).

A newborn of a mother in a methadone program develops irritability, poor feeding and sleeping, sweating, and a high-pitched cry. Should this infant have received naloxone at birth?

No. Although this infant is affected by narcotic abstinence syndrome, which occurs in 70% to 90% of the infant born to mothers treated with methadone, naloxone is contraindicated because it may precipitate an acute abstinence syndrome with seizures. Severe abstinence syndrome may be treated with phenobarbital, paregoric, diazepam, or methadone.

A mother drank six or more servings of alcoholic beverages per day during her pregnancy. What are the teratogenic effects that the fetus may experience?

This amount of alcohol exposure can lead to fetal alcohol syndrome. The baby may experience IUGR as well as mental retardation, microcephaly, characteristic facial anomalies such as a flat philtrum, a depressed nasal bridge and micrognathia, as well as kidney and heart defects.

What antibiotics must be avoided during pregnancy due to its effects on teeth and bone of the fetus?

Tetracyclines should be avoided as they produce a permanent discoloration of tooth enamel and a transient delay of bone growth.

CLINICAL VIGNETTES

As you examine a newborn infant in the delivery room, you note the infant is cyanotic, tachypneic, and has an asymmetrical chest with a caved-in appearing abdomen. The breath sounds and cardiac apex are felt stronger on the right than the left. What is your diagnosis and what simple measure can be both diagnostic and therapeutic?

This infant has a left congenital diaphragmatic hernia (CDH), where the contents of the abdominal cavity have herniated into the thoracic cavity, displacing the left lung and heart to the right side. Placement of a nasogastric tube will help decompress the bowel and allow for easier lung inflation. It also helps highlight the location of the stomach in the thoracic cavity once an x-ray is taken, thereby clinching the diagnosis.

Do congenital diaphragmatic hernias (CDH) occur more on the right or left? Why?

Eighty percent to ninety percent of CDHs occur on the left. This is not because the "liver is in the way" on the right side (a common misconception), but rather because the diaphragm closes in utero on the right side before the left.

What cardiovascular complication(s) are infants born with CDH prone to?

The presence of bowel contents in the thorax negatively impacts the growth of the lungs and heart, resulting in hypoplastic lungs and compression of the heart. Since a smaller effective lung mass is seeing the same amount of pulmonary blood flow that fully developed lungs would see, the pulmonary vasculature undergoes hyperplasia and becomes more muscular, leading to pulmonary hypertension.

What is the treatment for CDH?

Surgical repair is required soon after birth. However, these patients are often extremely unstable and may require extracorporeal membrane oxygenation (ECMO) as a bridge to surgery.

CHAPTER 2

Growth, Development, and Nutrition

GROWTH

What are normal growth patterns for the average child?

The average infant doubles their birth weight by 5 to 6 months of age and triples their birth weight by 12 months. Birth height increases 50% by 1 year, doubles by 4 years, and triples by 13 years.

A mother presents with an irritable infant and states that her child has started teething. What is the usual sequence of dental eruption?

Central incisors are first to erupt between 5 and 8 months of age, with mandibular teeth erupting before maxillary teeth. By 2½ years of age, a child should have all of his or her primary teeth, including molars. Secondary/permanent teeth begin to erupt at around 6 to 7 years of age.

What are dental caries and what are known risk factors in children?

Caries are formed from an infectious process that results in tooth decay or cavities. Infant teeth are especially susceptible to caries due to their thinner enamel. Major risk factors include prolonged exposure to carbohydrates (ie, falling asleep with the bottle), frequent carbohydrate intake, poor oral hygiene, decreased saliva production, and lower socioeconomic status.

A 3-year-old boy has consistently remained at the fifth percentile on his growth curves since birth, and his mother is concerned about his growth. How would you counsel her?

Assessment of growth over time is the most important way to evaluate a child's growth. By definition, 5% of the population will be below the range of growth parameters that is defined as normal. Children tend to grow along genetically determined percentiles, and this child is not deviating from his growth curve. Lastly, the standard growth curves used in practice were determined using mostly white, middle class children, so children of different races or ethnicities may not have the same standard parameters for growth.

A 1-year-old boy is failing to meet expected norms for weight and height and is noted to have loss of subcutaneous fat, loss of muscle mass, edema, distended abdomen, and hair loss. These symptoms are a sign of which condition?

This child is presenting with failure to thrive (FTT), defined as weight, height, or head circumference below the third to fifth percentile, falling off the growth curve by crossing two major percentiles, or weight less than 80% of ideal body weight for age. It is not a diagnosis; it is a sign of an underlying organic or non-organic disorder.

What is the first growth parameter to be affected in FTT?

Weight is generally the first to be affected, but with prolonged duration of malnourishment, length and head circumference may also adversely be affected.

What is the most common cause of FTT in the United States?

Nonorganic or psychosocial causes including abuse, neglect, and improper feeding are the most common causes of FTT; however, gastrointestinal, pulmonary, renal, endocrine, central nervous system, and other multifactorial organic causes must be considered as well.

How is organic FTT distinguished from nonorganic FTT?

A thorough history and physical examination, including observation of the parent-child feeding interaction, and screening tests such as a complete blood count (CBC), electrolytes, blood urea nitrogen (BUN), creatinine, albumin, and total protein should be done to differentiate organic from nonorganic causes of FTT. Organic causes of FTT may have other manifestations in addition to FTT.

When should you hospitalize a patient for FTT?

Patients are hospitalized for FTT when there is suspicion or evidence of abuse or neglect, severe malnutrition or medical complications, or if outpatient treatment is unsuccessful.

A newborn presents with weight, length, and head circumference significantly below age-matched norms. What is the most likely cause?

An intrauterine insult or genetic abnormality is most likely responsible when multiple growth parameters are below average at birth.

A newborn presents with weight and length below average and head circumference within normal limits. What are some possible causes?

Likely causes include constitutional growth delay, genetic short stature, or endocrine causes of growth failure.

A newborn presents with weight significantly below average with sparing of the height and head circumference. What are some possible causes?

Likely causes include insufficient caloric intake or a hypermetabolic state.

A mother brings in her 7-day-old, full-term newborn with concerns that the infant's current weight is 10% less than birth weight. What is the next step?

Term infants can lose up to 10% of their birth weight soon after birth, which is due to loss of extracellular water and calorie requirements that are initially higher than the infant can meet. The infant should stop losing weight by 5 to 7 days and regain birth weight by 10 to 14 days. Reassurance for the parent and monitoring of the infant's weight are important.

DEVELOPMENT

While examining the head of a 4-month-old infant, you are able to appreciate the anterior fontanelle but are unable to palpate the posterior fontanelle. When do the fontanelles usually close?

The anterior fontanelle closes between 4 and 26 months, with an average of 14 months. The posterior fontanelle usually closes by 2 months of age, it can even be difficult to palpate in normal newborns.

What is craniosynostosis?

Premature fusion of a cranial suture leading to skull deformity. It can be the result of primary or secondary causes.

How does positional plagiocephaly differ from lambdoidal craniosynostosis?

Positional plagiocephaly is seen with greater frequency after the "Back to Sleep" campaign due to prolonged time infants spend in the supine position. This often leads to asymmetric occipital flattening. In positional plagiocephaly the ear ipsilateral to the flattening will be more anterior and the ipsilateral frontal region will also be more anterior. However, in craniosynostotic posterior plagiocephaly the ear and frontal region contralateral to the occipital flattening will be anterior.

After a difficult delivery, a newborn is active and crying but does not move his right arm and has a unilateral Moro reflex. What is the most likely cause?

Brachial plexus palsy, with or without clavicular or humeral fracture, can occur in a traumatic delivery with traction to the head or neck. In this patient, consider an inspiratory x-ray to look for phrenic nerve injury and resulting paralysis of the diaphragm. (See Table 2-1.)

Why do infants have a positive Babinski reflex?

The central nervous system of infants is not fully mature at birth. As the corticospinal tracts become fully myelinated in the first few months of life, the Babinski reflex disappears. (See Table 2-1.)

Table 2-1 Primitive Reflexes

Reflex	Timing	Elicit	Response
Moro	Birth to 3-6 mo	Allow head to fall back suddenly about 3 cm while supine	Symmetric extension and adduction, then flexion, of limbs
Startle	When Moro disappears to 1 y	Startle	Limbs flex
Galant	Birth to 2-6 mo	Stroke paravertebral region of back while prone	Pelvis moves in direction of stimulated side
Sucking	Birth to 3 mo (then becomes voluntary)	Stimulate lips	Sucks
Babinski	Birth to 4 mo	Stroke outer sole of foot	Fanning of toes and dorsiflexion of great toe
Tonic neck	Birth to 4-6 mo	Rotate head laterally while supine	Extension of limbs on chin side and flexion of limbs on opposite side (fencing posture)
Rooting	Birth to 4-6 mo	Stroke finger from mouth to earlobe	Head turns toward stimulus and mouth opens
Palmar/ plantar grasp	Birth to 4-9 mo	Stimulation of palm or plantar surface of foot	Palmar grasp/ plantar flexion
Parachute	Appears at 9 mo	Horizontal suspension and quick thrusting movement toward surface	Extension of extremities

A child sits well unsupported, transfers objects between hands, rolls over, and babbles. What is the child's approximate age?

Six months. (See Table 2-2.)

Table 2-2 Developmental Milestones

Age	Gross Motor	Fine Motor	Language	Social/Cognitive
2-3 mo	• Head up prone	• Tracks past midline • Holds hands together	• Coos • Alerts to sound	• Social smile • Recognizes parent
4-5 mo	• Rolls front to back • Sits supported	• Grasps object	• Orients to voice	• Laughs
6-7 mo	• Rolls back to front • Sits unsupported	• Transfers objects between hands • Raking grasp	• Babbles	• Stranger anxiety • Sleeps all night
9-11 mo	• Pulls to stand • Cruises	• Pincer grasp • Finger feeds • Bangs blocks together	• Mama-dada (nonspecific) • Understands "no"	• Separation anxiety • Waves bye-bye • Responds to name
12-14 mo	• Walks • Throws object	• Mature pincer • Scribbles	• Mama-dada (specific)	• Imitates actions • Follows 1-step commands • Indicates wants
15-17 mo	• Walks backwards • Stoops to pick up toy	• Uses cup	• 4-6 words	• Temper tantrums
18-23 mo	• Runs • Kicks a ball	• Uses spoon • Builds tower of 3-4 cubes	• Names common objects • Names multiple body parts • Vocabulary increases from 10 words to approximately 50 (by 24 mo)	• Copies parent in tasks

(Continued)

Table 2-2 Developmental Milestones (*Continued*)

Age	Gross Motor	Fine Motor	Language	Social/Cognitive
2 y	• Walks up and down stairs (2 ft per step) • Jumps	• Builds tower of 6 cubes • Copies a line • Removes clothes	• 2-word phrases • Half of speech understood by strangers	• Follows 2-step commands • Parallel play • Knows first and last name
3 y	• Up stairs with alternating feet • Rides tricycle • Helps dress and undress self	• Builds tower of 8 cubes • Copies a circle • Uses utensils	• 3-word phrases • Three-fourths of speech understood by strangers • Recognizes 3 colors	• Knows age and gender • Group play • Brushes teeth and washes hands with help
4 y	• Up and down stairs alternating feet • Hops on one foot • Broad jump • Throws overhand	• Copies a cross • Catches ball • Dresses alone	• Counts to 10 • Speech completely understood by strangers • Tells a story	• Cooperative play • Imaginative play
5 y	• Walks backwards • Skips, alternating feet	• Draws square • Holds pencil • Prints letters	• Defines words	• Ties a knot

A child crawls, says "mama," and can pick up his food with his fingers. What is this child's approximate age?

Ten months, as this child has developed the pincer grasp. (See Table 2-2.)

A child walks up and down stairs, runs, says two-word phrases, and half of his speech is understood by strangers. What is his approximate age?

Two years. (See Table 2-2.)

A parent of a 7-month-old (ex-28 week GA) preterm infant is concerned that her son is not yet sitting by himself, when all her other children had achieved this milestone by 6 months of age. How would you counsel her?

An age correction for prematurity should be used when evaluating for developmental milestones during the first 18 to 24 months of life. When the age correction is applied to this patient, he should be evaluated in terms of milestones for a 4-month-old infant, and therefore he is not delayed. In addition, milestones are acquired in an age range, and it is the overall pattern of development that is important as an indicator of neurologic function.

A 2-year-old child presents for a well-child check. What screening test is used in the office to assess development?

The Denver Developmental Assessment Test (Denver II) is administered to screen for developmental milestones. The basis of the test is that development occurs in a predictable pattern, with new skills built on previously acquired skills. Any abnormal findings must be followed up with further diagnostic evaluation.

What skills does the Denver II assess?

It evaluates gross motor, fine motor, language, and social skills by both directly observing the child and obtaining information from caregivers about specific milestones.

A Denver II screening test is performed at a well-child visit of a 2-year-old girl. She has adequate fine and gross motor and social development, but is not meeting expected language milestones. What is your next step?

Isolated language delays may be suggestive of a hearing problem, inadequate environmental stimulation, mental retardation, or autism spectrum disorder. The first step should be to evaluate this child for hearing loss using behavioral testing, otoacoustic emissions testing, or brainstem-evoked response audiometry.

A mother notices that her 4-month-old son has good truncal control but poor finger dexterity. What is the normal sequence for development of motor control?

Motor development progresses in both a cephalocaudal and a central-to-peripheral manner, and therefore truncal and extremity control precede finger dexterity. Motor development parallels central nervous system development, with myelination beginning prenatally and continuing up to 2 years of age in a cephalocaudal direction.

A child identified with developmental delay is evaluated and found to have an intelligence quotient (IQ) of 55. What is the definition of mental retardation (MR)?

Mental retardation is defined as intellectual functioning, measured by an IQ less than 70 or more than two standard deviations below the population mean on standardized intelligence tests (eg, Stanford-Binet or Wechsler intelligence tests). MR is usually associated with functional deficits in areas such as self-care, communication, or social interactions. Mild MR is defined as an IQ of 50 to 70, and moderate-severe MR is defined as an IQ less than 50.

What is the best predictor of a child's subsequent cognitive performance?

Language and speech development are the best indicators of future intelligence in a normal child.

When is stuttering worrisome?

Stuttering can be part of normal development until age 3 or 4 years. However, persistence into the school age years requires further workup.

A 7-year-old boy is referred to you by his teacher for poor spelling, slow learning, and poor overall school performance. He has no known medical problems. What are you concerned about?

Learning disabilities occur in 5% to 10% of children, with dyslexia being the most common. This child may have dyslexia, which is the failure to acquire reading skills in the usual time course due to inability to properly interpret written language.

How is dyslexia diagnosed?

Dyslexia is not related to intelligence and may be diagnosed based on a discrepancy between reading ability estimated on the basis of IQ and actual reading ability. The patient should have a complete psychoeducational assessment.

A 3-year-old girl throws a temper tantrum in a store when her parents tell her that she can not have a toy. Suddenly, the child turns blue and syncopizes. What is the most likely cause of her syncope?

Breath holding spells involve sudden cessation of breathing in response to a strong emotional stimulus and may lead to unconsciousness if prolonged. Cyanotic breath holding spells occur predictably upon upsetting or scolding the child and resolve spontaneously. They are rare at less than 6 months of age, peak at 2 years of age, and resolve by 5 years of age. Pallid breath holding spells tend to occur with painful or frightening experiences, and they also resolve spontaneously. Both types of spells will resolve without intervention and have no sequelae, although oral iron therapy can be used to aid in resolution.

A first-time mother asks about the normal sleeping pattern for a newborn. How would you counsel her?

Infants sleep 18 hours per day, evenly distributed over day and night for short intervals of 2 to 3 hours. Fifty percent of this sleep is rapid eye movement sleep (REM).

When can you expect an infant to sleep through the night?

By 4 to 6 months of age, nighttime sleep becomes consolidated and most infants will sleep through the night.

NUTRITION

A mother of a 2-month-old infant states that her son has colic. What is colic?

Colic is excessive, unexplained paroxysms of crying lasting more than 3 hours a day for more than 3 days per week in an otherwise healthy infant, and it occurs in 10% to 30% of infants.

What treatment strategies are used for colic?

Colic usually begins in the first week of life and self-resolves by 3 to 4 months, regardless of treatment strategies used. Suggested interventions include decreased stimulation (swaddling, dark quiet room), gentle rhythmic stimulation (rocking, walking), pacifier, swing, car or stroller ride, rubbing or patting infant, and singing of music.

A first-time mother has just delivered a healthy, full-term infant, and she asks when she can start feeding and how often she should feed her baby. How should you counsel her?

Newborns generally start feeding within the first 6 hours of life. They should be fed with breast milk or formula on demand every 1½ to 3 hours in the first few weeks and should not go longer than 4 to 5 hours without feeding. Caregivers should be counseled to feed at signs of hunger and to stop at signs of satiety.

What is the breast milk expressed immediately after delivery?

Colostrum is expressed for 2 to 4 days after delivery, and it is high in protein and immunologic factors (especially IgA) but low in carbohydrates and fat. The yellowish color comes from the high levels of carotene.

A new mother is also concerned about producing enough milk for her child. How would you address her concerns?

Mother will likely supply enough milk for her child because the more the baby breastfeeds, the more milk will be produced (the baby suckling stimulates prolactin and oxytocin release). It is normal to feed every 1 to 2 hours, 8 to 12 times per day. If mother starts supplementing with formula milk, the infant will breastfeed less, and less breast milk will be produced. The child's weight should be monitored to ensure adequate growth.

How many calories per day are required by newborns?

Newborns require 110 to 115 kcal/(kg · day) and should grow about 30 g (or 1 oz) per day.

What are the benefits of breastfeeding?

For the infant, there is decreased incidence of infection (otitis media, pneumonia, bacteremia, meningitis) due to immunologic factors such as antibodies and macrophages present in breast milk and decreased exposure to enteropathogens. For the mother, there is decreased postpartum bleeding, more rapid involution of uterus, decreased menstrual blood loss, delayed ovulation, and decreased risk of ovarian and breast cancer. Other benefits include maternal-child bonding, convenience, and low cost.

What are the absolute contraindications to breastfeeding?

Contraindications to breastfeeding include some medications (lithium, cyclosporine, ergotamine, and bromocriptine, that suppress lactation), cancer chemotherapy, exposure to radioactive isotopes, illicit drugs (cocaine, heroin), herpes simplex breast lesions, untreated active tuberculosis, human immunodeficiency virus infection (in developed countries), and infant galactosemia.

An exclusively breastfeeding mother asks if she needs to give her newborn any supplements. How do you counsel her?

Breast milk may be deficient in vitamins A, D, K, B_{12}, thiamine, and riboflavin; infants that are exclusively breastfed should be given Vitamin D supplementation within a few days of life. Additional vitamin supplementation can then be given at 4 months of age. Commercial formulas are often fortified with vitamins and minerals, so that no additional supplements are required.

What is the current dosing recommendation by the AAP for Vitamin D supplementation in infants?

The AAP recommends that infants receive 400IU of Vitamin D daily. All patients who are breastfed should receive supplementation and those who take formula should also receive supplementation if their intake is less than 400IU of Vitamin D per day.

Is iron supplementation required for newborns?

In a full-term infant, iron stores are sufficient for 6 months, and iron supplementation is started at 4 to 6 months. In preterm infants, iron supplementation is started at 2 months. The iron content of breast milk is less than that of formula but has greater bioavailability due to the presence of lactoferrin in breast milk.

A breastfeeding mother presents with a tender, warm, erythematous lesion in the periareolar region of her right breast and a low-grade fever. What is the most common source of this infection?

This mother has mastitis, most commonly caused by *Staphylococcus aureus* from the oropharynx of her infant transferred during breastfeeding.

What is the treatment of mastitis, and should a mother with mastitis discontinue breastfeeding until the infection resolves?

The mother should be treated with compresses, analgesics, and possibly antibiotics, and the infant should continue breastfeeding on the affected breast.

What is the difference between breastfeeding jaundice and breast milk jaundice?

Breastfeeding jaundice is due to insufficient milk intake, which leads to infrequent bowel movements and increased enterohepatic circulation of bilirubin. It occurs during the first week of life. Breast milk jaundice is unconjugated hyperbilirubinemia due to a bilirubin conjugation inhibitor in the breast milk. It occurs after the first week of life, is usually transient, and no treatment is required.

A first-time mother of a healthy, full-term boy decides that she wants to use formula for her newborn son. What type of formula would you recommend?

Most formulas for healthy, full-term infants are cow's milk protein-based with lactose as the carbohydrate source. Soy protein formulas are also available and use sucrose or corn syrup solids as the source of carbohydrates. Formulas come in powders, concentrate, or ready-to-eat forms, which are all equivalent and are fortified with vitamins and minerals. They do not require supplements. Standard formulas contain 20 kcal/oz.

A mother of a 7-month-old infant who has started solids asks if she can give her son the same whole cow's milk that she gives to her 2-year-old daughter. What is your response?

Whole cow's milk is not recommended until 1 year of age because an infant's gastrointestinal tract is not mature enough, and it can predispose the infant to allergy, gastrointestinal blood loss, and iron deficiency anemia (due to both the low iron content of whole cow's milk and occult gastrointestinal blood loss). In addition, cow's milk has high phosphorous content which can predispose the young infant to hypocalcemia.

A 5-month-old infant taking cow's milk-based formula presents with frequent diarrhea, poor weight gain, and irritability. What is your next step in management?

Consider cow's milk protein allergy (occurs in 1%-7% of infants) or lactose intolerance in this child. The protein-based formula can be switched; however, there is significant cross-reactivity of 30% to 40% to soy protein (cross-reactivity decreases after 6 months), and a casein hydrolysate (elemental) formula may be required.

A mother of a 4-month-old infant asks about starting solid foods. When and how should solids be introduced?

Solid foods should be started between 4 and 6 months of age, and new foods should be introduced individually about a week apart to identify any allergic reaction the child may have. In order to start solids, a child should be able to sit with support, have hand-to-mouth coordination, and open mouth to the spoon. Avoid foods that can be choking hazards, such as peanuts, hard candy, or popcorn.

The mother of a 5-year-old boy with body mass index (BMI) in the 99th percentile asks for information about how to improve the health and weight of her son. How would you counsel her?

Emphasize an overall healthy lifestyle for the patient and the family, including a balanced diet, regular exercise, and decreased sedentary activity including television/computer use. The goal is not to lose weight but to meet all nutritional needs and slow the rate of fat deposition.

A 3-year-old boy presents with progressive weight loss and muscular atrophy. His mother states that they are going through a difficult time and food is short. What is the diagnosis?

This child has marasmus due to caloric deficiency. This is a general nutritional deficiency that can be caused by inadequate calorie consumption, poor feeding, metabolic disease, or congenital abnormalities.

While working in the refugee clinic, you see a 4-year-old child who is in the lower percentiles for weight, appears pale and thin, has frail hair, and edema. What is your diagnosis?

This child has kwashiorkor due to protein deficiency. While this is not very common in the United States, it is still seen in developing countries.

A newborn is given an injection of vitamin K in the delivery room. Why is vitamin K given?

Vitamin K is given to prevent hemorrhagic disease of the newborn. Newborns have transient vitamin K deficiency and resulting deficiency of vitamin K-dependent clotting factors (II, VII, IX, X) due to lack of free vitamin K in the mother and lack of bacterial intestinal flora that synthesize vitamin K. (See Table 2-3.)

Name the fat-soluble vitamins.

Vitamins A, D, E, and K are fat-soluble. Deficiencies of these vitamins can occur in malabsorptive processes such as cystic fibrosis and short-bowel syndrome.

An 18-year-old man was recently found to be purified protein derivative (PPD) positive and was started on isoniazid. What supplement should he take with the isoniazid?

Pyridoxine (vitamin B_6) should be given as well because isoniazid competitively inhibits pyridoxine metabolism and can cause peripheral neuropathy. Pyridoxine supplements are given to adolescents but generally not to children, as peripheral neuropathy is rarely seen in children. (See Table 2-3.)

A 5-year-old boy presents with diarrhea, rash, and altered mental status. What deficiency in his diet may cause these symptoms?

Niacin (vitamin B_3) deficiency causes pellagra, which is manifested by the three Ds, which are diarrhea, dermatitis, and dementia. Niacin is derived from tryptophan and is a constituent of nicotinamide adenine dinucleotide (NAD) and nicotinamide adenine nucleotide phosphate (NADP), which is important for electron transfer and glycolysis. (See Table 2-3.)

A 4-year-old boy with gastroenteritis presents to the emergency room with severe vomiting and diarrhea. He is tachycardic, hypotensive, and irritable, he has not urinated all day, and his mucous membranes appear dry. What is the next step in his management?

This child is moderately to severely dehydrated and requires fluid therapy to rapidly expand his vascular space, correct his fluid deficit, and restore tissue perfusion. Lactated Ringer or normal saline (isotonic solution) is the fluid of choice; a 20 cc/kg IV bolus is given.

Table 2-3 Vitamins

Vitamin	Function	Source	Deficiency	Excess
Vitamin A (retinol)	Constituent of visual pigments, immune system	Carrots, milk, eggs, liver, green leafy vegetables	Night blindness, dry skin, infections	Arthralgias, headaches, intracranial hypertension (pseudotumor cerebri) skin changes, alopecia.
Vitamin B_1 (thiamine)	Carbohydrate metabolism	Fortified breads, cereals, pasta, meat, fish, soy, whole grains	Beriberi: congestive heart failure, peripheral neuritis, confusion	—
Vitamin B_2 (riboflavin)	Carbohydrate, fat, and protein metabolism (constituent of flavin adenine dinucleotide [FAD]), vision	Meat, eggs, legumes, nuts, dairy, leafy green vegetables	Angular stomatitis, cheilosis, corneal vascularization, dermatitis, anemia	—
Vitamin B_3 (niacin, nicotinic acid)	Carbohydrate, fat, and protein metabolism (constituent of NAD/ NADP), nerve function	Red meat, poultry, fish, fortified cereals, peanuts	Pellagra: dermatitis, diarrhea, dementia	Vascular dilation causes "niacin flush": flushing, burning, itching
Vitamin B_5 (pantothenate)	Carbohydrate, fat, and protein metabolism (constituent of coenzyme A [CoA]), neurotransmitters	Meat, eggs, vegetables, legumes, whole wheat	Dermatitis, enteritis, alopecia, adrenal insufficiency	—

(Continued)

Table 2-3 Vitamins (*Continued*)

Vitamin	Function	Source	Deficiency	Excess
Vitamin B₆ (pyridoxine)	Important for brain and nerve function, erythropoiesis	Leafy green vegetables, potatoes, bananas, seeds, nuts	Peripheral neuropathy, convulsions, hyperirritability	Sensory neuropathy, pain, fever
Vitamin B₉ (folic acid, folate)	Important for DNA and RNA synthesis, erythropoiesis	Dried beans, legumes, citrus fruits, poultry, leafy green vegetables	Macrocytic, megaloblastic anemia	—
Vitamin B₁₂ (cobalamin)	Important for DNA and RNA synthesis, erythropoiesis, nerve function	Animal products—fish, red meat, poultry	Macrocytic, megaloblastic anemia with neurologic symptoms, glossitis	—
Biotin	Carbohydrate and fat metabolism	Fruits, nuts, rice, egg yolk, milk	Dry skin, fatigue, depression, muscular pain	—
Vitamin C (ascorbic acid)	Collagen synthesis, facilitate iron and calcium absorption, immune system	Citrus fruits, red berries, broccoli, spinach, peppers	Scurvy: swollen gums, bruising, anemia, poor wound healing	Kidney stones, cramps, diarrhea, nausea
Vitamin D (ergosterol)	Facilitate intestinal absorption of calcium and phosphate	Fortified milk, egg yolks, fish oils	Rickets: defective mineralization of bone matrix, rachitic rosary, craniotabes	Hypercalcemia, nausea, diarrhea, soft-tissue calcification
Vitamin E (tocopherol)	Antioxidant	Leafy green vegetables, nuts, whole grains	Increased fragility of erythrocytes, neuropathy	—
Vitamin K (menadione)	Carboxylation of clotting proteins	Leafy green vegetables	Hemorrhage	—

The child above weighs 23 kg. How much fluid would you administer for maintenance therapy?

The Holliday-Segar method can be used to determine total daily intravenous fluid requirements: give 100 mL/kg of water for the first 10 kg, 50 mL/kg of water from 10 to 20 kg, and 20 mL/kg of water for every kg over 20 kg. When divided by 24 hours, the 4-2-1 rule approximation can be used for an hourly rate: give 4 mL/(kg · h) for the first 10 kg, give 2 mL/(kg · h) from 10 to 20 kg, and give 1 mL/(kg · h) for every kg over 20 kg. In this example of a child weighing 23 kg:

Using the Holliday-Segar method:

(100 mL/kg × 10 kg) + (50 mL/kg × 10 kg) + (20 mL/kg × 3 kg) = 1560 mL over 24 hours (approx. 65 mL/h)

Using the 4-2-1 rule:

(4 mL/(kg · h) × 10 kg) + (2 mL/(kg · h) × 10 kg) + (1 mL/(kg · h) × 3 kg) = 63 mL/h

A child with nephrotic syndrome is found to have serum sodium of 115 mEq/L. He has a headache and his mother notices some mental status changes. How would you correct his serum sodium?

This child has hypervolemic hyponatremia due to fluid retention from nephrotic syndrome. His headache and mental status changes are due to cerebral edema as the water flows from the hyponatremic serum into the hypertonic intracellular fluid, and the serum sodium must be corrected in order to prevent brain herniation. The sodium deficit is calculated:

$$Na^+ \text{ deficit} = (Na^+ \text{ desired} - Na^+ \text{ observed}) \times \text{body weight in kg} \times 0.6.$$

Half of the deficit is given in the first 8 hours, and the rest is given over the next 16 hours. Hyponatremia should not be corrected greater than 2 mEq/(L · h) in order to prevent cerebral pontine myelinolysis (demyelination).

A 3-month-old infant presents to the emergency room with a generalized tonic clonic seizure and is found to be hyponatremic. The child is formula-fed. What would you ask the caregiver?

You would ask about formula preparation. If the formula is diluted to make it last longer, or simply not mixed correctly, the child is taking in too much water. This can cause hyponatremia and water intoxication, which then can cause seizures.

A child presents with mental status changes, irritability, and muscle twitching. His urine specific gravity is 1.003 and his serum sodium is 160 mEq/L. What is your next step in management?

This child most likely has diabetes insipidus (DI), causing a low urine specific gravity and hypernatremic dehydration. The serum sodium is lowered gradually at a rate of 10 to 15 mEq/(L · day) in order to prevent cerebral edema due to fluid shifts into the central nervous system. Hypernatremic dehydration puts patients at risk for shrinking of brain cells and tearing of bridging blood vessels as water goes from intracellular space to extracellular.

A diabetic child presents to the emergency room in diabetic ketoacidosis. She has tachycardia and hyporeflexia on physical examination, U waves on ECG, and serum potassium of 2.5 mEq/L. How would you treat the hypokalemia?

Immediately place the patient with hypokalemia on a cardiac monitor, as arrhythmias may occur. Oral repletion is preferred if patient is stable or asymptomatic, however, in a case such as this IV potassium is given at a slow rate.

A patient with hypoaldosteronism presents with arrhythmias, muscle weakness, and the serum potassium is 7.3 mEq/L. She has peaked T waves and widened QRS complexes on ECG. How would you treat the hyperkalemia?

Patients with hyperkalemia should also be placed on cardiac monitors, as arrhythmias may occur. Calcium chloride or calcium gluconate should be given to stabilize cardiac cellular membranes; sodium bicarbonate, albuterol, or glucose with insulin can be given to shift potassium into the cells. Kayexalate can be given to bind potassium in the gastrointestinal tract. Though it works more slowly, furosemide can be given to enhance urinary excretion of potassium, and hemo- or peritoneal dialysis can be used in extreme cases.

CLINICAL VIGNETTES

A 10-year-old boy presents for a well-child check and appears to be overweight. How is obesity commonly measured?

The body mass index (BMI) is the most effective measure for obesity. BMI is defined as the body weight in kilograms divided by the height in meters squared, and there are BMI standard charts for children that vary with age and sex. A BMI greater than the 95th percentile is generally considered obese, and a BMI between the 85th and 95th percentiles is considered overweight.

How do you evaluate an overweight patient?

A thorough history, including age of onset, is important. If obesity begins prior to age 2, then syndromic or genetic causes may be responsible. Some risk factors for childhood obesity include having an obese parent (2-3 times increased risk), having a high fat diet, and increased daily screen time (which decreases physical activity, decreases metabolic rates, and has adverse effects on diet).

What is the most common cause of obesity in children?

Environmental causes of obesity are most common, with 95% of cases due to sedentary lifestyle and caloric intake greater than the need. Genetic factors also play a role.

What are the medical complications of obesity in children?

The complications of obesity include diabetes mellitus, metabolic syndrome, hypertension, hyperlipidemia, fatty liver disease, cholelithiasis, obstructive sleep apnea, Blount disease (tibia vara), slipped capital femoral epiphysis (SCFE), and psychosocial stress. Twenty-five percent of children in the United States are significantly overweight.

What laboratory studies are important in the evaluation of a child with obesity?

Basic screening tests that may be useful to monitor for complications of obesity include fasting glucose and insulin to monitor for glucose intolerance and insulin resistance, lipid panels (total cholesterol, triglycerides, HDL-cholesterol) to monitor for cardiovascular disease, and alanine aminotransferase (ALT) to monitor for fatty liver. Additional tests may be required based on history and physical examination findings.

What is the likelihood of persistence of obesity into adulthood?

Older obese children, having an obese parent, and those with severe obesity are more likely to be obese as adults. In addition, those who have a sedentary lifestyle and poor diet and do not make lifestyle changes are likely to be obese as adults.

CHAPTER 3

Screening and Prevention

GENERAL SCREENING

What screening and preventative care should be performed at every visit?

Interval history, height, weight, development and behavior assessments, immunization status, and age-appropriate anticipatory guidance should be done at every visit. Head circumference should be measured until 3 years of age. Blood pressure should be checked regularly beginning at 3 years of age, or earlier if medically indicated.

What is the sensitivity of a test?

The sensitivity of a test is the proportion of individuals with a disease that have a positive test result. It is calculated by dividing the number of true positives by the sum of the true positive and false negatives. If a test has a high sensitivity, a negative test rules out the diagnosis (SnOut). This makes the test a good screening test.

What is the specificity of a test?

The specificity of a test is the proportion of individuals without disease who have a negative test result. It is calculated by dividing the number of true negatives by the sum of the true negative and false positives. If a test has a high specificity, a positive test rules in the diagnosis (SpIn). This makes the test a good confirmatory test.

A screening test has a sensitivity of 98% and a specificity of 65%. How would you interpret this information?

In this case with a high sensitivity, the test is likely to pick up the disease. Thus, a negative test would rule out the diagnosis. However, with the lower specificity, a positive test would have to be confirmed with further diagnostic testing.

NEWBORN TO 1 YEAR

What is a newborn screening test?

Newborn screening tests are blood tests performed on samples obtained during the first week of life in order to identify serious or life-threatening illness. These diseases are usually treatable when diagnosed early.

What diseases are tested for in the newborn screen?

Each state has its own laws regarding newborn screening tests. Currently, all states test for congenital hypothyroidism, congenital adrenal hyperplasia, and hemoglobinopathies like sickle cell, biotinidase deficiency, galactosemia, cystic fibrosis, and many other metabolic disorders such as phenylketonuria.

A first-time mother comes in with her 5-day-old newborn. What anticipatory guidance would you provide for her?

Feeding

Newborns should feed on demand and at least every 3 hours. Most infants feed between 8 and 12 times per day. You should counsel about proper breastfeeding techniques and/or formula preparation. Vitamin D supplementation should be given to exclusively breastfed infants or those getting less than the recommended daily dose. Bottles should not be warmed in the microwave and always held, not propped.

Sleeping

Parents should place the infant on his or her back to sleep and on a firm mattress. Blankets, pillows, or other soft or bulky items should be removed from sleeping area.

Safety

Keep the home tobacco-free (smoke is associated with sudden infant death syndrome [SIDS] and acute otitis media). Set the water heater temperature to less than 120°F. Discuss appropriate car seats and installation. Babies should always be closely supervised.

Illness

Parents should call their doctor if the baby has a temperature greater than 100.4°F, has yellowing of skin or eyes, or is not looking or acting well. Avoid contact with anyone who has cold or contagious condition.

The mother of a newborn comes for the first doctor's visit and appears very tired. What questions should you ask?

Screening for postpartum depression is an important part of the newborn visit. The majority of women experience some form of "baby blues" during the postpartum period. However, 10% of women experience true depression. The clinician should ask about mother's sleeping and eating habits, mood and emotions, support system available, and history of depression. If depression is suspected, the mother should be referred to her obstetrician or health care professional. However, if the mother is felt to be at risk of inflicting harm, immediate action is required.

What are the most significant risk factors for developmental dysplasia of the hip (DDH)?

Female gender, breech position during gestation, and a family history of DDH increase a child's risk of having this disorder. The hip examination is an important part of the well-baby examination through 1 year of age.

Why should infants be put to sleep on their backs?

The supine sleeping position has been shown to decrease the risk of SIDS. The "back to sleep" campaign encouraging placement of a baby on his or her back while sleeping has decreased the incidence of SIDS by more than 50%.

What are the identified risk factors for SIDS?

Identified risk factors include male gender, prematurity or low birth weight, African American or American Indian/ Alaskan native ethnicity, drug use during pregnancy, prone sleeping, soft mattresses, being overheated, smoke exposure, sibling who died of SIDS, and recent illness. SIDS usually occurs between 2 and 4 months of age. Rarely, SIDS can happen to younger infants and has been reported up to 1 year of age. More SIDS cases are reported in winter months.

The mother of a 1-year-old asks you why you are testing her child for anemia. What should you tell her?

Anemia is the most common hematologic disorder of young children and is a recommended screening test. Iron deficiency, the most common cause of anemia in children, has been shown to affect cognitive ability, behavior, and school performance. Iron deficiency is easily treated through dietary modification and/or supplementation.

A screening for blood lead level for a 12-month-old infant comes back as 22 μg/dL. What are the risk factors for lead poisoning? What is the acceptable level of lead?

The risk factors for lead poisoning include living in or regularly visiting a house or building built before 1950, living in or regularly visiting a house or building built before 1978 that is being or has recently been renovated, having a relative or friend with lead poisoning, having contact with someone who works with lead, living near an industrial plant likely to release lead, having plumbing with lead pipes, using home remedies or ceramics that contain lead, and eating candy imported from Mexico. Although blood lead levels less than 10 μg/dL are considered within normal range, one recent study found that 6 year olds with blood lead levels less than 5 μg/dL scored higher on IQ tests.

A mother brings in her 1-month-old infant and wants to know what immunizations are recommended in the first year of life?

The recommended vaccine schedule for children up to 1 year of age includes hepatitis B, rotavirus, diptheria, tetanus toxoids, and acellular pertussis (DTaP), *Haemophilus influenzae type b* (Hib), pneumococcal conjugate vaccine (PCV), inactivated poliovirus vaccine (IPV), influenza, measles, mumps, rubella (MMR), varicella, and hepatitis A. (See Table 3-1 for dosing information.)

A baby is born to a mother who is known to be hepatitis B antigen positive. What should be administered to the baby at birth?

Hepatitis B immunoglobulin and hepatitis B vaccine should be administered to the infant within 12 hours of delivery in order to provide both passive and active immunoprophylaxis. As well, serologies should be checked at 6 months of age and at 1 year to ensure the immunity status.

Table 3-1 Recommended Immunizations for Children Ages 0 to 6 Years

Vaccine	Route	Doses/Schedule	Content	Notes
Hepatitis B	IM	3 Given at birth, 1-2 mo, and 6-18 mo	Recombinant hepatitis B surface antigen proteins	• Given at birth along with hepatitis B immunoglobulin (HBIg) if mother is hepatitis B surface antigen positive (HBsAg$^+$) • Children born to hepatitis B$^+$ mothers should get vaccines at birth, 1 mo, and 6 mo.
Rotavirus	PO	2 or 3 Given at 2 and 4 mo, at 6 mo if using Rotateq	Rotarix: live, attenuated virus given in 2 doses. Rotateq: live, human-bovine reassortant virus given in 3 doses	• New vaccines not associated with intussusception
DTaP	IM	5 Given at 2, 4, and 6 mo, 15-18 mo, and 4-6 y	DTaP: diphtheria and tetanus toxoids with acellular pertussis	• DTaP preferred for children under 7 y
Hib	IM	4 Given at 2, 4, and 6 mo, and 12-15 mo	Capsular polysaccharide antigen conjugated to protein	• Does not protect against nontypable strains of *H influenzae* that cause upper respiratory diseases such as otitis media

Vaccine	Route	Doses	Timing	Type	Notes
Poliovirus	IM (oral version available but not recommended)	4	Given at 2 and 4 mo, and 6-18 mo	IPV: inactivated poliovirus types 1, 2, and 3	• Oral polio vaccine (OPV) associated with vaccine associated paralytic polio (VAPP) in 1/760,000. IPV is used to prevent VAPP • Contraindication: anaphylactic reaction to neomycin, polymyxin B, or streptomycin
Influenza	IM or intranasal	1 yearly	Earliest age is 6 mo, then yearly	IM: inactivated virus Intranasal: live attenuated virus	• First immunization in children <9 y should receive 2 vaccine doses 1 mo apart • Intranasal available for children >2 y old and no history of wheeze • Contraindications: anaphylactic reaction to egg
MMR	SC	2	Given at 12-15 mo, and 4-6 y	Live attenuated viruses	• Transient thrombocytopenia within 2 mo after immunization has been reported • Contraindication: anaphylactic reaction to gelatin or neomycin
Varicella	SC	2	Given at 12-15 mo, and 4-6 y	Live attenuated virus	• Those with no history of natural infection should be immunized • Contraindication: anaphylactic reaction to gelatin or neomycin
Hepatitis A	IM	2	Given between 12 mo and 2 y	Inactivated virus	• Series recommended for children older than 2 y in high-risk areas

EARLY CHILDHOOD

What are some of the risk factors for developing dental caries in children?

Living in a community with non-fluoridated water, lower socioeconomic status, history of caries in a sibling or caregiver, developmental disability, and decreased access to professional dental care increase a child's risk of developing dental caries.

A 10-year-old boy presents for a well-child check and appears to be overweight. How is obesity commonly measured?

The body mass index (BMI) is the most commonly used measure for obesity. BMI is defined as the body weight in kilograms divided by the height in meters squared. A BMI greater than the 95th percentile for age and gender is considered obese, and a BMI between the 85th and 95th percentiles is considered overweight. BMI has been found to correlate with body fat and complications of obesity. Newer recommendations also encourage measurement of waist circumference, which correlates with visceral adiposity and higher risk of cardiovascular disease.

What dietary habits most commonly lead to obesity in children?

High consumption of fast food and sweetened beverages, plus low consumption of fruit and vegetables, whole grains, and calcium and low-fat dairy foods lead to obesity in children.

What are the medical complications of obesity in children?

The complications of obesity include diabetes mellitus, metabolic syndrome, hypertension, hyperlipidemia, fatty liver disease, cholelithiasis, obstructive sleep apnea, exercise intolerance, Blount disease (tibia vara), slipped capital femoral epiphysis (SCFE), and psychosocial stress.

What laboratory studies are important in the evaluation of a child with obesity?

Basic screening tests that may be useful to monitor for complications of obesity include fasting glucose and insulin to monitor for glucose intolerance and insulin resistance, lipid panels to assist in monitoring for cardiovascular disease risk, and serum transaminases (AST and ALT) to help monitor for nonalcoholic fatty liver disease. Additional tests may be required based on history and physical examination findings.

What is the likelihood of persistence of obesity into adulthood?

Older obese children, children with one or more obese parents, and those with severe obesity are more likely to be obese as adults. In addition, those who have a sedentary lifestyle and poor diet are likely to become obese adults.

ADOLESCENCE

A 14-year-old adolescent girl comes in for a routine examination. What psychosocial physical screening questions would you ask?

A common approach is using the HEADSS assessment. This includes questions regarding Home (living situation and family relationships), Education/Employment (school and academic performance, jobs, or future plans), Eating (diet, body image), Activities (what does patient do in his/her spare time, sports, hobbies, peer groups, media usage), Drugs (tobacco, caffeine, alcohol, and drug use including friend or family), Sex (sexual activity, sexual orientation, contraception, sexually transmitted diseases [STDs], pregnancy), Suicidality (moods and emotions, thoughts or plans to harm self, suicide attempts), Safety (injury prevention, abuse/violence risk).

A 16-year-old adolescent girl reports that she is sexually active with one partner and uses condoms routinely. What screening tests should she have performed?

Sexually active teenage girls should be offered routine and periodic testing for sexually transmitted infections and counseled on safe sex practices. A Papanicolaou smear may be performed for patients at the age of 21 or within 3 years of sexual intercourse. Contraception options should also be discussed.

A 15-year-old adolescent girl asks for a prescription for oral contraceptive pills, and she asks you not to mention it to her mother who is waiting outside. What should you do?

Laws regarding confidential health care for children under 18 years of age vary by state. However, most allow teenagers to consent to their own medical care including sexual/reproductive health, treatment for drug and alcohol abuse, and mental health services.

IMMUNIZATIONS

A 15-year-old adolescent girl presents to the emergency room with a laceration to her right hand from injury involving a metal fence. What immunization should she receive?

If she received her recommended TDaP vaccine at 11 to 12 years, she does not need further vaccination. Otherwise, she will need a TDaP now and then routine tetanus-diptheria (Td) boosters every 10 years.

A 1-year-old girl with congenital HIV (CD4 count = 100 cells/mm^3, <15%) presents for her 1 year vaccines. Which immunizations should she not receive?

When CD4 percentage is less than 15 or absolute count is less than 200, patients should not receive the live virus vaccines: MMR and varicella. However, once their CD4 counts have recovered, as is commonly seen with HAART (highly active antiretroviral treatment), they should receive the same vaccines as other children.

What are the contraindications to an immunization?

- Severe allergy to a vaccine component or prior dose of vaccine, current moderate to severe illness, encephalopathy within 7 days of prior pertussis vaccination.
- Recent administration of antibody-containing blood products or current chronic steroid or immunosuppressive therapy are contraindications for live vaccines. Children can receive live vaccines 6 months after receiving intravenous immunoglobulin (IVIg) or gamma-globulin.

In addition to active immunizing antigens, what other constituents may be included in vaccines?

Vaccines also contain suspending fluids, preservatives, stabilizers, antibiotics to prevent bacterial overgrowth, and/or adjuvants to enhance immunogenicity. These added materials may contribute to side effects of the vaccine, and those with history of anaphylactic reactions to any of these components should have skin testing to determine the safety of further immunization.

A 12-year-old boy who emigrated from Haiti 2 years ago has a positive reaction to a purified protein derivative (PPD) test. His mother tells you that he received the Bacille Calmette-Guèrin (BCG) vaccine as a baby. Should you consider this a positive tuberculin skin test?

The BCG vaccine consists of an attenuated strain of *Mycobacterium bovis*. It is the most widely used vaccine in the world, but rarely used in the United States. Generally, a positive PPD is considered positive regardless of previous BCG vaccination and should be followed up with prompt radiographic and clinical evaluation.

INJURIES AND ABUSE

A 4-month-old infant is brought in for medical care 2 days after an accident in which she injured her leg. On x-ray, there is a spiral fracture of the right femur. What is your next step?

Treat the patient and notify child protective services to report suspected child abuse. A spiral fracture in a non ambulatory child, delay in obtaining medical attention, and lack of history to explain the injury are consistent with non-accidental trauma. The siblings of the child may need to be examined as well if abuse is strongly suspected. Of note, if an older toddler is found to have a spiral fracture of the distal tibia, this is not usually due to abuse.

What other tests may be indicated in this patient?

A complete skeletal survey, ophthalmic examination, and a bone scan to evaluate for other fracture sites may be indicated for suspected physical abuse.

A 5-month-old infant is brought in with sudden onset of vomiting and seizures. A head CT shows a subdural hematoma. What is your suspected diagnosis?

Abusive head trauma, formally known as shaken baby syndrome, occurs when a baby is held by the trunk or upper extremities and is vigorously shaken, causing acceleration/deceleration injuries. The baby may present with lethargy, vomiting, seizures, and a bulging fontanelle.

What are the major findings in abusive head trauma?

The major findings of abusive head trauma are subdural hematomas, retinal hemorrhages, and metaphyseal chip fractures. Abusive head trauma is the most common cause of death in child abuse.

A 6-year-old girl is diagnosed with chlamydia. Her mother states that she has been acting out in school recently. What should you suspect?

A sexually transmitted disease in a young child is likely sexual abuse, and you must report the case to child protective services.

Are most perpetrators known to the child?

Yes, most perpetrators are males who are well known to the child, like fathers, stepfathers, mother's boyfriends, etc. Ask about siblings at home, as they may be affected by abuse as well.

An 18-month-old who has not been seen by a pediatrician for over a year presents with a severe diaper rash. He has not received any immunizations since his 2-month vaccines because his mother states that they "have not had the time." The child appears to be developmentally delayed. What is your next step?

You should report the case to child protective services, as neglect is a form of child abuse. Neglect is defined as not meeting the nutritional or developmental needs of a child. Neglect is the most common form of child maltreatment. Patients who are neglected may present with failure to thrive, poor hygiene, developmental delay, and delayed immunizations.

What are factors that increase the risk of child abuse?

Lower socioeconomic status, parents who were abused as children, multiple children in the household under the age of 5 years, mothers less that 19 years old, single-parent household, and substance abuse are all risk factors contributing to child abuse. As well, children who are disabled or have special needs, of a multiple gestation pregnancy, or from an unwanted pregnancy are at increased risk of being abused.

A 5-year-old girl is admitted to the hospital for intractable vomiting. Physical examination and laboratory testing are within normal limits. It is noted that she only vomits while her mother is around. What is your diagnosis and treatment?

Munchausen syndrome by proxy, where an illness in a child is inflicted or fabricated by a caretaker so that the caretaker can gain satisfaction from attention, should be suspected as the patient only has symptoms while her mother is present. Diagnosis and treatment is achieved by removing the child from the caregiver and verifying that symptoms resolve. Munchausen by proxy is a form of abuse and must be reported to child protective services.

A 6-month-old infant who is unknown to you presents for a well-child check. You notice bluish gray lesions over his buttocks and lower back. What is your next step?

These lesions are most likely Mongolian spots, which are dense collections of melanocytes and a normal variant. They should not be mistaken for bruises or child abuse. They are more common in dark-skinned infants and usually spontaneously resolve by 2 years of age.

What patterns of bruises and burns should raise suspicions of abuse?

Bruises of different ages in low-impact areas of the body such as the buttocks and back are suspicious for abuse. Burn injuries consistent with cigarette burns, immersions, or "branding" with hot objects are also very suspicious.

What are the most common sites of drowning for children?

Drowning is the second leading cause of accidental death in children and it is estimated that 80% of these were preventable. The most common place for a child under 1 year of age to drown is in a bathtub. Parents should be advised that a baby can drown in less than an inch of water and they should never be left alone while bathing. For a toddler, a swimming pool is the most common site. Children should always be supervised when near bodies of water.

What are the most common mechanisms for burns in children?

Fires and contact with hot items in the home constitute the most common reasons for burns in children. The majority of burn injuries in young children are from scalding.

What is the most common food to be aspirated by children?

Nuts are the most common food to be aspirated. Additional foods that should be avoided in young children include hard candy, grapes, popcorn, hot dogs, and seeds. Other objects such as coins, small toys, marbles, and latex balloons are also common culprits of aspiration.

CHAPTER 4

Adolescent Medicine

PUBERTY

What is puberty?

Puberty refers to the process of becoming physically capable of sexual reproduction. It is defined by both hormonal and somatic changes.

What triggers the initiation of puberty?

The exact triggers for puberty are unknown, but following three changes must occur:

(1) Nocturnal pulsatile luteinizing factor (LF) release
(2) Decrease in sensitivity of hypothalamus to feedback inhibition by sex hormones
(3) In females, the development of a positive feedback system where critical levels of estrogen cause a large release of gonadotropin-releasing hormone (GnRH) leading to the luteinizing hormone (LH) surge

A 10-year-old boy has not yet developed secondary sex characteristics, but has noticed that he now needs to wear deodorant due to the development of body odor. He has also noticed the appearance of pubic hair. What stage of puberty is defined by increased steroid production by the adrenal glands?

Adrenarche is the onset of maturation of the adrenal cortex. These changes are distinct from the hypothalamic-pituitary-gonadal changes that occur during puberty. Physical changes are due to androgens, including the changed composition of sweat glands as well as pubic hair.

A 13-year-old adolescent girl with Addison disease has not yet developed pubic hair, while a girl of the same age with Turner syndrome has. What explains this difference?

A person with Addison disease, or chronic adrenal insufficiency, will not have adequate adrenal function for adrenarche. Turner syndrome is characterized by gonadal failure, but normal adrenal function allows for the androgenic changes such as the development of pubic hair.

A 13-year-old adolescent boy notices that many of the girls in his class have become taller over the past year, but he has not grown very much yet. What would be the most likely explanation for this difference?

Girls typically experience a growth spurt earlier in puberty, while boys start their growth spurt about 2 years after girls do.

How do body composition changes differ between girls and boys during puberty?

During puberty, lean body mass decreases from 80% to 85% of body weight to 75% in girls, whereas in boys it increases from 80% to 90%. In girls, adipose tissue increases from 15% to about 25% of body mass; in boys it decreases from 14% to 11% of body mass. The increase in muscle mass of boys is twice that of girls.

A pediatrician is checking to see that a 12-year-old boy is developing appropriate secondary sex characteristics. How are the stages of secondary sex characteristics assigned?

The sexual maturity rating (SMR) scale, also known as Tanner stages, assesses the levels of secondary sex characteristics. Stage 1 is a preadolescent and stage 5 is an adult. For both sexes there is SMR for pubic hair. SMR for genitalia describes breast development in females and testicle/penile development in males. (See Table 4-1.)

According to the SMR, what are the typical first signs of puberty in boys and girls?

In boys, growth of the testes is the first sign of puberty, which occurs on average at 11.5 years, followed by penile enlargement, height growth spurt, and pubic hair. In girls, the first sign is breast budding, starting at 10.5 years, followed by height growth spurt, pubic hair, and menarche.

Table 4-1 Tanner Stages

Tanner Stage	1	2	3	4	5
Pubic hair	Prepubertal, no hair	Light downy hair at base of scrotum and phallus in males and labia majora in females	Curly, coarser, more pigmented hair extending laterally	Similar to adults in coarseness and curliness, but no extension to medial thighs	Adult type and quantity, extending to medial surfaces of thigh
Testes	Volume <1.5 mL	Volume 1.6-6 mL; increased scrotum size; red, thin	Volume 6-12 mL; increased scrotum size	Volume 12-20 mL; increased scrotum size and darkening in color	Volume >20 mL; adult size scrotum
Penis	Child-like	Child-like	Increase in length	Increase in length and width	Adult length and width
Breasts	Prepubertal	Breast bud, small amount of glandular tissue, areola widens	Increased breast size with elevation; increased areola size but in contour with breast	Increased breast size with elevation; areola and papilla form mound projection from breast contour	Adult size breast; areola and papilla in plane with breast; papilla projects above areola

HEALTH MAINTENANCE

How frequently should healthy adolescents visit their doctor?

Adolescents should have yearly preventative visits.

A 17-year-old adolescent boy sees you for his annual health maintenance visit. What immunizations are recommended for his age group?

Immunizations recommended for healthy adolescents include: human papillomavirus (HPV), meningococcal, diptheria, tetanus toxoids, and acellular pertussis (TDaP), varicella 2, and influenza. Additionally the hepatitis A series can be offered.

What are the three major causes of death in adolescents?

The top three causes of death in adolescents are suicide, homicide, and motor vehicle accidents.

What behaviors should be addressed to reduce the risk of death as well as assess lifestyle in adolescents?

Addressing specific behaviors can help reduce the risk of death. Specifically, the following should be assessed: seat belt use, access to lethal weapon(s), and depression and/or suicidality. Additionally other risk behaviors to assess include: use of drugs, cigarettes and/or alcohol, use of condoms if sexually active, type of diet, and amount of exercise.

When should adolescent girls undergo their first pelvic examination? When should they undergo their first Papanicolaou (Pap) smear?

Pelvic examinations should occur after initiation of sexual activity. Even more important than the pelvic examination is screening for sexually transmitted infections (STIs). Thus a pelvic examination may be deferred if STI screening occurs. However, when the first Pap smear occurs is a source of debate. New American Congress of Obstetricians and Gynecologists (ACOG) recommendations say the first Pap smear should occur at age 21, then every 2 years until age 30. In contrast, the American Cancer Society (ACS) still recommends the first Pap smear within 3 years of first sexual encounter or age 21, whichever comes first.

A 15-year-old adolescent girl comes to the pediatrician concerned that she may be pregnant. She has been sexually active with her boyfriend and does not use condoms. Her last period was 5 weeks ago. She wants to know whether it is too soon to use a urine pregnancy test.

Urine pregnancy tests are rapid, inexpensive, sensitive, and specific. A urine test will show a positive pregnancy 7 to 10 days after conception, before missed periods, and before clinical symptoms.

The test is positive and the patient decides that she wants an abortion. The clinician does not feel comfortable discussing the option of abortion. What must the clinician do to help this patient?

The clinician must provide the patient with a physician who can educate the patient about all of her options.

A 16-year-old adolescent girl with heavy periods wants to go on "the pill" to reduce the bleeding. What other changes in her menstrual cycle will she experience?

Combined oral contraceptive pills (OCPs) prevent pregnancy but also affect menstruation. Regular cycles, decreased cramps and decreased blood loss, and elimination of mittelschmerz (midcycle menstrual pain associated with ovulation) make it advantageous for women with these menstrual complaints to take this medication. It also decreases hirsutism and improves acne.

The 16-year-old adolescent girl is concerned about side effects of being on OCPs. What are the major side effects of this medicine?

She should be aware that OCPs do not protect from STIs, so a barrier method must be used. It must be taken daily in order to be effective, which can be difficult for some people. Other side effects include nausea and breakthrough bleeding.

A teenage girl presents to clinic and states that she is hoping to get a hormone shot, like her sister, for birth control. What are hormonal alternatives to the OCPs?

Injectable contraceptives, such as Depo-Provera, are progesterone-only contraceptives. Other hormonal alternatives include subdermal implants, which release levonorgestrel at a steady rate for up to 5 years, and the minipill, which is progesterone-only, and therefore a good choice for women who can not tolerate estrogen. Other options include the transdermal patch or intravaginal ring, both of which release levonorgestrel.

What are the advantages and disadvantages to Depo-Provera compared to OCPs?

Depo-Provera has the same menstrual advantages as OCPs, and it may even eliminate menses completely. It is administered every 3 months, so it is a good alternative for women who have difficulty with daily dosing. The major disadvantages are weight gain, acne, hair loss, and breakthrough bleeding.

An 18-year-old woman presents to the emergency room requesting "the morning after pill" after having unprotected sex with her boyfriend 2 days ago. Is it too late for emergency contraception?

No, emergency contraception can be used up to 5 days or 120 hours after unprotected sex. The regimen consists of either combined (Plan B) or progesterone-only OCPs taken at the same time. It is intended for one-time protection due to accidents or assaults and is not a regular method of contraception.

SEXUALLY TRANSMITTED INFECTIONS

What is the most common STI in the United States?

Human papillomavirus (HPV) infection is the most common STI in the United States. There are about 100 different types, with about 30 causing genital lesions.

What are "high-risk" and "low-risk" forms of HPV?

The "high-risk" types of HPV cause abnormal Pap smears and can cause cervical, vulval, penile, and anal cancers. They include types: 16, 18, 31, 33, 35, 39, 45, 51, 52, 56, 58, 59, 66, 68, and 73. Types 16 and 18 account for 70% of cervical cancer. "Low-risk" types cause genital warts, recurrent respiratory papillomatosis, and low-grade abnormal Pap smears. The low-risk HPV types are more likely to regress and include types 6 and 11.

Does the HPV vaccine protect girls and women from all types of HPV?

The current available HPV vaccines only protect patients from types 6, 11, 16, and 18. A new HPV vaccine becoming available will protect against other types. However, until it is widely available, patients should continue to get regular Pap smears.

A sexually active 18-year-old man complains to his physician about recurrent painful lesions on his penis. Physical examination reveals painful vesiculopustular lesions, and culture reveals that he has herpes. What are his treatment options?

Systemic antiviral medication, such as valacyclovir, acyclovir, and famciclovir can help control the signs and symptoms of herpes but do not cure the infection. Patients with frequent recurrences may use suppressive treatment, while those with infrequent symptoms may take medication during "flare-ups."

Is it possible to transmit herpes in the absence of visible lesions?

Yes. Herpes simplex virus can be shed when a patient is asymptomatic. Of note, the lesions are a risk factor for HIV acquisition. This patient and his girlfriend should be tested for STIs and advised about safe sex practices. His girlfriend should also get a pregnancy test.

Why should all sexually active adolescents get screened for chlamydia and gonorrhea annually?

Both are common (highest rates in 15-24 years in the United States) and can be carried asymptomatically. They can cause pelvic inflammatory disease (PID) and infertility in women if left untreated.

A 16-year-old adolescent girl comes to the emergency room (ER) complaining of fever and abnormal vaginal discharge. She reports having unprotected sex with her boyfriend. On examination, she has lower abdominal tenderness, adnexal tenderness, and cervical motion tenderness. What is the likely diagnosis?

This patient likely has pelvic inflammatory disease. Criteria for diagnosis of PID include abdominal pain, cervical motion tenderness, and adnexal tenderness. She should be treated with broad-spectrum antibiotics promptly and rescreened in 4 to 6 weeks after completion of therapy. Additionally, her boyfriend should be evaluated and treated to prevent reinfection.

What organisms typically cause PID?

Causative pathogens are usually *Neisseria gonorrhea, Chlamydia trachomatis,* gram-negative facultative bacteria, and streptococci. Thus PID can be considered a multiorganism process.

How is a definitive diagnosis made?

Definitive diagnosis relies on histo-pathologic evidence, imaging studies, or laparoscopic evidence, although the diagnosis is usually made clinically. It is also important that the patient be offered and encouraged to undergo HIV testing.

MALE GENITOURINARY CONDITIONS

A 14-year-old adolescent boy complains to his pediatrician about a painless mass in his scrotum. The physician palpates what feels like a "bag of worms" along the left spermatic cord. What is the most likely diagnosis?

This painless testicular mass is most likely a varicocele, which is the most common cause of scrotal masses in teenagers. Varicoceles occur when the veins of the pampiniform plexus within the spermatic cord become elongated and dilated.

Why are such masses often palpated on the left side?

Although they can occur bilaterally, they are often more common or obvious on left side because of anatomic reasons including: lack of antireflux valves at the junction of the left testicular and renal veins, angle at which the left testicular vein enters left renal vein and increased renal vein pressure due to compression between superior mesenteric artery and aorta.

How do patients typically describe the sensation of a varicocele?

The "bag of worms" sensation is more prominent in the upright position, and usually occurs on the left side.

A third year medical student notices a painless testicular mass in a 10-year-old patient. How can she distinguish tumors from painless masses?

Painless testicular masses have a number of different etiologies, and physical examination can give important clues for a diagnosis, such as the location and characteristics of the mass on the testicle and transillumination.

If a testicular mass transilluminates, what are the two possible diagnoses?

A hydrocele is a fluid collection between layers in the tunica vaginalis. It presents as a soft, fluctuant, fluid-filled mass anterior to the testicle. A spermatocele is a retention cyst of the epididymis. It is less common than a hydrocele, is often posterior and superior to the testis, and is freely movable.

Table 4-2 Causes of Painful Testicular Swelling

	Testicular Torsion	Epididymitis
Cremasteric reflex present?	No	Yes
Decreased pain with elevation of testes?	No	Yes
Testes position normal?	No. Testes are horizontal and elevated	Yes

A 15-year-old adolescent boy presents to the ER with sudden onset of testicular pain and swelling that woke him from sleep. He is nauseous and in significant pain. What should the physician look for on physical examination to determine whether this is an emergency?

Two common causes of painful testicular swelling are torsion, which is a urologic emergency, and epididymitis, which is not. (See Table 4-2.)

What causes testicular torsion?

Torsion occurs when the testes and spermatic cord twist and result in venous obstruction. In some cases it is secondary to a "bell clapper deformity"—a congenital abnormality that occurs in 12% of males in which there is an abnormally high attachment of the tunica vaginalis to the testis. In such cases, the testes can freely rotate. In 40% of cases, the congenital abnormality is bilateral.

What causes epididymitis?

Epididymitis refers to swelling of epididymis secondary to retrograde extension of organisms from the vas deferens. Causative agents vary with age; for example, in sexually active males *C trachomatis* is the most common organism. Antibiotics are necessary to treat it.

What are the complications of testicular torsion?

Testicular torsion can lead to loss of the testicle if not diagnosed and treated promptly. Patients who present within 6 hours of pain have an 80% to 100% testicular salvage rate. From 6 to 12 hours the salvage rate steadily decreases, and at 12 hours salvage rate approaches 0%.

What diagnostic studies are indicated for testicular torsion?

Imaging studies are not required if the diagnosis is made clinically; if the diagnosis is not certain, radionuclide scans or color Doppler ultrasonography of the testis may be used to evaluate blood flow.

What are the treatment options for torsion?

Treatment involves manual detorsion outward and laterally as most testes twist inward toward the midline, and it is successful in 30% to 70% of patients. Surgery for detorsion may be required. At the time of repair, it is important to check the other side as bilateral torsion can occur.

ACNE

A 16-year-old adolescent girl presents to the dermatologist requesting Accutane for her acne. She has never been treated for acne before, and on examination, she has several open and closed comedones. What is the appropriate management of this patient?

Though very common, acne can cause emotional distress and embarrassment to adolescents. Treatment is important to prevent scarring and improve the appearance of the skin. In a patient with open and closed comedones (blackheads and whiteheads), a first approach would be topical agents, such as benzoyl peroxide and retinoic acid.

Should Accutane be prescribed for a patient with mild acne?

No. Accutane is best reserved for the most severe forms of acne due to its side effects. Side effects include: teratogenic effects, palpitations, neutropenia, hematuria, pruritus, fatigue, headache, and hepatitis.

CLINICAL VIGNETTES

A 16-year-old-adolescent girl who developed breast buds at age 11 still not has experienced menarche. Is this normal?

This is not normal and can be considered an example of delayed puberty.

What is the definition of delayed puberty?

Delayed puberty is defined as a lack of apparent sexual maturation by age 14 in boys or 13 in girls or the absence of menarche by 16 years or within 5 years of onset of puberty.

Is delayed puberty a common condition and what is the most common cause?

2.5% of adolescents meet these criteria with the majority secondary to constitutional delay.

An 18-year-old man presents for a health maintenance visit. His last visit was 3 years ago. What topics should you cover?

As previously stated, an adolescent health maintenance visit should include physical as well as psychosocial assessment where psychosocial assessment includes: Home environment, Education/Employment, Activities, Drugs, Sexuality, and Suicide/Mental Health (HEADSS). Additionally, a review of his immunization record is important as it is very much possible that there are vaccines that he is eligible to receive (meningococcal, TDaP).

The patient in the previous question reports that he is sexually active and his mother does not know. What advice should you give and what should you consider doing?

At the onset, it is important to emphasize to the patient that his sexual health is confidential information that you are not obligated to reveal to his mother. A thorough assessment of his sexual activity should be made to ascertain risk for STIs, coercion, etc. Additionally testing for STIs including syphilis, chlamydia, gonorrhea, and HIV should be offered.

CHAPTER 5

Cardiology

ARRHYTHMIAS

A 16-year-old adolescent boy presents to the emergency department (ED) after syncopating at school. An ECG shows a pattern of a short PR interval and a prolonged upstroke of the QRS, which is widened. What syndrome does he have?

This patient has Wolff-Parkinson-White (WPW) syndrome. (See Fig. 5-1.)

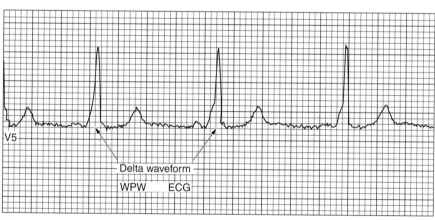

Figure 5-1

What causes the short PR interval, prolonged upstroke, or "delta wave," and widened QRS that are seen on an ECG in patients with WPW syndrome?

WPW syndrome is caused by an accessory bypass tract between the atria and ventricles. Normally, the AV node slows conduction prior to ventricular depolarization. The accessory pathway does not have this property, so impulses travel quickly and preexcite the ventricle.

Why are patients with WPW syndrome at risk for sudden death?

If patients with WPW syndrome develop atrial arrhythmias such as atrial fibrillation or atrial flutter, the accessory pathway may conduct these rapid beats to the ventricles without delay, causing an increased risk of ventricular fibrillation and sudden death.

How are orthodromic supraventricular tachycardias triggered in WPW?

A premature atrial complex may occur while the accessory pathway is refractory. As a result, the impulse goes down the AV node then travels retrograde back up the accessory pathway. This results in an orthodromic supraventricular tachycardia.

A 14-year-old adolescent girl syncopizes immediately after finishing an event at a swim meet. She has a family history significant for a brother who died suddenly while playing basketball at 16 years of age. What is the differential for young patients with syncope during exercise?

Syncope with exercise is concerning for cardiac pathology that could lead to sudden death. The most common cause of sudden death in young athletes is hypertrophic cardiomyopathy. Other cardiac causes of syncope and sudden death with exercise include conditions predisposing to arrhythmias, myocarditis, coronary artery anomalies, ruptured aortic aneurysm, other cardiomyopathies, valve stenosis, and pulmonary hypertension. If the patient syncopizes several minutes after exercise with a prodrome of dizziness, muffled hearing, and nausea, it may be due to vasodepressor syncope with dehydration. Referral to a cardiologist for syncope associated with exercise is recommended.

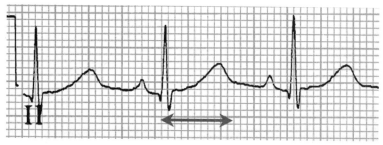

Figure 5-2   (Reproduced, with permission, from Knoop KJ, Stack LB, Storrow AS, et al. *Atlas of Emergency Medicine.* 3rd ed. New York: McGraw-Hill; 2010. Fig. 23.18B.)

The 14-year-old patient's ECG is shown below. (See Fig. 5-2.) What is the likely diagnosis?

This patient has a prolonged QT interval over 0.46 seconds. Her presentation, ECG, and family history are consistent with long QT syndrome (LQTS).

How do patients with LQTS present?

They present with syncope, seizures, and even cardiac arrest induced by exercise or strong emotions. There are several genetic mutations that have been identified; so a family history of sudden death should raise a suspicion for this disease.

What is the mechanism by which patients with LQTS are at risk of sudden death?

These patients have ion channel abnormalities that result in prolonged recovery of the myocardium from electrical excitation. This alters transmembrane voltage and can lead to dangerous tachyarrhythmias and sudden death.

If you suspect that a patient has LQTS but the ECG is normal, what other testing can be performed to further evaluate them?

An exercise stress test is an effective way to evaluate for prolonged QT syndrome. An electrophysiology study, pharmacologic provocation study, and/or genetic testing are also useful in diagnosis.

What are the treatment options for LQTS?

Treatment options include beta-blockers, antiarrhythmics, and implantable cardioverter defibrillator (ICD) to shock the patient out of dangerous tachyarrhythmias.

CARDIOMYOPATHIES AND HEART FAILURE

A 16-year-old adolescent boy presents to the office with syncope during exertion. Physical examination reveals a loud, harsh systolic ejection murmur at the right upper sternal border that increases during a Valsalva maneuver and decreases with release of Valsalva. What is the diagnosis?

This patient has hypertrophic cardiomyopathy (HCM) with obstruction of the left ventricular outflow tract (LVOT). The strain phase of Valsalva decreases preload and afterload and increases the intensity of the murmur due to increased dynamic obstruction. Release of Valsalva then increases preload and afterload, decreasing the intensity of the murmur. Squatting also decreases the intensity of the murmur, while exertion increases the intensity of the murmur.

An echocardiogram reveals a thick 4-cm septum with mild LVOT obstruction. What medications can be used to help this patient?

Medications to treat HCM include beta-blockers, such as atenolol, and calcium channel blockers, such as verapamil and diltiazem.

What is the mechanism by which these medications work in patients with HCM?

These medications are used to treat the impaired filling of the noncompliant, hypertrophied ventricle. The negative inotropic effects decrease dynamic obstruction by lowering the heart rate and enhancing diastolic filling. They do not decrease the amount of hypertrophy or the incidence of sudden death.

A 7-year-old girl develops an upper respiratory infection (URI) symptoms and fever and 1 week later develops malaise, abdominal pain, vomiting, and cough. On her cardiac examination, she has a gallop and her liver is distended 4 cm below the costal margin. What is the next step in diagnosis?

Viral myocarditis should be suspected and an ECG and echocardiogram (echo) should be performed. Children with low cardiac output states often present with gastrointestinal (GI) symptoms secondary to poor gut perfusion. The cough is secondary to pulmonary edema.

In a patient with viral myocarditis, what are the typical ECG and echo findings?

An ECG will typically show ST depressions, T-wave inversions, and ventricular arrhythmias. Meanwhile an echo will show poorly contracting ventricles as well as a possible pericardial effusion and dilation of the ventricles.

What is the mechanism by which viruses cause myocarditis?

The mechanism is not clearly known, but it is thought to be caused by an immunologic response to the virus or by direct viral invasion of the myocardium. Biopsy specimens show inflammation of the tissue and myocardial necrosis.

A 9-year-old boy with a history of cancer develops symptoms of congestive heart failure and is found to have a dilated cardiomyopathy. What is the most likely cause of the cardiomyopathy?

Patients with exposure to anthracyclines or radiation as cancer treatments are at increased risk for the development of cardiomyopathies later in life. There is a dose-related response between these treatments and the risk for development of cardiac dysfunction.

What are the oral medications typically used to treat dilated cardiomyopathy?

Diuretics are indicated to treat pulmonary edema or vascular congestion. Beta-blockade with carvedilol is commonly used. This medication helps to improve diastolic function, blocks the effects of sympathetic stimulation, and reduces afterload. Angiotensin-converting enzyme inhibitors such as enalapril also help to reduce afterload. Both of these medications have direct antifibrotic effects on the myocardium and modify the neurohumoral response to poor heart function.

What continuous infusions are commonly used to treat heart failure patients?

Milrinone is a phosphodiesterase inhibitor that improves lusitropy, enhancing diastolic function. It also causes vasodilation to decrease afterload. Sympathomimetic agents such as dopamine and epinephrine may also be used if hypotension is present to improve contractility and maintain blood pressure. A heparin drip may prevent clot formation in a poorly moving heart and a lidocaine drip may also be used if ventricular tachycardia develops.

A patient with heart failure develops a holosystolic murmur at the apex of the heart. What is the likely etiology of this murmur?

This murmur is likely secondary to mitral regurgitation (MR). The causes of MR in heart failure include dilation of the chambers of the heart leading annular dilatation and papillary muscle dysfunction or chordae tendineae rupture from ischemia or infarction.

A 10-lb newborn presents for his initial primary care evaluation and is found to have a systolic ejection murmur. His mother suffered from gestational diabetes. What is the most likely diagnosis?

This baby likely has hypertrophic cardiomyopathy secondary to exposure to elevated maternal glucose levels during gestation that stimulate fetal hyperinsulinemia. These infants typically have asymmetric septal hypertrophy that resolves spontaneously within the first year of life.

A 7-year-old boy presents to the clinic with complaints of weakness and difficulty walking. On physical examination, he has a gallop, hepatomegaly, and enlarged calves. What is the underlying disease?

This is a classic presentation for muscular dystrophy and the most common types are Duchenne or Becker dystrophy. These are X-linked disorders caused by mutations in the dystrophin gene found in muscle tissue. The enlarged calves are due to pseudohypertrophy from muscle breakdown and replacement with fibrofatty tissue. The cardiac symptoms are secondary to cardiomyopathy commonly seen in this patient population.

CARDIAC EXAMINATION

A tachypneic newborn baby arrives in the neonatal intensive care unit (NICU) with an oxygen saturation of 83%. What initial test can be performed to distinguish if this is a primary cardiac process or a primary pulmonary process?

A hyperoxia test can be performed. An arterial blood gas is obtained when the patient is on room air and again when the patient is on 100% FiO_2. If the PaO_2 is unchanged or is less than 100 mm Hg, congenital heart disease should be suspected. If the PaO_2 is greater than 200 mm Hg on 100% FiO_2, the process is likely not secondary to a shunt lesion.

A 3-year-old boy presents to his pediatrician with a new murmur. The doctor appreciates a 2/6 systolic vibratory murmur at the left lower sternal border while he is in the supine position and resolves when he sits upright. Does this patient need a further work-up?

No. This patient has a Still murmur, which is a benign functional murmur. The murmur is typically found in patients of 2 to 7 years of age and often resolves spontaneously (Table 5-1).

Table 5-1 Innocent Heart Murmurs

Murmur Type	Typical Age Group	Description of Murmur
Still murmur	2-7 y	Low frequency, vibratory, musical systolic murmur best appreciated at the left lower sternal border when supine
Peripheral pulmonary stenosis of the newborn	Newborns, typically resolves by 3-6 mo	Low-frequency systolic ejection murmur best appreciated at the left upper sternal border and radiates to the axilla
Cervical venous hum	3-6 y	Continuous murmur best appreciated above or below the right clavicle that changes intensity with head rotation and jugular vein compression and is inaudible when supine
Cardiac bruit	Any age	Crescendo/decrescendo systolic murmur best appreciated above the right clavicle; associated with a carotid thrill
Physiologic ejection murmur	8-14 y	Soft, blowing, crescendo/decrescendo, early to midsystolic murmur best appreciated at the left upper sternal border

A newborn baby has a low-pitched systolic ejection murmur that radiates to the axillae. An echocardiogram is performed showing mild branch peripheral pulmonary stenosis (PPS). What is the typical course of the lesion?

Physiologic peripheral pulmonary stenosis typically resolves by 6 weeks in two-thirds of babies and resolves in almost all babies by 6 months of age. (See Table 5-1.)

A 4-month-old infant presents with a weight below the third percentile for age. The mother reports that the baby only feeds for 5 minutes at a time and often sweats while feeding. The physical examination reveals a continuous machinery-like murmur accentuated in systole at the left upper sternal border with bounding pulses. What is the likely diagnosis?

This patient likely has a patent ductus arteriosus (PDA), which is the remnant of fetal circulation that connects the pulmonary artery to the aorta. The shunt is left to right once the pulmonary vascular resistance drops after birth. The baby has bounding pulses due to the diastolic runoff through the PDA.

What is the etiology of the baby's symptoms?

Feeding is analogous to exercise in babies. In infants with a patent ductus arteriosus, there is increased blood flow to the lungs and right-sided heart failure can occur. As a result, they have difficulty tolerating the increased metabolic demands during feeding and can develop failure to thrive.

How does a PDA murmur differ from that of a venous hum?

Both murmurs are continuous. However, the venous hum is best appreciated just below the clavicle or at the base of the neck. It disappears when the head is turned, the jugular vein is compressed, or with supine positioning. A PDA will not resolve with these maneuvers.

You are examining a neonate with cyanotic Tetralogy of Fallot (TOF) in the NICU. What murmurs can you appreciate?

The features of TOF include an overriding aorta, pulmonary stenosis, a ventricular septal defect, and right ventricular hypertrophy. This patient likely has a systolic ejection murmur appreciated best at the left upper sternal border due to the right ventricular outflow tract obstruction. There may also be a holosystolic murmur at the apex at the site of the ventricular septal defect. (See Fig. 5-3.)

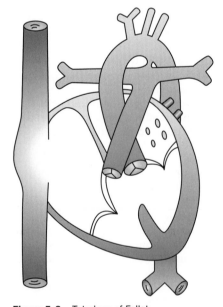

Figure 5-3   Tetralogy of Fallot.

STRUCTURAL HEART DISEASE

A 4-day-old newborn arrives in the emergency room (ER) and appears gray and unstable. The baby previously had a pulse oximetry of 99% upon discharge from the newborn nursery. On examination, the baby has good brachial pulses but femoral pulses can not be palpated. What is the likely inciting event that led to this presentation?

This patient's patent ductus arteriosus likely has closed at home and blood flow to its lower body is compromised due to an obstruction. This can be seen with aortic arch anomalies, such as an interrupted aortic arch and coarctation of the aorta.

A 14-year-old adolescent boy presents to cardiology clinic with an elevated blood pressure of 162/105 in his right upper extremity. This pressure measurement is confirmed by ensuring the patient has an adequate cuff size and is checked manually. What is the next step in your examination?

Once confirmed, an elevated blood pressure is concerning for a possible coarctation. Blood pressures should be obtained in four extremities. This is done to assess for a gradient between the upper extremity or extremities prior to the coarctation and the lower extremities. The radial and femoral pulses may also be checked to assess for a radiofemoral delay, which may also indicate coarctation. Renal disease and idiopathic hypertension should also be included in the differential.

What x-ray findings may be found in adolescent patients with coarctation of the aorta?

Rib notching of the posterior third to eighth ribs may be appreciated due to erosion from large collateral vessels. A "3" sign indentation of the aortic wall may also be seen.

Why are older patients with undiagnosed coarctation of the aorta often hypertensive even after the obstruction is relieved by surgical or balloon intervention?

In coarctation of the aorta there is diminished blood flow to the organs supplied by vessels distal to the obstruction. As a result, the kidneys appreciate this diminished flow and activate the renin-angiotensin-aldosterone system. This results in higher pressures that often persist after the coarctation is repaired.

What syndrome is most commonly associated with coarctation of the aorta?

Ten percent of patients with Turner syndrome (karyotype X,O) have coarctation of the aorta.

What other cardiac anomaly is most commonly associated with coarctation of the aorta?

A bicuspid aortic valve is commonly associated with coarctation. This association is often found in patients with Turner syndrome.

A neonate is born with pulmonary valve atresia with an intact ventricular septum. What medication should be started as a bridge to a balloon valve dilation or surgical intervention?

This patient should be started on prostaglandin E1 to keep the PDA open and to supply blood flow from the aorta and into the pulmonary arteries. Without other collateral blood vessels, this would be the only source of pulmonary blood flow to the lungs to allow for oxygenation.

An otherwise healthy 4-year-old boy has a systolic murmur on examination and an echo reveals an atrial septal defect (ASD). What is the physiologic reason for the systolic murmur?

The murmur is not caused by blood flow between the atria, but is a flow murmur across the pulmonic valve due to increased blood volume in the right heart from the left to right atrial shunt. A diastolic rumble may also be present from increased flow across the tricuspid valve.

What determines the direction of the shunt in patients with an ASD and otherwise normal cardiac physiology?

The shunt at the level of the atrial septum is determined by the relative compliance of the right and left ventricles rather than the pressure differences between the left and right sides of the heart. Typically the right ventricle is more compliant and blood preferentially flows from left to right.

What is Eisenmenger syndrome in a patient with an ASD?

Eisenmenger syndrome describes the condition that may occur in patients with ASD when the pulmonary vascular resistance rises due to the chronically increased blood flow through the lungs secondary to the shunt. When this occurs, the right ventricle may become more hypertrophied, resulting in decreased compliance and a right to left shunt at the atrial level.

How does the physiology of an isolated ASD differ from that of an isolated ventricular septal defect (VSD)?

Both of these lesions initially result in a left to right shunt, causing an increase in blood flow circulating through the lungs. ASDs result in an increased volume load on the right side of the heart, while VSDs typically result in a volume load on the left side of the heart. Over time, both lesions can lead to pulmonary hypertension and Eisenmenger syndrome.

What site of shunting in unrepaired D-transposition of the great arteries (D-TGA) is the most critical for supplying oxygenated blood to the body?

Shunting in D-TGA may occur via the PDA, ASD, and/or VSD. Due to the drop in pulmonary vascular resistance (PVR) during the transitional period after birth, blood typically shunts predominantly from the aorta to the pulmonary arteries through the PDA and from the right ventricle to the left ventricle through the VSD. As a result, the main source of oxygenated blood supplying the body comes from the shunt from the left atrium to right atrium via the ASD.

If a patient with D-TGA, with a restrictive atrial septum has low oxygen saturations and is becoming increasingly acidotic despite proper ventilation, what is the next step in management?

Unless the patient can be taken emergently to surgery, a balloon septostomy via cardiac catheterization should be performed to create an enlarged connection between the atria. This allows the oxygenated blood to get to the body and will improve acidosis.

What does the classic x-ray look like for patients with D-TGA?

These patients have an "egg-on-a-string" appearance due to the narrow mediastinal shadow made by the aorta and pulmonary artery overlying one another in the PA view.

What are the four basic features of Tetralogy of Fallot (TOF)?

The four basic features are an overriding aorta, VSD, hypertrophied right ventricle, and right ventricular (RV) outflow tract obstruction.

What is the physiology behind a "tet spell"?

"Tet spells" are hypercyanotic episodes that occur in patients with TOF when there is increased shunting from right to left across the VSD. This can occur when the pulmonary vascular resistance increases transiently, especially with increased irritability and agitation, or if the systemic vascular resistance drops.

Why do older, unrepaired patients with TOF feel better when they squat during tet spells?

Squatting increases systemic vascular resistance and increases preload. This decreases the right to left shunting to promote blood flow to the lungs and the patient becomes less cyanotic.

What is the classic chest x-ray finding in patients with TOF?

The chest x-ray shows a "boot-shaped" heart, reflecting right ventricular hypertrophy and an upturned ventricular apex. (See Fig. 5-4.)

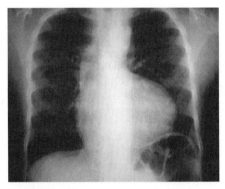

Figure 5-4   Chest x-ray of a patient with unrepaired Tetralogy of Fallot.

A newborn has total anomalous pulmonary venous return (TAPVR) with drainage of the pulmonary veins into the inferior vena cava (IVC). In what case is TAPVR a surgical emergency?

It is a surgical emergency when there is significant pulmonary venous obstruction at the site of the vessel's insertion. This leads to backup of blood causing pulmonary edema and decreased cardiac output as oxygenated blood is not draining into the heart.

Why should prostaglandin E_1 be avoided in this patient?

The PDA increases pulmonary blood flow, causing increased pulmonary venous return going to the obstructed pulmonary veins. This leads to worsening pulmonary edema.

A baby is prenatally diagnosed with hypoplastic left heart syndrome (HLHS). What are the features of this syndrome?

The left ventricle and ascending aorta are severely hypoplastic. In addition, the aortic and mitral valves are typically severely stenotic or atretic.

When this baby is born, how does blood reach the body from the lungs?

Pulmonary venous blood returns to the left atrium from the lungs and is shunted from left to right across an ASD or patent foramen ovale (PFO) to the right atrium. It then mixes with deoxygenated blood and flows to the right ventricle into the pulmonary artery. At that time some of the blood shunts from right to left through the PDA to the aorta. This provides systemic blood flow.

A baby is diagnosed with an interrupted aortic arch. He has other anomalies including a cleft palate, hypocalcemia, and frequent infections. What chromosomal deletion does this baby likely have?

This baby likely has a 22q11 deletion, indicating DiGeorge syndrome. This syndrome is associated with conotruncal cardiac defects, hypoparathyroidism resulting in hypocalcemia, an absent thymus resulting in frequent infections and cleft palate.

A 2-month-old infant presents to the emergency department with irritability associated with feeds and tachypnea. An ECG shows wide and deep Q waves in the anterolateral leads. An echocardiogram reveals a significantly dilated left ventricle but otherwise normal structural anatomy. What further testing is needed to make the diagnosis?

This patient needs a cardiac catheterization to confirm the origin of the coronary arteries. An echocardiogram can not rule out anomalous left coronary from the pulmonary artery (ALCAPA) as an etiology of a dilated cardiomyopathy.

Why do patients with ALCAPA often develop heart failure?

As the pulmonary vascular resistance drops, blood flows retrograde from the left coronary artery into the pulmonary artery. This creates a coronary steal, resulting in inadequate perfusion of the myocardium, subsequent ischemia, and heart failure.

A newborn patient presents to his primary care doctor. He has a history of dextrocardia, a midline liver, malrotation of the intestines that required correction with a Ladd procedure, and has multiple spleens. Why was this patient discharged on amoxicillin?

This patient likely has heterotaxy syndrome, which is a disorder that affects sidedness and development of asymmetric organs. This disorder is linked to a high incidence of congenital heart disease. Typically these patients are asplenic or polysplenic with functional asplenia. As a result, amoxicillin prophylaxis is started soon after birth to protect the patients from infection by encapsulated organisms.

What medication should be initiated at birth for patients with congenital heart disease that have ductal dependent lesions?

Prostaglandin E_1 should be started in order to prevent vasoconstriction and closure of the patent ductus arteriosus (PDA). In congenital heart lesions that cause obstruction to the right side of the heart, the PDA provides flow from the aorta into the pulmonary arteries to supply blood flow to the lungs. Meanwhile, obstructive lesions on the left side of the heart require the PDA for flow from the pulmonary artery into the aorta.

ACQUIRED HEART DISEASE

A 5-year-old girl presents to the ER with high fevers, conjunctivitis, cervical lymphadenopathy, a rash on the chest, and a strawberry tongue. What serious complication of this disease may be avoided with early intravenous immunoglobulin (IVIG) administration?

This patient has Kawasaki disease and early IVIG treatment may prevent a coronary artery aneurysm.

What additional medication may be given to decrease the incidence of a late coronary artery aneurysm in Kawasaki disease?

Aspirin may be given late in the course of Kawasaki disease to prevent a coronary artery aneurysm.

A 6-year-old girl comes to the ER with fever, arthritis, abnormal movements and muscle weakness, subcutaneous nodules, and a new heart murmur. She had untreated pharyngitis 3 weeks ago. What bacteria caused this illness?

This patient has rheumatic fever caused by an immunologic reaction to group A beta-hemolytic streptococcal infection. This may be avoided by early antibiotic treatment.

How does a streptococcal infection cause the sequelae of rheumatic fever?

Rheumatic fever is caused by the development of antibodies to the streptococcal antigens that cross-react with proteins on human tissues, such as heart valves, and lead to rheumatic fever.

What are the cardiac manifestations of rheumatic fever?

Valve damage from the cross-reaction of the anti-streptococcal antibodies can lead to scarring of the valves and subsequent mitral, aortic, and/or tricuspid regurgitation. The most commonly affected valve is the mitral valve. Pericarditis, myocarditis, and heart failure may also occur.

What criteria are used to diagnose rheumatic fever?

The Jones criteria are used to diagnose rheumatic fever. Two major symptoms or two minor symptoms and one major symptom are used to diagnose.

What are the major and minor symptoms of the Jones criteria?

The major criteria are arthritis, carditis, subcutaneous nodules, erythema marginatum, and Sydenham chorea. A common mnemonic for these criteria is:

J: Joints—Arthritis

♥: Carditis

N: Nodes—subcutaneous nodules

E: Erythema marginatum

S: Sydenham chorea

The minor criteria include fever, arthralgia, increased erythrocyte sedimentation rate (ESR) or C-reactive protein (CRP), a prolonged PR interval, previous rheumatic fever or rheumatic heart disease, and evidence of a preceding streptococcal infection.

A 12-year-old boy with a history of rheumatic fever goes to the dentist for a tooth extraction. He subsequently develops fever with dyspnea and malaise. An echo shows vegetation on the mitral valve. What organism is likely responsible?

This patient has endocarditis likely due to *Streptococcus viridans*, a bacteria found in the mouth that translocates into the bloodstream during dentistry procedures and seeds damaged valves. *Staphylococcus aureus* is also a common culprit in endocarditis.

How can endocarditis be avoided in patients with a history of infective endocarditis or with synthetic valves?

These patients should be given a prophylactic antibiotic, such as amoxicillin or clindamycin, prior to dental work, as well as prior to procedures of the GI, genitourinary (GU), and pulmonary systems.

Which additional patients with congenital heart disease should receive endocarditis prophylaxis during dental procedures?

A recent update to the endocarditis prophylaxis guidelines recommend dental prophylaxis for patients with unrepaired or incompletely repaired cyanotic heart disease, including those with palliative shunts or conduits. It also recommends that patients with completely repaired congenital heart disease using synthetic materials or devices should receive prophylaxis for 6 months. Patients with any residual shunting defects after repair using these synthetic materials or devices should also use endocarditis prophylaxis. Transplant patients with cardiac valvulopathy should also receive prophylaxis.

What dangerous complications may occur in patients with endocarditis?

Septic emboli from the vegetation may occur causing transient ischemic attack (TIA), stroke, red cell casts with hematuria, as well as clinical findings such as splinter hemorrhages, Roth spots, Janeway lesions, and Osler nodes. To prevent these phenomena, patient with endocarditis are treated for 4 to 8 weeks of antibiotics targeting the causative organism.

CARDIAC SURGERY

A baby is born with hypoplastic left heart syndrome (HLHS) that consists of an atrial septal defect, mitral atresia, a tiny left ventricle, and aortic atresia. He undergoes a Norwood procedure and a modified Blalock-Taussig (BT) shunt. What are the goals of this operation?

The goals of the operation are to enlarge the hypoplastic aorta to create an adequate size aortic arch with unobstructed flow to the body. This is done by surgically anastomosing the main pulmonary artery with the small aorta and augmenting this neo aortic arch with patch material during the Norwood procedure. A source of pulmonary blood flow must also be created. The modified BT shunt consists of a conduit from the innominate artery to the pulmonary artery to provide pulmonary blood flow. Of note, some patients will undergo a Sano operation with the formation of an RV to PA conduit rather than a BT shunt to provide blood flow to the lungs.

What is the second stage of repair in single-ventricle patients?

The BT shunt or Sano is taken down in the second stage. To provide pulmonary blood flow, the superior vena cava (SVC) circulation is connected to the pulmonary artery circulation. This is called the bidirectional Glenn anastomosis. A Hemifontan procedure is a similar but more complex procedure and also provides this circulatory physiology. The timing of this stage varies from center to center but is typically performed between 3 and 6 months of age.

What is the final stage of repair in single-ventricle patients?

This final stage of repair is a Fontan procedure and is typically performed at 2 to 3 years of age. In this operation the IVC is also connected to the pulmonary artery circulation. As a result, venous blood from the body passively flows into the lungs, bypassing the heart.

Why are there three stages of a single-ventricle repair rather than one operation in the neonatal period?

There are three stages to the single-ventricle repair because the pulmonary vascular resistance is too high in infants to allow for complete passive flow of the venous system through the pulmonary lung fields. (See Fig. 5-5.)

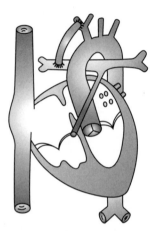

Blalock-Taussig shunt

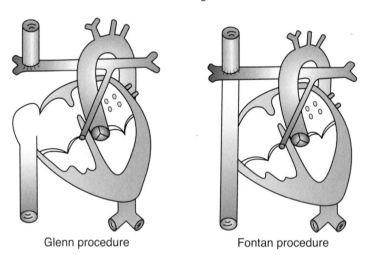

Glenn procedure   Fontan procedure

Figure 5-5   Blalock-Taussig shunt, Glenn procedure, and Fontan procedure in a patient with a hypoplastic right ventricle and right ventricle outlet tract obstruction.

What surgical repair is used to correct D-TGA if the pulmonary artery and aorta are of adequate size?

In D-TGA, the aorta arises from the right ventricle while the pulmonary artery arises from the left ventricle. An arterial switch operation is now widely used to correct D-TGA. In this repair, the aorta and pulmonary artery are divided just above the valve tissue and are transferred. The coronary arteries are typically translocated separately after the aorta is transferred to avoid kinking and obstruction.

CLINICAL VIGNETTES

An ex-35-week-old newborn is born without prenatal care in the newborn nursery. He is found to be tachycardic to 210 beats per minute (bpm). His blood pressure is stable and he is warm and well perfused. An ECG is performed and shows this pattern. (See Fig. 5-6.)

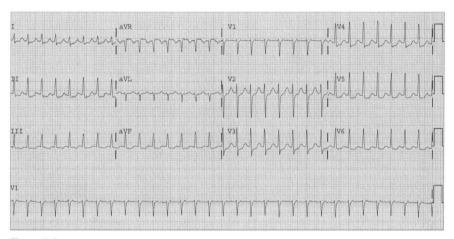

Figure 5-6

What abnormal rhythm is demonstrated in this ECG?

This is a narrow complex tachycardia that is at a rapid but regular rate and no P waves can be seen preceding the QRS complexes. This rhythm is consistent with supraventricular tachycardia.

What is the next step in treatment?

If the baby is stable, vagal maneuvers may be attempted, such as ice to the face. If this is not effective, adenosine 0.1 mg/kg may be administered.

What is the mechanism of action of adenosine?

Adenosine briefly slows conduction at the AV node. The reentry pathway circuit is interrupted and sinus rhythm is restored. Once the baby is in sinus rhythm, he continues to be tachypneic and has sweating with feeds. The heart is auscultated and he is appreciated to have a III/VI holosystolic murmur appreciated at the left lower sternal border. His oxygen saturation is 85%. A chest x-ray shows marked cardiomegaly. An echocardiogram is performed that shows a huge right atrium and a tiny right ventricle due to inferior displacement of the tricuspid valve, resulting in a dilated right atrium and hypoplastic right ventricle.

What congenital heart defect does this patient have?

This patient has Ebstein anomaly. (See Fig. 5-7.)

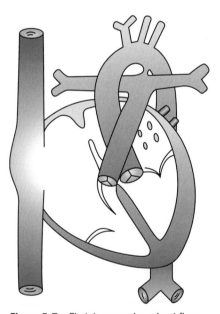

Figure 5-7   Ebstein anomaly—shunt flow.

Why is this patient cyanotic?

This patient likely has severe tricuspid regurgitation and may have an element of obstruction to the right ventricular outflow tract due to the displaced valve leaflet. As a result, desaturated blood flows from right to left through the patent foramen ovale or atrial septal defect.

If there is significant right ventricular outflow tract (RVOT) obstruction in this patient, how does blood get to the lungs?

Blood is likely delivered to the lungs through a left to right shunt through the patent ductus arteriosus. In some cases, multiple aortopulmonary collateral arteries (MAPCAs) may also develop to supply blood flow to the lungs.

If this patient's blood flow is supplied exclusively by a patent ductus arteriosus, what is the next step in management?

This patient should be started on prostaglandins in order to keep the PDA open to maintain blood flow into the lungs. If anterograde flow through the RVOT is not adequate, the patient may need to have a shunt placed surgically from the innominate artery to the pulmonary artery prior to a definitive surgical repair.

Is there an association between Ebstein anomaly and supraventricular tachycardia?

Yes. Patients with Ebstein anomaly have an increased incidence of SVT, occurring in one-fourth to one-half of all patients, as well as WPW syndrome.

CHAPTER 6

Pulmonology

UPPER AIRWAY CONDITIONS

During the winter, a 3-year-old boy presents to the office with a seal-like barking cough, retractions, nasal flaring, and tachypnea. A chest x-ray reveals a classic "steeple sign" in which the trachea appears narrowed below the vocal cords. What is the most likely diagnosis?

This patient has croup, a viral infection that causes inflammation of the larynx, infraglottic tissues, and trachea resulting in upper airway obstruction. Symptoms include inspiratory stridor, barking cough, hoarse voice, and fever. The incidence of croup peaks during late fall and winter, and typically affects children between the ages of 6 months and 3 years.

What viruses are typically responsible for this illness?

Parainfluenza viruses types 1 and 2 are the most common pathogens. Other viruses include respiratory syncytial virus (RSV), influenza A and B, adenovirus, Coxsackie virus, and measles.

What should be the management of this condition?

For mild cases, cool mist tent or vaporizer help reducing airway edema and improving clearing of secretions. For moderate to severe cases, racemic epinephrine and systemic steroids (dexamethasone 0.6 mg/kg) can be used. Minimal observation time in the emergency department (ED) should be 3 hours.

A 3-year-old boy with incomplete immunization presents with respiratory distress, drooling, and stridor on inspiration. On examination, he is toxic-appearing, extending his neck with an open mouth and leaning forward. An x-ray reveals the "thumb sign." What is the next step in treatment?

This patient has epiglottitis, a bacteria-induced inflammation of the supraglottic tissues. Epiglottitis is a medical emergency that can result in sudden irreversible upper airway obstruction. This patient should be taken to the operating room (OR) to perform an urgent intubation. ENT should be summoned in order to perform an emergent tracheostomy in the event of sudden airway obstruction.

What is the appropriate antibiotic treatment for this patient?

He should receive ceftriaxone for 7 to 10 days and close contacts should be treated with rifampin as prophylaxis.

What pathogens typically cause epiglottitis?

Pathogens include *Haemophilus influenzae* type b (Hib), *Streptococcus pyogenes* or *pneumoniae*, and *Staphylococcus aureus*.

Why is epiglottitis less frequent now than it was 20 years ago?

Hib caused the majority of epiglottitis before the vaccine was introduced. Currently it is much less common, although there are still some cases of epiglottitis due to HIB even in those who have been vaccinated. The primary series for the vaccine is at 2, 4, and sometimes 6 months, depending on the brand of the vaccine. Every child needs a booster at 12 to 15 months of age.

LOWER AIRWAY CONDITIONS

An 8-month-old infant presents to the office during the winter months with wheezing, crackles, cough, and tachypnea. X-ray reveals hyperinflation with increased anteroposterior (AP) diameter. What is the most common pathogen responsible for this respiratory infection?

This patient has bronchiolitis, an infection of the lower respiratory tract that results in distal airway obstruction. RSV causes 50% to 75% of cases. It is most common from November to April and usually affects children under 2 years of age.

How does RSV cause bronchiolitis?

RSV infects the epithelium of the lower respiratory airways, resulting in necrosis, inflammation, and submucosal edema that lead to obstruction of distal airways.

What is the typical course of the illness?

The typical disease course is 5 to 10 days of acute symptoms, followed by 1 to 2 weeks of slow recovery.

What is the treatment for a case of RSV without complications?

Most infants can be treated with supportive care (supplemental oxygen and chest physiotherapy). Bronchodilators and racemic epinephrine may transiently improve symptoms. For infants with reactive airway disease (RAD), corticosteroids early in the course of the disease may be beneficial.

Which patients typically receive antiviral agents and immunoglobulin therapy for RSV infections?

High-risk patients, such as those with chronic lung disease, congenital heart disease, immunodeficiency, neuromuscular disease, premature infants, or those with multiple congenital anomalies.

What is the appropriate prophylaxis and treatment for high-risk patient with RSV?

During RSV season, high-risk patients younger than 2 years of age can receive prophylaxis with RespiGam, an IV RSV immunoglobulin, and palivizumab, an RSV monoclonal antibody. During acute illness, aerosolized ribavirin, an antiviral that suppresses the RNA polymerase of the virus can shorten the duration of symptoms.

A 16-year-old adolescent girl presents to clinic with 10 to 14 days history of productive cough with associated rhinitis. On examination she has no sinusitis, pneumonia, or any other significant pulmonary disease. What is the most likely diagnosis?

This patient has bronchitis, an infection of the lower respiratory airways caused by viruses such as adenovirus, parainfluenza virus, influenza A and B, rhinovirus, and Coxsackie virus.

What treatment should be given to this patient?

Bronchitis is typically self-limiting. Treatment includes supportive measures and bronchodilators. Bacteria such as *Bordetella pertussis*, *Mycoplasma pneumoniae*, and *Chlamydophila pneumoniae* can also cause bronchitis, and in these cases antibiotics may be used.

A 5-year-old girl with a past medical history of multiple episodes of RSV-induced bronchiolitis presents with a cough for 6 months that is exacerbated by exercise, cold air, and seasonal allergies. A chest x-ray taken during an episode of coughing reveals hyperinflation. What is the cause of the patient's cough?

This patient has asthma, a chronic obstructive airway disease characterized by reversible episodes of airflow obstruction secondary to bronchospasm and inflammation of large and small airways. Irritation and cellular damage of the respiratory epithelium result in recurrent episodes of cough particularly at night or early in the morning.

Does a normal chest x-ray rule out a diagnosis of asthma?

No. A chest x-ray showing hyperinflation is consistent with asthma; however, a normal chest x-ray does not rule out this diagnosis because the findings are often completely reversible when a patient is asymptomatic.

What tests may be performed to further evaluate if this patient has asthma?

Spirometry is the test of choice for patients with RAD. It can demonstrate airway obstruction and assess reversibility of symptoms in patients more than 5 years of age.

What does spirometry show in a patient with RAD?

It shows an obstructive pattern with a forced expiratory volume at one second (FEV_1) less than 80% predicted and a decrease vital capacity (decreased FEV_1/FVC) of less than 65% of lower limit of normal.

How is reversibility determined in patients with RAD?

Reversibility is determined by an increase in FEV_1 of greater than 200 mL and more than 12% from baseline measure after inhalation of a short-acting beta-2 agonist (SABA).

If an 8-year-old child with asthma complains of symptoms three times per week, as well as symptoms during the night three times per month, which level of severity is her asthma?

This child has mild persistent asthma, defined as more than two episodes of symptoms per week but not daily, exacerbations that affect activity, and more than two episodes of symptoms during the night per month. Patients with mild persistent asthma have FEV_1 values more than 80%.

What is the basic treatment regimen for mild persistent asthma?

Treatment is SABA for symptoms relief and a low-dose inhaled corticosteroid for long-term control.

An 18-year-old man with moderate persistent asthma asks when he should use his SABA and when he should use his combined inhaled steroid and long-acting beta-2 agonist. What is your recommendation?

He should use combined inhaled steroid and long-acting beta-2 agonist daily to decrease inflammation and prevent acute exacerbations. SABA should be used only to relieve acute symptoms or to prevent acute attacks prior to exposure of known triggers.

What is the basic treatment regimen for moderate persistent asthma?

A SABA for acute symptom relief and a low-dose corticosteroid and long-acting inhaled beta-2 agonist for long-term relief. Other options for long-term relief include leukotriene receptor antagonists or medium-dose inhaled corticosteroids.

A 19-year-old patient presents to clinic with continuous, daily symptoms of asthma, as well as nightly symptoms and an FEV_1 of less than 60%. She has very limited activity and frequent exacerbations. What is the appropriate treatment for this patient?

This patient has severe persistent asthma. She should take high-dose inhaled corticosteroids, a long-acting beta agonist (LABA), and if necessary to stabilize symptoms, an oral systemic corticosteroid. She should also take a SABA for acute symptom relief.

A 2-year-old boy presents to the office after an episode of choking followed by persistent wheezing. On examination, he has hyperresonant lung fields and tracheal deviation to the left. An x-ray shows overinflation of the right lung and deviation of the mediastinum to the left. What is the next step in diagnosis?

This patient has a foreign body obstruction. The next step in diagnosis and treatment is rigid bronchoscopy to visualize and remove the foreign body.

Where are aspirated foreign bodies most commonly found?

Among toddlers, foreign body aspiration occurs equally in the left and right main stem bronchus. However, with normal growth, the angle of the right main stem bronchus in relation to the trachea becomes more acute making a straight path from the larynx to the bronchus. Thus, in older children, foreign body obstructions occur more frequently in the right main stem bronchus.

What are common long-term complications of foreign body aspiration?

Complications of objects not removed include recurrent pneumonia, abscesses, erosion and perforation, and bronchiectasis.

Why does the lung appear hyperinflated on the chest x-ray of this patient?

Partial obstruction due to a foreign body can cause a "ball-valve" phenomenon in which air flows into the lung during inspiration and becomes trapped on expiration, causing hyperinflation.

PNEUMONIA

A 2-month-old infant develops purulent conjunctivitis, followed by symptoms of tachypnea and a staccato cough, but remains afebrile. She is diagnosed with pneumonia. In what manner did this infant likely acquire this infection?

This infant has *Chlamydia trachomatis* pneumonia acquired from the genital flora in the birth canal of her mother. Intrauterine transmission of this organism has also been documented.

In the pediatric population, which age range does *C trachomatis* pneumonia typically affect?

Chlamydia conjunctivitis usually presents between 5 and 14 days of age while the respiratory symptoms are typically seen in patients between 2 and 12 weeks of age.

What is the appropriate management for this patient?

This infant should be treated with erythromycin for 14 days.

A 14-year-old adolescent boy presents with fever, headache, sore throat, and myalgia. These symptoms diminish over the course of a week. Meanwhile, he develops a prominent cough that persists for over 2 weeks. X-ray shows an interstitial infiltrate. What is the appropriate treatment for this illness?

This patient has *M pneumoniae*, an atypical or "walking" pneumonia that predominantly affects patients aged 5 to 15 years of age. Treatment consists of macrolides, such as erythromycin or azithromycin. Tetracyclines may also be used in older children.

A 6-year-old girl who recently had an upper respiratory tract infection (URI) presents to the emergency room (ER) with abrupt onset of respiratory distress with tachypnea, malaise, and fever. Pulmonary examination reveals diminished breath sounds and crackles in the left lower lung. What will a chest x-ray likely reveal?

This patient has a "typical," community-acquired, bacterial pneumonia. The chest x-ray will probably show a lobar consolidation. *S pneumoniae* is the most common source of community-acquired bacterial pneumonia.

What types of antibiotics are used to treat a community-acquired pneumonia?

Penicillin, ampicillin, second- or third-generation cephalosporins may be used depending on the sensitivities of the organism. Erythromycin may be used in patients allergic to penicillin.

What should be the management of community acquired pneumonia in areas with high prevalence of penicillin-resistant *S pneumoniae*?

High doses of penicillin, ampicillin, or macrolides must be used to overcome resistance mediated by penicillin-binding protein seen in pneumococci. Vancomycin can be used for highly resistant strains.

A 6-month-old infant presents with respiratory distress, tachypnea and diffuse wheezes, and crackles on examination. A chest x-ray shows hyperinflation, hilar adenopathy, and peribronchial thickening. She is diagnosed with viral pneumonia. What types of pathogens may be responsible?

Pathogens include adenovirus, RSV, influenza, and parainfluenza viruses. The majority of cases of pneumonia in children are caused by these viruses.

A toxic-appearing 5-year-old boy presents to the ER with rapidly progressive respiratory distress. An x-ray reveals an infiltrate in the left upper lobe, a pleural effusion, and a pneumatocele. What pathogen is likely responsible for this type of presentation?

The presentation of this patient is most consistent with a bacterial pneumonia caused by *S aureus*. Infections by this pathogen can become complicated by osteomyelitis, endocarditis, septic arthritis, and septic shock.

What is the most appropriate treatment for this condition?

The recommended antibiotic therapy for pneumonia associated with a pleural effusion is clindamycin plus cefotaxime. Alternative regimens include oxacillin plus cefotaxime, clindamycin alone, or vancomycin.

An 18-year-old man presents to clinic with a 2-week history of low-grade fever, congestion, and rhinorrhea, followed by 1 week of paroxysmal cough with a stridor upon inspiration. What is the most likely diagnosis?

This patient has pertussis or "whooping cough," an upper respiratory infection caused by *B pertussis*.

What is the typical course of this illness?

The condition presents in three stages: the "catarrhal phase" which consists of 1 to 2 weeks of low-grade fever, rhinorrhea, and cough; the "paroxysmal phase" in which patients have paroxysms of cough followed by a stridulous inspiration (the characteristic "whoop") and post-tussive emesis. This phase lasts 2 to 4 weeks; and the "convalescent phase" in which symptoms resolve, except for the cough that may persist for up to 8 weeks.

Why are college students particularly susceptible to epidemics of *B pertussis*?

College students are often susceptible to epidemics of this illness as their immunity from the *B pertussis* vaccine begins to wear off and they are living in close quarters with one another where the bacteria can spread more easily.

How is *B pertussis* treated?

Erythromycin is used to treat patients and close contacts. It shortens symptoms duration if given during the catarrhal phase. Afterward, it is mainly used to decrease the period of disease transmission. To prevent disease in adolescence and adulthood, a TDaP booster is recommended for all 11-year-olds.

NEONATAL CONDITIONS

A mother gives birth at 30 weeks' gestational age. The infant has grunting, nasal flaring, and tachypnea. A chest x-ray reveals diffuse atelectasis and a "ground-glass" pattern. What medical management of this premature infant will improve his survival and morbidity?

This infant has respiratory distress syndrome (RDS). He should receive respiratory support with oxygen and continuous positive airway pressure (CPAP) until symptoms improve. Exogenous surfactant may also be given to (3-5 mL/kg per dose) for two or more doses at 12-hour intervals to improve survival and morbidity. In addition, he should receive antibiotic treatment since symptoms of RDS are indistinguishable from congenital pneumonia.

What is the cause of RDS?

RDS is secondary to a deficient production of surfactant in premature infants.

What is the natural course of this condition?

The natural course of RDS is progressive worsening of symptoms during the first 24 to 48 hours of life, followed by improvement once surfactant production reaches adequate levels, usually by 72 hours.

When does endogenous surfactant begin to be produced in the fetus and what is its function?

Surfactant production is begun by type II pneumocytes at 32 weeks' gestational age. It is a phospholipid that lines the alveoli, decreasing alveolar surface tension, preventing alveolar collapse, and increasing lung compliance. Lack of surfactant results in the development of progressive atelectasis, intrapulmonary shunting, hypoxemia, and cyanosis.

What medication can be given to a mother prior to the birth of her premature infant in order to decrease the severity and incidence of RDS in her baby?

Antenatal corticosteroids such as betamethasone and dexamethasone can be given to mothers between 24 and 34 weeks of gestation. Corticosteroids accelerate surfactant production by acting on the baby's type II pneumocytes. They are more effective when given within 24 to 48 hours prior to the delivery.

A 4-month-old infant has a past medical history significant for premature birth at 30 weeks' gestational age, intubation, and mechanical ventilation for 2 weeks, and O_2 dependence beyond 36 weeks preconceptional age. What chronic lung disease did this patient likely develop in the first few months of life?

This child has bronchopulmonary dysplasia (BPD), a complication of preterm infants exposed to prolonged mechanical ventilation with high mean airway pressures and high oxygen tensions.

What is the cause of BPD?

BPD is caused by small airway and microvasculature injury by toxic factors such as oxygen, mechanical ventilation, inflammatory agents, and infections. Airway injury causes squamous metaplasia and hypertrophy of small airways, and results in arrested alveolar septation and decrease in the number of alveoli.

When should a diagnosis of BPD be considered?

A diagnosis of BPD is considered in infants who require oxygen support after 28 days of life and who fail a room air challenge at 36 weeks of corrected gestational age.

What are the goals of treatment in a patient with BPD?

Patients should be given oxygen therapy to maintain their SaO_2 from 92% to 95%. Bronchodilators can be used to improve lung compliance, diuretics to minimize fluid retention, and steroids to decrease inflammation.

What are the long-term complications of BPD?

Long-term complications include RAD, pulmonary hypertension, increased risk of sudden infant death syndrome (SIDS), and increased severity of common respiratory infections, such as RSV, that can cause severe respiratory distress in these patients.

A neonate presents with recurrent choking, vomiting, and cyanosis immediately following a feed. In utero, the patient's mother was found to have polyhydramnios. What simple procedure may be performed to make the diagnosis?

This patient has esophageal atresia with an associated tracheoesophageal fistula (TEF). It can be easily diagnosed by attempting to pass an orogastric tube down the esophagus and observing if the tube loops back on itself on AP and lateral chest x-rays.

What procedure should be performed to classify and confirm the diagnosis of a TEF?

Bronchoscopy and imaging with a contrast medium are ways to definitively diagnose and classify a TEF.

What type of TEF is the most common?

There are five different variants of TEF. The most common type is esophageal atresia with distal TEF, in which the superior portion of the esophagus ends in a blind pouch and there is communication between the distal esophagus and the trachea. Other less common types include isolated esophageal atresia without TEF, isolated TEF without atresia (H-type), esophageal atresia with proximal and distal TEF, and esophageal atresia with proximal TEF. (See Fig. 6-1.)

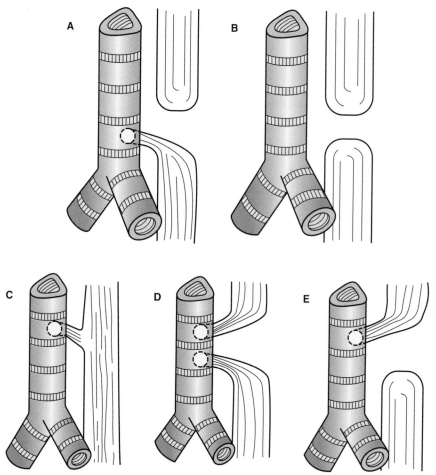

Figure 6-1   Types of tracheoesophageal fistula. **A**. Esophageal atresia with distal fistula (82%) **B**. Esophageal atresia without fistula (9%) **C**. H-type tracheoesophageal fistula (6%) **D**. Esophageal atresia with proximal and distal fistulas (2%) **E**. Esophageal atresia with proximal fistula (1%).

What is the appropriate management of these patients?

These patients are at risk for respiratory compromise secondary to aspiration. Infants require constant aspiration of secretions accumulating in the esophageal pouch. Definite treatment requires surgical intervention.

What are long-term complications of TEF?

Long-term complications include esophageal stenosis, esophageal dysmotility, and gastroesophageal reflux disease (GERD).

A full-term neonate presents soon after birth in respiratory distress. On examination, he appears to have a scaphoid abdomen. Lung auscultation reveals poor inspiratory breath sounds on the left side of the chest and a shift of the heart sounds to the right of the chest. What is the most likely diagnosis?

This patient has a congenital diaphragmatic hernia (CDH). CDH results from a defect in the diaphragm that results in herniation of abdominal contents into the thorax. It is usually associated with lung hypoplasia, pulmonary hypertension, and intestinal malrotation.

What are the most common findings in a chest x-ray?

Chest x-ray shows air and fluid-filled loops of bowel migrating into the chest cavity. The lung volumes are low and the mediastinum is displaced to the opposite side of the herniation.

Where is the most common location of CDH?

The majority of CDH result from a defect in the posterolateral diaphragm (foramen of Bochdalek). Ninety percent occur on the left side of the diaphragm. Bilateral hernias occur in less than 5% of cases.

What are other types of CDH?

Other less common types of CDH include paraesophageal hernias and those herniating through the anteromedial diaphragm (foramen of Morgagni). The latter ones are usually symptomatic after the neonatal period.

How can a congenital diaphragmatic hernia become lethal?

CDH results in pulmonary hypoplasia and pulmonary hypertension caused by the compromise of lung development. Inadequate surfactant production, congenital heart defects, and other congenital anomalies associated with CDH may also adversely affect survival.

What is the appropriate management of this patient?

Management should include immediate endotracheal intubation and mechanical ventilation. A nasogastric tube should be placed to decompress the gastrointestinal tract. In cases of sever pulmonary hypertension, patient may require high-frequency ventilation or extracorporeal membrane oxygenation (ECMO). Surgical repair of the defect should be performed once the patient is stable.

A 1-month-old newborn presents to clinic with noisy breathing, feeding difficulty, and occasional inspiratory stridor. This patient has a condition that is the most common cause of stridor in infants. What is the cause of this condition?

This patient has laryngotracheomalacia, caused by immature cartilage resulting in a flaccid larynx and/or trachea. Stridor occurs due to prolapse of the laryngeal or tracheal tissues during inspiration. Symptoms worsen with crying or agitation and on supine position.

What is the recommended management for this condition?

Mild to moderate cases can be managed conservatively with reassurance to family. Typically, with normal growth, the cartilage gradually stiffens and symptoms resolve by 18 months of age. For severe cases surgery may be necessary.

CONGENITAL LUNG LESIONS

What is the most common congenital lung lesion to present in the neonatal period and how does it present?

The most common congenital lung lesion is congenital lobar emphysema and it presents several days after birth with dyspnea, wheezing, and cyanosis. This congenital lesion is caused by over-expansion of a segment of the airspaces or a lobe of the lung.

What is the treatment for congenital lobar emphysema?

Treatment consists of a lobectomy or observation in mild cases.

A neonate presents with respiratory distress and recurrent respiratory infections. A chest x-ray shows several air-filled cysts, as well as a mediastinal shift away from the lesions and flattening of the diaphragm on the side of the lesions. What are these cystic lesions caused by?

This neonate has a congenital cystic adenomatoid malformation (CCAM) caused by overgrowth of the terminal bronchioles. It is the second most common congenital lung malformation. The cysts typically occur within one lobe and cause respiratory distress due to compression of the surrounding lung tissue.

What is the treatment for cystic adenomatoid malformations that compromise ventilation?

Treatment consists of surgical excision of the affected lobe of the CCAM.

What is the difference between at CCAM and a bronchopulmonary sequestration?

Perfusion of a CCAM is derived from the pulmonary circulation, whereas a bronchopulmonary sequestration is perfused separately from the pulmonary blood supply. It is typically perfused by collaterals arising from the aorta.

GENETIC CONDITIONS

A 3-year-old boy has had coughing, recurrent sinusitis, and otitis media since infancy. He subsequently develops nasal polyps and digital clubbing. Further evaluation reveals situs inversus and bronchiectasis. What autosomal recessive defect is the cause of this patient's frequent respiratory symptoms?

This patient has Kartagener syndrome, which is an autosomal recessive syndrome characterized by impaired function of the cilia lining the epithelium of sinuses, middle ear, and airway. It also affects the spermatozoa, causing male infertility.

A common symptom of Kartagener syndrome is bronchiectasis. What are signs and symptoms of bronchiectasis?

Bronchiectasis is a permanent dilation of the bronchi due to persistent inflammation and damage of the bronchial wall. Signs and symptoms include a recurrent cough with purulent sputum, wheezing, dyspnea, and hemoptysis.

A 2-year-old girl presents to the office with chronic cough associated with sputum. She has history of meconium ileus at birth and has had multiple episodes of sinusitis and pneumonia. On physical examination she is below the fifth percentile for weight. What is the most likely diagnosis?

This patient has cystic fibrosis (CF), an autosomal recessive disease characterized by dysfunction of exocrine glands.

What is the main defect in CF?

CF is secondary to a mutation on the cystic fibrosis transregulator (CFTR) gene, a cell membrane protein that functions as a chloride channel in epithelial cells of exocrine glands. Mutations in this gene lead to defective chloride secretion from cells and increased absorption of sodium from the airway lumen. As a result, secretions from these cells become thicker and more difficult to clear.

What are the most common pathogens responsible for respiratory infection among CF patients?

Pathogens include *S aureus, H influenzae,* and *Pseudomonas aeruginosa.*
Colonization with *Burkholderia cepacia* is particularly worrisome as this pathogen can cause rapidly progressive pulmonary failure and death.

What is the most common pathogen responsible for respiratory failure among patients with CF?

Pseudomonas aeruginosa is the most common cause of respiratory failure in patients with CF. Up to 90% of patients will get infected by this organism.

What tests may be performed to diagnose this patient?

The sweat chloride test remains the gold standard for diagnosis. A level greater than 60 mEq/L is considered abnormal. DNA testing is reserved for confirmation. Genetic and prenatal testing is also available for the most common gene mutations.

CLINICAL VIGNETTES

An 8-year-old patient with asthma presents to the emergency room (ER) with wheezing, increased work of breathing, and shortness of breath. What is the best initial treatment for this patient?

This patient is presenting with an acute asthma exacerbation. Initial treatment should include nebulized SABA such as albuterol which works immediately by reducing smooth muscle constriction. An anticholinergic, such as ipratropium, is often added to improve response.

After providing initial treatment for this patient, what other medications may be indicated?

A 5-day course of oral corticosteroids IV or PO may be recommended based on the severity of the symptoms and the response to albuterol. Corticosteroids begin to work 4 to 6 hours after administration and help treat the underlying inflammation preventing the late phase of asthma.

After receiving initial treatment with nebulized short-acting beta agonist and a first dose of systemic corticosteroids the patient's wheezing has subsided, but she looks sleepy. On examination, her breath sounds are diminished bilaterally. What is the next step in treatment?

Changes in mental status in patients with an acute asthma exacerbation are usually a sign of hypercarbia and impending respiratory failure. This patient may require administration of epinephrine (SQ or IM), magnesium sulfate IV, and terbutaline. An arterial blood gas that shows a falling pH and a rising Pco_2 is helpful in confirming impending respiratory failure and the need of intubation.

The patient is intubated and later recovers. Once the patient is discharged, what medications should be considered to try to prevent future asthma exacerbations?

In addition to avoidance of environmental triggers, there are several preventative medications that the patient could take. A leukotriene antagonist, such as montelukast, a long-acting beta-2 agonist, such as salmeterol, as well as an inhaled corticosteroid, such as fluticasone, are all options for asthma prevention.

CHAPTER 7

Gastroenterology

PEDIATRIC GASTROENTEROLOGY

A 2-year-old boy presents with gagging, drooling, and inability to swallow. His mother saw him playing with marbles earlier in the day. Where is the most likely location the marble would be lodged?

What diagnostic tests are available for esophageal foreign body?

Esophageal foreign body should be suspected. The three most common locations for objects to become lodged are the upper esophageal sphincter, the aortic impression on the esophagus, and the lower esophageal sphincter.

Plain x-rays are helpful for radiopaque foreign bodies, and barium or gastrografin swallow may be used when objects are radiolucent. On x-ray, the location of a coin can be determined by positioning. The coin will usually face you if it is lodged in the esophagus and will be on its side if lodged in the trachea (see Fig. 7-1). Endoscopy is also useful as it can be used to both localize and remove foreign bodies.

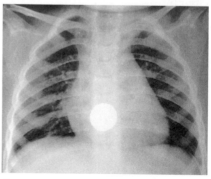

A

Figure 7-1 Chest x-ray depicting the foreign body ingestion of a coin in the esophagus. (Reproduced, with permission, from Stone CK, Humphries RL. *Current Diagnosis & Treatment: Emergency Medicine*. 6th ed. New York: McGraw-Hill; 2008: Fig. 48.10AB.)

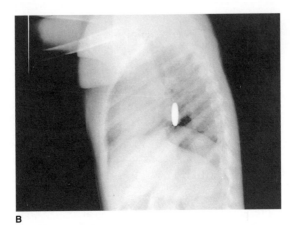

B

Figure 7-1 *(Continued)*

A 2-month-old infant presents with emesis after feeds, irritability, and cough. If an infectious etiology is ruled out, what diagnosis would you suspect?

This child likely has gastroesophageal reflux (GER), which is the retrograde passage of stomach contents into the esophagus due to an incompetent lower esophageal sphincter, and it is common in young infants. GER affecting a child's thriving is considered pathologic and is termed gastroesophageal reflux disease (GERD).

What recommendations can you give the caregivers of an infant with GERD?

Recommendations include giving small frequent meals, having the infant sit upright or elevating the head of the bed at a 20° to 30° angle after feeds, and thickening formula with rice cereal.

What tests may aid in the diagnosis of GERD?

GERD is typically diagnosed by clinical history. However, several tests may aid in diagnosis including esophageal pH monitoring, upper gastrointestinal (UGI) series, scintigraphy, and manometry. However, endoscopy remains the most accurate method of demonstrating esophageal damage by reflux.

A parent of a child with GERD has tried your recommendations for prevention without success. What other treatment options are available for a child with GERD?

Pharmacologic options include antacids, H$_2$ blockers, or proton pump inhibitors (PPIs). Prokinetic agents that stimulate gastric emptying such as metoclopramide or erythromycin may be helpful, although erythromycin has been associated with increased incidence of pyloric stenosis in young infants. Changing the source of nutrition to a protein hydrolysate formula may be an effective treatment for GERD associated with milk protein allergy.

What surgical options are available for GERD and at which point should they be considered?

A surgical Nissen fundoplication, where the fundus of the stomach is wrapped around the distal esophagus to reinforce the lower esophageal sphincter, may be considered for severe GERD but should be delayed as long as possible because patients will usually outgrow GERD by 1 to 2 years of age.

A 10-year-old boy complains of burning epigastric pain, choking, vomiting, and dysphagia that have not responded to antireflux medications for suspected GERD. He undergoes upper endoscopy, and pathologic specimens of the esophagus show greater than 15 eosinophils per high-powered field. What is the diagnosis?

Eosinophilic esophagitis is an inflammatory reaction that is thought to be caused by an allergic process, yet no responsible allergens are identified in the majority of cases. The disease process is not entirely understood, but diagnosis is suggested by greater than 15 eosinophils per high-powered field on biopsy. Treatment options include dietary elimination of possible food allergens, medical therapy (proton pump inhibitors, topical or systemic corticosteroids, antihistamines), and esophageal dilatation for scarring/strictures.

A 14-year-old adolescent girl presents to the emergency room after a syncopal episode at school and is found to have a hematocrit of 14. On further questioning, she states that she has been taking nonsteroidal antiinflammatory drugs (NSAIDs) for frequent headaches and experiencing epigastric abdominal pain recently. What is your next step in diagnosis and management?

Initial laboratory evaluation should include a complete blood count (CBC), coagulation profile, liver function tests (LFTs), blood type, and cross match. The goal of initial resuscitation is to restore hemodynamic stability with fluids or blood transfusion. An upper gastrointestinal (GI) endoscopy should be done to locate the source of GI bleeding, which is most likely a peptic ulcer in this patient on ulcerogenic medication.

What treatment options are available for peptic ulcer disease?

Treatment options include medications (antacids, sucralfate, misoprostol, H_2 blockers, PPIs), endoscopic cautery, or surgery for excessive bleeding or perforation.

What are the presentations of GI bleeding? How can the source of the bleed be identified?

Upper GI bleeding is defined as bleeding proximal to the ligament of Treitz. It can present as hematemesis (vomiting with bright red or coffee-ground blood) or melena (black tarry stool due to digested blood). Lower GI bleeding generally presents as bright red blood per rectum or hematochezia (grossly bloody stool), but may also present as melena if the bleeding is between the ligament of Treitz and proximal colon. If blood loss is brisk, upper GI bleeding can also present with bright red blood per rectum. A gastric lavage can be used to differentiate an upper GI bleed from a lower GI bleed. However, clear gastric aspirate does not eliminate a duodenal bleeding source. Upper and/or lower endoscopy is usually required to identify the exact source of bleeding and can provide therapeutic options such as cauterization.

What is the differential diagnosis for GI bleeding in children and adolescents?

Causes of upper GI bleeding are:

Mallory-Weiss tear

Medications: aspirin, NSAIDs, steroids

Caustic ingestion

Peptic ulcer disease

Esophageal varices

Esophagitis

Vasculitis

Crohn disease

Bowel obstruction

Causes of lower GI bleeding:

Anal fissures

Infectious colitis: Shigella, *Escherichia coli*

Polyps: juvenile polyps/polyposis, Peutz-Jeghers syndrome, familial adenomatous polyposis

Inflammatory bowel disease: Crohn disease, ulcerative colitis, or indeterminate colitis

Meckel diverticulum (younger children)

Intussusception (younger children)

Henoch-Schönlein purpura

A 10-year-old boy presents with abdominal pain after a bicycle accident. He is noted to have several broken ribs, pallor, tachycardia, hypotension, and dizziness. What diagnostic tests would you order?

In this patient, splenic rupture causing hypovolemic shock is likely. Imaging tests such as CT or ultrasound are performed to evaluate abdominal trauma and determine the necessity of surgery. In cases of suspected internal hemorrhage, exploratory laparoscopy/laparotomy may be indicated for both diagnosis and treatment.

A 1-month-old newborn presents with projectile, nonbilious vomiting after feeds that has progressively worsened over the past week. He is found to have a hypochloremic, hypokalemic metabolic alkalosis, and dehydration. An olive-shaped mobile mass is palpable in the epigastric area. What diagnosis would you suspect?

Pyloric stenosis occurs with a peak incidence at 2 to 4 weeks of life and is more common in males (4:1). Treatment is nasogastric tube decompression, fluid resuscitation, correction of electrolyte abnormalities, and then surgical pyloromyotomy.

What diagnostic test would you order for pyloric stenosis?

Ultrasound is the modality of choice for diagnosing hypertrophic pyloric stenosis, which is defined as a pyloric channel greater than 14 mm in length or a pyloric wall greater than 4 mm thick. An upper GI series may suggest the diagnosis with the "string sign," a thin stream of contrast coursing through the stenotic pylorus.

A 1-day-old newborn with trisomy 21 and prenatal history significant for polyhydramnios presents with bilious vomiting. What diagnostic test would you order?

An x-ray would show the double bubble sign and paucity of gas in the distal GI tract consistent with duodenal atresia, which has a higher incidence in Down syndrome (see Fig. 7-2). Treatment includes decompression with a nasogastric tube, intravenous fluid replacement, and surgical duodenoduodenostomy.

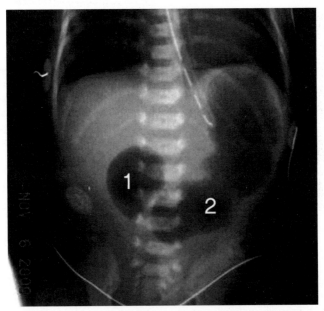

Figure 7-2   Chest x-ray depicting the double-bubble sign of duodenal atresia. (Reproduced, with permission, from Brunicardi FC, Andersen DK, Billiar TR, et al. *Schwartz's Principles of Surgery.* 9th ed. New York: McGraw-Hill; 2010: Fig. 39.13.)

A 2-week-old newborn with bilious emesis has an upper GI series with small bowel follow-through showing abnormal positioning of the ligament of Treitz. What is the diagnosis and next step in management?

Malrotation occurs due to abnormal rotation of the small intestine in utero and results in abnormal mesenteric attachments. The intestine is at risk for volvulus, or twisting of the intestine on its vascular supply, which can lead to bowel ischemia, metabolic acidosis, or death. Risk of volvulus is highest during the neonatal period. Urgent laparotomy is required after fluid and electrolyte resuscitation and nasogastric decompression.

A 2-year-old child presents with diarrhea, vomiting, abdominal distention, and failure to thrive consistent with celiac disease. What diagnostic tests would you order to evaluate for this disease?

To diagnose celiac disease, or gluten-induced enteropathy, serology can serve as the first-line test including antiendomysial, antigliadin, and antitissue transglutaminase antibodies. A duodenal or jejunal biopsy is the gold standard for diagnosis, showing villous atrophy and crypt hyperplasia. Treatment is elimination of gluten (wheat, barley, rye, oats) from the diet.

A child presents with abdominal pain. How would you evaluate the child?

A thorough history and physical examination are essential. In the history, ask about the location, quality, temporal characteristics, exacerbating and alleviating factors, previous surgeries, associated symptoms, vomiting, diarrhea, stooling, and family history. Physical examination of the abdomen includes inspection, auscultation, palpation, and percussion as well as assessing for rebound and guarding. A rectal examination should be considered to obtain stool for occult blood testing. A pelvic examination should be considered in adolescent females.

A 2-year-old boy presents with cough, congestion, and fever. His caretaker has been giving him aspirin for fever. Why is aspirin not recommended in children?

Reye syndrome, which is acute encephalopathy and fatty degeneration of the liver, is related to acetylsalicylic acid use in children, especially during influenza and varicella virus infections. Reye syndrome has a biphasic course, first with a prodromal upper respiratory or varicella infection followed by protracted vomiting. Neurologic symptoms including coma or death may occur.

A 6-year-old girl presents with episodic abdominal pain lasting 2 to 3 hours occasionally associated with nausea, vomiting, or headache, and she feels well between episodes. She has a maternal family history of migraines. What treatment would you suggest?

Abdominal migraines occur mostly in female children with a family history of migraines, and these patients tend to develop typical migraines as adults. Episodes self-resolve, but sleep in a dark, quiet room and analgesics may be beneficial. Abdominal migraines may also respond to medications used to control typical migraines.

A 2-year-old boy presents with painless rectal bleeding and is diagnosed with Meckel diverticulum. What is Meckel diverticulum and how can it present?

Meckel diverticulum is the persistence of the embryologic omphalomesenteric duct. Remember the rule of 2s: occurs in 2% of the population, is 2 inches in length, is 2 feet from the ileocecal valve, most commonly presents at age 2, and 2% are symptomatic. It most commonly presents with intermittent painless rectal bleeding, but may also present as intestinal obstruction, volvulus, or diverticulitis.

How is Meckel diverticulum diagnosed?

It is diagnosed with a technetium-99m pertechnetate scan, which identifies heterotopic gastric mucosa usually found in symptomatic Meckel diverticulum. Treatment is surgical resection of the diverticulum.

An 8-month-old infant presents with episodes of bilious vomiting, abdominal pain, and currant jelly stool. He has a right upper quadrant mass on physical examination. What diagnosis do you suspect?

Intussusception occurs when one part of the bowel telescopes into another part and is usually ileocolic in location. It can be seen at any age but is most common between 6 months and 2 years. Intussusception may occur at lead points, including Meckel diverticulum, a polyp, or lymphoma, but the cause is most likely idiopathic.

What diagnostic test could you order for suspected intussusception?

Air (or less commonly barium) enema can be used for both diagnosis and treatment via hydrostatic reduction. Ultrasound may also be used and can show a target sign representing the inner and outer layers of overlapping bowel (see Fig. 7-3). Abdominal x-ray may show lack of gas in distal bowel and/or air-fluid levels suggestive of obstruction.

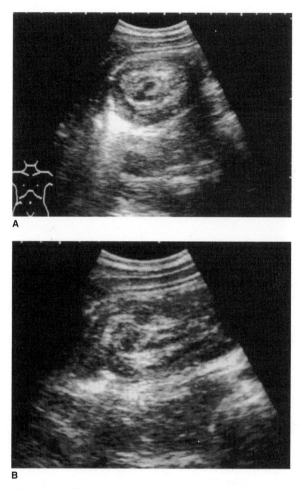

Figure 7-3 Ultrasound of a patient with intussusception. The target appearance is created by the telescoping of bowel seen in this disorder. (Reproduced, with permission, from Tintinalli JE, Kelen GD, Stapczynski JS. *Tintinalli's Emergency Medicine: A Comprehensive Study Guide.* 6th ed. New York: McGraw-Hill; 2004: Fig. 124.2.)

A 16-year-old adolescent boy presents with crampy abdominal pain, diarrhea, bloody stools, anorexia, and weight loss concerning for inflammatory bowel disease. What are the major differences between Crohn disease and ulcerative colitis?

Crohn disease has transmural involvement of the bowel wall, common ileal involvement, skip lesions, and is pan-enteric, meaning any segment from mouth to anus can be involved. Ulcerative colitis has mucosal involvement of the bowel wall, obligatory rectal involvement, bloody diarrhea, and a greatly increased risk of colon cancer. Extraintestinal manifestations are commonly seen in both Crohn and ulcerative colitis. (See Table 7-1.)

Table 7-1 Inflammatory Bowel Disease

Feature	Crohn Disease	Ulcerative Colitis
Bowel wall involvement	Transmural	Mucosal
Common areas of involvement	Any part of the GI tract (mouth to anus), commonly ileum	Rectum, colon
Lesions	Skip (discontinuous)	Continuous
Colonoscopic/ pathologic findings	Longitudinal ulceration, fibrosis, strictures, granulomas, rectal sparing	Diffuse superficial ulceration, easy bleeding, crypt abscesses, pseudopolyps
Risk of colon cancer	Slightly increased	Greatly increased; annual colonoscopy with rectal biopsy for disease >10 y
Clinical manifestations	Crampy abdominal pain, weight loss, diarrhea, rectal bleeding, perianal disease (skin tags, fissures, fistulas, abscesses) Growth failure may be the only presenting sign in pediatric patients	Bloody diarrhea, abdominal pain, tenesmus, rectal bleeding, weight loss, anemia
Complications	Obstruction, fistulas, malnutrition	Toxic megacolon, intestinal perforation
Extraintestinal disease	Polyarticular arthritis, primary sclerosing cholangitis, pyoderma gangrenosum, erythema nodosum, nephrolithiasis, aphthous stomatitis, episcleritis, iritis, uveitis	
Pharmacologic treatment	5-Aminosalicylic acids, corticosteroids, immunosuppression (6-mercaptopurine, azathioprine, cyclosporine A, methotrexate, infliximab [anti-TNF-a])	
Surgical therapy	Removal of diseased bowel is not curative and recurrence is common	Surgery in up to 40%: colectomy is curative

A 14-year-old adolescent girl presents with episodic abdominal pain and diarrhea interspersed with periods of constipation over the past year. She has undergone multiple workups in the past with no diagnosis. What is a probable cause of her symptoms?

Irritable bowel syndrome is defined by Rome criteria as abdominal pain with two of the following three features: relief of pain with defecation, onset of pain with change in stool frequency, and onset of pain with change in stool appearance. There is no identifiable organic cause, and it is a diagnosis of exclusion. Diagnosis is met if the patient has had symptoms for 12 weeks, not necessarily continuous, in the past year.

A 2-year-old girl presents with infrequent passage of hard stool and pain with straining to pass stool. Stool is palpable in the descending colon, and abdominal x-ray shows the colon filled with stool. What can you recommend to her caregivers?

For acute treatment of constipation, the patient should first be disimpacted with enemas, suppositories, or oral laxatives. For maintenance, dietary changes can be recommended such as increasing fluids such as prune juice, increasing fiber intake, and decreasing dairy products. In refractory cases, laxatives and stool softeners may be needed as chronic therapy.

What pharmacologic options are available for treatment of constipation?

Treatments include osmotic laxatives (polyethylene glycol [Miralax], lactulose, milk of magnesia), lubricants [mineral oil], stool softeners (docusate [Colace], stimulating laxatives [Senna, Senokot, bisacodyl [Dulcolax]), and rectal suppositories (glycerine, bisacodyl). GoLYTELY (polyethylene glycol-electrolyte solution) can be used for severe and intractable constipation. Routine use of enemas or suppositories is not recommended.

What is the most common cause of constipation in toddlers?

Voluntary withholding or functional constipation is most common, usually starting at the time of toilet training. It is caused by pain with defecation, which creates aversion to stooling and further withholding and constipation. Withholding stool over time leads to dilation of the rectum and colon, decreased rectal sensation, and a larger stool mass necessary to trigger the urge to defecate.

What complications can arise from constipation?

Complications include anal fissures, rectal bleeding, hemorrhoids, impaction, abdominal pain, and encopresis due to leakage of stool around the large fecal bolus contained in the rectum.

A 1-month-old infant presents with bilious vomiting, abdominal distention, poor feeding, and infrequent bowel movements that only occur with rectal stimulation. He did not pass meconium until 36 hours after birth. What is the diagnosis?

Hirschsprung disease, or congenital aganglionic megacolon, is due to absence of ganglion cells of the myenteric plexuses in the bowel wall, which leads to bowel obstruction and proximal bowel dilation.

What diagnostic test would you order for suspected Hirschsprung disease?

Abdominal x-ray may show proximal bowel dilation and paucity of gas or feces in rectum. Diagnosis is confirmed by a rectal suction biopsy or full thickness rectal biopsy to evaluate for presence of ganglion cells in the submucosa.

A 6-month-old infant presents with a swelling in the inguinal area that appears with crying and straining. What is the suspected diagnosis?

The child likely has an inguinal hernia, a protrusion of small bowel through the inguinal canal. Elective surgery is curative. If the hernia is not reducible, the bowel may become incarcerated or strangulated. These cases require emergent surgery due to the risk of gangrene.

What is the difference between an indirect and direct hernia?

The more common indirect hernia occurs when bowel protrudes through the internal and external inguinal rings into the scrotum lateral to the inferior epigastric vessels. It is due to the failure of the closure of the processus vaginalis. A direct hernia occurs when bowel protrudes through the Hesselbach triangle medial to the inferior epigastric vessels and goes through the external inguinal ring (see Fig. 7-4).

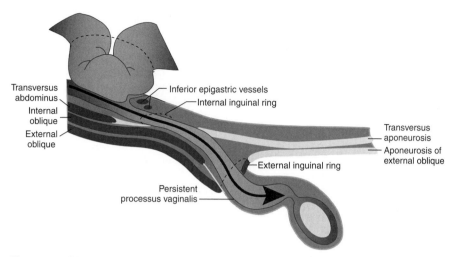

Figure 7-4 Direct inguinal hernia. (Reproduced, with permission, from *Emergency Ultrasound*. 2nd ed. New York: McGraw-Hill; 2008: Fig. 9.15.)

A newborn child has yellow skin discoloration on the second day of life. What are the main physiologic causes of neonatal hyperbilirubinemia?

There are three main contributing factors to indirect (unconjugated) hyperbilirubinemia in neonates: (1) defective conjugation of bilirubin due to low levels of glucuronyl transferase, (2) increased bilirubin load secondary to erythrocyte breakdown, and (3) increased enterohepatic circulations.

What is the treatment for neonatal hyperbilirubinemia?

Treatment via phototherapy allows bilirubin to be converted into a form excreted into the urine or feces. If left untreated, bilirubin deposition in the basal ganglia can cause kernicterus, a form of brain damage. In severe cases of jaundice, exchange transfusions may be needed.

INFECTIOUS GI DISEASE

A child presents with profuse, foul-smelling diarrhea containing blood and mucus, abdominal pain, fever, and vomiting. She was recently hospitalized for the treatment of an abscess with clindamycin for 1 week. What is the likely diagnosis?

Pseudomembranous colitis due to *Clostridium difficile* can occur days to weeks after antibiotic use, which disrupts the normal bowel flora and permits *C difficile* to proliferate. The diagnosis is made by finding *C difficile* toxin in the stool or by colonoscopy showing pseudomembranes which are exudates composed of inflammatory debris and white blood cells.

What is the treatment of pseudomembranous colitis?

Treatment is oral metronidazole or oral vancomycin for 7 to 10 days.

A 3-year-old child presents with vomiting, diarrhea, and fever and is unable to tolerate feeds. What is the most common cause of gastroenteritis in children?

Most gastroenteritis in children is viral, with rotavirus being the most common (others include enterovirus, adenovirus, Norovirus). One should consider looking at stool and evaluating for mucus, blood, or leukocytes and obtaining stool cultures to rule out other causes of gastroenteritis.

What is the treatment of viral gastroenteritis?

Treatment involves oral rehydration with electrolyte solutions such as Pedialyte, or intravenous hydration if the patient is severely dehydrated. Current recommendations are to continue feeds as tolerated throughout the diarrhea in order to minimize sloughing of the intestinal mucosa and facilitate return to normal stooling.

Would you recommend antidiarrheal medications in viral gastroenteritis?

No, they are contraindicated in viral gastroenteritis due to the risk of toxic megacolon.

A 4-year-old child presents with abdominal pain, distention, and flatulence for the past few days since recovering from a severe episode of gastroenteritis. What do you recommend to the caregivers?

After a diarrheal illness, there may be diffuse mucosal disease affecting lactase in the bowel wall. Therefore, children may have transient lactase deficiency after a diarrheal illness. You can suggest that the child use lactose-free milk products temporarily until the bowel recovers.

A 4-year-old boy presents with diffuse abdominal pain and a low-grade fever. On physical examination, he has positive obturator, psoas, and Rovsing signs. He also has tenderness at McBurney point. How are the above maneuvers performed?

The obturator sign is positive if there is pain when the right leg is internally rotated while the hip and knee are flexed at 90°. The psoas sign is positive if pain is elicited on extension of the right thigh. The Rovsing sign is positive when palpation of the abdominal left lower quadrant results in more pain of the right lower quadrant. McBurney point in the area of the abdomen is located two-thirds the distance from the umbilicus to the anterior superior iliac spine.

For the above patient, bloodwork shows an elevated white blood cell count with a left shift. What is your next step in management?

Consider appendicitis, call a surgical consult, and obtain imaging, an ultrasound (in experienced centers) or MRI (for older children who do not need to be sedated to tolerate the length of the scan) or CT scan.

The above patient has had symptoms for 4 days. What are you concerned about?

Perforated appendicitis tends to occur about 36 hours after pain begins. Broad-spectrum antibiotics need to be started immediately, and the surgery may need to be postponed until inflammation around the appendix resolves.

A 2-year-old boy in daycare presents with fever, vomiting, diarrhea, abdominal pain, and jaundice. Other children in his daycare have been sick with similar symptoms. The daycare is found to have an outbreak of hepatitis A. How is hepatitis A transmitted?

Hepatitis A is transmitted via the fecal-oral route and is highly contagious. (See Table 7-2.)

Table 7-2 Hepatitis Viruses

	HAV	HBV	HCV	HDV	HEV
Virus type	RNA Picornaviridae	DNA Hepadnaviridae	RNA Flaviviridae	RNA Delta virus	RNA Hepeviridae
Illness duration	Acute	Chronic	Chronic	Chronic	Acute
Transmission	Fecal-oral route, person-to-person contact	Infected bodily fluids, sexual contact, vertical transmission	Infected bodily fluids, transmission through sexual contact and vertical transmission less common	Infected bodily fluids, sexual contact	Fecal-oral route
Symptoms	Fever, fatigue, jaundice, vomiting, diarrhea, abdominal pain	Jaundice, mild flu-like symptoms, dark urine, light stools, fatigue, fever. May be asymptomatic			

Screening assays	IgM anti-HAV present for 4 mo, then IgG anti-HAV detectable	HBsAg: acute or chronic infection HBsAb: immunity through vaccination or infection HBcAb: IgM highly infectious phase within 6 mo of infection; IgG distant infection that has cleared or persists HBeAg: high viral replication, marker of infectivity HBeAb: low viral replication	Anti-HCV Ab	IgM anti-HDV	Anti-HEV IgM, IgG
Treatment		Antivirals, inteferon	Interferon, ribavarin	Interferon	
Notes	Most cases in children, developing countries, vaccines available, IVIg postexposure prophylaxis	Vaccines available, IVIg postexposure prophylaxis. Chronic infection can progress to hepatocellular carcinoma or liver cirrhosis	Can progress to cirrhosis, end-stage liver disease, or primary hepatocellular carcinoma	Requires infection with hepatitis B virus to be active. Higher incidence of cirrhosis and hepatocellular carcinoma than HBV alone.	Can progress to fulminant hepatic failure and death in pregnant women

What prophylaxis can be given to close contacts of patients with hepatitis A to prevent illness?

Healthy close contacts may receive hepatitis A vaccine or immunoglobulin within 2 weeks of exposure to prevent transmission. The vaccine is preferred because it offers long-term protection, as immunoglobulin will only prevent infection for 1 to 2 months.

A 17-year-old is found to be antibody to hepatitis B surface antigen (HBsAb) positive but hepatitis B surface antigen (HBsAg) negative on routine screening. How is this test result interpreted?

This patient has been immunized against hepatitis B.

GENETIC DISEASES AND SYNDROMES

A newborn with feeding difficulties and respiratory distress is diagnosed with esophageal atresia. What other congenital anomalies are seen in VACTERL association?

VACTERL association includes the following: Vertebral defects, Anal atresia, Cardiac defects, Tracheoesophageal fistula, Esophageal atresia, Renal anomalies, and Limb anomalies.

A 10-year-old girl with deeply pigmented spots on her lips and gums has crampy abdominal pain and bleeding. Her mother had similar symptoms in the past and died of breast cancer at a young age. What is the likely diagnosis?

Peutz-Jeghers syndrome is an autosomal dominant condition where there are multiple benign hamartomas in the GI tract and hyperpigmented mucocutaneous lesions. It significantly increases the risk of cancers of the gastrointestinal tract, pancreas, cervix, ovaries, and breasts.

A 5-year-old boy presents with abdominal pain, jaundice, hepatomegaly, and tremors, and on examination he has greenish-brown rings (Kayser-Fleischer rings) at the limbus of the cornea. What diagnostic tests would you order?

Wilson disease is an autosomal recessive disease of excessive copper deposition in the brain and liver. Diagnosis is made via laboratory testing showing low ceruloplasmin and high serum copper levels. Twenty-four-hour urine copper collection is recommended as the next diagnostic step. Liver biopsy with quantitative copper analysis can confirm the diagnosis.

What is the treatment for Wilson disease?

Treatment involves zinc to block intestinal absorption of copper, copper-chelating agents such as penicillamine, dietary copper restriction, and liver transplant for hepatic failure.

A 1-year-old girl with Beckwith-Wiedemann syndrome presents with a large abdominal mass. What types of cancer is she at risk for?

Children with Beckwith-Wiedemann have an increased incidence of childhood cancers, especially Wilms tumor and hepatoblastoma. Screening includes routine abdominal ultrasounds and blood tests to check alpha-fetoprotein levels.

A 16-month-old girl is brought to the office. Her parents report that she has had foul-smelling, greasy stools for many weeks. She is in the 10th percentile for growth. The patient's past medical history is significant for frequent respiratory infections. Also of note, the child's parents reveal that she did not have a bowel movement in the first 48 hours after birth. What is an appropriate diagnostic test to further evaluate this patient?

A sweat test would be an appropriate test to evaluate the patient for a suspected diagnosis of cystic fibrosis (CF). A chloride concentration greater than 60 mEq/L is a positive test result.

What test would confirm this suspected diagnosis?

DNA analysis revealing a mutation in the cystic fibrosis transmembrane conductance regulator (CFTR) gene on chromosome 7 would confirm the diagnosis. The most common mutation is the delta F508 mutation of the CFTR gene.

What is the cause of the patient's greasy, foul-smelling stools?

These stools indicate malabsorption of fat due to impaired pancreatic function. Viscous exocrine fluid leads to obstruction of pancreatic ducts and decreased or absent pancreatic amylase, lipase, colipase, and phospholipases. This causes malabsorption of fats and proteins, steatorrhea, fat-soluble vitamin deficiencies (A, D, E, K), failure to thrive, and hypoproteinemic edema. Pancreatic enzyme and vitamin replacement are indicated.

Why are respiratory infections common in CF patients?

Frequent respiratory infections are a common feature of CF due to thickened, viscous mucous that becomes colonized with bacteria in the lungs.

What is significant about the fact that this patient did not pass meconium in the first 48 hours after birth?

This patient has a history of meconium ileus, in which she was unable to pass meconium in the first 48 hours after birth. This is due secondary to thick, tenacious meconium that obstructs the distal ileum.

What are some other GI manifestations of CF?

GI manifestations of CF include pancreatic insufficiency, distal intestinal obstruction syndrome (the counterpart of meconium ileus in an older child), steatorrhea, neonatal cholestasis, cholelithiasis, liver disease, gastroesophageal reflux, rectal prolapse, hypoproteinemic edema, and prolonged neonatal jaundice.

CLINICAL VIGNETTES

A mother presents to your office with her 1-month-old daughter. The baby was full term and there were no prenatal/postnatal complications. The baby's appetite has been normal and she has been consistently in the 25th percentile for length and weight. Two days ago the mother noted that the baby's stool was pale, while her urine appeared slightly darker when she was changing the diapers. She also noted that the baby's skin was more yellow than usual. On examination, the baby's liver edge is palpated 3 cm below the costal margin. What initial laboratory tests will aid with diagnosis?

Initial basic laboratory tests should include a set of liver function tests with total and indirect bilirubin as well as gamma-glutamyl transferase (GGT), a basic metabolic panel, a CBC with differential to evaluate for infection.

The laboratory tests are significant for elevated total and direct bilirubin, GGT, and alkaline phosphatase but only mildly elevated aspartate aminotransferase (AST) and alanine aminotransferase (ALT). An ultrasound is ordered and it reveals an absence of a gall bladder. What test would be helpful for further evaluation in this infant?

This infant has neonatal cholestasis as evidenced by the jaundice, acholic stools, and dark urine, as well as hepatomegaly and abnormal laboratory values. Neonatal cholestasis may result from multiple infectious, metabolic, anatomic, and idiopathic conditions. Hepatobiliary scintigraphy, in particular a hydroxy iminodiacetic acid (HIDA) scan may be helpful in diagnosis. In this test, an isotope is injected into the blood. In a normal patient, it is absorbed by the liver then excreted via the biliary tree into the intestine and films are made to show the isotope as it travels through the body.

The baby undergoes a HIDA scan and it shows normal uptake by the liver of the isotope, then very limited excretion of the isotope from the liver with lack of visualized flow into the gall bladder or intestine. What is the possible interpretation of this test?

Non-excretion on HIDA scan suggests that this patient may have biliary atresia (BA), a condition in which the extrahepatic biliary tree becomes obliterated. Non-excretion on HIDA scan, however, is not specific for BA and may be seen in other causes of neonatal cholestasis. Liver biopsy may be further helpful in diagnosis by demonstrating evidence of extrahepatic bile duct obstruction.

What is the next step in treatment for this patient with biliary atresia?

The mean lifespan of untreated patients is 11 months. A Kasai procedure (hepato-portoenterostomy) that connects the intestine directly to the liver in order to achieve bile drainage may be performed. The results of this procedure are dramatically improved if done before 2 months of age. Twenty percent to forty percent of the patient may eventually require a liver transplant after Kasai.

v

CHAPTER 8

Hematology and Oncology

HEMATOLOGY

What is the difference between an antibody screen and a direct antiglobulin test (DAT)?

An antibody screen looks for the presence of unbound RBC antibodies in the plasma. A DAT looks for antibodies bound to RBCs. If the antibody screen is positive but the DAT is negative, this indicates a previous sensitization to a foreign antigen (ie, alloimmunization) without active hemolysis. If both are positive, this indicates ongoing auto- or alloantibody mediated hemolysis.

A 12-month-old infant is found to have Hgb 8 and mean corpuscular volume (MCV) 65 on routine complete blood (cell) count (CBC) screen. What is the likely cause of these abnormal laboratory values?

Iron deficiency anemia is the most common type of anemia in children, especially in children 6 months to 3 years old. In this age group, it is commonly caused by inadequate nutritional intake. This child's diet likely consists of only milk, which would not supply adequate iron. A thalassemia disorder may also be considered in this patient.

An 8-month-old infant is found to have low hemoglobin and low MCV on a routine CBC. He is treated with iron supplementation for 5 months, but on repeat CBC, he is still anemic. What is the likely cause of his anemia?

One option for his continued anemia is noncompliance with medications. However, assuming he had good compliance with his medications, he likely has alpha or beta thalassemia trait in addition to a treated iron deficiency anemia, diagnosed by hemoglobin electrophoresis.

How can you distinguish between iron deficiency and alpha- or beta-thalassemia traits (both microcytic anemias) using only the numerical values provided from a CBC?

Distinguishing between these two microcytic anemias can sometimes be difficult. The Mentzer index: defined as the ratio of MCV: RBC count, a value of 13 or more suggests iron deficiency while a value less than 13 suggests thalassemia. The red blood cell distribution width (RDW) is often elevated in iron deficiency and within normal limits in thalassemia trait.

What other laboratory tests would you like to perform to confirm a diagnosis of iron deficiency anemia?

Typically in iron deficiency anemia, serum ferritin is decreased, serum iron is decreased, and total iron-binding capacity is increased. Under the microscope, RBCs are hypochromic and microcytic in iron deficiency anemia.

You hand a mother a prescription for iron supplements (ferrous sulfate) for her 1-year-old child who has iron deficiency anemia. She asks you how to administer the iron in relation to the child's meals.

Iron is best absorbed in its ferrous form (2^+) and in an acidic environment because the low pH promotes the activity of an enzyme that reduces iron from its ferric form (3^+) to the ferrous form (2^+) and keeps it in this state. Iron should be given in the morning on an empty stomach (when gastric acidity is high) and with vitamin C (ie, ascorbic acid in the form of orange/grapefruit juice) which helps maintain iron in its ferrous (2^+) form.

You are working up a patient with isolated macrocytic anemia and an otherwise normal CBC. You find that his B_{12} and folate levels are normal. What else should be considered in the differential?

Hypothyroidism is another cause of isolated macrocytic anemia that should be considered if B_{12} and folate levels are normal (ie, check [thyroid-stimulating hormone] TSH).

A 7-month-old African-American infant presents to his pediatrician with symmetric swelling of his hands and feet. For what type of infections will he be at risk in the future?

Dactylitis or hand-foot syndrome is a common presenting symptom of sickle cell disease; it is often the child's first vaso-occlusive crisis. After their spleen has been removed or auto infarcted, patients with sickle cell disease are at risk for infection with encapsulated organisms, such as *Streptococcus pneumoniae, Haemophilus influenzae,* and *Salmonella.*

In a patient with sickle cell disease and osteomyelitis, what is the most common cause of infection?

Staphylococcus aureus, which is the most common cause of osteomyelitis in all other patients, is also the most common cause of osteomyelitis in sickle cell patients. Although *Salmonella* is also a frequent cause of osteomyelitis in sickle cell patients, *S aureus* still predominates.

What is the etiology of sickle cell disease?

Substitution of glutamine for valine at the sixth position on the beta globin chain. Sickle cell disease is autosomal recessive—therefore, both parents must be carriers.

What cardiovascular complications are sickle cell patients at risk of developing and why?

1. Anemia-related complications: Severe anemia leads to a hyperdynamic circulation from a compensatory increase in cardiac output.
2. Hemolysis-related complications: When sickled cells undergo hemolysis, they release arginase, which breaks down arginine. Since arginine is a precursor of nitric oxide (NO), a known vasodilator, these patients develop increased basal pulmonary vascular tone, secondary to decreased NO levels.
3. Vaso-occlusion-related complications: Microinfarctions in the heart over time can lead to rupture of chordae tendineae and valvular disease.

An Rh positive (+) infant is born to an Rh negative (–) mother and is jaundiced. The mother is upset and states, "My first child was also Rh+ but never got jaundiced!" How do you counsel this mother?

During the mother's first pregnancy with an Rh+ child, she was sensitized and began developing antibodies late in the pregnancy. These antibodies crossed the placenta during her second pregnancy, were exposed to the baby's Rh+ RBCs and caused hemolysis. While this happened in the intrauterine environment, the bilirubin was cleared via the placenta and by the mother's liver. Jaundice (indirect hyperbilirubinemia) results postnatally because the baby's liver is immature and cannot effectively clear the bilirubin.

What is erythroblastosis fetalis (EF)? How do you diagnose EF postnatally?

EF is caused by transplacental passage of maternal antibodies directed at paternal antigens that are present on fetal RBCs (from either Rh or more commonly ABO incompatibility), resulting in increased RBC destruction. Clinical signs include severe anemia, hepatosplenomegaly, edema, and hydrops (fluid throughout the body's tissues). After birth, a direct Coombs test will be positive, indicating antibodies are present on the patient's RBCs. The blood types and Rh status of the infant and the mother should also be determined.

A 6-year-old girl is found to have splenomegaly on a routine physical examination. Blood tests show Hgb 8.5, an increased reticulocyte count, and hyperbilirubinemia. Coombs test is negative. Further questioning reveals that her father had a cholecystectomy in the past. What do you see on a peripheral smear?

Spherocytes on peripheral smear are crucial in diagnosing hereditary spherocytosis. RBCs will also have increased osmotic fragility.

A 5-year-old patient with hereditary spherocytosis is scheduled for splenectomy. What vaccines does he need before his surgery?

Splenectomy predisposes patients to infections with encapsulated organisms such as *S pneumoniae*, *Neisseria meningitides*, and *H influenzae*. Therefore he must be given pneumococcal, meningococcal, and Hib vaccinations prior to splenectomy.

A 4-year-old girl is brought to her pediatrician after her mother noticed bruising on her thighs, calves, and forearms. Her only recent past medical history (PMH) includes varicella infection 1 month ago. Her CBC shows a normal WBC and Hgb with a low platelet count. What is the appropriate treatment?

Idiopathic thrombocytopenic purpura (ITP) is treated with IV immune globulin (IVIg) or WinRho in Rh+ patients and IV steroids. Splenectomy is reserved for patients with severe or chronic ITP, or for children older than 4 years.

A patient admitted to the hospital had a routine tonsillectomy surgery 3 days ago and on a routine CBC is noted to have an Hgb of 8. She is not tachycardic, tachypnic, or diaphoretic. Do you want to give her a blood transfusion?

No. The patient is not symptomatic from her anemia, and the risks of transfusion are too great to transfuse with no clinical indication. We need to treat the patient, not the "numbers," especially since this was a benign surgery. Risks of transfusion include immune-mediated reactions (such as with blood group system [ABO] incompatibility), infections, and fever.

A child presents to the emergency room (ER) with vomiting, diarrhea, and marked cyanosis. She is lethargic, is not in respiratory distress, and has a normal O_2 saturation by pulse oximetry. With what should she be treated?

This patient has gastroenteritis complicated by methemoglobinemia, which is treated with methylene blue. Methemoglobin is produced by the oxidation of ferrous iron in hemoglobin into ferric iron, which prevents oxygen transport. In acquired methemoglobinemia, toxins (such as antimalarial drugs and nitrates in well water) can increase the percentage of methemoglobin, interfering with oxygen transport. Methylene blue helps convert the ferric iron back to ferrous iron, thus allowing hemoglobin to transport oxygen.

A 3-year-old girl, recently recovered from a diarrheal illness, now presents with pallor, irritability, and hematuria. What type of RBCs do you expect to see on a peripheral blood smear?

Schistocytes are commonly seen with hemolytic anemia, secondary to mechanical disruption. Given the history of diarrhea and the current symptoms, hemolytic uremic syndrome (HUS) is a likely diagnosis.

What regulates RBC production? Does this change after birth?

Erythropoietin (EPO) regulates RBC production in the bone marrow. Prior to birth, EPO is produced in the liver, and after birth, it is produced in the kidney. RBCs are produced in the marrow of almost the entire skeleton during the last third trimester and early infancy. With age, only the marrow of the vertebrae, sternum, pelvis, scapula, and the proximal ends of the long bones are involved in RBC production.

A 4-week-old newborn comes into your office for a regularly scheduled newborn visit. The infant is growing and feeding well, but you decide to check a CBC anyway. Compared to his CBC at birth, his hemoglobin has decreased from 17 mg/dL to 12 mg/dL. What is wrong with this infant?

Nothing is wrong with this newborn. This drop in hemoglobin is expected and is termed "physiological anemia of infancy." RBCs last only 90 days in infants, compared to 120 days in adults. Furthermore, rates of erythropoeisis are much decreased after birth, especially relative to the overproduction of RBCs in utero. This combination of increased destruction and decreased production of RBCs leads to this drop in hemoglobin immediately after birth.

When would you expect hemoglobin to rise again?

Erythropoiesis starts again after 6 to 8 weeks of life, leading to an increase in hemoglobin and reticulocyte count. Hemoglobin is then maintained at approximately 12.5 mg/dL.

An infant is born preterm, and is admitted to the neonatal intensive care unit (NICU). As you monitor his laboratory values, you notice his hemoglobin decrease to as low as 9 mg/dL. What is happening?

This is likely "anemia of prematurity" and represents an exaggerated physiologic anemia. Like the term infant, there is increased destruction and decreased production of RBCs. However, in the premature infant, EPO production is not adequate for the degree of anemia. Other factors also contribute to the anemia of prematurity, including frequent phlebotomy and rapid expansion of blood volume with growth.

A 5-year-old boy is found to have elevated levels of fetal hemoglobin. What conditions may this child have, which would explain the increased levels of fetal hemoglobin?

Fetal hemoglobin is the predominant type of hemoglobin in newborns and continues to constitute 90% of hemoglobin at 6 months. By 1 year, levels usually fall to almost zero. However, in patients with hemoglobinopathies, aplastic anemia or thalassemias, fetal hemoglobin declines much slower and may persist throughout life.

A 4-year-old girl, recently immigrated from a developing country, is found on a routine screening CBC to have what appears to be iron deficiency anemia. What further test must be performed to understand the etiology?

The patient's stool must be checked for occult blood loss. Hookworm infection is the most common cause of gastrointestinal blood loss worldwide, and chronic blood loss can lead to iron deficiency anemia. Other causes of chronic gastrointestinal blood loss include peptic ulcer disease and Meckel diverticulum.

A 6-year-old girl is brought to her pediatrician for complaints of pallor and fatigue for the past 2 weeks. She is afebrile. Her CBC shows anemia, neutropenia, and thrombocytopenia. What did you see (and not see) on examination?

With aplastic anemia you would expect to see pallor and bruising on physical examination, but would not see hepatosplenomegaly or lymphadenopathy.

A newborn boy continues to bleed after routine circumcision. What is the most likely diagnosis?

Hemophilia A (factor VIII deficiency) is the most common type of hemophilia, and is X-linked. Fifty percent of males with severe hemophilia will bleed after circumcision. However, boys with von Willebrand (vWF) disease may also bleed after circumcision, so further testing must be done.

Why will children with hemophilia complain of joint pain and swelling?

Patients with hemophilia are at risk to develop hemarthroses, which are defined as bleeding into the joints. This occurs usually at first in the ankles, then the knees, and elbows.

A premenstrual young girl is brought to the ER for continued epistaxis. On further questioning, the parents report that the child has had multiple episodes of epistaxis in addition to frequent ecchymoses. What will you see on CBC?

A normal platelet count! This child likely has von Willebrand disease, the most common hereditary bleeding disorder. This disorder is autosomal dominant, and results in defective platelet function. Platelet count will be normal, but bleeding time and partial thromboplastin time (PTT) will be prolonged.

You are working up an 8-year-old boy who bruises easily and has trouble stopping his nosebleeds. You find that his prothrombin time/international normalized ratio (PT/INR), PTT, and platelet count are all normal with a prolonged bleeding time. What should be considered in the differential?

This could still be von Willebrand disease as it does not always cause a prolonged PTT. However, if testing for vWF is negative on at least two occasions consider a platelet function disorder such as Bernard-Soulier (defect in glycoprotein 1b) or Glanzmann thrombasthenia (defect in glycoprotein 2b/3a). Also factor 13 is the only factor not accounted for in the PT/PTT tests, and would not produce abnormal results, but the bleeding is more severe and would likely have presented earlier than age 8.

You see target cells under the microscope in a patient's blood smear. What is your differential diagnosis?

Liver disease, iron deficiency, sickle cell disease, thalassemia, and postsplenectomy all result in target cells, which are caused by an increased surface area to volume ratio.

You see spiculated red blood cells known as burr cells under the microscope in the blood smear of a patient with hyperkalemia, hypocalcemia, and a pericardial effusion. What is the underlying diagnosis?

This patient likely has uremia and chronic renal failure, which has resulted in the production of burr cells. Burr cells are also seen in liver disease but this patient's electrolyte abnormalities are more indicative of kidney disease. Burr cells are thought to develop in kidney disease due to deficiency in erythroid precursors in the patient's bone marrow.

A child returns from his vacation to southeast Asia with periodic high fever, chills, and splenomegaly. What diagnostic test would make the diagnosis?

The patient likely has malaria, which is the most common cause of hemolysis worldwide. Other signs and symptoms of malaria include jaundice and diaphoresis. Malaria is diagnosed by identification of the organisms on blood smears obtained when the patient is actively febrile.

What is the appropriate treatment for this illness?

Treatment depends on the specific organism and the geographic location, as some areas are resistant to chloroquine. If chloroquine resistant, mefloquine should be used.

A 3-year-old boy with a family history of nosebleeds and excessive bleeding after surgical procedures presents to your office with his third episode of epistaxis this month. In reviewing his most recent CBC, you notice a normal platelet count. What medications should be avoided in this patient?

This patient likely has von Willebrand disease, the most common hereditary bleeding disorder. A mutation on chromosome 12, inherited in an autosomal dominant fashion, results in a deficiency of factor VIII-R, which is necessary for normal platelet function. Aspirin and nonsteroidal antiinflammatory drugs (NSAIDs) should not be used in patients with von Willebrand disease as they further interfere with platelet function.

Define Virchow triad.

The triad of endothelial damage, hypercoagulability, and stasis describe the states which predispose to thrombus formation. This can then lead to deep vein thromboses, pulmonary embolisms, or strokes. Trauma, immobilization, lupus, protein C or protein S deficiency, polycythemia vera, and sickle cell anemia can all predispose to thrombus formation.

ONCOLOGY

A child complaining of severe abdominal pain associated with vomiting is brought to the operating room (OR) for an appendectomy. Instead of an inflamed appendix, however, the surgeons find a mass. Biopsy reveals that this mass originated from cells within Peyer patches, close to the ileocecal junction. What is the associated genetic mutation?

The cancer described is likely Burkitt lymphoma, and often involved translocation of the c-myc oncogene. Of note, Burkitt lymphoma is the fastest-growing malignant tumor in humans.

Who is at an increased risk for acute lymphoblastic leukemia (ALL)?

ALL is the most common childhood malignancy. Children with Down syndrome, siblings of children with ALL, children with congenital immunodeficiency syndromes, and those exposed to ionizing radiation are at increased risk for developing ALL.

A 9-year-old Caucasian girl has been recently diagnosed with ALL. Her WBC on diagnosis was 60,000. She has no central nervous system (CNS) involvement and pathology has not revealed any chromosomal translocation abnormalities. Is she a "high-risk" patient with a poorer prognosis or is she considered to be "standard-risk?"

She is a "high-risk" patient because her WBC count on diagnosis was greater than 50,000. Other determinants of high-risk patients are: (1) age less than 1 year and greater than 10 years, (2) chromosomal translocation abnormalities, (3) CNS involvement, (4) African-American or Hispanic patients, (5) males, (6) malignant cells with hypoploidy (<45 chromosomes).

What is the Philadelphia chromosome?

A translocation between chromosomes 9 and 22 results in the coding of a new tyrosine kinase with increased activity. This translocation is highly associated with chronic myelogenous leukemia (CML) (it is seen in >90% of patients with CML), but is also seen in less than 5% of children with ALL and in less than 2% of children with acute myelogenous leukemia (AML). When present in ALL, it is associated with a worse prognosis, placing the child in the "high-risk" category.

The mother of a 2-year-old boy reports that she has noticed when bathing him that he has a swelling in his abdomen. What else should you look for on physical examination?

The abdomen must be examined to determine the nature of this "swelling" or mass. Wilms tumor is the most common abdominal tumor in children. If suspected, the signs of Wilms tumor-associated syndromes must be investigated, such as partial or complete hemihypertrophy, aniridia, and genitourinary abnormalities, including hypospadias, cryptorchidism, and ambiguous genitalia.

A 17-year-old adolescent boy presents to the ER complaining of knee pain and swelling, although he denies any recent trauma or injury. He also denies weight loss, fever, and lethargy. X-ray reveals a "sunburst lesion." What is the next step in treatment?

A "sunburst lesion" is typical of osteosarcoma, the most common primary malignant bone tumor in children and adolescents. Unlike Ewing sarcoma, systemic signs and symptoms are usually not present on presentation of osteosarcoma. The most important next step for this patient is determining whether metastasis is already present, as this determines prognosis. Therefore, this patient needs further imaging to look for metastatic lesions.

A parent brings his child to your office because she is "just not acting like herself." The physical examination at first appears normal, but on further inspection, you notice nystagmus. If this child has an intracranial mass, where is it likely located?

Two-thirds of pediatric intracranial tumors are located in the posterior fossa. In addition, nystagmus is a classic finding in posterior fossa tumors.

An 8-year-old child is brought to the ER because of worsening headache and changes in mental status. Imaging of the head reveals hydrocephalus and a mass. Rosenthal fibers are seen on biopsy. What is this child's prognosis?

Rosenthal fibers are diagnostic of cerebellar astrocytoma, the most common pediatric posterior fossa tumor. Hydrocephalus is a common finding in all posterior fossa tumors because the mass obstructs the flow of cerebrospinal fluid (CSF). Astrocytomas are treated with surgical resection; with good prognosis the 5 year survival rate is greater than 90%.

A 6-year-old child complains of early morning headache, and constant back-pain. The headache has been worsening over the past month, and is now associated with vomiting. A magnetic resonance imaging (MRI) shows a posterior fossa tumor. What is the most likely diagnosis?

Medulloblastomas are the second most common type of pediatric posterior fossa tumors, but are the most prevalent type of brain tumor in children under 7 years of age. Furthermore, the patient's backpain implies metastasis, and "drop metastases" are common in medulloblastoma.

An infant is noted to have a white pupillary reflex at a routine well-visit. What is the most likely diagnosis?

Cataracts are the most common cause of leukocoria, but the patient must be evaluated for retinoblastoma. The diagnosis of retinoblastoma is made by direct visualization during a detailed eye examination.

A 2-year-old child is brought to the pediatrician with the complaint of constipation. Further questioning reveals a 3-month history of fatigue and loss of appetite. Physical examination is significant for an abdominal mass, and eventual biopsy shows small, round, blue cells. What tumor markers would be elevated in the urine?

With neuroblastoma, homovanillic acid (HVA) and vanillylmandelic acid (VMA) are elevated in the urine.

What genetic characteristics if found on the biopsied neuroblastoma cells would suggest a poor prognosis?

Amplification of myc-n, a protoonco-gene, as well as diploidy (having a chromosome number of 46) both portend a poor prognosis in neuroblastoma.

List the most common toxicities of the following chemotherapy agents: (1) cisplatin (2) bleomycin (3) doxorubicin (4) vincristine

It is important to be aware of toxicities in addition to patient comorbidities when choosing a chemotherapy regimen: (1) cisplatin—acoustic nerve damage and renal toxicity; (2) bleomycin—pulmonary fibrosis; (3) doxorubicin—cardiotoxicity; (4) vincristine—peripheral neuropathies.

A 5-year-old patient, previously growing well, begins to "fall off his growth curve." Further investigation reveals hypothyroidism, with low thyroid-stimulating hormone (TSH) and low free T4. Imaging reveals a cystic calcified lesion in the suprasellar region. What is the most likely diagnosis?

Craniopharyngiomas are derived from Rathke pouch and commonly present with pituitary hypofunction. This patient has presented with growth failure caused by central hypothyroidism. The calcifications and cysts seen on imaging are very typical of craniopharyngiomas.

CLINICAL VIGNETTES

A toxic-appearing patient, admitted with fever and signs of sepsis, is now bleeding from this morning's venipuncture site. His capillary refill time is delayed and his hands and feet are cool, while a new petechial rash and purpura are developing. What is the etiology of this disorder?

This patient is most likely in disseminated intravascular coagulation (DIC). DIC is caused by the deposition of fibrin in the microvasculature, consumption of coagulation factors, and generation of thrombin. The process is primarily thrombotic; consumption of the clotting factors leads to bleeding.

What conditions can precipitate DIC?

Severe sepsis, leukemias, and other malignancies, lupus, obstetric calamities, severe hepatic dysfunction, immunologic reactions, and trauma can all precipitate DIC.

What laboratory abnormalities do you expect with DIC?

Prothrombin time (PT) and partial thromboplastin time (PTT) are prolonged, fibrinogen and platelet count are low, and the d-dimer level is elevated.

What is most effective treatment for DIC?

The most effective therapy for DIC is to treat the underlying cause.

CHAPTER 9

Infectious Disease

A 2-day-old newborn develops respiratory distress that leads to shock and disseminated intravascular coagulation (DIC). What organisms may cause this illness and where was the baby exposed to the pathogens?

This baby has early-onset sepsis after exposure to pathogens from mother's reproductive tract during delivery. Common organisms that cause early-onset sepsis include the "GEL" organisms, group B *Streptococcus* (GBS), *Escherichia coli*, and *Listeria*. Other pathogens include herpes simplex virus (HSV) (though it typically presents in 2nd-3rd week of life), nontypeable *Haemophilus influenzae* and *Klebsiella.*

What is appropriate antibiotic coverage for patients with early bacterial sepsis?

Ampicillin and a third-generation cephalosporin, such as cefotaxime, are good choices for antibiotics in these patients. Ampicillin works to combat *Listeria* and GBS, while cefotaxime also fights GBS as well as *E coli*. Gentamicin is another option to target gram-negative organisms such as *E coli.*

If a 20-day-old newborn develops fever, what systems could be the source of infection?

Possible locations of infection include the urinary tract, the blood, and the meninges, so cerebrospinal fluid (CSF) cultures, protein, glucose, and cell counts, blood cultures, and urine cultures should be sent. The bones and joints may also be seeded when a patient is bacteremic and lung infections causing pneumonia are other sources.

Why is a third-generation cephalosporin good choice for late-onset sepsis?

Cefotaxime or ceftriaxone may be used for late-onset sepsis because they cover common organisms in late-onset sepsis that include *Streptococcus pneumoniae, Neisseria meningitidis, E coli,* and GBS. Note that this class of antibiotics does not provide ideal coverage for *Staphylococcus aureus.*

A premature 24-day-old infant in the neonatal intensive care unit (NICU) with an indwelling central venous line develops signs of sepsis. What organisms should be considered in addition to the pathogens that cause late-onset sepsis?

This patient likely has been exposed to nosocomial pathogens and may have developed sepsis from a line infection. Causative organisms may include methicillin-resistant *S aureus* (MRSA), *Staphylococcus epidermidis, Klebsiella, Serratia, Pseudomonas,* and *Candida albicans.* Vancomycin and amphotericin B may be added for coverage based on the suspected pathogen.

A 1-year-old boy is brought to the emergency department (ED) due to fever and increased crying at nighttime. He is bottle-fed and attends day care. On physical examination, his left tympanic membrane is erythematous and has decreased light reflex. What is the most likely causative organism?

Streptococcus pneumoniae causes about 50% of all bacterial acute otitis media infections. Nontypeable *H influenzae, Moraxella catarrhalis,* and group A *Streptococcus* come in second, third, and fourth, respectively. Group A *Streptococcus* is usually seen in older children.

What is the recommended antibiotic treatment for uncomplicated otitis media?

American Academy of Pediatrics (AAP) recommendations include: high-dose amoxicillin (90 mg/kg/d) for 10 days. Alternative option for mild cases is ceftriaxone IV/IM for one dose (50 mg/kg). Severe infection, treatment failure cases may change antibiotic to amoxicillin/clavulanate or ceftriaxone for 3 days.

The father of your patient tells you that this is the patient's third ear infection in 6 months and that the past two involved "yellowish drainage." What is your next step?

Chronic suppurative otitis media is usually caused by *Pseudomonas aeruginosa* or *S aureus.* In addition to antibiotic treatment, this patient may be referred to ENT for possible tympanostomy tube placement.

Which organism is most likely responsible for "otitis conjunctivitis syndrome"?

Nontypable *H influenzae.*

A 1-year-old boy with multiple food allergies comes to the clinic for his first flu shot. You are called into the vaccine room as the patient appears to be having an anaphylactic reaction. What is the most likely cause?

The influenza vaccine contains egg protein, thus this patient most likely is allergic to eggs. In such children, the vaccine should not be given. If it is necessary, allergy skin testing should be done prior.

A pregnant adolescent presents to clinic asking for the varicella vaccine as she realized she had never received it. She wants to make sure her fetus is protected from the virus. Should the physician give her the vaccine at this time?

The varicella vaccine is a live-virus vaccine and should not be given in pregnancy or in immunodeficiency states. Other live virus vaccines include measles, mumps, rubella (MMR), rotavirus, oral typhoid, and yellow fever. Oral polio was live-attenuated as well, but is no longer used in the United States.

What are the original six exanthems of childhood?

1. Measles, rubeola
2. Scarlet fever
3. Rubella
4. Filatov-Dukes
5. Erythema infectiosum
6. Roseola infantum

An 11-month-old infant presents to the ED with a rash that started on her head and is now spreading downward. Her eyes are red and she has a cough. On examination you confirm the presence of a maculopapular rash with confluent areas, conjunctivitis, and Koplik spots on the buccal mucosa. What future complications would you worry about in this patient?

This patient most likely has measles. Known complications are pneumonia, myocarditis, blindness (more in underdeveloped countries or with malnutrition), and subacute sclerosing panencephalitis.

A worried grandmother brings her grandchild into the clinic because of a rash. She states she noticed that the 3-year-old's cheeks were "bright red" this morning and now his extremities appear red also. On examination, you immediately identify the "slapped-cheek" appearance with a reticular rash. What is the diagnosis?

Parvovirus B19 is the cause of erythema infectiosum (Fifth disease). *Parvovirus* can also cause aplastic crises in sickle cell patients and hydrops fetalis in cases of intrauterine infection.

A 9-year-old boy comes to your office with fever and headache for 3 days and a rash that started yesterday on his extremities and now has spread to his chest and back. About 1 week ago, he went on a camping trip in the mountains. On examination you notice petechiae with some blanching erythematous macules involving the palms and soles. What is the most likely diagnosis and how is it spread?

Given the characteristic rash, the most likely diagnosis is Rocky Mountain Spotted Fever (RMSF). This is seen mostly in the southeastern United States and is transmitted by ticks (*Dermacentor variabilis, Dermacentor andersoni*) which serve as the vector for the causative organism *Rickettsia rickettsii*. Symptoms generally appear 5 to 11 days after tick bite.

In Rocky Mountain Spotted Fever, what laboratory findings occur?

There is no appropriate diagnostic test; however, antibodies can be detected approximately 10 days after symptoms. In addition, patients are found to have low albumin, decreased platelets, increased transaminases, and hyponatremia.

Name and describe the three stages of Lyme disease.

Early localized: 7 to 10 days (can be up to 30 days) after tick bite; erythema migrans rash at site of bite, fevers, headache, generalized malaise, myalgias. Early disseminated: days to weeks after early localized; multiple erythema migrans, CN VII palsy (facial nerve), meningitis, heart block, carditis. Late: more than 6 weeks after bite; arthritis, subacute encephalopathy.

A child comes into the ED with a classic erythema migrans rash (single lesion) and complaints of fever. What would be your treatment of choice for Lyme disease in this patient?

Treatment of early localized Lyme disease is usually with amoxicillin or cefuroxime. Children greater than 8 years old and nonpregnant adults generally use doxycycline.

A 2-year-old child with chickenpox is brought into the office with his mother. She is concerned about her other children acquiring chickenpox as they all attend the same day care. When was the affected child most likely exposed to varicella?

Most patients develop symptoms (fever, fatigue, classic rash) approximately 10 to 20 days postexposure.

Describe the typical varicella rash.

Erythematous lesions usually start on the face and spreading downward. Lesions begin as macules, then evolve to vesicles, and then develop a crusted surface—various stages of lesions may be seen at once. The lesions are usually very pruritic in nature.

The same worried mother from above asks you what complications of varicella to expect. What do you tell her are known complications of untreated varicella infections?

The most common complications include secondary bacterial infection, pneumonia, and encephalitis. Current recommendations do not indicate treatment with acyclovir in routine, uncomplicated cases.

A 12-year-old boy comes to your office with 2 weeks of clear nasal discharge, pain over the frontal sinuses, and cough. Which organisms are most commonly involved?

Similar to acute otitis media, *S pneumoniae, H influenzae,* and *M catarrhalis* are the most common causative organisms in sinusitis. Thus, antibiotic coverage is generally the same.

In addition to that described above, what is the other common presentation of acute sinusitis?

The two common presentations of acute sinusitis in children include persistent headache, photophobia, and pain over the sinuses exacerbated by moving the head forward, nasal discharge and cough, or acute onset of high fever and purulent nasal discharge.

In chronic sinusitis, which additional organisms must be considered?

Chronic sinusitis is defined by at least 12 weeks of symptoms. In addition to above organisms, one must also consider *S aureus,* anaerobes, fungus (especially in immunocompromised), and *P aeruginosa* (especially in cystic fibrosis patients).

Name potential complications of sinusitis.

Meningitis, cavernous sinus thrombosis, orbital cellulitis, brain abscess

During your adolescent medicine rotation, you see a 15-year-old girl who tells you immediately that she has a fever, sore throat, and "no energy." Her best friend has the same symptoms. On examination you find the classic signs of Epstein-Barr virus infection (EBV)—pharyngitis, lymphadenopathy, and splenomegaly. What laboratory findings would support your diagnosis?

In EBV-associated mononucleosis, the WBC count may be increased or decreased. There are usually more than 50% lymphocytes and more than 10% atypical lymphocytes. Thrombocytopenia and increased aspartate aminotransferase (AST) and alanine aminotransferase (ALT) may be seen. The monospot test detects the heterophil antibodies (which cause RBC agglutination). This test is less sensitive in younger children. The Epstein-Barr viral capsid IgM will present first, usually in the first week. The Epstein-Barr nuclear antigen (EBNA) will not be positive for 4 to 6 months.

Before leaving the clinic, the patient above asks you if she can play in her soccer tournament tomorrow. What advice do you give her?

No. Patients with EBV-associated splenomegaly should be advised against contact sports due to the increased risk of splenic rupture for 3 to 6 weeks and should be cleared by their doctor.

What is the major difference in the presentation of EBV infection in young children versus adolescents/adults?

Most EBV infections in young children are asymptomatic compared to the adolescent population who commonly present as the patient described earlier.

A 5-year-old girl is brought to the ED with chief complaint of fever to 103°F, headache, photophobia, and increased irritability. What examination findings may you see in a child with meningitis?

Signs of increased intracranial pressure may present as full fontanelle in infants, or as papilledema or cranial nerve palsies in older children. Signs of meningeal irritation include nuchal rigidity, Brudzinski sign (hip and knee flexion with passive neck flexion), and Kernig sign (pain with knee extension when hips are flexed). In infants and younger children signs and symptoms are more general (ie, irritability, sleepiness, hypo- or hyperthermia, poor feeding).

In our patient above, a lumbar puncture was performed by the ED resident. The cerebrospinal fluid results showed: 2000 WBC, 80% neutrophils, glucose 30, protein 150. How would you use these results to determine the type of meningitis?

Based on her presentation and the CSF values, this patient most likely has bacterial meningitis. General guidelines exist to aide in the differentiation of meningitis causes (to help in treatment decisions)—mainly between septic and aseptic. (See Table 9-1.) It is important to remember that cerebrospinal fluid (CSF) findings may differ by age and by stage of disease.

Table 9-1 CSF Findings in Bacterial Versus Viral Meningitis

	Bacterial	Viral
WBC (per mm^3)	>500	<500
Neutrophils	>80%	<50%
Protein	>100	<100
Glucose	<40	>40

What is the most common etiology of meningitis in this patient?

The most common bacterial organisms in this age group are *S pneumoniae* and *N meningitidis*. See Table 9-2 for lists of the most common organisms by age group.

Table 9-2 Common Organisms in Bacterial Meningitis by Age

<1 mo	Group B *Streptococcus, E coli, Listeria monocytogenes*, gram-negative rods, *S pneumoniae, H influenzae* (non type B) (in hospitalized preterm infants—coagulase-negative *Staphylococcus*)
1-23 mo	*Streptococcus pneumoniae, N meningitidis*, group B *Streptococcus*
2-18 y	*Streptococcus pneumoniae, N meningitidis*

Which antibiotics should be added to broad-spectrum coverage in cases of neonatal meningitis?

In childhood meningitis, broad-spectrum antibiotics usually include third-generation cephalosporin and vancomycin. In neonates, ampicillin should be started for group B *Streptococcus* and *L monocytogenes*.

Which vaccine routinely given to infants has decreased the overall incidence of bacterial meningitis in children?

Haemophilus influenzae type b (Hib) was a common cause of bacterial meningitis, especially in infants and young children, prior to administration of the vaccine. It is important to remember that non type B and non typeable strains of *H influenzae* still remain possible causes of infections in this age group. The pneumococcal 7-valent vaccine protects children from meningitis caused by *S pneumoniae*.

Name the most common hepatitis viruses and their modes of transmission.

Hepatitis A, B, C, D are the most common in the United States (hepatitis E is also found outside of the United States). Hepatitis A and E are transmitted via fecal-oral route, commonly via contaminated water supply. Hepatitis B, C, and D are transmitted via infected bodily fluids or via vertical transmission of mother to fetus.

A 5-year-old boy presenting with scleral icterus, and jaundice had a hepatitis B panel sent as part of his workup. His results were the following: hepatitis B surface antibody (HBsAb)—positive; hepatitis B core antibody (HBcAb)—negative; hepatitis B surface antigen (HBsAg)—negative. What disease state do these results indicate for this patient?

This laboratory finding implies appropriate immunity to hepatitis B in a child who has received his immunization series. Thus, the findings of clinical jaundice in this patient must be worked up further.

See Table 9-3 for details on diagnosing hepatitis B virus (HBV) disease states through laboratory findings.

Table 9-3 Hepatitis B Disease States

	Acute HBV	Resolved HBV	Chronic HBV	Immunized
HBsAg	+	−	+	−
HBsAb	−	+	−	+
HBcAb	+	+	+	−
HBeAg	+/−	−	+/−	−
HBeAb	−	+	+/−	−

In addition to routine neonatal care, how should infants born to hepatitis B surface antigen (HBsAg)-positive mothers be managed?

These infants should receive both the first dose of the hepatitis B vaccine and the hepatitis B immune globulin within 12 hours of birth to reduce the risk of transmission.

Similarly, how should infants born to hepatitis C infected mothers be managed?

Although there has been shown to be a risk of vertical transmission of hepatitis C, there is currently no preventive therapy for newborns.

A 3-year-old child with fever and diarrhea comes into your clinic. On history, you find that the patient returned from a family vacation to southeast Asia a few days ago. As per the mother, the patient has decreased energy, frequent crying episodes associated with the frequent stooling, and abdominal pain. Which common causes of bacterial diarrhea are part of your differential diagnosis?

Infectious diarrhea can be viral, bacterial, or parasitic. The most commonly seen bacterial organisms are *Shigella* species, *Salmonella* species, *Yersinia enterocolitica, Campylobacter jejuni,* and *E coli* ("SSYCE").

Of the bacterial organisms above, which two are associated with hemolytic uremic syndrome (HUS) and what is the believed mechanism?

Endotoxins (Shiga toxin, Shiga-like toxin) produced by *Shigella dysenteriae* and *E coli* (O157:H7) are believed to cause HUS. *Streptococcus pneumoniae* can also cause HUS. This disease is characterized by a triad of microangiopathic hemolytic anemia, acute renal failure, and thrombocytopenia.

A 10-year-old child who is currently on a prolonged course of antibiotics for a persistent leg abscess present with crampy abdominal pain and loose stools. In addition to advice on hydration, what treatment would you initiate?

Given the antibiotic regimen and the symptom history this patient most likely has *Clostridium difficile* pseudomembranous colitis. Metronidazole is the recommended treatment.

Which parasite found in the United States is associated with acute gastroenteritis, abdominal cramps, nausea, vomiting, and weight loss and what is the treatment of choice?

Giardia lamblia can cause symptoms as mentioned earlier, but can also cause chronic malabsorption and failure to thrive in children. Treatment is usually with metronidazole.

A 17-year-old adolescent girl presents to the adolescent clinic with severe abdominal pain and fever. She has had multiple sexually transmitted infections and she is still having unprotected sex. On examination, she has severe cervical motion tenderness and adnexal tenderness. In cases of pelvic inflammatory disease (PID), what two organisms are most commonly found and treated?

Neisseria gonorrhoeae and *Chlamydia trachomatis* are the most commonly found in the United States. Treatment regimens differ based on severity, follow-up, and age. Outpatient regimens include third-generation cephalosporins for *Neisseria* and azithromycin and/or doxycycline for *Chlamydia*.

What are the known infectious complications of PID?

Neisseria can spread and cause oligo-or polyarthritis. Untreated *Chlamydia* can lead to reactive arthritis (formerly known as Reiter syndrome) which includes urethritis, conjunctivitis, and arthritis. Either organism can lead to Fitz-Hugh-Curtis syndrome (perihepatitis), decreased fertility, increased risk of ectopic pregnancy, and tubo-ovarian abscess.

How is HPV (human papillomavirus) transmitted and what can be done to prevent it?

HPV is transmitted through genital contact, even when infected partner has no signs or symptoms of infection. Vaccines are now available for both male and female adolescents. While the vaccines do not contain all existing serotypes, they have been shown to help prevent genital warts and cervical cancer.

What are the most common bacteria when dealing with skin or musculoskeletal infections?

Staphylococcus aureus and *Streptococcus pyogenes.*

What is the mechanism of resistance for MRSA (methicillin-resistant *S aureus*) and what treatment options exist for MRSA infections?

Resistance mechanism involves alteration of the penicillin-binding protein. Thus one cannot use beta-lactam antibiotics effectively. Antibiotic options to treat MRSA include: clindamycin, TMP-SMX, vancomycin, linezolid. Local resistance/sensitivity patterns must be taken into account.

What is the most common cause of severe diarrhea among children worldwide?

Rotavirus. Prior to initiation of the rotavirus vaccine, rotavirus was responsible for approximately 520,000 deaths globally per year.

CLINICAL VIGNETTES

A 6-month-old infant recently adopted from a small village in southern Africa is brought to your clinic for a routine visit. On the limited history you obtain from the adoptive parents, you learn that the baby has been very "sick," and has not been gaining weight appropriately. The biological mother also is reportedly "very sick." On examination you notice generalized lymphadenopathy, failure to thrive (<5% for height and weight), hepatosplenomegaly, oral candidiasis, and developmental delay. You immediately suspect HIV, what tests should you perform to confirm diagnosis in this patient?

In cases of possible perinatal/vertical transmission of HIV, the test of choice for confirming infection is usually HIV DNA polymerase chain reaction (PCR). In most settings, two positive results on separate samples give you the diagnosis of HIV. HIV antibody and cultures are also available, though are used less routinely. It is important to remember that this patient may still have maternal antibodies in his system.

What are the established risk factors for perinatal HIV transmission?

The following are believed to increase the risk of perinatal transmission of HIV: monotherapy of antiretrovirals during pregnancy, high maternal viral load, prolonged rupture of membranes, fetal instrumentation during labor, vaginal delivery, and breastfeeding.

While HIV-positive infants and young children may present as described above, how would you expect an affected neonate to present?

Infants and young children usually present with generalized lymphadenopathy, hepatosplenomegaly, recurrent infections, failure to thrive, and even neurological disease—whereas newborns are mostly asymptomatic at birth. Some newborns may have lymphadenopathy and hepatosplenomegaly.

What types of infections are HIV-positive children at risk for acquiring?

Due to the helper T-cell deficiency, these children are at risk for recurrent bacterial infections, fungal disease, disseminated HSV or cytomegalovirus (CMV) infections, and *Mycobacterium avium* infections. In children, the AIDS-defining illnesses are *Pneumocystis carinii* pneumonia, lymphocytic interstitial pneumonitis, and CNS lymphoma.

What are the treatment options for children with HIV?

Just as in adults, the available treatment options are constantly changing. The currently recommended regimens include: nucleoside reverse transcriptase inhibitors (NRTIs), nonnucleoside reverse transcriptase inhibitors (NNRTIs), protease inhibitors, fusion inhibitors, and immune modulators. Each regimen is tailored to the specific disease stage of the individual child; however, it is believed that polytherapy is superior to monotherapy.

On a busy clinic day in December you see a 10-year-old girl with complaint of fever and a sore throat. She reports multiple sick contacts at school and begs for relief as it feels like "knives in the back of my throat every time I swallow." On examination, she has enlarged erythematous tonsils covered with exudate, bilateral cervical lymphadenopathy, and a "sandpaper-like" rash. What would you do next?

> In such a patient, you would want to rule out streptococcal pharyngitis. You can do a "Rapid Strep" (rapid antigen detection) test in the clinic; if the test is negative the recommendation is to send a throat culture. The Rapid Strep test has been shown to have a sensitivity of greater than 80%.

What diagnosis would you give to the combination of fever, rash on trunk and extremities, and streptococcal pharyngitis?

> This combination makes up the diagnosis of scarlet fever. Treatment is the same for streptococcal pharyngitis and scarlet fever.

Why is it important to test for group A beta-hemolytic *Streptococcus*?

> It is important to test for beta-hemolytic *Streptococcus* so that antibiotic therapy (with penicillins or macrolides) can be initiated. Untreated infections can lead to potentially serious consequences. Stay tuned.

The 10-year-old patient returns for follow-up in about 2 weeks after initial infection and states her throat feels much better but she has not been urinating as much as normal. In fact, at times, she noticed that her urine is more orange in color. You glance at her chart and see that her vitals show a blood pressure of 145/80. What laboratory tests would aid you in this diagnosis?

> This patient most likely has poststreptococcal glomerulonephritis which presents about 10 days postinfection with elevated blood pressure, decreased urine output, hematuria, and edema. Important laboratory tests to perform would be electrolytes (specifically looking at blood urea nitrogen [BUN] and creatinine), urinalysis, and complement level. Remember, this is *not* prevented by antibiotic treatment of streptococcal pharyngitis.

Which poststreptococcal sequelae is prevented by appropriate therapy and how is it diagnosed?

> Acute rheumatic fever is a consequence of untreated group A streptococcal infections. It typically occurs a few weeks after initial pharyngitis.

CHAPTER 10

Nephrology and Urology

PHYSIOLOGIC DISORDERS AND GENERAL SYMPTOMS

A 9-month-old infant is noted to have failure to thrive, vomiting, and only one wet diaper a day. Urinary pH is noted to be 7. A blood gas shows acidosis. Acid load test from NH_4Cl would confirm the diagnosis. What is the most likely finding on renal ultrasound?

Medullary nephrocalcinosis or nephrolithiasis associated with type 1 or distal renal tubular acidosis (RTA) is caused by increased hydrogen ion secretion by distal tubule and collecting duct. This presents with failure to thrive, anorexia, vomiting, dehydration, constipation, decreased urine output, acidosis, increased serum chloride, and decreased serum potassium. Type 1 RTA is commonly caused by decreased H^+-ATPase ion pump activity.

A child with cystinosis develops acidosis secondary to Fanconi syndrome. What is the mechanism that causes this acidosis?

Fanconi syndrome is identified as a type 2 or proximal renal tubular acidosis due to the decreased ability of the proximal tubules to reabsorb filtered HCO_3. These patients will have urine with low pH, likely less than 5.5, on initial presentation. Fanconi syndrome can be primary (inherited) or secondary (acquired). Several inborn errors of amino acid or carbohydrate metabolism (ie, cystinosis, galactosemia, tyrosinemia, glycogen storage diseases, etc) are associated with Fanconi syndrome.

A 3-week-old newborn has been projectile vomiting for 3 days and has just been diagnosed with pyloric stenosis. What is the most likely electrolyte abnormality?

The patient is expected to have hypochloremic, hypokalemic metabolic alkalosis which is the classic electrolyte and acid-base imbalance of pyloric stenosis. Persistent emesis causes progressive loss of fluids rich in hydrochloric acid, which causes the kidneys to retain hydrogen ions in favor of potassium. The duration of symptoms affects the severity of the imbalance.

An 11-year-old girl recently has developed meningitis as a result of untreated recurrent otitis media. During hospitalization, patient's sodium falls from 140 to 126. She has no swelling or signs of edema. Her fluid balance was diligently monitored during hospitalization. Her serum osmolality is low and her urine osmolality is high. What caused this hyponatremia?

The girl has developed syndrome of inappropriate secretion of antidiuretic hormone (SIADH). SIADH is associated with neurologic disorders and tumors. The patients are usually euvolemic and sometimes present with seizures due to hyponatremia.

How is this patient managed?

Patients with SIADH need strict fluid restriction until serum sodium normalizes. Acutely hypertonic saline should only be used if the patient is not stable. Rapid correction of long-standing hyponatremia can lead to central pontine myelinolysis.

How is proteinuria diagnosed in children?

The gold standard for diagnosis is an analysis of 24-hour urine collection. A 24-hour urinary creatinine excretion should be determined at the same time to assure that the child has collected all urine. Proteinuria is defined as excretion of 4 mg/$(m^2 \cdot h)$ of protein over this 24-hour span. If the patient has gross hematuria, up to 500 mg/$(m^2 \cdot h)$ of protein must be considered normal.

How is the hypertension diagnosis defined in children who have not yet hit puberty?

Unlike adults, no set numeric pressure cutoffs are utilized. Rather average systolic and/or diastolic blood pressure greater than or equal to 95th percentile on three occasions is used for diagnosis. Prehypertension is defined as greater than 90th but less than 95th percentile.

GLOMERULOPATHIES

A 4-year-old boy went to his pediatrician yesterday for vaccines and today returns with confirmed gross blood in urine but is otherwise asymptomatic and has a normal physical examination. A diagnosis of immunoglobulin A (IgA) nephropathy is presumed by the pediatrician. How would this be confirmed?

A diagnosis is confirmed by light, immunofluorescence, and electron microscopy demonstrating IgA in the glomerular mesangium. Serum IgA level is elevated in only a small percentage of children. IgA nephropathy commonly occurs 1 to 3 days after upper respiratory infection (URI), gastrointestinal infections (GIs), vaccinations, or exercise.

A 3-year-old boy who had "flu" per mother 2 weeks ago presents with worsening swelling around both of his eyes, some mild abdominal pain, and mild decrease in urine. Urinalysis of the patient is negative for blood but has 3+ protein. What is the most likely diagnosis?

Minimal change nephrotic syndrome (MCNS) is the most common form of nephrotic syndrome in children. The etiology of MCNS is unknown. Two-thirds of patients with minimal change nephrotic syndrome present between ages 2 and 6 years. The long-term prognosis for MCNS is excellent. Eighty percent of patients enter a sustained remission during adolescence.

What is the mainstay of therapy for this patient?

Corticosteroids are the mainstay of therapy for patients with minimal change nephrotic syndrome. In a responsive patient, proteinuria typically resolves within the first 3 weeks of therapy. Relapses do occur in 80% of children.

The patient above continues to have edema and proteinuria despite two attempts at corticosteroid therapy. All urinalysis results continue to show isolated large proteinuria. The patient has now developed hypertension. What is the next action taken toward diagnosis?

Renal biopsy is recommended in children who fail trials of prednisone therapy or have significant hypertension for etiology. Considering isolated large proteinuria, the biopsy may be significant for focal segmental glomerulosclerosis, mesangial nephropathy, or membranous nephropathy.

An 8-year-old boy with a recent history of throat infection that was treated with amoxicillin now has tea-colored urine and a headache. He has no rash. What is the most likely diagnosis?

Poststreptococcal glomerulonephritis. With the history of recent possible streptococcal pharyngitis and now hematuria, poststreptococcal or postinfectious glomerulonephritis is the likely diagnosis. His headache may stem from mild hypertension. Some of these patients may present with mild edema.

What are some important diagnostic laboratory findings in this patient?

A laboratory evaluation for streptococcal infection is helpful including a serum antistreptolysin-O (ASO) and anti-DNase B (ADB) titers. Throat and skin lesion cultures may also be positive at the time of nephritis, though in this case that patient was recently treated for streptococcal pharyngitis. The most important diagnostic laboratory finding in poststreptococcal glomerulonephritis however is depressed serum C3 concentration. Activation of the alternative pathway of complement results in reduced serum C3 levels.

The patient above returns to the nephrologist who saw him in the emergency room (ER) for a follow-up appointment 3 weeks later. His serum complement levels are now lower than initial presentation and he is persistently hypertensive. A renal biopsy shows electron microscopy with subendothelial humps. What is the new most likely diagnosis?

Membranoproliferative glomerulonephritis is consistent with this picture of continued decreased complement levels and hypertension. This is often initially confused as a postinfectious glomerulonephritis. The renal biopsy is the hallmark of the diagnosis.

A 14-year-old adolescent girl presents with hemoptysis. She has been considerably weak as of late and has also noticed swelling in her legs and around her eyes. Her creatinine is found to be 2.4. A renal biopsy reveals crescentic glomerulonephritis and linear IgG deposits along the capillaries of the glomeruli. What is the most likely diagnosis?

Goodpasture syndrome is the most likely diagnosis and is caused by anti-glomerular basement membrane (anti-GBM) antibodies in the alveolus in the lung and the basement membrane of the glomerulus in the kidney.

A 2-year-old girl with no past medical history hit her elbow after playing outside. Her mother gave her ibuprofen for the pain and the next morning found her to have a fever, a dry diaper, and periorbital swelling. The urinalysis shows leukocyturia and hematuria. Eosinophils are found on smear. What is the most likely diagnosis?

Acute interstitial nephritis is characterized by diffuse or focal inflammation and edema of the renal interstitium. Secondary involvement of the renal tubules may also be found and is most often related to drugs including nonsteroidal antiinflammatory drugs (NSAIDs), antibiotics, and diuretics.

A 10-year-old boy comes to the pediatrician with complaint of abdominal pain and scrotal edema. On further examination he is found to have a palpable, non-blanching maculopapular rash on buttocks and legs. Urinalysis shows mild hematuria and proteinuria. What is the most likely diagnosis?

Henoch-Schönlein purpura (HSP) would most likely fit this constitution of symptoms. HSP nephritis is a systemic vasculitis that typically affects children and presents as a triad of purpuric rash, crampy abdominal pain, and arthritis. Signs and symptoms of nephritis may not appear until days or weeks into the disease.

Two days following the diagnosis of HSP, the patient returns to the emergency room with colicky severe abdominal pain with melena. What are complications of the disease process that must be evaluated for?

In patients with HSP and history of severe abdominal pain, it is important to rule out intussusception, bowel perforation, bowel ischemia, or pancreatitis. Immediate radiographic abdominal obstruction series is advised in this situation to rule out acute surgical emergencies of bowl perforation and intussusception.

A 5-year-old boy with speech delay presents to his pediatrician with confirmed gross blood in urine. Audiometry shows bilateral hearing loss to high tones in frequency. What is the likely diagnosis?

Alport syndrome is characterized by progressive hereditary nephritis and deafness usually presenting with gross hematuria. It shows a male predilection due to autosomal dominant/X-linked transmission. Eye abnormalities are also associated with it.

A 14-year-old adolescent girl with known systemic lupus erythematosus (SLE) and history of protein casts in urine presents with edema and 4+ protein on urinalysis. Why would this patient undergo a renal biopsy?

Every patient with SLE is likely to have some abnormality demonstrated on renal biopsy. In the case of this patient, her lupus nephritis has apparently progressed to nephritic syndrome. A biopsy would be appropriate to distinguish membranous glomerulonephritis from diffuse proliferative glomerulonephritis, as this would require much more aggressive therapy.

NEWBORN UROLOGY

An expecting mother comes to her pediatrician for a prenatal consult. She states that on prenatal ultrasound it was found that her son has posterior urethral valves. She asks "How would this be identified in a child without prenatal diagnosis?"

Fortunately, with the advent of prenatal ultrasonic monitoring, posterior urethral valves are typically diagnosed by the presence of bilateral hydroureteronephrosis, a thickened bladder wall, and a widened and elongated posterior urethra. Discovery during the newborn period is usually prompted by findings of a distended bladder, palpable kidney, urinary tract infection (UTI), renal insufficiency, and rarely a poor urinary stream. Delayed diagnosis of posterior urethral valves may result in failure to thrive, abdominal distention, and vomiting.

How is the diagnosis of posterior urethral valves confirmed in the postnatal period?

The diagnosis can usually be confirmed by a voiding cystourethrogram.

What is the treatment and prognosis for patients with posterior urethral valves?

Treatment is directed toward relief of bladder neck obstruction. Initial therapy, especially in the neonate, includes transurethral catheter placement, electrolyte normalization, and treatment of any infection. Transurethral valve ablation is performed as safely as possible following birth.

What is the best predictor of prognosis in patients with posterior urethral valves?

The best predictor of prognosis is the nadir serum creatinine following ablation. Renal failure with resultant dialysis is common in those with elevated creatinine. Most renal damage occurs early in fetal life, and despite effective valve ablation, bladder dysfunction is usually a lifelong problem resulting in incontinence and poor emptying.

A nervous mother comes into a pediatrician's office concerned that she only feels one testicle in her 1-month-old son and is fearful of cancer. On examination the pediatrician feels the left testicle in the scrotum and the right testicle in the inguinal canal. What cancer is she afraid of and what advice can be given?

Patience. Most cases of undescended testicles do resolve by 3 to 6 months of age. She is correct that failure of descent by 6 months, or cryptorchidism, will result in increased risk of seminomas as well as testicular torsion, infertility, and hernias.

A parent of a 2-month-old infant with bilateral undescended testicles asks when he should be referred to urology. At what age should this child be referred for orchidopexy?

Cryptorchidism, or undescended testicle(s), is usually diagnosed during the newborn examination. Orchidopexy is a surgical procedure to move the undescended testicle down into the scrotum. Orchidopexy as early as 6 months and up to 2 years has been shown to increase the likelihood of fertility in these patients. Orchidopexy should be performed between 6 and 12 months of age. It does not change rates of testicular cancer in these children, but allows for regular testis examination.

What is the most common congenital anomaly of the penis?

Hypospadias, a congenital penile deformity resulting from incomplete development of the distal or anterior urethra occurs in 1 in 250 live births. The urethral meatus may be located at any point along the ventral shaft of the penis, midline of the scrotum, or perineum. Hypospadias is a clinical triad including a malpositioned urethral meatus, ventral chordee (curvature), and a dorsal hooded prepuce. Any child suspected to have hypospadias should not be circumcised at birth, and should be referred to pediatric urology for further evaluation.

What is phimosis?

Phimosis is the inability to retract the distal prepuce over the glans penis. Congenital phimosis is physiologic, even into the teenage years, and typically does not cause urologic problems. Acquired phimosis can result from poor hygiene, chronic balanoposthitis, or forceful retraction of a congenital phimosis.

In what situation does surgical intervention need to be undertaken for this problem?

If phimosis is causing urinary obstruction, significant voiding symptoms, or recurrent UTIs, a urologic evaluation for circumcision or preputial plasty is recommended to enlarge the preputial opening without actually removing tissue. Topical betamethasone cream can usually obviate the need for surgery in most children with congenital phimosis.

URINARY INFECTION AND REFLUX

A 1-month-old newborn presents with fever and irritability. Rule out sepsis workup yields white blood cells on smear of urine and 50 WBC on urinalysis. What is the most common organism to grow from urine culture?

Escherichia coli is the culprit for 80% to 90% of initial UTIs in infants.

Why does this patient require aggressive antibiotic treatment of the infection?

Infants less than 2 months of age are at an increased risk for urosepsis or other concomitant infections.

What would be the best imaging modality to assess for an abnormality of the urinary tract in the above patient?

These infants should receive a renal ultrasound to screen for urinary tract obstruction or other structural abnormalities. The infant should also receive a voiding cystourethrogram (VCUG) to evaluate for vesicoureteral reflux.

Why is VCUG preferred to direct radionuclide cystogram (DRC) by most pediatric urologists?

VCUG is more accurate and sensitive for grading vesicoureteral reflux. The VCUG also provides more precise anatomic detail of the urethra and bladder and therefore is better for analysis of bladder dysfunction. The DRC attempts to minimize radiation exposure to the gonads, and is an acceptable alternative to the VCUG for follow-up imaging in children with a known history of reflux.

On VCUG this patient was found to have mild dilation of the ureter and renal pelvis with some blunting of the renal calyces. What grade vesicoureteral reflux is this patient diagnosed with? See Fig. 10-1.

This patient has grade III reflux.

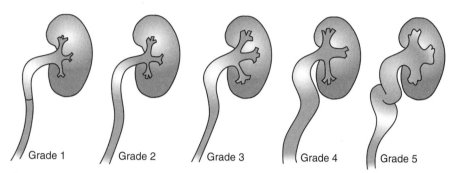

Figure 10-1 Vesicoureteral reflux.

What would be the medical management of this low-grade vesicoureteral reflux?

Prophylactic low-dose antibiotics would be given until the reflux resolves. The patient should have a repeat VCUG every year. The patient should also get a renal ultrasound twice a year to evaluate renal growth. A urinalysis and urine culture should be performed to evaluate any significant fever. If a child with grade III unilateral reflux has breakthrough febrile UTIs on prophylaxis, definitive surgical management is indicated.

RENAL FAILURE

A 2-year-old with severe growth failure, low serum calcium, elevated serum phosphate level, and drastically elevated alkaline phosphatase is found to have chronic renal insufficiency (CRI). What hormone will be drastically elevated in this patient?

Parathyroid hormone (PTH) is increased secondary to the decreased filtration rate leading to phosphate retention and decreased production of 1,25-dihydroxyvitamin D by the kidney. This causes decreased calcium absorption from GI tract and increased production of PTH by the parathyroid gland.

How should this patient with hyper-parathyroidism and chronic renal insufficiency be treated?

Renal osteodystrophy, also known as "renal rickets" is seen in patients with CRI and hyperparathyroidism. Treatments are based on hyperphos-phatemia via dietary restriction, dietary phosphate binders (ie, calcium carbon-ate), and vitamin D to maintain serum calcium at normal levels.

What is the cause of anemia in chil-dren with CRI?

Erythropoietin production is decreased in CRI. Subcutaneous administration of erythropoietin is standard in these children.

ACQUIRED ADOLESCENT DISORDERS

A 13-year-old adolescent boy presents to the ER with several hours of unre-lenting right flank pain with no change with position change or movement. The urinalysis is positive for blood. What is the most likely diagnosis?

This is a very typical presentation of renal colic likely secondary to urolithia-sis or kidney stones.

After lithotripsy, stone examination is consistent with calcium oxalate. On 24-hour urinalysis, it is found that this 13-year-old secretes high amounts of calcium and oxalate in the urine. What pharmacologic intervention would be taken to prevent further stone formation?

Thiazide diuretics increase renal cal-cium reabsorption and therefore decrease the urinary calcium excretion. Potassium citrate is often added if the urinary citrate is low or the urine is acidic. Although vitamin B_6 has been shown in some studies to decrease oxalate absorption from the gut, it is not typically used clinically.

A 12-year-old boy presents to the ED with a history of severe right-sided hemiscrotal pain starting 30 minutes ago. There is no history of trauma. On examination the patient has an elevated, exquisitely tender right testicle. The cremasteric reflex is lost on the right side. What is the most appropriate next step?

This patient most likely has testicular torsion and your most appropriate next step is to arrange prompt surgical exploration and detorsion. Though an ultrasonography with Doppler can be helpful to assess blood flow and to differentiate torsion from other conditions, these studies should preferably be ordered once urologic consultation has been completed and only for equivocal presentations. If treatment is not prompt, orchiectomy may be required. The optimal window for saving the testis occurs between 4 and 6 hours following the onset of symptoms.

CLINICAL VIGNETTES

A 3-year-old girl comes to a pediatrician's office with a 2-day history of abdominal pain, vomiting, and bloody diarrhea after eating at a barbeque. As the physician waits for the stool culture sent off in the clinic, the patient returns the next day with some swelling around the eyes, a pale appearance, and decreased urine output. What is the most likely diagnosis?

Hemolytic uremic syndrome (HUS) is the most common glomerular vascular cause of acute renal failure in childhood.

What is most likely to grow from the stool culture taken by the pediatrician in this diagnosis?

Escherichia coli serotype O157:H7 is the most common source of this syndrome. Other bacterial causes include Shigella, Salmonella, Yersinia, and Campylobacter species. The Shiga and Shiga-like toxins, produced by some strains of Shigella dysenteriae and E coli O157:H7, respectively, have been associated with approximately 70% of cases of HUS in children.

What is likely to be seen on a blood smear of this patient with HUS?

Red blood cell fragments, burr cells, and schistocytes are noted in patients with hemolytic uremic syndrome. The mechanism is microangiopathic hemolytic anemia.

Why would the physician be very cautious about this child bumping herself as she is taken from the waiting room into the examination room?

The last part of the triad of hemolytic uremic syndrome is thrombocytopenia (acute renal failure and microangiopathic hemolytic anemia are the other two). The pathogenesis of thrombocytopenia is related to anemia. Circulating verotoxin causes microvascular occlusion with subsequent hemolysis and thrombocytopenia.

The parents of the patient understand the severity of their child's disease and therefore demand "the strongest antibiotic possible to fight this bacterium." Why should the pediatrician resist this urge to treat with antibiotics?

Antibiotics have been shown to worsen hemolytic uremic syndrome by causing the release of large amounts of bacterial Shiga toxin. Therefore, treatment is based on management of fluid and electrolyte disturbances. Transfusions and dialysis may be necessary. Most children recover from acute episode in 2 to 3 weeks. End-stage renal disease does occur in 15% and some lasting renal disease in 30%.

CHAPTER 11

Neurology

NEURAL TUBE DEFECTS

A pregnant woman is found to have an elevated alpha-fetoprotein (AFP) at her 16-week obstetrics visit. An ultrasound done at the visit shows that the fetus is anencephalic. What supplements should this mother have taken in early pregnancy to decrease the chance of this defect from occurring?

This baby has a neural tube defect (NTD) that results in elevated AFP levels in the amniotic fluid and maternal serum. NTD appears to be associated with a combination of genetic and environmental factors. Folic acid fortification for women 3 months before as well as during pregnancy is necessary to reduce NTD.

A baby with a lumbar NTD develops fecal and urinary incontinence and impaired movement of his lower extremities. Which NTD does he have if it consists of a herniated sac of neural tissue covered by meninges?

The baby has a meningomyelocele, which is the most serious and most common defect. Another type of NTD is a meningocele, which is a defect of protruding meninges only. Spina bifida occulta is a closed defect that does not result in a sac but a defect in the vertebrae and is often asymptomatic.

CEREBRAL PALSY

A baby suffers from meconium aspiration with presumed hypoxic damage to her brain. She is hypotonic for several months but then develops bilateral hypertonicity, especially in her lower extremities. Is this condition progressive?

Cerebral palsy (CP) is a nonprogressive, static disorder affecting motor activity and posture. Physical and occupational therapy will be extremely important for maximizing independent skill.

If a patient with CP has spasticity in both of his lower extremities only, how is his CP classified?

It is classified as spastic diplegia. In hemiplegia, one side of the body is primarily affected, and in quadriplegia, all limbs are affected. Seventy percent to eighty percent of patients with CP have the spastic type.

What treatments are now being offered to treat spasticity in children with cerebral palsy?

Injections of botulinum toxin are now routinely used for treatment of localized spasticity in CP patients. Diazepam is also often used for short-term antispasticity treatment.

SEIZURE DISORDERS

What is the difference between a simple and a complex partial seizure?

There is alteration of consciousness in a complex partial seizure while consciousness is preserved with simple partial seizures.

A 2-year-old girl has a generalized tonic clonic seizure that lasts 1 minute while she is febrile. If the patient recovers and a source for the fever is identified, should she be placed on an antiepileptic or undergo further testing?

No. This child had a simple febrile seizure and the underlying cause of the seizure should be treated. No additional workup is needed if she is otherwise neurologically intact with no meningeal signs.

What is the typical age range of children who develop febrile seizures?

Febrile seizures occur in children between 6 months and 6 years of age and peak between 1 and 2 years of age. Seizures that occur with fever in infants under 6 months or children over 6 years of age, should not be termed "febrile seizures."

What are the basic features of a simple febrile seizure?

A simple febrile seizure lasts less than 15 minutes and affects children between 6 months and 6 years old. It does not recur within the day of the event and is generalized without focal features.

In what cases would a further workup be warranted with a febrile seizure?

Complex febrile seizures usually warrant further studies. These seizures last longer than 15 minutes, have focality, or recur within 24 hours. Children with neurological sequelae following a simple febrile seizure, as well as children with meningeal signs or other abnormalities on neurologic examination should undergo further testing.

An 8-year-old boy is observed by his teacher to be staring and unresponsive for several seconds at a time throughout the day, but is able to return to his classwork without a problem after the episodes. If this child is experiencing absence seizures, what would his electroencephalograph (EEG) show?

The characteristic EEG pattern for absence seizures is a 3 per second spike and wave pattern. Although brief, absence seizures may occur so frequently that they interfere with learning.

What is the typical treatment and prognosis of absence seizures?

First-line treatment is ethosuximide (most effective), valproic acid, or lamotrigine. With appropriate treatment, the prognosis is good with most patients experiencing complete resolution of seizures by adolescence. Children with absence seizures are at increased risk for generalized tonic–clonic seizures as they grow older; ethosuximide is not effective for this type of seizure in contrast to valproic acid and lamotrigine.

A 4-month-old infant develops jerky movements involving flexion of her neck and extension of her arms that occurs for 5 to 10 seconds and recur throughout the day. EEG reveals a hypsarrhythmic pattern, characterized by random, high-voltage, slow waves and spikes from foci throughout the cortex. What medications have been shown to be effective for this condition?

This patient has infantile spasms. The American Academy of Neurology published a practice guideline for treatment of infantile spasms in 2004. Adrenocorticotropic hormone (ACTH) is generally considered the treatment of choice and vigabatrin has been noted to be possibly effective. Corticosteroids have been used but there is limited evidence supporting their utility. Overall, the prognosis is poor in infants with infantile spasms and major or minor neurologic deficits are noted in 50% and 40%, respectively.

A 14-year-old adolescent boy is being evaluated for new onset generalized tonic–clonic seizures. With further questioning, it is found that he has also had episodes of "daydreaming" at school and "jerking" of his extremities in the early morning. What type of epilepsy does he most likely have?

This child most likely has juvenile myoclonic epilepsy, which is characterized by a combination of myoclonic seizures (usually upon awakening), generalized tonic–clonic seizures, and absence seizures. Onset is usually in late childhood and patients may have cognitive deficits. A very specific EEG pattern is noted in such children. Treatment is generally lifelong and usually includes valproate, lamotrigine, or levetiracetam.

HEAD INJURIES

A 5-year-old boy falls off a jungle gym onto his head. Bruising is noted behind his ear and underneath both of his eyes. During your examination you note a clear nasal discharge coming from one nostril that is positive for glucose. What is his clinical presentation concerning for?

This child's ocular physical finding is termed "raccoon eyes" and a "Battle sign" denotes the bruising behind the ear which is pathognomonic for basilar skull fracture. The clear rhinorrhea is likely cerebrospinal fluid (CSF), indicating a dural leak in association with the fracture. Other indications of this type of fracture include hemotympanum and CSF otorrhea.

How does a coup injury differ from a contra-coup injury?

During acceleration injuries, damage to the brain is found at the point of impact, such as in a coup injury. Contra-coup injuries are deceleration injuries and are located opposite the site of impact.

An 18-year-old man is involved in a motor vehicle accident and undergoes a severe head injury that leads to death. Autopsy shows diffuse white matter brain damage. How did this occur?

This patient had diffuse axonal injury caused by shearing forces that occurred at the time of the accident. Diffuse axonal injury can cause long-term brain damage, coma, and death.

A 17-year-old adolescent boy is tackled during a football game with his friends. After the tackle, he begins to vomit and develops a headache and a subsequent seizure. A CT scan of his brain shows a crescent-shaped hematoma that crosses suture lines (See Fig. 11-1). What type of closed head injury did he develop?

This patient has a subdural hematoma caused by a tearing of the cortical bridging veins between the dura and the brain.

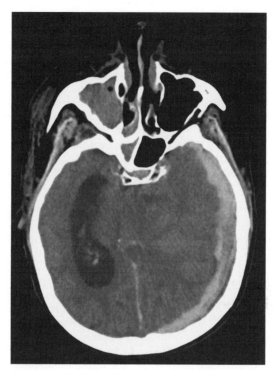

Figure 11-1   (Reproduced, with permission, from Knoop
KJ, Stack LB, Storrow AS, et al. *Atlas of Emergency
Medicine*. 3rd ed. New York: McGraw-Hill; 2010: Fig. 1.52.
Photo contributor: Lawrence B. Stack, MD.)

A teenager is involved in a physical
altercation and is hit on the side of his
head with a blunt object. Immediately
after the event, he is able to answer
questions appropriately. However,
when he arrives to the ER, he becomes
confused and his pupil is dilated on
the same side as the trauma. What
vessel was likely injured during
the fight?

This patient likely has an epidural
hematoma caused by injury to the middle meningeal artery. The blood is
located between the skull and dura
mater and forms a convex collection
that can be seen on CT scan. Most individuals with epidural hematoma, have
a so-called "lucid interval" that is a
period of time that they seem entirely
normal following the injury, before presenting with deteriorating neurologic
status.

What should be done for an acutely decompensating patient with an epidural hematoma?	This patient may be herniating and should be mildly hyperventilated to decrease hypercapnia. Mannitol or hypertonic saline can be given to decrease intracranial pressure, and the head of the bed should be elevated to 30° to optimize cerebral perfusion pressure. The neurosurgeon should be immediately consulted as urgent neurosurgical intervention is often necessary.

HEADACHES

How are migraine headaches typically described?	Pain associated with migraines is generally unilateral and described as pounding or throbbing. Patients often prefer to be in dark, quiet rooms, experience nausea and sometimes vomiting, and find relief after sleeping. Auras consisting of visual phenomena or other neurological symptoms may occur prior to the headache. Childhood migraines may have atypical presentations which do not follow the classic pattern.
What are treatment options to abort migraine headaches?	Nonsteroidal antiinflammatory drugs (NSAIDs) and acetaminophen may be used to treat migraine headaches. Promethazine and other phenothiazines are also used for nausea associated with migraine, but these agents can have side effects. Triptans can also be used for abortive therapy.
What is the mechanism of action of triptans?	Triptans are serotonin agonists that cause vasoconstriction of cranial blood vessels and prevent the release of inflammatory vasoactive peptides. They also work within the pain pathways of the brain to block transmission of pain signals.

What are treatments used to prevent migraine headaches?

A patient should identify headache triggers and avoid those foods or stressors. Various antidepressants, antiepileptics, calcium channel blockers, and beta-blockers are also used as prophylactic medications.

An overweight 16-year-old adolescent girl enters your office complaining of frequent headaches. An ophthalmologic examination reveals bilateral papilledema. If a mass is ruled out and the child is presumed to have pseudotumor cerebri, what procedure may be performed to alleviate her headaches?

A lumbar puncture (LP) revealing a high opening pressure would indicate pseudotumor cerebri once a mass is ruled out. This procedure is not only diagnostic, but may also be therapeutic, and repeated removal of CSF will decrease pressure to alleviate the patient's symptoms. Acetazolamide is typically the drug of choice, other causes for pseudotumor cerebri need to be investigated. In rare cases, surgical fenestration of the optic nerve sheath are additional treatment options. Eye damage is a major morbidity with this condition, so prompt consultation with a pediatric ophthalmologist is recommended.

A teenager with known polycystic kidney disease presents to the ER with the worst headache of his life. What defect may be causing these symptoms?

Patients with polycystic kidney disease are predisposed to developing berry aneurysms within the brain. These may rupture and cause a subarachnoid hemorrhage and are classically associated with "the worst headache" of one's life. Cerebral aneurysms occur most commonly in adults but can occur at any age. A number of inherited disorders as well as certain risk factors (ie, hypertension, cocaine use) are noted to be more common in those with ruptured cerebral aneurysms. Angiography can be used to diagnose brain aneurysms and surgical clipping or endovascular coiling are used to treat them.

WEAKNESS AND NEUROMUSCULAR DISEASES

A 16-year-old adolescent girl notes her feet and ankles feel "funny." She complains of weakness that travels up her legs. On examination, reflexes are not appreciated in her legs. She has an antecedent history of diarrhea that occurred 2 weeks ago. What is the next step in diagnosis? What results would you expect to see?

A lumbar puncture may be performed to confirm the diagnosis. A normal WBC count and elevated protein in the CSF would be suggestive of Guillain-Barre syndrome (GBS). Enteric infection with *Campylobacter* has been associated with immunoreactive complications including GBS though in many cases an antecedent illness is not confirmed.

Should a patient with ascending paralysis secondary to Guillain-Barre syndrome be discharged home?

GBS is characterized by symmetric ascending weakness due to peripheral nerve demyelination secondary to a cross-reaction of antibodies from a recent infection to the myelin surrounding the nerves. This patient should be observed in the hospital because the ascending weakness could affect the diaphragm and accessory muscles, which could lead to respiratory distress. Intravenous immune globulin infusion is now considered the treatment of choice for patients with significant deficits associated with GBS.

A 19-year-old woman presents to your office complaining of diplopia. She also reports a generalized weakness associated with exertion and occasional trouble eating and speaking. An electromyogram (EMG) is performed and shows a decreased response after repeated stimuli. What is underlying pathophysiology of this disorder?

This patient has myasthenia gravis (MG), a disorder in which autoantibodies attack the postsynaptic acetylcholine receptor and inhibit its action.

What treatment is effective for myasthenia gravis?

An anticholinesterase agent such as Mestinon or pyridostigmine can be used to decrease the breakdown of acetylcholine and allow more acetylcholine to act on its postsynaptic receptors.

ATAXIA

A 2-year-old girl is at her pediatrician for follow-up for an upper respiratory tract infection. On examination she is noted to have an ataxic gait. She is otherwise asymptomatic. An LP is performed and is normal. What is the likely cause of the symptoms?

This patient likely has acute cerebellar ataxia secondary to a postviral autoimmune response.

A 2-year-old boy develops ataxia. He has not had any recent viral infections, but a chart review shows multiple previous hospitalizations for infections. On examination, blood vessels visible within the skin are noted on his nose, face, and neck. What further testing should the patient have?

After obtaining a thorough family history, this patient should receive genetic testing for ataxia-telangiectasia, which is an autosomal recessive disease that can lead to neurodegenerative disabilities as well as brain and lymphoid tumors later in life. These patients may also be tested for alpha-fetoprotein (AFP), which is typically elevated in people with this disorder.

How does the presentation of Friedreich ataxia differ from that of ataxia-telangiectasia?

Friedreich ataxia often presents later in childhood, with symptoms initially occurring between age 5 and 15. Friedreich ataxia is also associated with wasting and weakness of muscles, sensory deficits, scoliosis, and cardiomyopathies. It affects the dorsal column, the spinocerebellar tracts, the pyramidal tracts, and the cerebellar hemispheres.

NEUROCUTANEOUS DISEASES

A baby is born with a "port-wine" stain in the distribution of the first branch of cranial nerve V. What syndrome must you consider and what sequelae of the disease should the parents anticipate in the coming years?

Sturge-Weber must be considered. The parents should be aware of the possible development of ophthalmologic disease, such as glaucoma, as well as neurological sequelae such as seizures, hemiparesis, and mental retardation.

A patient with retinal hamartomas undergoes testing and is diagnosed with von Hippel Lindau disease. What oncologic processes are associated with this disease?

Von Hippel Lindau disease is associated with retinal and cerebellar hemangioblastomas and renal cell carcinomas.

A patient's mom reports that she has noticed freckling on the inguinal and axillary regions of her 3-year-old son's body. When seen by an ophthalmologist, Lisch nodules and pigmented hamartomas are noted on his iris. There are also 12 coffee-colored macules on his skin. What disease does this patient likely have?

This child has many characteristics of neurofibromatosis (NF) type 1.

What additional findings are often associated with NF type 1?

Other characteristics of this disease include a first-degree relative with NF1, 2, or more neurofibromas (or one complex/plexiform neurofibroma), osseous lesions, and optic gliomas. Onset is typically in childhood and long-term effects include learning disabilities, seizures, and increased risk of central nervous system (CNS) tumors.

How does NF2 differ from NF1?

NF2 is less prevalent than NF1. Onset is in the teenage years and the disease is associated with bilateral acoustic neuromas as well as neurofibromas, meningiomas, schwannomas, and astrocytomas.

A 2-year-old child presents with new-onset seizures. On examination, you note acneiform lesions over the nose of the child and several hypopigmented macules on his trunk. What are the skin lesions and what is his diagnosis?

This patient has tuberous sclerosis. The hypopigmented macules are called ash-leaf spots; sometimes the use of a Wood lamp is needed to identify such lesions in fair-skinned patients. The acneiform lesions are called adenoma sebaceum. The child might also have skin thickening (in the lumbosacral region or nape of the neck) called shagreen patches.

Why is it important that patients with suspected tuberous sclerosis receive head imaging?

These patients should get serial head imaging because they may develop brain "tubers" within the periventricular regions of the brain. These calcify and can lead to seizures and obstructive hydrocephalus.

SYNCOPE

A 15-year-old otherwise healthy adolescent girl loses consciousness 15 minutes after receiving a routine immunization. She remembers feeling nauseated and dizzy prior to the episode but does not recall subsequent events. She returns to her normal self immediately after the episode. What is this episode most characteristic of?

The story is most consistent with an episode of vasovagal syncope. Syncope results from inadequate cerebral perfusion pressure and is associated with a transient loss of consciousness. Vasovagal syncope is associated with a prodrome of dizziness and nausea, and often occurs in an upright position. Cardiac and metabolic etiologies must also be ruled out as causes of these syncopal events, though the history that the episode follows a noxious event and has a typical prodrome is most often seen in typical vasovagal syncope. Workup might include checking an ECG to exclude long QT syndrome.

SLEEP DISORDERS

A father is awakened by his 3-year-old son's blood-curdling screams. When he arrives to the room, his son is sitting up in bed, but subsequently falls back asleep and does not remember the incident in the morning. In what stage of sleep did this episode occur?

This child had a night terror, also known as pavor nocturnus, which occurs in stage 4 (non-REM) sleep. Night terrors generally occur from 18 months to 5 years of age. Episodes can last 10 to 20 minutes and usually occur within 2 hours of a child falling to sleep. The episodes are not remembered by the child and generally require no treatment.

ABNORMALITIES IN HEAD SIZE AND SHAPE

A baby is found to have a rapidly enlarging head circumference. A head ultrasound reveals an absence of the roof of the fourth ventricle with cystic dilation and enlargement of the posterior fossa. What is this defect called?

This patient has a Dandy-Walker malformation, which is associated with agenesis or hypoplasia of the cerebellar vermis. The condition often causes obstructive hydrocephalus and definitive treatment consists of a shunt to prevent or alleviate the hydrocephalus.

What is the most common Arnold-Chiari malformation.

Type 1. It is characterized by caudal displacement of the cerebellar tonsils, causing subsequent downward displacement of the fourth ventricle. It is generally asymptomatic in childhood. Type 2 and 3 are much more severe, are associated with meningomyeloceles and encephaloceles.

A baby is born with severe microcephaly. You do not have any information about the mother's pregnancy or her past medical history. What etiologies of the baby's microcephaly should you be most concerned about?

Microcephaly is defined as a head circumference more than two standard deviations below the mean. The patient should be evaluated for other dysmorphic features as he may have an underlying genetic cause for his microcephaly. Congenital infections, maternal drug use, and maternal diabetes can also be potential causes.

What neurological disorders are associated with microcephaly?

Microcephalic patients should be closely followed as they are more likely to have developmental and learning disorders, seizures, cerebral palsy, vision, and hearing problems.

NEUROPATHIES

You are seeing a newborn for his first follow-up visit after discharge from this hospital and you notice that his right arm is internally rotated with his elbow extended. Mother reports that the delivery was "difficult" and the baby was born breech. What is the prognosis for this type of lesion?

This patient has an Erb palsy secondary to birth trauma. This palsy involves damage to the C5 and C6 nerve roots and patients often have weakness of their deltoid and biceps. Seventy percent to eighty percent of patients have full recovery with the help of physical therapy, usually in the first 6 months of life.

COMPLICATIONS OF ANTIEPILEPTICS

A 12-year-old girl comes to the emergency room with flu-like symptoms, a diffuse rash, and new mouth and lip ulcers. She was started on lamotrigine 1 week ago for treatment of her seizure disorder. What reaction is she experiencing?

This patient has Stevens-Johnson syndrome secondary to her lamotrigine. This reaction, which generally occurs within the first 8 weeks of treatment, is a form of erythema multiforme, a hypersensitivity reaction, which affects the skin and mucous membranes. Patients are often hospitalized due to the extent of mucosal sloughing.

NEURO-ONCOLOGY

You are seeing a 4-year-old boy for new-onset clumsiness. For the past few weeks, he has been unable to keep his balance while walking. In addition, his parents note that he has been vomiting frequently, usually in the mornings, and complaining of headaches. What should you do next?

The history is concerning for a brain tumor, especially one located in the posterior fossa. The combination of new onset ataxia, morning emesis, and increasing headaches is typical and the patient should have a magnetic resonance imaging (MRI) to further characterize this area of the brain as it is often not well imaged on a CT scan.

A previously healthy 18-month-old infant develops difficulty sitting-up and standing without support. She has also been noted to have intermittent rapid eye movements in all directions. What diagnosis do you suspect?

This patient is exhibiting features of opsoclonus–myoclonus, which often heralds a paraneoplastic complication related to an underlying neuroblastoma, one of the most common malignancy of childhood. She should have further testing to locate the primary tumor, which is typically abdominal in origin. The prognosis is poor and residual neurologic sequelae may occur even if the neuroblastoma is cured.

TIC DISORDERS

An 8-year-old boy was recently diagnosed with Tourette syndrome. What other disorders are associated with this syndrome?

Patients with Tourette syndrome often have comorbid conditions of obsessive-compulsive disorder and attention deficit disorder. These disorders may be seen in immediate family members as well.

CLINICAL VIGNETTES

A 12-year-old girl is in class and suddenly screams and falls to the ground. She subsequently develops body stiffening with extension of her arms and legs for about 1 minute followed by bilateral, rhythmic shaking with foaming of her mouth. Her teacher notes that she is not responsive during the episode. What type of seizure is she having?

She is having a generalized tonic–clonic seizure. The tonic stage is the stiffening of the arms and legs and the clonic stage involves the shaking of the body.

The teacher calls for help then rushes to the patient's side. What should she do to protect the patient from hurting herself?

The child should be placed on her side in case she vomits. Nothing should be placed in her mouth and a soft shirt or pillow can be placed under her head in an effort to avoid head trauma. She should not be held down and the seizure should be timed if possible.

Seizure activity continues and she is brought to the ER across the street. The teacher estimates that the seizure has lasted about 5 minutes thus far. The teacher is a substitute and is unaware of the patient's medical history or medications. What is the immediate management of the patient?

As always, airway, breathing, and circulation should be evaluated first. The child may be given oxygen and IV access should be obtained immediately. The patient's glucose as well other laboratory values, such as an electrolyte panel, antiepileptic drug levels, and a toxicology screen can also be checked. Lorazepam or diazepam should be prepared.

Her glucose is normal and the patient is treated with rectal diazepam and the seizure continues. Diazepam is repeated but the seizure continues. What is the next step in treatment?

The patient should be given a loading dose of fosphenytoin or phenytoin. Intubation should be considered if her airway or breathing is impaired.

The seizure resolves after a loading dose of fosphenytoin and the two doses of rectal diazepam. At this time, the patient's mother arrives and reports that her daughter has idiopathic epilepsy and this is the 12th seizure of her life. She believes her daughter has been missing doses of her antiepileptic medicine for several weeks. After the patient is stabilized, what anticipatory guidance and follow-up should be suggested?

The child should be referred to the neurology clinic for close follow-up. The importance of compliance with the antiepileptic medicine should be emphasized to both mother and the patient, and information regarding support groups and websites for patients with epilepsy should be discussed.

CHAPTER 12

Musculoskeletal Disease

INJURIES

A 3-year-old daughter presents to the emergency department (ED) because she suddenly refuses to move her arm after her mother grabbed her hand while crossing the street. On examination the child's arm is flexed at the elbow and the hand is pronated. How was this injury likely inflicted?

This patient likely has nursemaid's elbow, also known as subluxation of the radial head. It likely occurred when her mother pulled on her extended arm and pronated forearm. Traction along the axis of the radius in this position can cause the displacement of the radius under the annular ligament.

How is a nursemaid's elbow corrected?

It can be fixed by supinating the forearm, then fully flexing the elbow. Hyperpronation of the arm may also be attempted if the previous technique is unsuccessful.

A 6-year-old girl falls from a tree and develops marked point tenderness along the growth plate but has a normal x-ray. What Salter-Harris fracture is this classified as and what is the prognosis of this fracture?

This is a type 1 Salter-Harris fracture, a transverse fracture through the physis causing the width of the physis to increase. It has an excellent prognosis. These fractures are often not visible on x-rays. Treatment typically involves casting or splinting to hold the leg in place during healing. (See Fig. 12-1.)

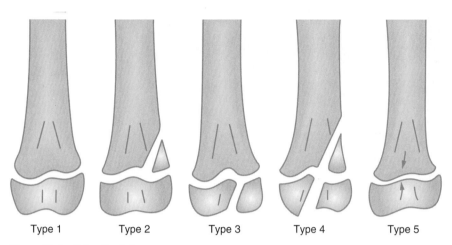

Type 1   Type 2   Type 3   Type 4   Type 5

Figure 12-1   Salter-Harris fractures.

An 8-year-old boy falls from a jungle gym and develops a type 2 Salter-Harris fracture. How does this fracture appear on an x-ray in comparison to a type 3 fracture?

A type 2 Salter-Harris fracture seen on an x-ray goes through the physis and a portion of the metaphysis. A type 3 fracture goes through the physis and epiphysis.

Why do type 4 and 5 Salter-Harris fractures have a worse prognosis?

A type 4 Salter-Harris fracture goes through the metaphysis, physis, and epiphysis, while the type 5 Salter-Harris fracture is a crush injury to the physis. Both of these fractures are associated with increased complications such as growth arrest of the affected limb. Type 4 fractures often require surgical alignment.

What mneumonic is helpful to remember the different types of physis fractures?

Slipped physis (Type 1)

Above the physis (Type 2)

Lower than the physis (Type 3)

Through the epiphysis, physis, and metaphysis (Type 4)

Raised physis (Type 5)

How does a greenstick fracture differ from a torus fracture?

A greenstick fracture incompletely fractures the bone and breaks one side of the cortex and bends the other side. Torus fractures are buckle fractures and are caused by compressive injuries to the bone. (See Figs. 12-2 and 12-3)

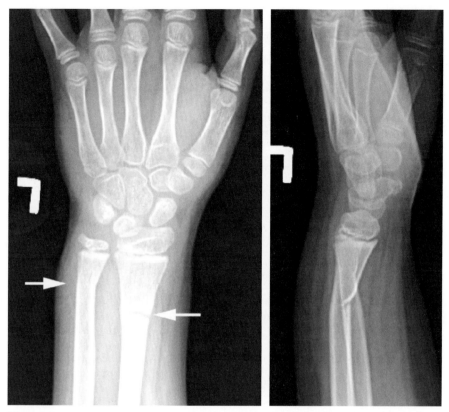

Figure 12-2   Anteroposterior and lateral x-rays of greenstick fracture. (Reproduced, with permission, from Strange GR, Ahrens WR, Lelyveld S, et al. *Pediatric Emergency Medicine*. 2nd ed. New York: McGraw-Hill; 2002.)

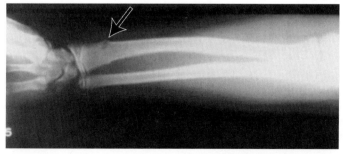

Figure 12-3   X-ray of a torus fracture of the distal radius. (Reproduced, with permission, from Simon RR, Sherman SC, Koenigsknecht SJ. Emergency *Orthopedics, The Extremities*. 5th ed., New York: McGraw-Hill; 2007.)

GROWING PAINS

A 14-year-old basketball player presents to the office with knee pain reproduced when he squats on the ground. Mother reports a recent growth spurt. If Osgood-Schlatter disease is suspected, what will you look for examination?

Osgood-Schlatter disease, often referred to as "growing pains," typically presents with swelling and discomfort on palpation to the tibial tuberosity.

What causes Osgood-Schlatter disease?

It is caused by chronic microtrauma as the stress of the contracting quadriceps is transmitted to the tibial tuberosity.

What type of patient is Osgood-Schlatter commonly seen in?

This overuse injury is common in adolescent athletes who play sports involving jumping or running, such as soccer or gymnastics.

What is the appropriate course of treatment for Osgood-Schlatter disease?

Treatment typically involves stretching before exercise, icing the knee, and use of antiinflammatory medications. If significant pain is present, limitations of physical activity are recommended and casting may be performed for severe cases.

Is idiopathic scoliosis symptomatic?

Typically, idiopathic scoliosis is asymptomatic, without complaints of pain or fatigue.

A 14-year-old adolescent boy has a lateral curvature of the spine of 30°. What is the appropriate treatment for each of the varying degrees of curvature?

This patient has a curvature over 25° and is skeletally immature. As a result, bracing is indicated. If his curvature was less than 25°, observation with follow-up imaging is recommended. For curvatures over 40°, surgical fusion of the vertebra may be indicated to stabilize and improve the shape of the spine.

Is bracing curative for scoliosis?

Bracing does not typically correct the problem, but it does halt the progression of the scoliosis and optimizes spinal growth.

GENETIC CONDITIONS

A 3-year-old boy presents to the office when his parents note that he has difficulty rising up from a seated position and often must use his arms to stand up. On examination you note hypertrophied calf muscles. What condition do you suspect, and how is it inherited?

Duchenne muscular dystrophy (DMD) should be suspected. It is an X-linked disorder.

How does it present?

Weakness with easy fatigability is typically noted symmetrically in the proximal muscles. Early signs are delay in walking, frequent falling, and difficulty getting up from a sitting position. This weakness is demonstrated in this patient by the clinical maneuvers known as "Gower Sign."

What is the defect that causes DMD?

The defect is typically caused by a deletion in the dystrophin gene found on the X chromosome, secondary to a frame-shift mutation. Dystrophin protein provides integral structural stability to the myofiber. Without it, the muscles are susceptible to mechanical injury and undergo repeated cycles of necrosis and regeneration. This results in breakdown of muscle fibers by proteases.

What is the next step in diagnosis?

A serum creatinine phosphokinase (CPK) and a muscle biopsy should be obtained. Serum CPK levels in patients with DMD are often elevated to levels 50 to 100 times the reference range. Muscle biopsy with dystrophin immunostaining shows necrotic muscle fibers and an absence of the dystrophin complex at the sarcolemmal membrane.

What is the prognosis of DMD?

This is a progressive disorder and often leaves patients wheelchair-bound. Death typically occurs in the teens and twenties due to respiratory failure or dilated cardiomyopathy.

How does Becker muscular dystrophy compare and contrast to DMD?

Becker muscular dystrophy (BMD) is also an X-linked disorder that affects the dystrophin gene, but differs in the type of mutation. BMD results from a reading frame or in-frame mutation, causing the production of abnormal but functional dystrophin. BMD typically presents later in life than DMD and has a slightly milder course.

A newborn baby is found to be hypotonic at birth despite an alert expression and normal eye movements. He dies of respiratory failure at 6 months of age. If this patient has spinal muscle atrophy (SMA), what changes may be found on a muscle biopsy?

Patients with SMA have biopsies that show large areas of atrophic type 1 and 2 muscle fibers interspersed among bundles of hypertrophied type 1 fibers. This is consistent with a pattern of atrophy and reinnervation.

What other method can be used to make the diagnosis?

Electromyography (EMG) may also assist with making a diagnosis of SMA.

What would an autopsy of the spinal cord show in a patient with SMA?

Autopsy shows degeneration of the anterior horn cells. This is due to mutations in the survivor motor neuron gene found on chromosome 5q, which is thought to promote motor neuron formation and inhibit apoptosis.

How is SMA type 1 differentiated from the other forms of SMA in its presentation?

The SMAs comprise a group of autosomal recessive disorders characterized by progressive lower motor neuron weakness. SMA type 1 is diagnosed in early infancy, with signs and symptoms appearing usually by age 3 months. Infants may show progressive muscle weakness and hypotonia along with poor suck and difficulty swallowing. Most children die by age 18 months.

How does SMA type 2 differ?

SMA type 2 typically presents between 6 and 18 months, and is the most common form of SMA. Patients with SMA type 2 often show developmental motor delay as the first indication of the disease. Lifespan varies and patients can survive to the third decade. Most deaths are secondary to respiratory failure.

How does SMA type 3 differ?

SMA type 3 is a mild form of SMA, presenting after 18 months. Patients have slowly progressive proximal weakness with an overall mild course. Many patients have normal life expectancies.

Why do these three types of SMAs differ in their presentation?

The different types of SMAs are typically due to different mutations on the survival motor neuron (SMN) gene on chromosome 5.

An adopted 1-year-old boy comes into the emergency room (ER) when his mother notes that he "broke his leg" when he slipped out of his stroller. Multiple fractures are noted on x-ray in both the left and right legs. The baby is noted to have blue sclera and is below the third percentile for length. What is the most likely diagnosis?

This patient may have osteogenesis imperfecta, which is an autosomal dominant abnormality of type 1 collagen and results in bone fragility. There are four different levels of severity of this disease due to different types of genetic mutations.

What is the defect that causes achondroplasia?

The defect occurs in the fibroblast growth factor receptor gene-3 (*FGFR-3*). Increased function of the *FGFR-3* results in decreased endochondral ossification and inhibited proliferation of the chondrocytes in the growth plate cartilage. This alters normal formation of cartilage, causing early ossification and stunted growth, resulting in a short-limbed dwarfism.

What are the skull defects often associated with achondroplasia?

Children with achondroplasia often have ear infections secondary to eustachian tube defects, tooth overcrowding, and characteristic facies. Homozygous patients may develop brain stem compression due to a narrow foramen magnum.

What is the major cause of pulmonary complications in patients with achondroplasia?

These patients often have kyphoscoliosis, which can cause compression of the lungs.

What hand defects are appreciated in patients with achondroplasia?

These patients often are double-jointed and have shortened metacarpals and phalanges.

INFLAMMATION AND INFECTION

A 3-year-old girl wakes up in the morning and refuses to walk on her right leg. She had no previous trauma to the leg and on examination the hip is externally rotated and flexed. The leg has minimally limited range of motion and does not appear painful, red, or swollen. Mother reports that the child recently recovered from a bad cold but has been afebrile. What is the likely diagnosis and what diagnoses should be ruled out?

The clinical presentation is consistent with toxic (or transient) synovitis. However, a septic arthritis, osteomyelitis, and fracture should be ruled out.

How does toxic (or transient) synovitis present?

Toxic synovitis usually presents with unilateral hip pain, limp, and recent history of a viral infection. It is caused by transient inflammation of the hip synovium. Patients are typically afebrile and respond quickly to nonsteroidal antiinflammatory drugs (NSAIDs). The exact cause is unknown.

How does septic arthritis present differently than toxic synovitis?

Patients with septic arthritis can be more toxic-appearing and will usually have a painful joint with limited range of motion and associated fever. The joint may appear erythematous and warm, with signs of swelling. These patients also tend to have an elevated white blood cell (WBC) count and erythrocyte sedimentation rate (ESR).

What organisms are commonly found in septic joints?

Staphylococcus aureus and *Streptococcus* are the most common organisms found in septic joints. *Neisseria gonorrheae* can also be found in sexually active patients.

What is the treatment for a septic joint?

In addition to IV antibiotics, surgical drainage of the joint with irrigation is often performed to prevent permanent damage to the affected joint. A septic joint is an orthopedic emergency unless proven otherwise.

A 6-week-old infant develops fever and refuses to move his right leg with some swelling and erythema of the thigh. The baby has an elevated WBC count and an elevated ESR and C-reactive protein (CRP). A bone scan shows osteomyelitis. What are the most common organisms to cause osteomyelitis?

The most common organism to cause osteomyelitis is *S aureus*. In neonates, group B *Streptococcus* and *Escherichia coli* are common pathogens, while in older children, group A *Streptococcus* and *Haemophilus influenzae* are often the culprits.

An 11-year-old boy steps on a nail through his shoe and subsequently develops osteomyelitis in his foot. What is the likely pathogen?

Puncture wounds often cause osteomyelitis by *S aureus* and *Pseudomonas aeruginosa*.

Which bacterial species are sickle cell patients with osteomyelitis particularly susceptible to?

These patients are more prone to *Salmonella* bone infections.

Why does osteomyelitis tend to occur at the metaphysis?

The metaphysis is more prone to infectious seeding from the bloodstream due to its degree of vascularization. Vessels at the distal metaphysis make sharp angles causing slowed blood flow and low oxygen tension. If microthrombi form in these small vessels, the bone can undergo localized necrosis and bacterial seeding.

What is the typical length and type of treatment for osteomyelitis?

The typical length of treatment is 4 to 6 weeks of antibiotics. Initially treatment must be parenteral but the patient can be transitioned to oral antibiotics as an outpatient depending on the type and location of the infection. Aspiration of the bone can aid with identifying and targeting the bacterial antibiotic coverage.

NONINFECTIOUS LIMP

A 6-year-old boy suddenly develops a limp and reports mild discomfort in his left hip. No trauma has occurred. On examination, the range of motion of the leg is limited when flexed, abducted, and internally rotated. X-ray shows fracture of the femoral head. If this patient has Legg-Calve-Perthes disease, what caused this fracture?

Legg-Calve-Perthes disease occurs due to idiopathic osteonecrosis of the femoral head. Upon revascularization, the soft, previously ischemic bone can develop a fracture and collapse, which has occurred in this patient. The bone will subsequently remodel.

How do a bone scan and an MRI aid in the diagnosis of Legg-Calve-Perthes disease?

A bone scan evaluates for ischemia of the femoral head and any resulting bony changes. This is helpful, especially in cases where initial x-rays are normal. An MRI can give more specific information regarding bony changes and bone marrow edema.

What is the treatment for Legg-Calve-Perthes disease?

Treatment varies based on the symptoms and the degree of damage to the bone of the femoral head. If the patient is young and asymptomatic and the head remains smooth and round, likely observation is the only treatment. Meanwhile, if there is hip stiffening with a flattened femoral head, bracing and surgery may be necessary.

A 13-year-old adolescent boy with a body mass index (BMI) of 32 presents to the office with a limp and aching left hip pain that developed without trauma. On examination, internal rotation is limited and the left leg appears shorter than the right. An x-ray shows anterior and superior displacement of the proximal femur distal to the physis. What is the diagnosis?

This patient has a slipped capital femoral epiphysis (SCFE). This is actually a misnomer, since the epiphysis remains in place but appears to have posterior, inferior displacement.

How does a SCFE occur?

An SCFE occurs when shearing forces exceed the strength of the capital femoral physis, causing the femoral head to be displaced posteriorly and inferiorly in relation to the femoral neck. Increased risk is associated with obesity, growth spurts, inflammation, trauma, and endocrine or metabolic disturbances.

NEWBORN EXAMINATION

On a routine newborn examination, you appreciate a right hip clunk during the hip examination. What maneuvers are performed to evaluate for developmental dysplasia of the hip (DDH) in babies?

The Barlow and Ortolani maneuvers are used to evaluate for DDH in infants. The Barlow test adducts the legs and applies posterior pressure to dislocate the hip posteriorly and superiorly. The Ortolani maneuver abducts the hip while applying gentle pressure over the greater trochanter. The hip will "clunk" as the femoral head is relocated in the acetabulum. The examiner should also evaluate for the presence of asymmetric gluteal and leg folds.

What are risk factors for DDH?

Risk factors include a breech presentation, limited fetal mobility, family history of DDH, a first-born child, and female sex.

What is your next step in diagnosis?

Patients with suspected DDH should be referred for a bilateral hip ultrasound to evaluate if the head of the femur is dysplastic, subluxable, dislocatable, and/or dislocated. If there is an abnormal result, orthopedics should be referred to evaluate and treat.

What is the treatment for DDH?

A Pavlik harness is recommended for children less than 6 months with dislocatable or subluxable hips. This prevents hip extension and adduction and keeps the femoral head in the acetabulum, allowing surrounding ligamentous structures to tighten over time. Open or closed reduction may be required in children over 6 months.

The mother of your newborn patient reports that her child's right foot appears to be inverted. If you are able to easily mold the foot into its anatomically correct position, what is the next step in treatment?

No further intervention is required. This is a common finding on the newborn examination.

A fetus is born after the mother is diagnosed with oligohydramnios. The baby is found to have club foot, or talipes equinovarus, with inversion of foot, plantarflexion, and medial rotation of the tibia. What is the appropriate treatment?

The aim of therapy for a club foot is to correct the deformity early and to maintain the correction until growth stops. These children often require manipulation of the foot, followed by casting or splinting. This is best performed as early as possible but can usually be done between 3 and 6 months of age. Surgery is indicated only if nonsurgical treatments fail (see Fig. 12-4).

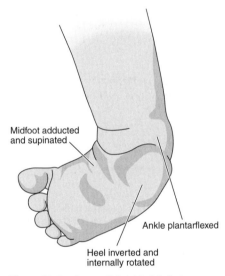

Midfoot adducted and supinated

Ankle plantarflexed

Heel inverted and internally rotated

Figure 12-4   Congenital right club foot. (Reproduced, with permission, from Skinner HB. *Current Diagnosis & Treatment in Orthopedics.* 4th ed. New York: McGraw-Hill; 2006: Fig. 11.15.)

How does congenital torticollis differ from acquired torticollis?

Congenital torticollis typically occurs during delivery when the sternocleidomastoid muscle is injured, whereas acquired torticollis occurs from cervical spine rotary subluxation.

What additional study should be obtained if congenital torticollis is suspected?

A hip ultrasound may also be obtained due to the association of congenital torticollis with DDH.

How do the treatments of congenital versus acquired torticollis differ?

Treatment for congenital torticollis consists of physical therapy, whereas treatment for acquired torticollis is dependent on the cause. Most commonly antiinflammatory medications, stretching, and a cervical collar may be utilized.

CLINICAL VIGNETTES

An 8-year-old boy presents to your office with a history of 1 week of intermittent left anterior thigh and knee pain. Both parents and child deny a history of trauma. You note a limp as he walks into the examining room. On examination he has decreased range of motion of the left hip, particularly with internal rotation and abduction. The complete blood count (CBC) is within normal limits and the ESR is not elevated. A plain x-ray of the hips shows no abnormalities. What additional medical history should you obtain to narrow your differential?

Rule out other conditions that can cause avascular necrosis of the femoral head, such as a history of sickle cell anemia or other hemoglobinopathies, and chronic diseases requiring frequent or long-term corticosteroid use, such as systemic lupus erythematosus or asthma.

You obtain a technetium 99 bone scan, which shows avascular changes to the left femoral head. The CBC and ESR are within normal limits. What is the most likely diagnosis?

Legg-Calve-Perthes disease, or idiopathic avascular necrosis of the femoral head.

What are two potential long-term complications for this patient.

Permanent deformity of the hip and higher risk for osteoarthritis of the joint later in life.

A 9-month-old infant is at your office for her well-child checkup. The parents are concerned because she appears weaker and more floppy than similar-aged babies in her playgroup. Looking through your records, you note that she was unable to sit independently at the 6-month well-child checkup. Today, she cannot get to the sitting position independently but can stay sitting if placed in that position by her mother. You also note poor pincer grasp, and diffuse bilateral hypotonia in the proximal muscle groups. A fine postural tremor is seen when the child reaches out for a toy. What is the next step in diagnosis?

A neuromuscular disorder is suspected, most likely spinal muscular atrophy type 2 based on this patient's age and history. A muscle biopsy is necessary to differentiate the type of neuromuscular disorder.

The muscle biopsy shows large areas of atrophic types 1 and 2 muscle fibers interspersed among bundles of hypertrophied type 1 fibers. What will be the most likely cause of death for this child?

Although children with SMA type 2 can live into the third decade, severe respiratory failure or pulmonary infection is the typical cause of death for these patients.

The parents come to see you a few months later. They are planning to have a second child and would like more information. What should you tell them?

The SMAs are an autosomal recessive disorder caused by a genetic mutation on chromosome 5q. Due to the inheritance pattern there will be a 25% chance the next child could have SMA. The parents should be referred to a genetic counselor for a complete family history and education about the role of prenatal diagnosis.

CHAPTER 13

Endocrinology

DIABETES, DIABETES INSIPIDUS, AND SYNDROME OF INAPPROPRIATE ANTIDIURETIC HORMONE

An 8-year-old girl presents with progressive fatigue, polyuria, polyphagia, and reports losing 7 lb over the past month in spite of a healthy appetite. What test(s) would you perform next?

This patient is likely presenting with type 1 diabetes. Blood glucose levels should be obtained. In a symptomatic patient, a single random glucose level ≥200 mg/dL is sufficient for the diagnosis. If asymptomatic, a fasting blood glucose ≥126 mg/dL or an oral glucose tolerance test (OGTT) with a 2-hour post load blood glucose level of greater than 200 mg/dL is diagnostic. A urinalysis should also be performed to determine the presence of ketones in the urine.

If the above patient had a random blood glucose level of 300, what would be the proper treatment?

Type 1 diabetes is caused by beta-cell loss resulting in insulin deficiency. Ketosis may also occur. Therefore, this patient will require insulin therapy. Education and counseling will be critical in helping the family master diabetes self-management.

What human leukocyte antigen (HLA) types are commonly associated with type 1 diabetes?

HLA-DR3 and HLA-DR4 located on chromosome 6 are both associated with an increased risk for type 1 diabetes.

A 13-year-old adolescent boy with type 1 diabetes presents with nausea, vomiting, severe abdominal pain, fatigue, and increased polyuria and polyphagia. On physical examination, a fruity odor to the breath, tachycardia, and rapid, shallow breathing are noted. What is the diagnosis and appropriate treatment?

The patient's signs and symptoms are consistent with diabetic ketoacidosis (DKA), a dangerous condition characterized by hyperglycemia, ketosis, dehydration, and acidosis. This is a medical emergency that needs to be judiciously treated with an insulin drip and IV fluid/electrolyte replacement. The patient must be monitored frequently for electrolyte changes and any neurological changes that could herald symptomatic cerebral edema.

What are Kussmaul respirations?

Kussmaul respirations are rapid, shallow breaths that often occur in DKA. It is the respiratory response to compensate for the metabolic acidosis.

A 16-year-old Latino adolescent girl presents with a body mass index (BMI) of 33 and reports a family history of diabetes. On physical examination, a velvety hyperpigmentation and thickening of the skin is noted under the axilla and at the back of the neck. What diagnosis is suspected?

Type 2 diabetes, which is characterized by insulin resistance and an inability to compensate by increasing insulin levels adequately, should be ruled out in this patient. Obesity and acanthosis nigricans are frequently observed and those findings along with the family history place this patient at high risk.

What complications is this child at risk for in the future?

Complications of poorly controlled diabetes include retinopathy, nephropathy, neuropathy, and accelerated large-vessel atherosclerosis leading to stroke or myocardial infarction.

A 7-year-old boy presents to clinic 3 months after being hospitalized for bacterial meningitis. His mother has noted that he wet his bed at night six times since returning home from the hospital and has been drinking a lot of water. What laboratory values do you expect to find in this condition?

The patient has central diabetes insipidus (DI) in which decreased antidiuretic hormone (ADH) release from the brain results in polyuria, enuresis, and excessive thirst. Urine osmolality and urine specific gravity will be low and serum sodium and serum osmolality will eventually increase over time. Treatment includes administering desmopressin acetate (DDAVP), an ADH analogue.

Describe how one would differentiate between central and nephrogenic DI.

A DDAVP challenge will help alleviate symptoms of polyuria and excessive thirst in central DI and will not alleviate symptoms in nephrogenic DI, in which the collecting ducts do not respond to ADH.

The parents of a 21-month-old infant rush their child to the emergency room (ER) after a witnessed seizure. Laboratories are significant for Na 118, serum Osm 255, increased urine Na, and urine Osm 800. What diagnosis is most likely?

This patient has syndrome of inappropriate antidiuretic hormone (SIADH) in which increased levels of ADH lead to hyponatremia, decreased serum osmolality, increased urine Na, and increased urine osmolality.

What is the treatment for SIADH?

Treatment of chronic hyponatremia in a symptomatic patient is slow correction with hypertonic saline. Patients are usually asymptomatic until Na less than 120, in which case fluid restriction and occasionally demeclocycline are the treatments of choice.

THYROID DISORDERS

What is the most common cause of acquired hypothyroidism?

Hashimoto thyroiditis, which is a chronic lymphocytic thyroiditis that results in autoimmune destruction of the thyroid, is the most common cause of acquired hypothyroidism. Other causes of hypothyroidism include radioactive iodine or surgical ablation for treatment of hyperthyroidism, use of antithyroid meds, panhypopituitarism, and ectopic thyroid dysgenesis.

What are common symptoms of acquired hypothyroidism? What is the diagnostic test?

Signs and symptoms include goiter, growth failure, cold intolerance, lethargy, constipation, coarse puffy facies, dry thin hair and skin, and deep tendon reflexes with a delayed relaxation time.

What markers are diagnostic for hypothyroidism?

A decreased total T4 and T3, or free T4, and elevated thyroid-stimulating hormone (TSH) are diagnostic for hypothyroidism. Antimicrosomal antibody titers may also be increased.

An 18-month-old infant born in Africa presents to clinic with a large goiter, late milestone development, sluggishness, and an occasional hoarse cry. Physical examination reveals macroglossia, mottled skin, abdominal distention, and hypotonia. What newborn screening test was not performed?

Congenital hypothyroidism should be diagnosed by neonatal thyroid function test screening after 24 hours of life and within 10 days of birth. Consequences of undiagnosed hypothyroidism include: lowered IQ, gross and fine motor difficulties, ataxia, decreased attention spans, and speech problems.

What is the appropriate treatment for congenital hypothyroidism?

Treatment with levothyroxine should begin as soon as the diagnosis of congenital hypothyroidism is made. If treatment begins within the first month of life, the prognosis for intellectual performance is much improved.

A 13-year-old adolescent girl presents with "nervousness, sweatiness, a huge appetite, and bulging eyes" over the past 9 months. Physical examination is significant for exophthalmos, fine tremor, goiter, and warm skin. What treatment is needed?

This patient likely has juvenile Graves disease and should be treated with an antithyroid agent such as methimazole (the only indication for use of propylthiouracil or PTU is thyroid storm). A beta-blocker may also be used to relieve symptoms of anxiety, tachycardia, tremor, and diaphoresis.

What is thyroid storm?

Thyroid storm is a medical emergency caused by excess release of thyroid hormone. It is characterized by severe tachycardia that may lead to cardiogenic shock, marked fever, central nervous system (CNS) manifestations (agitation, psychosis, confusion), and GI symptoms (nausea, vomiting, diarrhea). It is treated with antithyroid agents such as PTU, iodine, beta-blockers, steroids, and often cooling blankets.

A concerned parent brings her 10-year-old boy into the clinic for a "big growth in the center of his neck." Further history and physical is significant for an asymptomatic, asymmetrical 2 × 2 cm thyroid nodule. Thyroid function tests (TFTs) are normal. What is the next step in management?

Ultrasonography can be performed followed by fine-needle aspirate (FNA). Ultrasound can help better define the nodule. FNA is more difficult in children as compared to adults and as such success of the procedure as well as cytopathologic interpretation is dependent upon the experience of the center. Additional studies that can be done include iodine scan and CT if malignancy is suspected.

What is the significance of the terms "cold nodule" and "hot nodule" on a radioactive iodine scan?

A cold nodule has poor uptake of radioactive iodine and represents hypo or nonfunctional thyroid tissue. It is more concerning of malignancy (considered rare in childhood) and should be treated with surgery. A hot nodule has increased intake of radioactive iodine and represents thyroid tissue that is functioning autonomously with minimum or no regulation. It may be closely observed with periodic physical examination of the thyroid and TFTs.

What are the different types of malignant thyroid cancers and which is the most common form?

Malignant thyroid cancers include papillary, follicular, medullary, and undifferentiated carcinomas, sarcomas, and lymphomas. Papillary carcinoma is the most common and has the best prognosis due to its slow-growing nature.

What are the pathologic features of thyroid papillary carcinoma?

The pathologic features of thyroid papillary carcinoma are Orphan Annie eyes (nuclei that are uniformly light-blue staining and appear empty), psammoma bodies, and nuclear grooves (lines that run across the nuclei).

PARATHYROID DISORDERS

A previously healthy 11-year-old boy develops severe abdominal pain with constipation, polyuria, and polydipsia. He has been more moody in days prior to presentation. While in the ER, he passes a kidney stone in his urine. Laboratory evaluation reveals an elevated calcium (Ca) level. What condition does this patient likely have and what is the treatment?

This patient likely has primary hyperparathyroidism. During childhood the etiology is usually a single parathyroid adenoma. The treatment of choice is to give fluids, furosemide (which increases Ca excretion), and prednisone in more refractory cases (decreases intestinal absorption of Ca). Surgical removal may be necessary.

Name three causes of secondary hyperparathyroidism.

1. Vitamin D deficiency
2. Chronic renal failure
3. Liver disease

A 4-year-old boy with a known history of cleft palate, abnormal facies, truncus arteriosus, and mental retardation presents to the ER with new onset of seizures, tetany, and carpopedal spasms. What laboratory values do you expect to find?

This patient has DiGeorge syndrome. The new onset of seizures and tetany are due to hypocalcemia secondary to congenital underdevelopment of the parathyroid glands. Thus, one would expect the following laboratory values: decreased serum Ca, increased serum phosphorous, and decreased serum parathyroid hormone (PTH).

What is the appropriate immediate treatment for the above patient?

Hypocalcemia is treated with 10% calcium gluconate and vitamin D. Seizure medications may also be used to immediately stabilize the patient; however, they will not treat the underlying cause.

HPA AXIS DISORDERS

A 15-year-old adolescent girl presents to clinic complaining of intermittent severe palpitations, headaches, sweating, and flushing. While at the doctor's office, she experiences another episode and her BP is recorded at 190/110. An abdominal mass is palpated on examination. What tests would you order next?

This patient likely has pheochromocytoma, a catecholamine-secreting tumor that is located in the adrenal medulla (70%) or in the extra-adrenal sympathetic chain (30%). Serum vanillylmandelic acid (VMA), metanephrine, and normetanephrine levels should be sent as well as a urine sample for catecholamines or metabolites. Imaging studies such as an abdominal ultrasound, CT, or MRI may also be considered. Surgical excision is the accepted treatment.

A 3-week-old newborn girl who was born at home is rushed to the ER for intractable vomiting and listlessness for 5 hours. On physical examination, ambiguous genitalia are noted. What is the likely etiology for this disorder?

This patient likely has salt-wasting congenital adrenal hyperplasia (CAH). In a 46 XX child 21-hydroxylase deficiency is the most common cause of CAH.

What laboratory values do you expect in the above patient?

Hyponatremia and hyperkalemia are the result of a low aldosterone level and hypoglycemia is the result of a low cortisol level. There are markedly increased levels of 17-hydroxyprogesterone and testosterone. Ambiguous genitalia is the result of excess 17-hydroxyprogesterone being shunted over to the overproduction of androgens.

What is the accepted treatment of the above patient?

IV fluid and electrolyte replacement are essential as patients with 21-hydoxylase deficiency are dehydrated, hyponatremic, hypochloremic, and hyperkalemic. Normal saline is given along with dextrose for management of hypoglycemia. Hydrocortisone and fludrocortisone replacements are necessary for life.

Describe the difference between 21-hydroxylase deficiency and 11-hydroxylase deficiency.

While in 21-hydroxylase deficiency there is an accumulation of 17-hydroxyprogesterone, in 11-hydroxylase deficiency there is an accumulation of 11-deoxycortisol and deoxycorticosterone, which has mineralocorticoid activity. Thus, patients with 11-hydroxylase deficiency usually have hypertension, hypernatremia, and hypokalemia.

A 17-year-old adoloscent girl presents with complaints of fatigue, increased acne, facial hair, and 15-lb weight gain over the past 3 months in spite of attempts to diet. Physical examination is significant for moon facies, buffalo hump, virilization, and BP of 150/90. What is the next clinical step?

Cushing syndrome is the most likely diagnosis. Initial laboratory tests include both a.m. and p.m. serum cortisol levels and a 24-hour free urine cortisol collection. If cortisol levels are elevated, a stepwise dexamethasone suppression test is performed. A magnetic resonance imaging (MRI) of the pituitary and CT of the adrenal glands are also appropriate imaging studies.

What are several different etiologies of Cushing syndrome?

Endogenous causes of overproduction of cortisol include Cushing disease or bilateral adrenal hyperplasia, and adrenal adenomas and carcinomas. Cushing disease is usually caused by a microadenoma of the pituitary secreting excess amounts of adrenocorticotropic hormone (ACTH). Exogenous causes of Cushing syndrome include pharmacologic use of steroids.

What is the treatment for Cushing syndrome?

Treatment is determined by etiology. In cases of excessive exogenous steroid use, the medications are tapered or discontinued. In patients with Cushing disease, transsphenoidal resection of the pituitary adenoma is curative. In patients with adrenal tumors, adrenalectomy and radiotherapy are needed.

A 20-year-old man presents with fever, severe nausea, vomiting, abdominal pain, weakness, and a suntan in the middle of January. BP at supine position is 90/50 and BP while standing is 85 per palp. What is the treatment of choice?

This patient has acute adrenal insufficiency and Addison disease. The treatment of choice is to give IV fluids to facilitate volume replacement and IV steroids. Glucocorticoid and mineralocorticoid treatment must continue for 48 hours and doses must be increased during times of stress.

What laboratory values would you expect in this patient?

A patient with acute adrenal insufficiency will be hyponatremic, hyperkalemic, and hypoglycemic due to the failure of the adrenal cortex to produce enough glucocorticoids and mineralocorticoids.

Name several etiologies of Addison disease.

Addison disease may either be caused by primary adrenal insufficiency as a result of autoimmune destruction, tuberculosis, meningococcal septicemia, or HIV therapy. Secondary causes of adrenal insufficiency include hypothalamic or pituitary tumors, congenital hypopituitarism, and adrenal suppression.

A 16-year-old adolescent girl presents to clinic complaining of worsening headache and amenorrhea for 3 months. She is not sexually active and a urine pregnancy test is negative. Physical examination is significant for galactorrhea. What is the next step in management?

This patient needs a serum prolactin level and an MRI of the pituitary to establish the size and location of the prolactinoma. Measurement of other pituitary hormones such as growth hormone (GH), ACTH, and TSH are also necessary to determine the secreting activity of the adenoma. Treatment includes a dopamine agonist such as bromocriptine or transsphenoidal surgical resection.

Explain how dopamine agonists help to reduce symptoms of prolactin-secreting adenomas.

In normal physiology, prolactin secretion is inhibited by dopamine in the pituitary. Dopamine serves as an antagonist to prolactin secretion. Thus, dopamine agonists, such as bromocriptine, help relieve symptoms of prolactin-secreting adenomas.

A 22-year-old man presents with headache, coarsened facial features, frontal bossing, and complains that his shoes and gloves no longer fit him comfortably. What tests would you order next?

This patient likely has acromegaly, a condition caused by an excess of GH after the epiphyses close. Workup for acromegaly includes serum insulinlike growth factor 1 (IGF1), serum GH, oral glucose challenge test (failure to suppress GH <5 ng/dL is diagnostic), and an MRI of the pituitary.

What treatment options may be offered to the above patient?

Medical therapy with somatostatin analogues such as octreotide or with dopamine agonists such as bromocriptine may be offered to treat this patient's GH excess. Transsphenoidal resection of well-circumscribed pituitary tumors may be curative.

Name two hormones that oppose the actions of insulin (ie, insulin counter-regulatory hormones)?

1. GH
2. Cortisol

A 7-hour-old newborn is noted to have persistent hypoglycemia and physical examination is significant for micropenis. What diagnosis is suspected and what other signs/symptoms may arise in the future from this diagnosis?

This infant likely has hypopituitarism. Luteinizing hormone (LH) and follicle-stimulating hormone (FSH) deficiency will lead to micropenis and pubertal delay while ACTH deficiency will lead to decreased cortisol levels. TSH deficiency will cause secondary hypothyroidism and GH deficiency will result in hypoglycemia and poor linear growth.

PUBERTAL DISORDERS

A 7-year-old girl begins to develop breasts and 4 months later she begins to develop axillary and pubic hair. Her first menses is at age 8. What diagnosis do you suspect and what is the treatment?

This patient has precocious puberty. In girls it is defined as having secondary sexual characteristics before the age of 8 years and in boys before the age of 9 years. Treatment involves the use of gonadotropin-releasing hormone (GnRH) analogues for central precocious puberty.

What is the most common cause of precocious puberty in girls and what is the most common cause of precocious puberty in boys?

While precocious puberty in girls is usually idiopathic, in boys there is usually an organic cause including a greater incidence of CNS pathology including infection, head injury, gliomas, and congenital malformation.

A 17-month-old girl presents to the clinic with Tanner stage II breasts. You suspect premature thelarche. Describe how the levels of hormones, growth rate, and bone age differ between premature thelarche and precocious puberty.

In premature thelarche, there are prepubertal levels of LH, FSH, and estrogen as opposed to precocious puberty in which there is pubertal levels of LH, FSH, and estrogen. Furthermore, there is advanced bone age and growth acceleration in precocious puberty while in premature thelarche there is normal bone age and growth rate. Premature thelarche is self-limiting and does not progress. It is most common in the first few years of life.

Name the three classic signs/symptoms of McCune-Albright syndrome.

McCune-Albright syndrome consists of the following:
1. Polyostotic fibrous dysplasia
2. Café au lait skin pigmentation
3. Precocious puberty

A 15-year-old adolescent boy presents complaining that he does not look like other boys in his class. Physical examination is significant for absence of pubertal development. What is your differential diagnosis?

This patient has pubertal delay. The differential diagnosis includes: underlying systemic disease, constitutional delay, primary gonadal failure including Klinefelter syndrome and hypothalamic/pituitary axis dysfunction.

What is the most common cause of pubertal delay?

The most common cause of pubertal delay is constitutional delay. In these patients, there is usually a family history of constitutional delay and bone age is delayed.

A 5-year-old girl has consistently presented to clinic below the fifth percentile in height. Name five possibilities for this child's condition.

Short stature is defined as height below the fifth percentile. The differential diagnosis for short stature includes: genetic short stature, constitutional delay, nutritional deficiencies, GH deficiency, hypothyroidism, Cushing syndrome, panhypopituitarism, Turner syndrome, Down syndrome, and psychosocial deprivation. The most common etiology is familial short stature.

Describe the normal pattern of female secondary sexual characteristics development.

Breast development (<8 years → precocious puberty; >14 years → delayed puberty); height growth spurt; development of pubic hair; menarche

Describe the normal pattern of male secondary sexual characteristics development.

Testicular enlargement (<9 years → precocious puberty; >15 years → delayed puberty); penile enlargement; height growth spurt; pubic hair

A 17-year-old adolescent girl presents to clinic complaining that she has not had her first menses yet. On physical examination, she has Tanner stage 4 breasts, sparse armpit and pubic hair, and a short, blind-ending vagina. What syndrome is suspected and what is this patient's karyotype?

Testicular feminization or androgen insensitivity syndrome occurs when a developing fetus with a XY karyotype is insensitive to androgen hormones. When androgen insensitivity is complete, the patient is genetically a male but appears to be a female. This occurs 1 in 20,000 live births.

What malignancy is this patient at increased risk for?

This patient is at increased risk for malignant transformation of gonadal tissue (gonadal blastoma). A physical examination and/or imaging studies should be performed to detect undescended testicles.

A 15-year-old adolescent girl has complained of painful menstruation for 8 months. What is the most likely cause of this patient's pain?

This patient's dysmenorrhea is most likely caused by excess production of prostaglandins E_2 and F_2, which cause uterine contractions, increased sensitization of pain receptors, and uterine tissue hypoxia and ischemia. Treatment includes the use of NSAIDs and hormonal contraceptives. This is an example of primary dysmenorrhea, in which there is no pathology of the pelvis present.

What are several causes of secondary dysmenorrhea?

Causes of secondary dysmenorrhea include:

1. Congenital abnormalities of the vagina, cervix, or uterus
2. Endometriosis
3. Pelvic adhesions
4. Foreign bodies (IUDs)
5. Sexually transmitted infections (STIs)
6. Ectopic pregnancy

A 16-year-old adolescent girl presents to clinic stating that she has yet to get her first period. She reports normal sexual development up until now and denies recent weight loss or strenuous physical activity. Physical examination is within normal limits. What laboratories do you want to order?

The absence of menses by age 16 is the definition of primary amenorrhea. Laboratories that are needed for the workup of primary amenorrhea include: urine beta human chorionic gonadotropin (β-hCG), prolactin, FSH, LH, testosterone, DHEA-S, estradiol, TSH, and free T4.

What are several common causes of secondary amenorrhea?

Several common causes of secondary amenorrhea include pregnancy, extreme exercise, weight loss, and polycystic ovarian syndrome with pregnancy being the most common.

What common cause of primary amenorrhea can be diagnosed by a karyotype?

A common cause of primary amenorrhea is Turner syndrome. Turner syndrome (45, XO) is a rare chromosomal disorder of females characterized by short stature, a lack of sexual development at puberty, infertility, cardiac abnormalities, webbed neck, broad chest, low posterior hairline, puffy hands and feet, and kidney abnormalities.

CLINICAL VIGNETTES

A 19-year-old woman with a known history of medullary thyroid cancer presents with intermittent headache, palpitations, and diaphoresis. On further questioning, she also reports muscle weakness, nausea, vomiting, constipation, polyuria, polydipsia, and subjective fevers. What condition do you suspect?

This patient likely has multiple endocrine neoplasia type 2a (MEN2a), an inherited disorder. The triad of MEN2a is medullary cancer of the thyroid, hyperplasia or adenoma of the parathyroid gland(s), and pheochromocytoma.

What causes MEN type 2a?

MEN2a is caused by a mutation in the *RET* gene. The major risk factor of MEN 2a is a positive family history.

Should this patient have been screened for MEN2a after being diagnosed with medullary cancer of the thyroid?

A detailed family history should have been taken at the time of the diagnosis of medullary thyroid cancer and a screening test for MEN2a and MEN2b should have been performed. Furthermore, medullary thyroid tumors are present in over 90% of MEN2a cases. This condition affects patients of all ages and men and women equally.

How is the diagnosis of MEN2a made?

The diagnosis is dependent on the identification of the *RET* mutation through a blood test. The endocrine organs are also evaluated with several tests including: ultrasound of thyroid revealing a thyroid nodule, thyroid scan showing cold nodule, thyroid biopsy significant for medullary carcinoma cells, urinary metanephrines and catecholamines, adrenal CT/MRI, elevated calcitonin, increased calcium, and decreased phosphorus.

What is the treatment for MEN2a?

Medullary carcinoma of the thyroid is treated by total thyroidectomy and removal of surround lymph nodes. Pheochromocytoma and parathyroid hyperplasia or adenoma are treated with surgical resection as well. Screening of close relatives of patients with MEN2a should be performed.

CHAPTER 14

Immunology and Rheumatology

IMMUNOLOGY

Why are human immunodeficiency virus (HIV) antibody tests on neonates born to mothers with HIV not reliable for diagnosing HIV?

Maternal serum antibodies are transferred across the placenta during pregnancy and may be found in the infant until 6 to 12 months of age when the child begins to develop his or her own antibodies. Thus, neonates born to mothers with HIV may have a false-positive HIV antibody test.

What testing should be done on an infant of an HIV-positive mother?

Babies born to HIV-positive women should have a DNA or RNA polymerase chain reaction (PCR) test at 14 to 21 days of life, 1 to 2 months of age, and again at 4 to 6 months of age. Two negative tests are needed to confirm a negative HIV status. Breastfeeding is a source of continued HIV exposure, and is therefore not recommended for HIV-positive mothers in the United States. A baby must have two negative blood tests collected at a minimum of 6 months after cessation of breastfeeding to confirm negative status.

What treatment should be initiated on HIV-exposed infants?

PCP (*Pneumocystis jiroveci* pneumonia) is a common opportunistic infection encountered in HIV-positive children. Therefore, it is recommended that HIV-exposed infants are started on prophylactic cotrimoxazole until negative infection status is confirmed.

Patients with a history of recurrent infections with encapsulated organisms such as *Haemophilus influenzae* and *Streptococcus pneumoniae*, along with a failure to respond to antibiotic therapy, suggests what type of immunodeficiency?

This history is strongly suggestive of a primary B-cell deficiency disorder, which includes Bruton agammaglobulinemia, common variable immunodeficiency, and selective IgA deficiency.

A 3-month-old infant has a history of recurrent pneumonia, diarrhea, skin rashes, sepsis, and failure to thrive has an absent thymic shadow on radiographic studies. What is the diagnosis?

This patient has severe combined immunodeficiency (SCID) in which a defect in stem cell maturation results in complete absence of lymphocyte function. Patients typically present during infancy with chronic diarrhea, failure to thrive, and opportunistic infections. There are multiple genetic mutations which may cause SCID, all of which cause the absence of functioning T-lymphocytes. Thus, the absent thymic shadow is suggestive of thymic aplasia, which can also be seen in other T-lymphocyte disorders such as DiGeorge syndrome.

What precautions are necessary for this patient?

Patients with SCID should never receive blood products without prior irradiation due to the high likelihood of developing a graft versus host reaction. As well, defects in T-lymphocyte function is a contraindication to receiving live virus vaccines.

A 6-month-old infant presents with eczema, recurrent bacterial infections, and thrombocytopenia. What type of immunodeficiency is suspected?

Wiskott-Aldrich syndrome is an X-linked recessive combined (cellular and humoral) immunodeficiency disorder characterized by the triad of eczema, recurrent bacterial infections, and thrombocytopenia.

What is the inheritance pattern of the above syndrome?

This illness results from a defect in the Wiskott-Aldrich syndrome protein (*WASP*) gene that affects the organization of actin during interactions between antigen-presenting cells and T-cells.

A 4-year-old girl presents to clinic with a history of chronic sinopulmonary infections, regression of motor milestones, and small, dilated vessels along the bulbar conjunctiva and skin surface. An alpha-fetoprotein level is found to be elevated. What condition is this patient at future risk for?

This patient's clinical history is consistent with ataxia telangiectasia, a rare autosomal recessive disorder characterized by humoral and cell-mediated immunodeficiency, oculocutaneous telangiectasia, and progressive cerebellar ataxia due to Purkinje cell degeneration in the cerebellum. This disease is a result of mutations on the ataxia telangiectasia mutated (*ATM*) gene, which is involved in DNA repair. Therefore, these patients are at increased risk for malignancy, particularly leukemias and lymphomas, as well as radiation sensitivity.

What diagnostic tests would be needed to diagnose disorders of cell-mediated immunity?

An absolute lymphocyte count (ALC), T-cell panel, mitogen stimulation response, and delayed hypersensitivity skin testing are often used to diagnose cell-mediated immunity disorders.

A 4-month-old infant presents with a hypocalcemic tetany, ventricular septal defect, abnormal facies, and thymic hypoplasia. What is the etiology of this patient's condition?

This patient has DiGeorge syndrome, which results from the abnormal development of the third and fourth pharyngeal pouches. It is characterized by the mnemonic CATCH-22: **C**ardiac abnormalities, **A**bnormal facies, **T**hymic hypoplasia, **C**left palate, **H**ypocalcemia, chromosome **22**q11 deletion. There is a strong overlap between this syndrome and velocardiofacial syndrome.

Why do patients with the above condition have disorders of cell-mediated immunity?

Patients with DiGeorge syndrome have varying degrees to thymic hypoplasia, and thus differing degrees of T-lymphocytes function. The thymus is a primary lymphoid organ for the development of T-lymphocytes. Those with complete DiGeorge syndrome have thymic aplasia and therefore no functioning T-lymphocytes. Others have mild thymic hypoplasia and are classified as partial DiGeorge.

The concerned parents of the infant in the previous question want to know the treatment options for their child. What do you tell them?

Thymus transplantation and human leukocyte antigens (HLA)-identical bone marrow transplants have been successful in patients with complete DiGeorge syndrome. Some patients with partial DiGeorge have improved in time without treatment. However, initial therapy should be directed toward treating hypocalcemia and repairing associated congenital heart defects and cleft palate.

A 5-year-old girl has a history of multiple respiratory, gastrointestinal, and urinary tract bacterial infections. Serum IgA is less than 5 mg/dL. What diagnosis is suspected?

Selective IgA deficiency is the most common primary immunodeficiency syndrome and is most often asymptomatic. It is found in approximately 1 out of every 600 people.

What medical treatments are contraindicated in the above condition?

Characterized by low levels or absence of serum and secretory IgA immunoglobulin, selective IgA deficiency patients may have fatal anaphylactic reactions to blood products and intravenous immunoglobulin. Thus, immunoglobulin treatment is contraindicated in these patients.

A 10-month-old infant presents with a condition in which he has recurrent sinopulmonary infections, no tonsillar tissue, and extremely low or absent levels of immunoglobulins and mature B-lymphocytes. What is the name and cause of his disorder?

X-linked agammaglobulinemia (XLA), also known as Bruton agammaglobulinemia, is an X-linked recessive disorder in which a defect in the gene coding for Bruton tyrosine kinase causes arrest of early B-cell development. Symptoms occur after 6 to 9 months when maternally derived antibody levels fall.

A 9-year-old boy with a history of liver abscesses and chronic pyogenic skin infections is found to have leukocytosis and hypergammaglobulinemia. What are the next steps needed to make the diagnosis?

This patient likely has chronic granulomatous disease (CGD) in which phagocyte dysfunction leads to an inability to kill catalase-positive microorganisms. A nitroblue tetrazolium test (NBT) will be negative as neutrophils in this patient are unable to reduce NBT to insoluble blue formazan. A dihydrorhodamine (DHR) test is used to confirm the diagnosis. This test uses flow cytometry to show lack of superoxide production.

What is the treatment for the above patient?

Treatment for CGD includes prophylactic trimethoprim-sulfamethoxazole and itraconazole, antibiotic treatment during infections, and recombinant interferon-gamma, which reduces the incidence of serious infections. Human stem cell transplant is the only know cure for CGD.

A 22-month-old child presents with a history of recurrent sinusitis, pneumonia, and impetigo. Physical examination is significant for oculocutaneous albinism and laboratories are significant for pancytopenia. What treatment should be offered to the patient?

This patient has Chediak-Higashi syndrome, an autosomal recessive disorder characterized by abnormal intracellular protein transport which affects neutrophil function. Treatment includes antibiotics for acute infections, high-dose ascorbic acid, and bone marrow transplant.

A 2-month-old female infant presents with labial cellulitis and an intact umbilical stump. Blood testing reveals a very high WBC count. What condition should you suspect?

Although very rare, this patient could have leukocyte adhesion deficiency, in which a defect on chromosome 21 causes a failure in CD18 expression. CD18 is essential for leukocyte adhesion to vascular endothelium and phagocytosis. Clinical manifestations include delayed umbilical cord separation, recurrent bacterial and fungal infections, absence of pus at wound sites, and persistent leukocytosis.

Patients with complement disorders are at higher risk of what three conditions?

Disorders of the complement system can manifest in increased susceptibility to *Neisseria* infection, hereditary angioedema, and a higher incidence of autoimmune disease.

What tests are performed to establish the diagnosis of complement disorders?

Total hemolytic complement tests of the classical or terminal pathway and alternative pathways known as CH_{50} and AH_{50}, respectively, are used to establish the diagnosis of complement disorders. Further testing may be necessary to identify the causative protein involved.

An 18-month-old boy status post bone marrow transplantation for SCID presents 3 weeks post-op with severe diarrhea and intense, widespread reddening of the skin with exfoliation. Laboratories are significant for elevated liver function tests (LFTs). What is the etiology of this patient's condition?

Graft-versus-host disease (GVHD) is a complication of bone marrow transplantation. It is characterized by grafted and immunocompetent donor T-cell activation against an immunocompromised host's major histocompatibility complex antigens (HCA).

What could have been done to prevent the above condition and what treatment can be offered to the patient?

GVHD may be prevented by a careful preoperative screening for blood group (ABO) and HLA-compatible donors. The treatment for GVHD includes the use of high doses of corticosteroids, antibodies to T-cells, or other immunosuppressive medications.

ALLERGY

One hour after a CT scan with iodinated contrast, a 19-year-old patient becomes short of breath, tachypneic, tachycardic, and has a BP of 80 per palp. The patient's friend tells you that she thinks there is a history of an allergic reaction to shellfish. What is the next clinical step?

The patient has anaphylaxis secondary to the administration of iodinated radioactive contrast. The next clinical step is to establish ABCs (airway, breathing, circulation). IM epinephrine should be given simultaneously as well as diphenhydramine. Vital signs should be monitored frequently.

What is the difference between anaphylaxis and anaphylactoid reaction?

Although anaphylactoid reaction is clinically similar to anaphylaxis, anaphylactoid reaction is not IgE-mediated and does not require previous exposure to the antigen.

What are the causes of acute urticaria?

Urticaria, or hives, is caused by a type I hypersensitivity reaction or other immunologic response. Etiologies include viruses, bacteria, food, medications, insect stings, autoimmune diseases, and malignancies. The most common cause of acute urticaria in children is viruses.

What is the difference between acute and chronic urticaria?

Chronic urticaria is defined as symptoms that last for more than 6 weeks. Many cases are autoimmune and are associated with autoantibodies directed against the high-affinity IgE receptor on mast cells and basophils. Food and aeroallergen testing is not recommended in cases of chronic urticaria.

A 7-year-old girl presents with a long history of nasal congestion, sneezing, and profuse watery rhinorrhea. On physical examination, the nasal mucosa are blue and boggy, there are dark circles under the eyes, and a horizontal crease across the middle of the nose. What is the next clinical step and what is the treatment?

This patient has allergic rhinitis, a type I hypersensitivity reaction to environmental allergens. Skin testing may be needed to determine the causative allergen(s). Allergen avoidance, nasal steroids, and non-sedating H_1 histamine blockers are first-line treatments. If a particular allergen is the culprit, immunotherapy (allergy shots) would be a second-line treatment.

What is the atopic triad?

Allergic rhinitis, asthma, and atopic dermatitis make up the atopic triad.

A 13-year-old adolescent girl presents with a rash on her arms and legs that appeared 3 days following a camping trip in the woods. The rash is red, linear, with raised small vesicles filled with clear fluid. She reports that it is extremely itchy. What are the most common exposures that could cause this type of reaction?

This patient has contact dermatitis, which is a T-cell mediated, type IV hypersensitivity reaction. The most common exposures are to plants in the *Toxicodendron* genus which include poison ivy, poison sumac, and poison oak. The allergen urushiol is found in the sap of these plants. It is also cross-reactive with allergens found in mango, gingko, cashew, and pistachio trees.

RHEUMATOLOGY

A 12-year-old girl with complaints of bilateral knee, elbow, wrist, and neck pain for 4 months presents to your office. She denies any systemic symptoms. Rheumatoid factor tests are positive. X-rays of affected joints are significant for soft tissue swelling and minimal narrowing of the joint spaces. What is your diagnosis?

Juvenile idiopathic arthritis (JIA) is characterized by arthritis in at least one joint for longer than 6 consecutive weeks in a patient younger than 16 years of age when all other types of arthritis have been excluded. This child likely has rheumatic fever (RF)–positive polyarthritis JIA, which involves five or more joints in the first 6 months of disease, and is more common in females and in those who are HLA-DR4 positive. Unlike other forms of JIA, these patients are at greater risk of developing severe erosive disease and adult-type rheumatoid arthritis (RA).

What is the treatment for the above patient?

The goals of treatment of JIA include the relief of joint pain, restoration of joint function, and decrease further joint damage. This is provided by a combination of physical and occupational therapy with antiinflammatory medications. Nonsteroidal antiinflammatory drugs (NSAIDS) are the first-line pharmacotherapy for the control of joint pain, and disease-modifying antirheumatic drugs (DMARDs) are used to slow progression of disease. Also, steroids are often used during acute manifestations of the disease to decrease overall inflammation. If functional or cosmetic surgery is indicated, it is performed after growth is complete.

When does juvenile rheumatoid arthritis (JRA) typically present?

Although systemic JIA can affect children of any age, there is a peak incidence between 1 and 6 years of age.

What are the clinical manifestations of systemic juvenile idiopathic arthritis?

Classic symptoms of JRA include daily or diurnal fever, a maculopapular rash that is typically faint pink, evanescent, and blanching, lymphadenopathy, hepatosplenomegaly, and serositis. These systemic symptoms usually precede the arthritis, which is most often symmetric and prolonged.

What are the classic laboratory findings in patients with active JRA?

Laboratory findings are usually significant for elevated WBCs and platelets, anemia, and increased acute phase reactants. Antinuclear antibodies (ANAs) can be positive in a small subset and RF is usually negative.

A 17-year-old adolescent boy with a past history of urethritis and conjunctivitis presents with frequent stiffness and pain in the lower back and buttocks. What is the likely etiology of this patient's joint pain?

Reactive arthritis, or Reiter syndrome, is a triad of symptoms: urethritis, conjunctivitis/uveitis, and arthritis. Patients affected are most often HLA-B27 positive, and symptoms usually occur following a bacterial infection. Bacteria associated with reactive arthritis include: *Salmonella, Shigella, Chlamydia, Yersinia, Campylobacter,* and *Mycoplasma.*

A 12-year-old girl presents with a violaceous rash on the eyelids and a pink, smooth rash on her elbows and ankles. She reports weakness and difficulty in climbing stairs. On further questioning, she also reports intermittent fevers, fatigue, and a 6-lb weight loss over 2 months. What is the next clinical step?

Measurement of serum concentration of muscle enzymes (CK, aldolase, AST, and LDH) can help in the diagnosis of dermatomyositis. MRI and muscle biopsy can also aid in the diagnosis. Dermatomyositis is vasculopathic disorder that affects muscles and skin. Typical findings include a heliotrope rash around the eyes, proximal muscle weakness, and Gottron papules.

What are appropriate treatments for the above patient?

Treatment includes steroids and physical therapy. Other treatment options include intravenous immunoglobulin (IVIg), cyclosporine, cyclophosphamide, or methotrexate.

What three symptoms are extremely worrisome in patients with polymyositis or dermatomyositis?

Dysphagia, dysphonia, and dyspnea caused by oropharyngeal, chest wall, and respiratory muscle weakness are symptoms that suggest increased risk of aspiration and respiratory failure.

A 4-year-old boy who had suffered from an upper respiratory infection 2 weeks ago presents to the emergency room (ER) with severe abdominal pain, vomiting, acute renal failure, and a maculopapular rash over the buttocks and lower extremities. What is the diagnosis?

Henoch-Schönlein purpura (HSP) is the most common systemic vasculitis of childhood. HSP typically involves the GI tract, skin, kidneys, and joints. It may be preceded by a group A streptococcal or viral upper respiratory infection.

What is the appropriate treatment for the above disorder and what is the prognosis?

Treatment is supportive and the prognosis is generally good. However, patients with significant renal involvement need frequent and long-term follow-up.

A 7-year-old girl is brought into the ER with high fevers and bilateral conjunctivitis for 5 days. Physical examination reveals erythema of the hands and feet, enlarged cervical lymph nodes, and a red tongue with prominent papillae. What is the diagnosis?

Kawasaki disease is a systemic vasculitis characterized by fever for 5 or more days plus four out of five of the following: cervical adenopathy; mucous membranes changes such as cracked lips or strawberry tongue; polymorphous rash; bilateral conjunctival injection; extremity changes such as peripheral edema, peripheral erythema, periungual desquamation.

What laboratory findings help diagnose Kawasaki disease?

Typical laboratory findings in Kawasaki disease include leukocytosis, thrombocytosis, anemia, elevated erythrocyte sedimentation rate (ESR) and C-reactive protein (CRP), elevated transaminases (particularly AST), and hypoalbuminemia. Urinary findings may be consistent with a sterile pyuria.

What is the most serious complication of the above patient's disease process?

Coronary dilatation and coronary artery aneurysm formation are the most serious complications of Kawasaki disease. This may lead to arrhythmias, myocarditis, congestive heart failure, or ischemic heart disease.

What is the treatment for the above patient?

IVIg and high-dose aspirin are needed during the acute phase of Kawasaki disease to reduce the risk of coronary artery aneurysms.

A 16-year-old adolescent girl presents to the clinic with an erythematous rash over the nose and cheeks, photosensitivity, and pain in her wrists and hands. Laboratories are significant for leukopenia, positive ANA, and positive double-stranded DNA (dsDNA). What is the diagnosis?

This patient has systemic lupus erythematosus (SLE), a systemic autoimmune disease characterized by fever, weight loss, rash, mucositis, nephritis, arthritis, hematologic abnormalities, and positive immunoserology.

What is the most important next test that should be performed on the above patient?

Since lupus nephritis is the most common cause of morbidity or mortality in SLE, a urinalysis and 24-hour urine collection for protein should be performed. If these tests are abnormal, then a kidney biopsy is indicated.

What treatment options should be offered to this patient?

A variety of treatment options exist for SLE. NSAIDS, methotrexate, and hydroxychloroquine are common first-line medications. Steroids are used to treat exacerbations and are sometimes needed as a maintenance therapy. Other immunosuppresants such as cyclosporine, azathioprine, or cyclophosphamide may be used. Newer therapies with mycophenolate mofetil and other biologic agents have been used to treat severe or refractory disease.

What lifestyle changes should the patients with the above diagnosis make?

All patients should also be counseled in lifestyle management such as the avoidance of direct sunlight and careful monitoring of nutritional and fluid status. Compliance with medications should also be encouraged.

What cardinal laboratory tests indicate an impending lupus flare?

Patients with SLE who are experiencing a flare typically have increased titers of dsDNA and decreased levels of C3 and C4. The level of dsDNA antibodies parallels renal disease severity as well.

The above patient presents 9 months later with increased fatigue, malaise, weight loss, and laboratory findings significant for elevated creatinine, elevated dsDNA, and decreased C3 and C4. What treatment is indicated?

High-dose oral or intravenous pulse steroid therapy is indicated during acute exacerbations of SLE.

The same patient develops persistently elevated blood pressure and her kidney biopsy shows class IV lupus nephritis. What other laboratory findings are expected in a patient with type IV lupus nephritis?

Class IV lupus nephritis, or diffuse proliferative glomerulonephritis, is caused by massive deposits of immunoglobulin and complement in the mesangial and subendothelial areas of glomeruli. These patients have hypertension, elevated creatinine secondary to reduced renal function, elevated blood urea nitrogen (BUN), hematuria, and nephrotic range proteinuria.

A 9-year-old boy presents with persistent, periodic fevers. Each episode lasts 2 to 3 days, with fevers ranging from 102°F to 103°F, left hip pain, and a red, swollen, painful rash to the top of his feet. These symptoms always self-resolve, and the parents report that he is completely well between episodes. He is of Armenian descent. What is the most likely cause of his symptoms?

This patient likely has familial Mediterranean fever (FMF), the most common autoinflammatory hereditary recurrent fever syndrome. This disease in autosomal recessive inherited disorder characterized by periodic fever, peritonitis, erysipelas-like rash, oligoarthritis, and amyloidosis. The gene responsible, MEFV, is located on the short arm of human chromosome 16p and codes for the protein pyrin. Altered pyrin causes ineffective downregulation of inflammatory responses.

In the above patient, what laboratory findings would help make the diagnosis?

During an attack, serum CRP and ESR levels will be elevated, as well as an elevated white blood cell count. Serum amyloid A values also rise significantly during attacks. Between episodes, concentrations of these often remain slightly elevated. Genetic testing for MEFV is also available.

What is the treatment and prognosis of FMF?

Daily therapy with colchicine has been shown to limit recurrent attacks and prevent the development of renal amyloidosis, the most significant complication of the illness. With consistent adherence to this drug regimen, the majority of affected children have complete remission from symptoms.

You are called to the delivery room to evaluate a baby born to a mother with SLE. The baby has a multiple discrete red lesions on his face and trunk. What is the most likely diagnosis?

Neonatal lupus erythematosus (NLE) is caused by the placental transfer of antibodies from mothers with SLE to their babies. These mothers are typically anti-Ro or anti-La positive. Infants can also have positive antibody titers.

What are features of this disease? What is the prognosis?

NLE usually manifests with cutaneous lesions that may be present at birth or appear several weeks later. They usually self-resolve within 6 months, once maternal antibodies have cleared. Infants may also have asymptomatic thrombocytopenia. The most dangerous clinical manifestation of NLE is congenital heart block. These children have significant mortality and may require permanent pacemakers.

CLINICAL VIGNETTES

A 9-year-old girl presents to your office with complaint of right (R) knee swelling and pain. She also has a rash that comes and goes and a low-grade fever. Her parents deny any recent trauma and report that 2 days ago she had similar pain and swelling in her left (L) ankle. Prior to this, she has been well except for a throat infection about 1 month ago. What is the most likely diagnosis to explain this patient's new arthritis?

Acute rheumatic fever (ARF) is a consequence of untreated group A streptococcal infections. It usually occurs a few weeks after initial pharyngitis. Diagnosis is made by either two major or one major plus two minor Jones criteria plus evidence of streptococcal infection. The major Jones criteria include: polyarthritis, carditis, subcutaneous nodules, erythema marginatum, and Sydenham chorea. Minor criteria are fever, arthralgia, elevated ESR/CRP, prolonged PR interval.

What is the etiology of this disorder?

Rheumatic fever is thought to occur when antibodies formed during an untreated streptococcal infection cross-react with cells found in the heart, skin, joints, and central nervous system.

What is the most significant complication of acute rheumatic fever?

Inflammation of the layers of the heart is an important complication of acute rheumatic fever and can lead to rheumatic heart disease. Therefore, patients suspected of having ARF should have a thorough cardiac evaluation.

What is the treatment for ARF?

Because the risk of rheumatic fever recurrence is greatest within 5 years following the initial attack, long-term penicillin treatment is recommended. For patients with rheumatic heart disease, indefinite antibiotic prophylaxis is recommended.

CHAPTER 15

Genetic Disease

MODES OF INHERITANCE

A 17-year-old adolescent boy is found to have mental retardation, large ears, and large testicles. The genetic disorder this patient has is most likely transmitted in what way?

This patient has fragile X syndrome, an X-linked genetic disorder.

A male infant who has been diagnosed with pneumonia on three separate occasions now presents with purpura, prolonged bleeding, and eczema on physical examination. This patient's disorder is most likely transmitted in what way?

This patient has Wiskott-Aldrich syndrome (WAS), an X-linked recessive condition characterized by thrombocytopenia, atopy, as well as cellular and humoral immunodeficiency.

A previously well teenager presents to your clinic with progressive unilateral hearing loss. A magnetic resonance imaging (MRI) of the head shows a right-sided mass of the eighth cranial nerve. Why is family history very important in this patient's case?

This patient may have neurofibromatosis 2, which has an autosomal dominant inheritance pattern. These patients often present with a unilateral schwannoma of the eighth cranial nerve.

The parents of an 18-month-old infant with achondroplasia want to know what are the chances that his offspring will have the same disorder. What is the likelihood of that happening?

Fifty percent, if he has a child with a woman without achondroplasia. Achondroplasia is an autosomal dominant disorder.

How are Angelman syndrome (AMS) and Prader-Willi syndrome (PWS) examples of genetic imprinting?

These syndromes both involve a deletion of the 15q 11 to 13 gene but have their own unique characteristics. Angelman syndrome is due to a deletion of the maternal copy of the gene and Prader-Willi syndrome is due to a deletion of the paternal copy of the gene.

SCREENING

A baby in the neonatal intensive care unit (NICU) was born with an omphalocele. The patient's chart also indicates that he was large for gestational age with hemi-hypertrophy and macroglossia. What cancer screening is particularly important in this patient?

This patient has Beckwith-Wiedemann syndrome (BWS) and has an increased risk for hepatoblastoma and Wilms tumor. He should get a screening ultrasound as well as serum alpha-fetoprotein (AFP) levels checked every 6 months until 6 years of age.

What screening test is most important in a patient first diagnosed with Turner syndrome?

Patients with Turner syndrome should be screened for coarctation of the aorta with measurement of blood pressure and pulse in both upper and lower extremities as well as an echocardiogram.

On physical examination of a 12-year-old boy complaining of blurry vision, you note that the patient has eight café au lait spots (CALS) less than 2 cm in size. You also examine the patient's mother who appears to have many of the same spots and flesh-colored growths on the skin. What diagnostic test should be performed?

This patient likely has neurofibromatosis 1 and should have a brain MRI to evaluate for the possibility of an optic glioma.

An infant presents to the emergency department (ED) after a seizure. On examination, he has a port wine nevus on the right cheek. What referral does this patient need?

This patient likely has Sturge-Weber syndrome and should undergo an eye examination due to the increased likelihood of glaucoma on the side of the port wine stain. The patient should also have an MRI of the brain looking for intracranial calcifications.

Antenatal testing for an expectant mother shows a low alpha-fetoprotein level. What is this low level associated with?

Low AFP is often associated with chromosomal abnormalities, particularly the trisomies. Elevated AFP can be associated with neural tube defects and kidney abnormalities.

MALFORMATIONS

A patient with oligohydramnios in utero is born with poorly developed lungs and club feet. What is the likely diagnosis?

This patient has Potter syndrome. The constellation of findings results from decreased urine production in utero.

An infant is born with a tracheo-esophageal fistula and an imperforate anus. What other anomalies are important to evaluate for in this particular patient?

This patient may have VACTERL association which is a constellation of congenital anomalies often found together. In this patient, vertebral and cardiac anomalies, renal anomalies, or malformation of the radial limbs may also be present.

A baby who was born at home with both coloboma and choanal atresia arrives in the ER in moderate respiratory distress. Once this patient is stabilized, what diagnostic test should be performed that may have been missed at birth?

This patient may have CHARGE syndrome which stands for Coloboma of the eye, Heart anomaly, Atresia (choanal), Retardation of mental and somatic development, Genitourinary malformation, and Ear abnormalities and/or deafness. This patient should have an echocardiogram, newborn hearing screen, and renal ultrasound once stabilized.

TRISOMIES

On the initial newborn examination you find that a patient has a flat occiput, upward slanting palpebral fissures, short fingers with bilateral simian creases, and marked hypotonia. What imaging should this patient have during the newborn period?

This patient has Down syndrome and should have an echocardiogram during the newborn period as these patients are at an increased risk of endocardial cushion defects and other types of congenital heart disease.

A 2-day-old newborn infant with trisomy 21 presents with frequent episodes of green emesis that the parents report occurs each time they try to feed the baby. What diagnostic test is appropriate at this time?

This patient has bilious emesis. Children with Down syndrome are at increased risk of duodenal atresia. He should have an upper gastrointestinal (GI) series or an abdominal x-ray looking for a double bubble sign showing air bubbles in the stomach and the duodenum.

The mother of a 10-year-old female patient with Down syndrome brings her daughter to your clinic regularly. After a visit, one day she pulls you aside and asks whether or not her daughter can potentially become pregnant as she has heard conflicting information.

As opposed to males, females with Down syndrome are fertile.

The mother of the same patient with Down syndrome also would like to know if her daughter will need any special screening blood work done. Which screening tests should be ordered?

Children with Down syndrome are at increased risk of hypothyroidism and should have yearly thyroid function tests.

You have a young male patient with Down syndrome in your clinic who is interested in participating in the Special Olympics and his father asks you if he needs any special tests beforehand.

All patients with Down syndrome should have a screening cervical spine x-ray with flexion to look for atlanto-axial instability. This testing is particularly important prior to participation in any contact sports.

A patient with Down syndrome is found to have a 21, 21 translocation. The father is also found to have the 21, 21 translocation. The family would like to know what the chance of recurrence will be in subsequent offspring.

There is a 100% chance of recurrence of Down Syndrome in live births by a parent with a 21, 21 translocation. This is because there is a 50% chance of a lethal monosomy and a 50% chance of trisomy 21.

A fetus is diagnosed in utero as having trisomy 13. The mother asks what malformations this child could be born with.

Children born with trisomy 13 (Patau syndrome) often have cleft lip and palate, polydactyly, holoprosencephaly, eye abnormalities, heart defects, and profound developmental delay. Ninety percent of patients with trisomy 13 die by 1 year of age.

Following an emergent delivery of a mother with no prenatal care, an infant is born who has malformed ears, a small jaw, small face, and rocker-bottom feet. The patient also has a harsh holosystolic murmur on examination. A karyotype is performed that shows 47, XX+18. What is the prognosis?

Ninety percent of patients with trisomy 18 die by the age of 1 year.

SYNDROMES AND INHERITED DISORDERS

An 18-year-old woman comes to your clinic with a complaint of amenorrhea. On physical examination the patient is short for her age with a broad chest. What diagnosis should be suspected?

This patient may have Turner syndrome.

A prenatal ultrasound of a baby girl shows a cystic hygroma and her fetal karyotype is found to be 45, X. The parents are concerned that the child will have mental retardation. What can you tell them?

This patient has Turner syndrome and is not likely to have mental retardation although patients with this disorder have an increased risk of learning difficulties.

The parents of an 18-month-old male patient with achondroplasia are concerned because the boy still does not walk. On physical examination, he has significant external rotation of the hips. What should you tell the family?

External rotation of the hips is very common in patients with achondroplasia and it will commonly resolve once the child begins weight-bearing. Many patients with achondroplasia will also not begin walking until 2 to 2½ years of age.

If a child has a deletion of the maternal copy of chromosome 15q 11 to 13, what syndrome is he or she likely to have?

This child will likely have Angelman syndrome, characterized by mental retardation, ataxic movements, facial dysmorphic features, and frequent smiling and laughter. It is also known as the "happy puppet" syndrome.

An infant presents to genetics clinic with failure to thrive, hypotonia, and small hands and testicles. Chromosomal analysis reveals a loss of a paternal copy of chromosome 15q 11 to 13. What are the risk factors for this patient as he ages?

This patient has Prader-Willi syndrome. These patients develop hyperphagia and obesity as well as global developmental delay, short stature, and hypogonadism.

A teenage boy is tall for his age and on examination is noted to have small testicles and early gynecomastia. What additional chromosome do patients with this genetic disorder have?

This patient has Klinefelter syndrome which affects males who have an extra X chromosome, or 47, XXY.

You are providing anticipatory guidance to the family of a 10-year-old boy with a history of mental retardation, large ears, and strabismus who was found on genetic testing to have repeat expansion of 500 cytosine-guanine-guanine (CGG) trinucleotides on the X chromosome. The family questions whether his having large testicles influences his fertility.

Patients with fragile X syndrome like this patient have normal fertility despite the macroorchidism.

A male teenager with a history of eight café au lait spots greater than 2 cm in size, axillary freckling, and two Lisch nodules is now sexually active. What can you tell him about his chances of having a child with the same disorder?

This teenager with neurofibromatosis 1 has a 50% chance of having a child with the disorder due to its autosomal dominant pattern of inheritance.

A 1-year-old boy comes into the ER with vomiting. His mother tells you that he has Williams syndrome. An ECG shows a shortened QT interval. Renal stones are found on an abdominal CT scan. What electrolyte abnormality could you find?

This patient has Williams syndrome, a genetic syndrome due to a microdeletion of chromosome 7. This boy likely has hypercalcemia, which, along with the dysmorphic facies, cardiovascular disease, and mental retardation, is one of the hallmarks of the disorder.

A 5-year-old boy has been diagnosed with pneumonia five separate times over the course of the past year. On physical examination, he has lung findings as well as difficulty walking in a straight line and nystagmus. You also note that he has a fairly large telangiectasia on his face. How is the disorder that this patient has transmitted?

This patient has ataxia telangiectasia which is an autosomal recessive disorder caused by mutations in the ataxia telangiectasia mutated (*ATM*) gene. Patients have progressive ataxia and dysarthria combined with variable immunodeficiency with a particular susceptibility to pulmonary infections.

What is the prognosis for a child with ataxia telangiectasia?

Most children with ataxia telangiectasia die during adolescence or early adulthood secondary to pulmonary infections.

The mother of a 2-week-old newborn comes into clinic because results of her daughter's newborn screening test show that she has congenital hypothyroidism. Why does this child need treatment even if she is clinically well at this time?

Congenital hypothyroidism causes mental retardation and is preventable with prompt treatment.

At the first clinic visit for a newborn infant with no prenatal care, the parents inform you that the patient had intestinal obstruction secondary to meconium ileus at birth. What further tests can be done?

Immunoreactive trypsinogen testing may have been performed as part of the newborn screen to evaluate for a possible diagnosis of cystic fibrosis, an autosomal recessive disorder that affects the lungs, pancreas, intestine, liver, and sweat glands. DNA-based molecular testing can be performed to test for the most common mutations on cystic fibrosis transmembrane conductance regulator (CFTR), the cystic fibrosis gene. The patient can also have sweat testing performed at a few weeks of age.

A 1-month-old infant with a known diagnosis of cystic fibrosis since birth presents with failure to thrive. The patient is shown to have low levels of elastase in fecal testing. What therapeutic intervention may be helpful at this point?

This infant with failure to thrive secondary to cystic fibrosis could benefit from pancreatic enzyme supplementation and nutritional support.

An 18-year-old male patient presents to the ER with acute onset of chest pain and shortness of breath. You note on physical examination that he wears glasses and has a pectus excavatum, hypermobile joints, long arms, and scoliosis. The patient is mildly tachypneic but otherwise stable. What should you order next?

This is a patient with Marfan syndrome, an autosomal dominant connective tissue disorder. He is at risk for spontaneous pneumothroax and should get a chest x-ray done. Patients with Marfan syndrome are also at increased risk of aortic dissection.

CHAPTER 16

Metabolic Disorders

OVERVIEW

What is the general pathophysiology of the inborn errors of metabolism?

Usually a defect in a single gene that results in abnormalities in the synthesis or catabolism of proteins, carbohydrates, fats, or complex molecules.

If the single gene defect results in a structurally abnormal protein, which mode of inheritance is more likely?

Autosomal dominant. Many generations are affected, non-sex specific.

If the single gene defect results in decreased activity or deficiency of an enzyme, which mode of inheritance is more likely?

Autosomal recessive. Twenty-five percent of offspring from two carrier parents are affected. Usually seen in only one generation.

How can the categories of inborn errors of metabolism be divided?

1. Disorders that result in toxic accumulation of a substance (disorders of protein metabolism, disorders of carbohydrate intolerance, lysosomal storage disorders)
2. Disorders of energy production or utilization (fatty acid oxidation defects, disorders of carbohydrate production/ utilization, mitochondrial disorders, peroxisomal disorders)

What are the three most common lab abnormalities for an acute life-threatening presentation of an inborn error of metabolism?

Metabolic acidosis, hypoglycemia, and hyperammonemia.

SUGAR METABOLISM

A 3-week-old neonate presents with hepatosplenomegaly, jaundice, irritability, poor weight gain, and a positive reducing substance in the urine after being fed with breast milk. What diagnosis do you suspect and what is the treatment?

This child has galactosemia, a congenital absence of galactose-1-phosphate uridyltransferase that results in elevated levels of galactose and its metabolites in the blood and urine. Excluding galactose and lactose from the diet is the standard treatment.

What infection is a neonate with galactosemia at increased risk for?

A neonate with galactosemia is at increased risk for *Escherichia coli* sepsis.

What other laboratory findings do you expect to find in the above patient?

Laboratory findings in patients with galactosemia include elevated aminotransferases, elevated direct bilirubin, hypoglycemia, aminoaciduria, a positive reaction for reducing substances on urine test strips, and prolonged prothrombin and partial thromboplastin times.

A 9-month-old infant has jaundice, hepatosplenomegaly, and is found to be hypoglycemic. His mother reports recently introducing fruit juice into his diet. What enzyme is deficient in this child?

This child likely has fructosemia (hereditary fructose intolerance) in which there is a deficiency of fructose-1, 6-biphosphate aldolase B. Patients with fructosemia are asymptomatic until fructose is introduced into their diet.

PURINE METABOLISM

A concerned parent brings her 4-month-old son to clinic reporting decreased motor activity, hypotonia, and occasional choreoathetosis. Laboratories are significant for elevated uric acid and macrocytic anemia. What condition do you suspect?

This patient's symptoms are suspicious for Lesch-Nyhan syndrome, an X-linked disorder of purine metabolism caused by a deficiency of hypoxanthine-guanine phosphoribosyl transferase (HGPRT). Without HGPRT, the purine salvage pathway is interrupted and there is an increased degradation of purine bases leading to an overproduction of uric acid. Elevated levels of uric acid cause precipitation of uric acid into body tissue causing the classical clinical syndrome.

What further test is necessary to establish a definitive diagnosis?

Since an elevated uric acid level may be caused by several disorders, the definitive test for Lesch-Nyhan syndrome is made by measuring HGPRT enzyme activity and/or by identifying the *HGPRT* gene mutation.

What are the treatment options for the above patient?

Treatment of Lesch-Nyhan syndrome is supportive. Hyperuricemia is treated through hydration and allopurinol. Benzodiazepines and antispastic agents may help to relieve extrapyramidal neurologic symptoms. Prevention of self-injury and mutilation is also important.

AMINO ACID METABOLISM

A 5-month-old infant who was delivered at home by a midwife presents with eczema, musty body odor, fair skin and hair, and blue eyes. What is the etiology of this patient's condition?

The patient has phenylketonuria (PKU), an autosomal recessive disorder in which a deficiency of phenylalanine hydroxylase or its cofactor tetrahydrobiopterin results in the accumulation of phenylalanine and its metabolites. The excess accumulation of phenylalanine is toxic to the brain and leads to mental retardation. Treatment involves a lifelong restriction of dietary phenylalanine.

What amino acid becomes an essential amino acid in the above disorder?

Normally phenylalanine is converted into tyrosine by phenylalanine hydroxylase. Thus, tyrosine is deficient and becomes an essential amino acid in PKU. Rashes, anemia, diarrhea, lethargy, and anorexia are all signs of tyrosine deficiency. The classic physical features of PKU are also secondary to the tyrosine deficiency as tyrosine is a precursor for melanin.

A 4-year-old boy who recently emigrated from Africa presents to clinic with a photosensitive, dry, scaly, red rash on sun-exposed areas of his skin, and a wide-based gait. Laboratories are significant for elevated levels of neutral amino acids in the urine with normal plasma amino acid levels. What diagnosis is suspected?

This patient has Hartnup disease, an autosomal recessive disorder in which decreased activity of a sodium-dependent transport system results in a defect in the transport of neutral amino acids in the intestinal mucosa and renal tubules. Most children with this disorder are asymptomatic; however, a deficiency of tryptophan due to poor nutrition results in clinical manifestations.

What is the treatment for the above patient?

Symptomatic patients are treated with a high-protein diet and nicotinic acid.

A 2-week-old female neonate is brought into the emergency room (ER) for incessant vomiting, poor feeding, lethargy, and alternating muscular hypertonia and hypotonia. The nurse notes that her urine smells of maple syrup. What is the next clinical step?

This patient has maple syrup urine disease, an autosomal recessive disorder in which a defect of branched-chain ketoacid dehydrogenase results in an accumulation of branched-chain amino acids in body fluids. The next clinical step would be to measure blood and urine levels of leucine, isoleucine, valine, and alloisoleucine.

What treatment must be given to the patient in the ER?

In an acute situation such as this, IV administration of glucose with insulin is needed. Hemodialysis and peritoneal dialysis is needed to remove branch-chain amino acids and ketoacids. Long-term treatment includes a restricted branch-chain amino acid diet and frequent serum-level monitoring to prevent future exacerbations and complications, as well as liver transplantation.

CHOLESTEROL METABOLISM

A 20-year-old man is called back into clinic for a serum cholesterol level of 540 mg/dL. On further questioning, he reports a history of extremely elevated cholesterol on his father's side of the family. What diagnosis is likely and what is the etiology?

This patient has the autosomal dominant form of familial hypercholesterolemia in which large elevations of serum cholesterol (>500 mg/dL) results in early atherosclerotic cardiovascular disease. It is caused by a genetic defect in the low-density lipoprotein (LDL) receptor.

If the above patient also had an extremely elevated triglyceride level, how would your diagnosis change?

Patients with both very high cholesterol and elevated triglyceride levels may have dysbetalipoproteinemia due to an apoprotein E (ApoE) mutation. Patients with this condition usually have cholesterol levels ranging from 300 to 600 mg/dL. Triglyceride concentrations can be greater than 400 mg/dL and may exceed 1000 mg/dL. ApoE mutations cause a decreased ability to convert very low-density lipoprotein (VLDL) and intermediate-density lipoprotein (IDL) to low-density lipoprotein (LDL) particles.

GLYCOGEN STORAGE DISORDERS

A 6-month-old infant presents to the emergency department (ED) after a seizure. Her last feed was 5 hours ago and she is found to be extremely hypoglycemic. Her workup is also significant for failure to thrive, metabolic acidosis, lipemia, and hepatosplenomegaly on examination. What by-product of metabolism is extremely elevated in this patient?

Von Gierke disease, or type I glycogen storage disease, is characterized by a deficiency of glucose-6-phosphatase. Deficiency of G-6-P blocks the final steps of glycogenolysis and gluconeogenesis, resulting in severe hypoglycemia. Excessive glucose-6-phosphate is shunted to other metabolic pathways and results in increased lactic acid, uric acid, and triglycerides. Glycogen accumulates in the liver, kidney, and intestine (see Fig. 16-1).

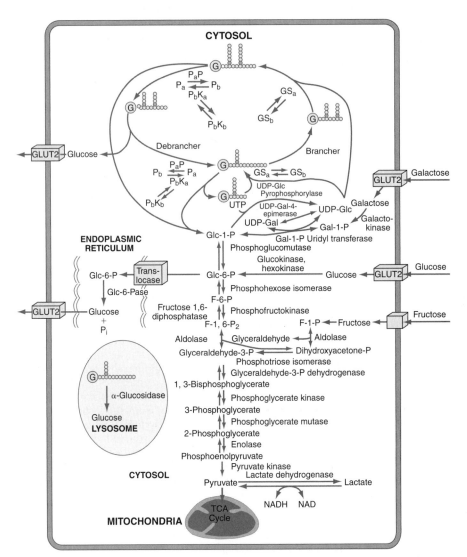

Figure 16-1 Metabolic pathways related to glycogen storage diseases and galactose and fructose disorders. (Reproduced, with permission, from Fauci AS, Kasper DL, Braunwald E, et al. *Harrison's Principles of Internal Medicine.* 17th ed. New York: McGraw-Hill; 2008: Fig. 356.1.)

What is the treatment for the above patient?

The key to treating von Gierke disease is to maintain consistent levels of blood glucose through frequent, high-carbohydrate meals and to avoid fasting, even at night. Severe cases may be treated with organ transplant.

A 6-month-old male infant presents with weakness, respiratory distress, and feeding difficulties. Further evaluation is significant for hypertrophied left ventricle with outflow obstruction on echocardiogram. What disease is suspected and what is its etiology?

This patient has the infantile form of Pompe disease, an autosomal recessive type II glycogen storage disease, caused by a deficiency of acid α-1, 4-glucosidase. Acid maltase is a lysosomal enzyme that catalyzes the hydrogenation of branched glycogen compounds. This results in the accumulation of glycogen within the lysosomes of cardiac and skeletal muscle.

Describe the differences in presenting signs/symptoms in infantile and juvenile forms of Pompe disease.

As described above, the infantile form presents in the first 6 months of life with weakness, hypotonia, rapid, progressive cardiomyopathy with massive cardiac hypertrophy, and death by 1 to 2 years. Children with the juvenile form of Pompe disease present later in life with a slowly progressive, milder myopathy, and little-to-no cardiac abnormalities. Treatment for this disorder consists of enzyme replacement therapy with α-1, 4-glucosidase.

A 14-year-old adolescent girl presents to clinic complaining of temporary cramping and weakness of the muscles after exercise. She also notes that her urine was darker after intense exercise. What diagnosis do you suspect?

McArdle disease, or type V glycogen storage disease, is an autosomal recessive disorder in which a deficiency of muscle glycogen phosphorylase results in muscle weakness following exercise, proximal muscle stiffness, and muscle wasting. The treatment includes a high-fat and protein diet, providing alternative sources of energy to the muscles, thus reducing the requirement for glucose.

What laboratory values would you expect in the above patient following exercise?

Elevated creatine kinase (CK) and normal levels of serum lactate. Additionally, up to 50% of patients with McArdle disease develop myoglobinuria after exercise.

LIPIDOSES

Define lipidoses and describe the type of definitive test that is used for diagnosis.

Lipidoses refers to a spectrum of diseases caused by inherited deficiencies of lysosomal hydrolases. This causes lysosomal accumulation of sphingolipids in the brain and visceral organs. Cultured fibroblasts or leukocytes from the patient are used to measure specific enzymatic activity to definitely diagnose any number of lipidoses.

A 12-month-old Ashkenazi Jewish male presents to clinic with developmental stagnation, hypotonia, increased startle response, and swallowing and breathing difficulties. Physical examination is significant for a cherry-red spot on the macula and no hepatosplenomegaly. What enzyme is deficient in this child?

Tay-Sachs disease is an autosomal recessive disorder more common in Ashkenazi Jewish populations that results from a deficiency in hexosaminidase A. This leads to an accumulation of GM 2 gangliosides in the brain. Most children are normal at birth and begin to exhibit neurologic symptoms as early as 6 months of age.

Describe the similarities and differences between Tay-Sachs disease and Sandhoff disease.

Tay-Sachs and Sandhoff disease are so similar in presentation (developmental stagnation, hypotonia, hyperacusis, cherry-red spot on macula, seizures, swallowing, and breathing difficulties) that it is almost impossible to tell the two apart aside from biochemical laboratory tests. However, Sandhoff disease is more common in non-Jewish populations and results from a mutation on a different chromosome that leads to a deficiency in both hexosaminidases A and B. Furthermore, hepatosplenomegaly may be seen in Sandhoff disease and not in Tay-Sachs disease.

A 7-month-old infant presents with developmental delay, severe hepatosplenomegaly, thrombocytopenia, and easy bruising. An x-ray is performed that demonstrates on Erlenmeyer flask appearance to the femur. What enzyme is deficient in this patient?

β-Glucosidase is deficient in Gaucher disease. This results in an accumulation of glucocerebroside in macrophages and monocytes in the reticuloendothelial system. Glucosylceramide accumulation in the bone marrow, liver, spleen, lungs, and other organs contributes to hepatosplenomegaly and pancytopenia. Deposition within the bone marrow may also lead to cortical thinning and pathologic fractures.

What test should be performed and what pathologic cells are found on this test?

Diagnosis can be confirmed by measuring the glucocerebrosidase activity in peripheral blood leukocytes. Although bone marrow aspiration is no longer recommended as a diagnostic tool, aspiration may reveal Gaucher cells with a characteristic "crinkled paper" cytoplasm as a result of intracytoplasmic glycolipid deposition.

A 4-month-old Ashkenazi Jewish male infant presents with hepatosplenomegaly, psychomotor retardation, and a cherry-red spot on his macula. Acid sphingomyelinase activity is found to be low. What is the diagnosis and what is his prognosis?

This patient has Niemann-Pick disease type A, an autosomal recessive disorder in which a deficiency of acid sphingomyelinase results in the accumulation of sphingomyelin. Most patients are normal at birth and are diagnosed by 4 months. Death usually occurs by 3 years of age.

How are the different subtypes of Niemann-Pick disease related?

Niemann-Pick disease types A and B are both due to deficiencies of acid sphingomyelinase. Type A is more severe and has an earlier age of onset than type B and is found almost exclusively in Ashkenazi Jewish population. Niemann-Pick disease type C (NPC) is due to impaired esterification of cholesterol and is caused most frequently by mutation in *NPC1* and less frequently by mutations in a second gene, *NPC2*.

An 11-year-old boy presents with fatigue, angiokeratomas on his buttocks and scrotum, and distal neuropathy. What is the inheritance of his condition?

Fabry disease is an X-linked recessive disorder where a deficiency of ceramide trihexosidase or α-galactosidase A results in an accumulation of glycosphingolipids in nerves, vascular endothelium, and other organs. Symptoms begin to manifest in childhood or early adolescence. This condition can be treated with enzyme replacement therapy.

A 6-month-old infant with failure to thrive, developmental regression, optic nerve atrophy, and seizures presents to clinic. A brain magnetic resonance imaging (MRI) is significant for diffuse cerebral atrophy and hypodensity of the white matter. What enzyme is deficient in this patient?

The patient may have Krabbe disease, or globoid cell leukodystrophy, which is an autosomal recessive disease. A deficiency of galactosyl-ceramide β-galactosidase or galactocerebrosidase results in the accumulation of ceramide galactose in lysosomes in the white matter of the brain.

What is the name of the cells that are found in areas of demyelination in Krabbe disease?

Globoid cells are large, multinucleated bodies that are found in the demyelinated areas of cerebellar white matter, pontine nuclei, and basal ganglia in patients with Krabbe disease.

LYSOSOMAL STORAGE DISORDERS

A 4-year-old girl is found to have no activity of the enzyme α-L-iduronidase. What lysosomal storage disease does this patient have and what signs/symptoms will be evident in this patient?

A deficiency of α-L-iduronidase indicates that this patient has Hurler syndrome, an autosomal recessive mucopolysaccharidoses. A deficiency in this lysosomal enzyme leads to an inability to degrade glycosaminoglycan within the cell, leading to an accumulation of glycosaminoglycan in the lysosome and ultimately tissue and organ damage. Signs and symptoms exhibited by patients with Hurler syndrome include coarse facial features, hepatosplenomegaly, mental retardation, corneal clouding, dyostosis multiplex, obstructive airway disease, hearing loss, and macroglossia.

Name an X-linked recessive mucopolysaccharidoses.

Hunter syndrome is an X-linked mucopolysaccharidoses characterized by a deficiency of iduronate sulfatase. Iduronate sulfatase deficiency leads to an accumulation of glycosaminoglycans, particularly dermatan and heparan sulfate, within the lysosome.

UREA CYCLE DISORDERS

A 4-day-old newborn infant is rushed into the ER for vomiting, lethargy, and seizures. Laboratories are significant for severe hyperammonemia and increased levels of orotic acid in the urine. What diagnosis is suspected and what is its etiology?

This patient has ornithine transcarbamylase deficiency, a urea cycle defect, resulting in hyperammonemia. The disorder impairs the reaction that leads to condensation of carbamyl phosphate and ornithine to form citrulline and therefore an inability to effectively excrete nitrogen. Excessive carbamyl phosphate is shunted into an alternative pathway leading to increased levels of orotic acid. Patients usually present within 24 to 48 hours after birth.

What is the inheritance pattern and treatment for the above disorder?

Ornithine transcarbamylase deficiency is an X-linked disorder. Treatment includes a low-protein diet and exploitation of other methods of nitrogen excretion using benzoic acid and phenylbutyrate.

CLINICAL VIGNETTES

A mother brings her 7-month-old infant to the ED after an episode of jerking movements of his arms and legs and deviation of his eyes to the left. She reports that she noted this behavior after waking him up from a long nap that afternoon. Mother is also concerned because the baby's belly has been becoming large and distended, even though he has not been gaining weight. A dextrose stick reveals blood glucose of 42, and an arterial blood gas shows a pH of 7.24, with a HCO_3 of 18.

What is your diagnosis?

Glycogen storage disorder type 1, or von Gierke disease, an autosomal recessive disorder due to a deficiency of glucose-6-phosphatase enzyme.

What is your immediate next step?

Give glucose in the form of dextrose 10% in water (D10W) or if the patient is stable, feed orally to increase his blood glucose level and prevent further seizure activity.

What electrolyte abnormalities do you expect to see with this patient?

An elevated anion gap and lactate level secondary to lactic acidosis from glucose-6-phosphate shunting.

How do you explain the patient's enlarged abdomen to the mother?

Due to a glucose-6-phosphatase deficiency, the patient cannot convert glycogen stores in the liver to glucose for the blood stream. This leads to an accumulation of glycogen in the liver and the liver becomes massively enlarged over time.

An 11-year-old girl comes to see you in your office complaining of small, soft, flat yellow papules on her Achilles tendon and over her eyelids. If you were to biopsy the papule, what would you expect to find?

Xanthomas and xanthelasmas are caused by cholesterol deposition in the skin.

What further history should you elicit?

A thorough family history is important to determine if there are first-degree relatives with signs or symptoms of hypercholesterolemia, including early death. The patient should also be asked about symptoms of ischemic heart disease.

A blood test shows grossly elevated LDL levels, but normal triglycerides. What is the metabolic defect?

The patient likely has familial hypercholesterolemia due to an absent or malfunctioning LDL receptor leading to severely diminished hepatic uptake of LDL.

CHAPTER 17

Dermatology

DISORDERS OF THE EPIDERMIS

An 8-year-old boy with a history of asthma and allergic rhinitis presents to clinic with dry, pruritic lesions with lichenification on the antecubital surfaces of his arms. What is the appropriate treatment for this patient?

He has atopic dermatitis, or eczema, which is treated with topical corticosteroids and emollients. Topical immunomodulators and oral antihistamines may be used in chronic eczema with frequent exacerbations, while oral antistaphylococcal antibiotics are necessary if there is a superimposed infection.

How does the presentation of atopic dermatitis differ in an infant versus an older child?

Infants typically have a pattern of erythematous, crusted, and sometimes vesicular lesions on the extensor surfaces and the cheeks or scalp. In childhood eczema, the lesions are drier and on the flexural surfaces (ie, neck, antecubital, and popliteal fossae).

What is the atopic triad?

The atopic triad consists of asthma, allergic rhinitis, and eczema. These three conditions are type 1 hypersensitivity responses in which there is excess production of IgE released by sensitized mast cells toward various antigens in the environment.

What is the appropriate treatment for contact dermatitis?

Contact dermatitis is divided into two categories: allergic and irritant. Treatment consists of removal and avoidance of the causative agent, topical corticosteroids, and lubrication. Systemic corticosteroids are indicated when greater than 10% of the skin surface is involved.

A 12-year-old girl presents to clinic with erythematous plaques and vesicles on her calves and shins. A thorough history reveals that she recently went hiking in the woods. What steps should be taken to make this diagnosis?

This patient likely has allergic contact dermatitis due to poison oak or poison ivy exposure. The diagnosis can be made clinically based on the history and characteristics of the rash. If treatment fails, a potassium hydroxide (KOH) test may be performed to rule out a fungal infection.

A mother presents to clinic with her 2-month-old infant girl. She reports that the baby has greasy scales on her scalp and dry erythematous patches on her cheeks bilaterally. What is the likely cause of this rash?

This infant has seborrheic dermatitis. Mineral oil can be used on the scalp prior to washing the hair, followed by combing out the scales. Antidandruff shampoo (often selenium-based) may also be used to treat and if necessary, topical corticosteroids may be applied to the face. See Fig. 17-1.

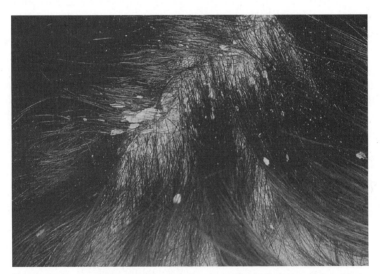

Figure 17-1   (Reproduced, with permission, from Plewig G, Jansen T. Seborrheic dermatitis. In: Freedberg IM, Eisen AZ, Wolff K, et al., eds. *Fitzpatrick's Dermatology in General Medicine.* 6th ed. New York, NY: McGraw-Hill; 2003:1198.)

A 19-year-old woman presents with a rash symmetrically distributed on her elbows and knees. The rash is nonpruritic, and involves erythematous papules with overlying silver scale. What is the etiology of this disease, and can it be cured?

The rash is caused by psoriasis, a common cutaneous disorder that is immune-mediated. It is a chronic disease characterized by exacerbations and remissions and at present cannot be cured. See Fig. 17-2.

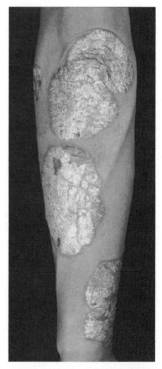

Figure 17-2 (Reproduced, with permission, from Freedberg IM, Eisen AZ, Wolff K, et al., eds. *Fitzpatrick's Dermatology in General Medicine.* 6th ed. New York, NY: McGraw-Hill; 2003:407.)

What is an Auspitz sign?

An Auspitz sign refers to pinpoint bleeding on a psoriatic rash where scales have been removed.

What is the proper treatment for psoriasis?

Treatment for mild to moderate disease consists of topical corticosteroids, emollients, tar, retinoids, vitamin D, and ultraviolet B (UVB) phototherapy. Severe disease may require systemic immunomodulators such as methotrexate, cyclosporine, or monoclonal antibodies (ie, alefacept).

What is the Koebner phenomenon?

The Koebner phenomenon describes when a rash emerges at sites of physical or thermal trauma. It is most classically a feature of psoriasis, but also may be found with the rash of juvenile idiopathic arthritis (JIA).

A 16-year-old male football player reports that he has developed dry, scaling lesions on his head. He has lost hair in certain areas overlying the rash. A Wood lamp shows bright green fluorescence of the hair shaft. What will a KOH preparation likely show?

A KOH preparation will likely show multiple, septated hyphae as this patient has tinea capitus, caused by fungi such as *Trichophyton, Microsporum,* and *Epidermophyton.*

What does a KOH preparation reveal in a patient with a *Candida* infection?

Candida albicans causes a yeast infection in moist cutaneous regions of the body. KOH preparation will show pseudohyphae and budding spores.

A 14-year-old adolescent boy presents to the office with 15 erythematous, oval-shaped patches covered in scales located on his back in a "Christmas tree" distribution. The most prominent plaque is 4-cm wide and is located on his shoulder blade. What disease are these lesions characteristic of?

This rash description is classic for pityriasis rosea. The prominent plaque described is the "herald patch" that appears first and is followed by a secondary eruption of smaller lesions.

What is the cause of pityriasis rosea?

The cause is unknown but it is thought to most likely have a viral etiology. It is self-limiting and resolution occurs in 6 to 12 weeks.

When making the diagnosis of pityriasis rosea, what other diseases should be in your differential?

The diagnosis of pityriasis rosea is made clinically with a good history and physical, and does not involve any laboratory abnormalities. It often very closely resembles tinea corporis, and a KOH preparation may be done to exclude the presence of fungal infection. Your differential diagnosis should also include secondary syphilis, psoriasis, drug eruptions, and human immunodeficiency virus (HIV) seroconversion illness.

SKIN INFECTIONS, INFESTATIONS, AND EXANTHEMS

A 12-year-old boy who recently emigrated from Africa enters the clinic with a maculopapular rash that began on his head and spread down the rest of his body. His illness began 5 days ago when he developed a high fever, conjunctivitis, cough, coryza, and malaise, followed by the appearance of erythematous lesions with a blue and gray center on his buccal mucosa. What are these lesions called?

This patient has measles, and the lesions on his buccal mucosa are Koplik spots. These are transient lesions that persist 2 to 3 days during the illness. The measles, mumps, and rubella (MMR) vaccine is used to prevent measles and it is typically administered at 12 to 15 months and again at 4 to 6 years of age.

A 19-year-old college student enters the clinic complaining of a painful vesicular rash that occurs on the right side of her back in a dermatomal distribution. This is a reactivation of what childhood illness?

This patient currently has herpes zoster (also known as shingles). She likely had varicella, or chickenpox, as a child. This rash represents a reactivation of the varicella virus that has been dormant within the dorsal root ganglia.

A mother calls the office to let you know that her daughter has chickenpox and that her lesions have crusted over on some areas of her body, while 2 mm clear vesicles remain on other areas of her body. Is this patient still infectious?

Yes. Varicella can be spread 24 hours prior to the development of the rash and she will continue to be infectious for about 1 week until all of the lesions have crusted over.

With what illness do you see the characteristic malar ("slapped cheek") rash?

Erythema infectiosum, also known as fifth disease.

What virus causes erythema infectiosum?

Parvovirus B19, a small single-stranded DNA virus.

A 3-year-old girl is brought to your office with a maculopapular rash that appeared after the resolution of 4 days of fever. What virus is the likely cause?

Human herpes virus 6 (HHV-6), which is manifested here as roseola infantum (also known as exanthem subitum and sixth disease).

A baby is born to a mother who recently emigrated from Mexico, whose immunization record is not known. The infant is found to have a "blueberry muffin" rash, as well as sensorineural deafness, cataracts, and a patent ductus arteriosus. She was most likely exposed to what virus in utero?

This baby's mother was likely infected with rubella virus during her pregnancy. Infants born with congenital rubella syndrome may also demonstrate intra-uterine growth restriction, microcephaly, radiolucent bone disease, hepatospleno-megaly, and thrombocytopenia. The resultant purpura is the "bluberry muffin" rash.

An 8-year-old boy presents to the clinic with pruritic lesions on his chin covered with a honey-colored crust. Which types of bacteria are likely responsible for this infection?

This patient has impetigo, which is typically caused by *Staphylococcus aureus* or group A beta-hemolytic *Streptococcus pyogenes*. Treatment consists of warm water soaks, topical antibiotics, and antibacterial washes.

In the case of cellulitis, which layer of skin is typically infected?

Cellulitis is an infection primarily of the dermis, creating an erythematous, edematous region of tender, warm skin with nonelevated borders.

What would the infection be called if it spread to the subcutaneous fat and fascia?

Necrotizing fasciitis is a bacterial infection that has spread to the subcutaneous fat and fascia.

A 4-year-old boy is hospitalized with skin that was erythematous with flaccid bullae. Within several days, the child's skin sloughs off around the axillae, groin, and neck, but does not involve the mucous membranes. What pathogen causes this syndrome?

This boy has staphylococcal scalded skin syndrome, which results from an epidermolytic toxin released by the *S aureus* bacteria. This bacteria colonizes the nose and conjunctiva and then produces toxins that travel through the blood to the skin, causing bullae formation and sloughing of the epidermis.

How is staphylococcal scalded skin syndrome (SSSS) treated?

Therapy for SSSS is directed toward the eradication of *S aureus*, which generally requires hospitalization and IV anti-staphylococcal antibiotics. Supportive skin care and IV fluids may be needed due to the disruption of the skin barrier.

A 10-year-old girl with a fever and a sore throat develops a sandpaper rash on her chest that spreads to her arms and legs. A strawberry tongue is also seen on examination. What is the appropriate treatment?

This patient has scarlet fever. It is caused by group A *Streptococcus* and is treated with penicillin or amoxicillin, which is more palatable.

A 6-year-old girl presents to clinic with several 3 mm pearly, dome-shaped papules with an umbilicated center on her axilla. How do these lesions typically spread from person to person?

This patient has molluscum contagiosum, which spreads via direct contact.

Does molluscum contagiosum need to be treated?

The infection is often self-limited and resolves after several months. Treatment outside of the genital region would be for cosmetic purposes only, and would involve curettage, cryosurgery, or laser treatment.

Which virus causes verruca, or warts, and what types of warts typically affect children?

Human papillomavirus causes verruca. Common warts that affect children are verruca plantaris on the plantar surface of the foot and verruca vulgaris, which are skin-colored warts on the hands. Verruca planar are small, flat warts on the hands and fingers.

What causes scabies?

The mite *Sarcoptes scabiei*, which tunnels into the skin leaving visible burrows and resulting in severe pruritis.

What is the classic distribution of the rash caused by scabies?

The distribution of scabies classically involves the finger webs, the flexor surface of the wrists, axillary folds, and the waist.

A school nurse observes nits in the hair of an elementary school student. What is the recommended treatment?

This child has lice and all of the student's hair implements should be discarded or boiled and her hair should be meticulously combed to remove nits. A 1% permethrin cream rinse is recommended, but must be repeated at 7 to 10 days because it does not effectively kill the eggs that will subsequently hatch.

GENETIC, IMMUNOLOGIC, AND RHEUMATOLOGIC SKIN DISORDERS

A 7-year-old boy presents to the office with blisters on his oral mucosa. Several months later, he develops generalized flaccid bullae that rupture and crust over. A biopsy is performed that reveals acantholysis, or detachment of keratinocytes. What will direct immunofluorescence of this biopsy sample likely show?

This patient likely has pemphigus vulgaris, which is caused by autoantibodies that adhere to keratinocyte desmosomes and other surfaces of the keratinocyte. This results in defects in cell-to-cell adhesion, causing blisters. Direct immunofluorescence of the biopsy will show the IgG deposits between epidermal cells.

What is the treatment for pemphigus vulgaris?

This disease is autoimmune in nature, so systemic steroids and immunosuppressive medications are used to treat it.

A 14-year-old adolescent boy is treated with trimethoprim/sulfamethoxazole and subsequently develops multiple target lesions varying in size on his torso. There is no involvement of his eyes or mucous membranes What is the cause of this patient's rash?

This patient has erythema multiforme, which is a self-limited hypersensitivity reaction, likely to the sulfonamide medication he took. Discontinuation of the medication, moist compresses, antihistamines, oatmeal baths, and reassurance should be provided for this patient.

If the 14-year-old adolescent boy with target lesions associated with a drug reaction had malaise, fever, diarrhea and vomiting, arthritis, and arthralgias several days prior to the development of the rash, as well as mucosal lesions. What treatment should he receive?

This patient has Stevens-Johnson syndrome (SJS), a rare and life-threatening reaction. Treatment is mainly symptomatic: hospitalization, IV fluids, topical anesthetics, mouthwashes with lidocaine for mucosal lesions, and additional supportive care, in addition to immediate discontinuation of the offending drug that triggered the reaction. An ophthalmology consult is recommended to evaluate for uveitis, conjunctivitis, and corneal ulceration.

How are TEN and SJS similar to staphylococcal scalded skin syndrome (SSSS)?

Both SJS and toxic epidermal necrolysis (TEN) are characterized by skin and mucous membrane involvement with widespread blistering and denudation of the skin. They are severe and life-threatening hypersensitivity reactions, most commonly triggered by medication, and are identical processes that differ only in the percentage of skin surface involved. SSSS also involves blistering and denudation of the skin, but is the result of *S aureus*-mediated release of exfoliative toxin and, in most cases, is not life threatening.

What is the difference between urticaria and angioedema?

Both urticaria and angioedema are type 1 hypersensitivity reactions that cause edema. Urticarial lesions, mediated by the cutaneous mast cell in the superficial dermis, have well-defined borders and appear as wheals or welts as they become red and raised. Angioedema is edema that involves not only the skin, but also the submucosa and other subcutaneous layers of tissue.

What causes urticaria and how is it treated?

Urticaria is caused by a triggering agent, such as an ingested food or infectious or environmental stimulus that leads to the trigger and release of histamine by mast cells, causing vascular permeability and vasodilation. Antihistamines, as well as steroids and epinephrine may be used to treat in severe cases.

A 6-year-old girl presents with a salmon-colored macular rash around her waist and on her legs. She has also been suffering from pain in her wrists and knees, and was initially brought to see her pediatrician because of intermittent high-spiking fevers. The rash is likely due to what systemic illness?

This patient likely has juvenile idiopathic arthritis (JIA, formerly known as juvenile rheumatoid arthritis). A JIA-associated rash is often found in the axilla and around the waist but can be found anywhere on the body. The rash is brought out by heat and is most prominent when the child is febrile, but will fade when the temperature returns to normal.

VASCULAR MALFORMATIONS AND MELANOCYTIC LESIONS

The mother of a 3-day-old newborn girl calls the office and reports that her newborn developed a red nodule on her brow that looked like a "strawberry" spot. What is the likely cause of this growth?

This neonate likely has a capillary hemangioma caused by vascular proliferation secondary to abnormal angiogenesis induced by beta fibroblast growth factor (β-FGF) and vascular endothelial growth factor (VEGF) cytokines. These growths typically resolve by 5 years of age.

A newborn baby has a speckled brown and black plaque on his back that is 20-cm wide. What is this patient's risk of developing melanoma?

This newborn has a giant congenital melanocytic nevus. The risk of melanoma is proportional to the size of a congenital nevus. The lifetime risk of melanoma for a giant congenital melanocytic nevus is estimated to be about 5%.

CLINICAL VIGNETTES

A 14-year-old adolescent boy presents with closed comedones and is concerned that his acne is worsening. What is the progression of the lesions of acne vulgaris?

Acne vulgaris begins with closed comedones, or whiteheads, to open comedones, or blackheads, to pustules, then papules, followed by cystic nodules. Eventually hypertrophic and atrophic scars may develop.

What causes acne vulgaris?

Acne vulgaris is caused by stimulation of sebaceous glands and hair follicles by circulating androgens, as well as by the infection of *Propionibacterium* acnes.

What do different treatments of acne vulgaris target?

Benzoyl peroxide decreases surface-free fatty acids and works to decrease the amount of bacteria within the lesions. Topical antibiotics also target the *Propionibacterium*, while oral contraceptives may be used in women to decrease androgen production. Retinoic acid, steroids, and estrogens also suppress sebaceous gland production of sebum.

CHAPTER 18

ENT and Ophthalmology

NEONATAL OPHTHALMOLOGY

A neonate is born at a gestational age of 29 weeks with a birth weight of 1050 g. The patient is initially mechanically ventilated. The neonate is extubated at 4 weeks of life in the neonatal intensive care unit. At 6 weeks of age, you walk by the neonate's incubator and the patient's nurse is administering dilating ophthalmic drops. What is the most likely reason this child is receiving an ophthalmologic evaluation?

This infant is receiving ophthalmologic evaluation for assessment of retinopathy of prematurity (ROP). ROP is a vasoproliferative retinopathy seen in premature infants exposed to high concentration of oxygen for prolonged periods. Most cases are detected from 6 to 10 weeks postpartum. Two phases can occur: Acute proliferative phase (90%) and a cicatricial phase in which scarring and tractional retinal detachment occur (only 10% progress to this).

Why is this neonate in a high-risk group for this condition?

ROP risk factors include:

Birth weight less than 1250 g (most important)

Gestational age less than 32 weeks

Mechanical ventilation

Is long-term ophthalmologic evaluation necessary for all ex premature infants?

Yes. Those with ROP should be closely followed for progression of the disease requiring laser photocoagulation or cryotherapy, which may improve visual outcome. Whether or not ROP is present, premature infants are at higher risk for other eye disorders including myopia, angle-closure glaucoma, amblyopia, and strabismus.

A 6-day-old newborn boy is brought to the emergency room (ER) by his parents due to "crankiness" and "irritability." The parents state the patient crawled off the couch and has acted this way since. A fundoscopic examination shows retinal hemorrhages with bleeding into the optic nerve. What is the most likely diagnosis?

The fundoscopic examination and history are most consistent with shaken baby syndrome, also known as abusive head trauma. Six-day-old newborns do not crawl and retinal hemorrhages especially with bleeding into optic nerve are very commonly found in cases of child abuse. At times, fundoscopic findings are the only evidence of abuse.

During a routine well-child examination, a 3-year-old girl is found to have leukocoria in the left eye when her red reflex is checked. What are the most common and most dangerous causes of leukocoria?

Leukocoria is a loss of the red reflex which appears as a white pupil on examination. The most common cause of leukocoria is pediatric cataract, which occurs in 1 of every 250 newborns and may be congenital or acquired, in one or both eyes. The most dangerous etiology of leukocoria is retinoblastoma, which is the most common intraocular malignancy that occurs in childhood and may present as leukocoria, strabismus, or red eye. Retinoblastoma may be treated with chemotherapy, cryotherapy, or laser photocoagulation, but may require enucleation.

How should leukocoria be managed?

The most important step after leukocoria is identified on physical examination is referral to an ophthalmologist. If not removed promptly, cataracts will affect the development of normal vision. If left untreated, retinoblastoma almost always metastasizes and leads to death. When retinoblastoma is treated, cure rates exceed 90%.

A 2-week-old newborn girl is brought to the pediatrician with red, swollen eyelids. Today she developed purulent blood-tinged discharge from the eyes. Prenatal care was minimal and sexually transmitted infection (STI) status is uncertain. After the eyelids are cultured, what treatment is necessary?

Due to the time and severity of presentation, chlamydial conjunctivitis is suspected. Therefore, oral erythromycin for 14 days is ideal therapy. The child's parents should be treated as well. Although chlamydial conjunctivitis is not as destructive as gonococcal conjunctivitis, it may last months and be complicated by pneumonia if not treated. Besides these two infections, herpes simplex conjunctivitis may also be transmitted to the newborn during labor. The incidence of neonatal conjunctivitis has declined due to the routine use of silver nitrate or antibiotic drops at birth. Table 18-1 compares these three serious causes of neonatal conjunctivitis.

Table 18-1 Cases of Neonatal Conjunctivitis

	N gonorrhoeae	*C trachomatis*	HSV-2
Incubation period	2-3 d	5-12 d	2-3 d
Presentation	Lid edema Corneal ulceration Profuse purulent exudate	Red, puffy eyelids Initial watery discharge followed by copious purulent discharge	Red, puffy eyelids May have corneal involvement or vesicles on the skin
Complications	Rapid development of blindness	Pneumonia	Systemic dissemination
Treatment	1 dose IM ceftraixone Treat parents	Oral erythromycin for 14 d Treat parents	Acyclovir for 14 d

OPHTHALMOLOGIC INFLAMMATION AND INFECTION

A 4-year-old boy presents to the pediatrician with the feeling that something is stuck in his eye. According to his parents, he woke up this morning with his eye "crusted shut." On examination, he has right eye conjunctival edema and erythema, and a mucopurulent discharge. What is the most likely diagnosis?

The patient has classic signs of bacterial conjunctivitis. *Streptococcus pneumoniae* and *Haemophilus influenzae* are common causes of this infection. Bacterial conjunctivitis can be treated with topical antibiotics and frequent handwashing to prevent spread of the infection to close contacts.

A 3-year-old girl presents to the pediatrician with several days of itchy, red eyes. On examination, both eyes are watery and erythematous. Preauricular lymph nodes are palpable. What is the diagnosis?

Conjunctivitis with palpable lymph nodes usually has a viral etiology. Viral conjunctivitis is most commonly caused by adenovirus or coxsackievirus. No antibiotic treatment is necessary, but frequent handwashing to prevent transmission should be encouraged.

A 6-year-old boy presents to the pediatrician with several days of itchy, red eyes. On this spring day, the examination shows both eyes that have a stringy mucoid discharge, mildly erythematous conjunctivae, and no lymphadenopathy. The patient also has a linear mark across his nasal bridge. What is your diagnosis?

This patient has seasonal allergic conjunctivitis with the hallmark of itching. This type of conjunctivitis is seasonal, associated with allergies (as evidenced by allergic salute mark on nose) and best treated with decongestant or mild steroid drops. Elimination of allergen for this type I (IgE-mediated) hypersensitivity is always the best treatment.

A 5-year-old boy presents to the pediatrician with eye pain, decreased vision, and red eye for several days. His mother thinks he may have had a sinus infection in the recent past. On examination, his right eye is erythematous and edematous, and appears proptotic. When you test his extraocular muscles, he complains of severe pain in his right eye. What is the likely diagnosis?

The patient most likely has orbital cellulitis, which is a true emergency. Orbital cellulitis is a bacterial infection of the soft tissues posterior to the orbital septum (as opposed to preseptal cellulitis, which does not extend posterior to the septum and features painless eyelid swelling without extraocular eye movement restriction or visual changes). Orbital cellulitis is most commonly caused by ethmoid sinusitis; other causes include facial cellulitis and dental infections.

What organisms are commonly associated with orbital cellulitis?

Organisms most commonly involved are *Streptococcus aureus* and *S pneumoniae*; the incidence of *H influenzae* has declined since the *Haemophilus influenzae* type b (Hib) vaccine became widespread.

What is the most important next step in management of this patient?

The patient should have a CT scan to determine the extent of the disease process (exclude subperiosteal or orbital abscess), and needs IV antibiotics started as soon as possible.

If left untreated, what are the complications of orbital cellulitis?

If left untreated, orbital cellulitis can lead to meningitis, cavernous sinus thrombosis, central nervous system abscess, or permanent loss of vision.

A 12-year-old boy presents to his pediatrician complaining of red, burning, itching eyes for several months. On examination, his lids are erythematous, with ulceration of the lid margins and scaling at the roots of the lashes. How should he be treated for this condition?

Blepharitis is an inflammation of the lid margins, which may have either a bacterial (*S aureus* or *Staphylococcus epidermidis*) or seborrheic etiology, or a combination of both. Patients with blepharitis can be told to cleanse their eyelids daily with a mild soap like baby shampoo to remove scaling. Topical antibiotics may also be used.

A 17-year-old adolescent girl presents to the pediatrician complaining of severe pain and tearing in her right eye. She wears contact lenses and has not removed her contact lenses at night for the last several nights. She reports no other history of trauma or foreign body in the eye. On examination, she is wearing sunglasses and asks you to turn off the lights in the room. Examination is limited due to her extreme discomfort, but her cornea appears hazy. What is the probable diagnosis?

The patient has a corneal ulcer. These ulcers are usually caused by trauma or foreign body in the eye with subsequent infection. Microbial agents include *Neisseria gonorrhoeae* or *Pseudomonas aeruginosa*. Fungal infections leading to corneal ulcer are especially common in contact lens users.

What is the most appropriate next step in management of this patient?

The patient should be referred as soon as possible to an ophthalmologist for slit-lamp examination and further treatment. Slit-lamp examination with fluorescein will show a corneal defect or corneal cloudiness. The ophthalmologist may also take corneal scrapings to determine the etiology of an infectious corneal ulcer. An infection will need to be treated with antibiotic eyedrops. If left untreated, corneal ulcers may lead to perforation, scarring, or even blindness.

COMMON OPHTHALMOLOGIC PROBLEMS

A 2-week-old newborn presents to the pediatrician with a "teary and crusty" left eye. The conjunctivae are clear but the parents state the eye is always crusting over and always tearing even when the patient is not crying. What is the probable diagnosis?

Dacryostenosis is a congenital obstruction of the nasolacrimal duct caused by failure of the distal membranous end of the nasolacrimal duct to open. This occurs in approximately 5% of all infants.

How should this problem be treated?

Treatment of nasolacrimal duct obstruction includes massage of the lacrimal sac area with massage directed inferiorly to mimic the course of the duct. Chronic antiobiotic therapy should be avoided. Most obstructions (90%) resolve after a year. If dacryostenosis is still present after 1 year of age, the membrane may be ruptured with a probe or ultimately silicone stents may be placed if probing does not help.

An 8-year-old girl presents with a "growth" on her eyelid that her mother thinks has been present for several weeks. On examination, she has a firm, nontender nodule on her left eyelid, without erythema, that measures about 2 mm in diameter. What is the diagnosis?

This patient most likely has a chalazion, an inflammation of a meibomian gland that eventually forms a granuloma. Most chalazia resolve spontaneously, given several months. Warm compresses may be used, and a chalazion may be excised if necessary. Granulation tissue and chronic inflammation distinguishes a chalazion from an internal or external hordeolum, which is an acute pyogenic inflammation with necrosis and pustule formation.

An 8-year-old boy presents with a "growth" on her eyelid that has become red and painful over the past several days. On examination, she has an erythematous swelling on her left eyelid that is tender to palpation. What is the diagnosis?

The patient probably has a hordeolum. They come in two varieties: external hordeolum (also known as a stye), which is an infection of the glands of Zeiss or Moll; and internal hordeolum, an infection of the meibomian gland. They are usually caused by *S aureus* and can be treated with warm compresses. If the hordeolum does not rupture after treatment, incision and drainage may be necessary.

A 4-year-old girl's parents state that she has trouble seeing the television clearly. A family member in the medical field has told them that their daughter may have amblyopia. What are three common causes of amblyopia?

Amblyopia, which means "dull sight," is decreased visual acuity caused by a distortion in the images received by the retinas and can subsequently cause interference with the normal development of the visual cortex. It may be unilateral or bilateral, and almost always presents before the child turns 7. The most common cause of amblyopia is strabismus, or a misalignment of one or both eyes. Other common causes of amblyopia include refractive errors and opacities in the pathway anterior to the retina (eg, corneal cloudiness or cataracts).

A 5-year-old boy is referred to the pediatrician after a routine school vision screening reveals decreased visual acuity. His parents have not noted any decrease in their son's vision, but state that he does seem to favor one eye over the other. What two tests can help to diagnose strabismus?

Corneal light reflex and cover-uncover test. Strabismus is a misalignment or deviation of one or both eyes. There are four types of deviation: "eso-" (inward), "exo-" (outward), "hypo-" (downward), or "hyper-" (upward) tropia.

How is the corneal light reflex tested?

The corneal light reflex is tested by having a child look directly at a penlight about 3 ft away. If the locations of the corneal reflexes differ from one eye to the other, you should suspect strabismus. The corneal light reflex is not as specific as the cover-uncover test, although corneal light reflex may be the only test possible in very young children.

| How is the cover-uncover test performed? | The cover-uncover test is done by having the child stare at an object in the distance. Then one eye is covered. If there is movement of the uncovered eye after the other eye is covered, a strabismus exists. |

NEWBORN ENT

| A full-term newborn boy is noted to have breathing and feeding difficulties on the second day of life. His mother notices that he turns blue while he is being breastfed, but that his color improves while he is crying. The child's physical examination is otherwise normal. What is the diagnosis? | Choanal atresia is a condition in which the nose and pharynx are separated by a membrane and/or bone, either unilaterally or bilaterally. Unilateral cases are usually asymptomatic. Bilateral cases present in the first days of life, usually with cyanosis, which may be worse during feeding, and respiratory distress that improves with crying. Severity will vary with the infant's ability to mouth breathe, though most are obligate nose breathers at birth. |

| How is the diagnosis of choanal atresia made? | Diagnosis is based on inability to pass a catheter through one or both of the child's nostrils. CT scan may further define the location and nature of the atresia, as well as other related anatomy, as repair is planned. |

| What is the management of this patient? | Definitive treatment of bilateral choanal atresia is surgical correction, although stenosis of the choana often occurs postoperatively. Nasal stents may be left in for 4 to 6 weeks to decrease the chance and degree of restenosis. While awaiting repair, temporary maintenance of the airway may be achieved with an oral airway; intubation or tracheostomy may be needed in severe cases, or if the child needs other surgeries. A McGovern nipple can assist in feeding during the pre- and perioperative period. |

AUDIOLOGY

A 2-year-old boy is brought to the pediatrician for a well-child visit. His parents state that he has met most developmental milestones, but they are concerned that he does not speak much and has said only 20 words. Since his last visit, he was treated for meningitis, but has had no other health problems. What is the most appropriate next step in management?

Refer the patient for audiologic testing. By age 2, he should have a vocabulary of about 50 to 75 words. Given his history, some hearing loss from the meningitis may have caused his language delay. After a meningitis infection, hearing loss is the most common long-term complication (10%-20% of cases).

What organisms are most commonly associated with meningitis and hearing loss?

Most often, the organisms associated with hearing loss are *S pneumoniae*, *N meningitides*, or *H influenzae*. After a meningitis infection, children should have annual hearing evaluations for several years. Vaccinations starting at 2 months age against *H influenzae* and *S pneumoniae* have reduced rates of meningitis caused by these organisms and in turn, decreased the rate of hearing loss in infants.

You are seeing a 27-month-old boy for the first time in your office. His mother states that she still cannot understand more than "mama" and "dada" from the child. He has no history of infections and is otherwise very healthy and has normal gross and fine motor development. What screening tool would you first use in this patient to evaluate the etiology of his speech delay?

A normal 27-month-old should say at least sentences of 2 to 3 words and have speech that is at least 50% understandable. Any significant delay of speech or language milestone should be followed by a thorough history and physical examination as well as a hearing evaluation. The examination may reveal cerumen, foreign body, or chronic otitis media causing conductive media. If normal as in this patient, an auditory brainstem response test can be done in addition to tympanometry to delineate the hearing loss.

ENT INFECTIOUS DISEASE

A 3-year-old girl is brought to the pediatrician with 1 day of fever, runny nose, cough, and sore throat. On examination, the girl has nasal discharge, conjunctival erythema, exudative pharyngitis, and no lymphadenopathy. What is the most likely etiology of the pharyngitis?

Among children of 3 or younger, viral etiology for pharyngitis or tonsillitis is most common. This girl also has rhinitis and conjunctivitis which makes this most likely a viral etiology. Adenovirus, parainfluenza, and influenza are the most likely viral agents in this age-group. Treatment is based on supportive care as the disease process is self-limited, lasting 4 to 10 days. The well-known group A beta-hemolytic *Streptococcus* is an exudative pharyngitis most commonly seen after 6 years of age and is associated with lymphadenopathy usually without other signs of upper respiratory infection.

A 15-year-old adolescent boy presents with trouble swallowing, chills, inability to open his mouth, and right-sided throat pain for 1 day after a few days of sore throat. On examination the patient is speaking in a "hot-potato" voice, has trouble opening his mouth, has tender right cervical adenopathy, and a uvula deviated toward the left. What is the most likely diagnosis?

The teenager has a peritonsillar abscess. They follow a virulent tonsillitis and most commonly present with bad breath, trismus, dysphagia, and fever. Aspiration of the abscess and oral antibiotics has been shown to be effective treatment. Formal incision and drainage can be done bedside in older patients or under general anesthesia in younger children. Untreated peritonsillar abscess may spontaneously rupture, but it can extend to the parapharyngeal or retropharyngeal spaces, with potentially fatal complications, including mediastinitis.

A 7-year-old girl presents to the emergency room with fever, neck pain, drooling, and trouble swallowing. On examination she can open her mouth but has a stiff neck. A large fluctuant mass is palpated in the posterior pharynx. The patient is also mildly tachypneic with stridor on auscultation. What is the treatment of choice?

This patient has history and physical of retropharyngeal abscess. These abscesses are most common in young children and are thought to be secondary to suppurative adenitis of retropharyngeal nodes. Causative organisms include aerobic, anaerobic, and gram-negative bacteria. Immediate intervention must be taken due to high-mortality complications such as airway obstruction, mediastinitis, aspiration pneumonia, epidural abscess. Treatment is with a broad-spectrum intravenous antibiotic covering anaerobic bacteria and incision and drainage under general anesthesia. A tracheostomy may be required if the airway is compromised.

Why must vigorous examination of this child's neck be avoided?

Vigorous palpation should be avoided because the abscess may rupture into the upper airway.

A 3-year-old un-immunized boy presents to the emergency room with a 1-hour history of drooling, fever, and dysphagia. As you approach the bedside, you see the ill-appearing boy is sitting up and gasping for air. A lateral neck x-ray at this point would show "thumb" sign and ballooning of hypopharynx. What is the appropriate first step in management of this patient?

The most important component of treatment of epiglottitis is securing the airway. Depending on the situation, tracheal intubation or tracheostomy is the next step. Epiglottitis, also termed supraglottitis, is an inflammation of the epiglottis and/or the supraglottic tissues surrounding the epiglottis. The clinical triad of drooling, dysphagia, and distress is the classic presentation.

What does the "thumb sign" on x-ray represent?

Radiographically, lateral neck radiographs may show an enlarged epiglottis protruding from the anterior wall of the hypopharynx called the "thumb sign."

What is the treatment for epiglottitis?

Treatment consists of IV antibiotic therapy and possible drainage of an epiglottic abscess, if present.

Why could vaccination have prevented this disease process?

Haemophilus influenzae type b (a constituent of the childhood vaccination schedule given in first 2 years of life) causes more than 90% of supraglottitis involving the epiglottis. Other *Staphylococcus* and *Streptococcus* organisms and parainfluenza are also reported to cause epiglottitis, but occurrences are rare.

A 2-year-old boy presents to the pediatrician with 2 days of coryza, congestion, and hoarse voice. Now the patient has developed a seal-like cough. On examination the patient has good air entry but inspiratory stridor upon agitation. What would be the most likely radiologic finding on the anterior-posterior x-ray of the neck?

The posterior-anterior chest radiograph classically reveals a steeple sign, which signifies subglottic narrowing in acute laryngotracheitis or croup. Croup is the most common etiology for stridor in febrile children.

What is the etiology of croup?

The etiology is most commonly parainfluenza, influenza, respiratory syncytial virus, or adenovirus. Treatment consists of supportive therapy and inhaled/oral steroids.

If the patient develops bacterial tracheitis, how does the treatment differ?

Bacterial tracheitis involves a superimposed bacterial infection of the trachea and presents with a more toxic clinical picture. Treatment includes IV antibiotic therapy and possible bronchoscopic debridement of suppurative tracheal secretions.

A 10-year-old boy presents to his pediatrician in April complaining of several weeks of nasal congestion, sneezing, runny nose, and itchy eyes and throat. Physical examination reveals a well-developed, well-nourished boy who frequently wrinkles his nose, with swollen, pale, boggy nasal mucosa, and dark circles under the eyes. What is the most likely diagnosis?

This presentation strongly suggests seasonal allergic rhinitis. Allergic rhinitis is the most common allergic disease, presenting in early childhood or the teenage years, and is often found together with atopic dermatitis and asthma. This combination is known as the allergic triad. Patients may present with any of the above symptoms, including "allergic shiners" (dark infraorbital circles) and "rabbit nose" (frequent nose wrinkling due to pruritus). Smears of nasal secretions will predominantly show eosinophils.

What is the most appropriate next step in the management of allergic rhinitis?

Management may include skin reactivity testing, antihistamine, and decongestant therapy. Treatment centers on avoidance of triggers (including pollen, grass, animals, or dust mites), antihistamines and decongestants, or anti-inflammatory medications such as topical steroids.

An 11-year-old boy presents in August to his pediatrician with ear pain for several days. Examination shows a healthy-appearing male with periauricular lymphadenopathy. He is very resistant to an ear examination, complaining of pain when his right pinna is moved. His right ear canal is erythematous and edematous, with whitish exudate in the canal. His tympanic membranes are pearly and mobile. What is the diagnosis?

This patient has otitis externa, an inflammation of the external auditory canal and auricle. It can be precipitated by trauma (cleaning with cotton swabs), high humidity, or abnormally wet or dry ears (frequent swimming or dermatitis), all of which may compromise the ear's defenses and allow the introduction of bacteria. Swimming in chlorinated pools is most likely etiology because the chlorinated water changes the acidic profile of external canal.

What bacteria usually cause these findings?

Otitis externa is most commonly caused by *Pseudomonas* or *S aureus*.

How should this patient be managed?

Otitis externa can be treated with eardrops that contain neomycin, polymyxin B, and hydrocortisone. Recurrences can be prevented by returning the canal to its normal acidity with a mixture of water and vinegar or by sterilizing canal with alcohol.

A 6-year-old girl presents with several days of left ear pain, fever, and decreased appetite. On examination, she is irritable and has an opaque, erythematous left tympanic membrane, as well as a red, swollen area behind her left ear. The pinna appears to be protruding forward as compared to her right ear. What is the diagnosis?

Mastoiditis, a complication of acute otitis media, is an inflammation of the mastoid cells. It may simply involve the mastoid cells, or progress to include periosteitis or acute mastoid osteitis, which destroys the mastoid cells and creates an empyema or subperiosteal abscess.

What is the appropriate treatment for this process?

Treatment of acute mastoiditis includes IV antibiotics and, depending on the extent of the infection, possibly myringotomy tube placement or mastoidectomy. If it involves only the mastoid cells, it usually resolves after treatment of the otitis media. Acute mastoiditis with periosteitis requires IV antibiotics and myringotomy tube placement. Acute mastoid osteitis requires IV antibiotics and may require mastoidectomy as well. Subperiosteal abscesses require surgical drainage. Chronic mastoiditis should be treated with antibiotics and may need mastoidectomy to treat osteitis if it has occurred.

A 15-year-old adolescent girl presents to the doctor complaining of frontal headache, postnasal drip, and cough for almost 2 weeks. On examination, she has purulent nasal discharge and swollen nasal mucosa, tenderness to palpation over her forehead and maxillary area, and opacity on transillumination of the left maxillary area. What is her diagnosis?

Sinusitis. Symptoms of sinusitis include persistent nasal congestion, clear or purulent nasal discharge, cough, and halitosis. Facial pain or pressure is common in older children and adults. Headache is an uncommon symptom in sinusitis. Symptoms that persist for more than 10 days help to differentiate sinusitis from a common cold, which would likely improve in 7 to 10 days.

How might sinusitis present differently in older and younger children?

Facial pain and pressure, although common in adults, may not be seen in younger children. On examination, tenderness to palpation over the sinuses may be observed in older children, but it is less common in younger ones. Transillumination of the maxillary sinuses may be useful as a diagnostic test in children over 10 years old. Young children may present with nonspecific signs and symptoms, such as an upper respiratory infection that lasts over 10 days or is accompanied by fever.

How should sinusitis be treated?

Sinusitis can be treated initially with antibiotics like amoxicillin-clavulanate or a broad-spectrum cephalosporin for 14 to 21 days. Children with chronic rhinosinusitis may benefit from topical steroid sprays and/or nasal saline rinses. Adenoidectomy may also provide some benefit in eradicating the nidus for many of these infections.

ANATOMIC PROBLEMS

An 18-month-old boy presents with tachypnea to the emergency room. The parents report that he had a coughing spell while he was playing with toys a few minutes before the onset of tachypnea. On examination the patient is noted to be tachypneic and wheezing is appreciated in the right lung field. What is the most likely treatment to relieve the symptoms?

Endoscopic removal of the foreign body in the right main stem bronchus is likely to improve the symptoms. The patient has right-sided wheezing and a history consistent with a small toy stuck in the right stem bronchus. Radiographically, obstructive emphysema involving the lung segment is the hallmark of a foreign body partially occluding the airway.

A 4-year-old girl is having her first nosebleed and her parents call the pediatricians office asking how to handle the bleed. What do you say?

Stable patients should be instructed to grasp and pinch their entire nose, maintaining continuous pressure for at least 10 minutes. The parents should do this with the girl's head tilted forward. You can also apply cold compresses to her nose. Bleeding for greater than 20 minutes or changes in the hemodynamic state needs medical attention.

What is included in the workup for the child who has frequent nosebleeds for extended periods of time?

Recurrent nosebleeds as the first symptom for a bleeding disorder are rare but if suspected obtain a complete blood count, bleeding time, and clotting factors. For children remember to investigate recurrent trauma and chemical irritants. Juvenile nasopharyngeal angiofibroma can also be seen in teenage boys, and suspicion warrants investigation with CT scan and/or magnetic resonance imaging (MRI).

An overweight 9-year-old boy presents to pediatrician with worsening school performance. Upon further questioning of patient and teachers it appears patient is falling asleep often in class. His mother states he sleeps for 10 hours at night but his snoring is heard throughout the house and he is often heard gasping in the middle of his sleep. What study would support the presumptive diagnosis?

Polysomnography is the study of choice in obstructive sleep apnea (OSA), although it is difficult to obtain in children and may not be cost-effective. OSA is usually seen in childhood between 3 and 10 years of age. The children are usually discovered to have trouble staying awake during the day. Parents may report that the child wakes frequently or falls out of bed, nighttime enuresis, and behavioral problems. Many of these children benefit from adenotonsillectomy.

CLINICAL VIGNETTES

A 3-year-old girl presents to the pediatrician with ear pain and fever of 101°F for several days. On examination, she is irritable and crying, and frequently tugs on her left ear. Both tympanic membranes appear erythematous, and the left appears opaque and bulging, with decreased mobility on pneumatic otoscopy. What three organisms are the most common bacterial causes of this condition?

Although acute otitis media may also be caused by respiratory viruses, *S pneumoniae*, *H influenzae*, and *Moraxella catarrhalis* are the three most common bacteria involved. On physical examination, pneumatic otoscopy showing decreased tympanic membrane mobility is the gold standard for diagnosis, since a crying child's tympanic membranes may appear red with or without infection.

Why are children so susceptible to otitis media?

Children are particularly susceptible to otitis media because of the anatomy of their eustachian tubes, which are shorter, run more horizontally, and have lower tone than those of adults. This anatomic configuration predisposes to dysfunction and also provides a route for nasopharyngeal bacteria to enter the middle ear space. Furthermore, children frequently have adenoid hypertrophy which causes further eustachian tube dysfunction. An immature immune system also plays a role in susceptibility.

The above 3-year-old is brought to the pediatrician again by her father because of a cold that has recently worsened. She also has a decreased appetite and a new discharge from her right ear. On examination, she is irritable and febrile to 101.5°F. Her right ear canal shows a yellowish exudate, and her tympanic membrane appears perforated. What is the treatment of choice?

Acute otitis media may be treated empirically with antibiotics. The first-line treatment remains 7 to 10 days of amoxicillin, although an increase in penicillin-resistant *S pneumoniae* has been documented. Antibiotics should be chosen with local resistance patterns in mind. In this situation with a non-intact tympanic membrane, topical antibiotics may be of added benefit to oral therapy. Antibiotic use seems to be associated with a decrease in complications, although antibiotics are not routinely prescribed for otitis media in all nations. The efficacy of a "no-treatment" approach has not yet been fully explored.

Five days into her course of antibiotics, the same 3-year-old girl is brought back to the pediatrician with no improvement. Should you make any changes in her care?

Otitis media symptoms should improve within 2 to 3 days of starting antibiotics. If first-line therapy fails, consider the possibility of a penicillin-resistant organism, and think about starting a second-line drug such as amoxicillin-clavulanate, erythromycin/sulfa drugs, or a cephalosporin.

What are some risk factors for recurrent otitis media?

Males, children in day care, those with a family history of recurrent ear infections, lack of breast feeding, and children exposed to cigarette smoke are particularly susceptible to recurrent infections.

The above patient presents to the pediatrician again, now with her fourth episode of ear pain in the past 6 months. The last three episodes were diagnosed as otitis media and treated with antibiotics, with complete resolution of symptoms. Today, the examination shows an opaque right tympanic membrane with decreased mobility. The girl's parents ask if there are treatment options that might help limit her frequent infections. What do you tell them?

This patient has recurrent otitis media, which is defined as three or four separate infections in 6 months, or six separate episodes within a year. This patient may benefit from the use of myringotomy tubes, which maintain a hole in the tympanic membrane, allowing middle ear fluid to drain without the use of the obstructed eustachian tubes. The tube also functions as an equilibrator of pressure between the middle ear and canal. It takes an average of 12 months for myringotomy tubes to fall out spontaneously, and they may need to be reinserted in some children. Adenoidectomy is recommended for children requiring a second set of myringotomy tubes.

The pediatrician's next patient of the day is a 2-year-old with Down syndrome. Is this child more susceptible to otitis media than other children?

Yes. Children with Down syndrome often suffer from chronic and recurrent otitis media. Up to 60% of children with Down syndrome suffer from this problem leading to a hearing disorder. The most common etiology for these children is eustachian tube dysfunction.

CHAPTER 19

Psychiatry

DEVELOPMENTAL PSYCHOLOGY

The parents of an 18-month-old boy want to know when to initiate toilet training with their son. In what ways can a child demonstrate readiness for toilet training?

A child's readiness for toilet training is determined by a number of factors including gender, physiologic and developmental status, cultural and behavioral expectations, and social stressors. Physiologically, the child must have voluntary control over the sphincter muscles and demonstrate more than 2 hours of remaining dry. Developmentally, he needs the motor skills required for pulling pants up and down and sitting on a toilet. Also, he must be able to follow directions, interpret his body's urges, and have a desire to remain dry.

What is the average age that children are able to achieve toilet training?

In the United States, the average age of achieving toilet training is around 37 months, with girls reaching this milestone 3 to 4 months ahead of boys. African-American ethnicity and lower socioeconomic status also tend to predispose to earlier toilet training. Factors that prolong toilet training readiness include stressors such as divorce, new sibling, death in the family, and moving.

A mother asks at what age would you consider lack of daytime bladder control to be a medical problem requiring intervention.

Enuresis, or involuntary urinary incontinence, is further classified as daytime wetting (daytime incontinence) and nighttime wetting (nocturnal enuresis). For daytime incontinence, since most children achieve daytime control prior to starting school, a child over the age of 5 should be evaluated. However, the prevalence of daytime incontinence at age 7 is still 2% to 3% in boys and 3% to 4% in girls.

The mother of an 8-year-old girl comes to you because her daughter still wets the bed at night. She wants to know if this is still normal for her age.

Primary nocturnal enuresis (PNE) is defined as persistent nighttime wetting in a child who has never achieved dryness previously. At age 7, 10% to 15% of children still wet the bed at night. With each subsequent year, 15% of these cases resolve. Therefore, 99% of children at age 15 are dry during the night. Many factors contribute to PNE including genetics, sleeping patterns, bladder dynamics, abnormal release of antidiuretic hormone (ADH), psychosocial stressors, and developmental delay.

A mother then asks if there are treatment options available to help her daughter achieve nighttime continence.

Treatment for PNE include both behavioral modification and pharmacotherapy. Parents should avoid blaming the child and work with their physician to identify the cause of enuresis. Avoidance of fluid intake after 6 PM or at least 2 hours before bedtime is the first step. As well, voiding prior to going to sleep is essential.

If enuresis continues despite these changes, the most effective treatment for curing PNE is a bed wetting alarm. Advantages include high success rate with no adverse effects. However, it does require significant parental involvement.

Pharmacotherapy options include desmopressin, anticholinergics, and tricyclic antidepressants. These therapies help treat, rather than cure, PNE and depend on the child to naturally grow out of incontinence. Adverse side effects can be serious and life-threatening. Therefore, parents should be notified of these risks, and what signs to look for, prior to initiating therapy.

A 7-year-old boy has had episodes of fecal soiling in his underpants twice each month for 5 months. His parents want to know why he is having these accidents.

The most common cause of encopresis is functional and is related to withholding stool. This pattern of behavior can arise from a painful stooling experience, association of punishment with toilet training, or irrational fears such as falling into the toilet. Other common etiologies include oppositional behaviors, anxiety regarding place of defecation, or psychosocial stressors leading to regression or attention-seeking behaviors.

Although organic causes are less common, anatomic, neurologic, and endocrinologic factors should be considered.

The mother of an 18-month-old boy describes events in which her son starts crying, holds his breath during expiration, and then briefly loses consciousness. She is concerned that he may suffer brain damage or even die if these episodes continue. What is the appropriate response?

This child is having breath-holding spells, which involve breath holding following a crying episode and are associated with color change, limpness, and collapse. They often occur in response to a strong emotional or physical stimulus. The episodes typically last less than 1 minute and then the child promptly returns to baseline. These behaviors are common in young children, peaking at around age 2 to 3 years, and are sometimes seen in infants as well. Most children grow out of breath-holding spells by age 5.

This mother needs reassurance that these episodes are generally benign and self-limited, and need no intervention. The child will start breathing on his own, and will not suffer brain damage or die from lack of oxygen. Breath-holding spells can be associated with iron deficiency anemia and this may need to be investigated by the child's physician.

What are the two types of breath-holding spells?

Breath-holding spells are classified as either cyanotic or pallid spells. Cyanotic spells are ones in which the child cries, holds breath, and turns blue prior to the loss of consciousness. Pallid spells are very rare, are often associated with painful events, and are thought to be due to increased vagal tone. In these cases, the child typically gasps, breath holds, and then turns pale prior to losing consciousness.

A 3-year-old boy is brought to the pediatrician by his mother, who complains that his temper tantrums are getting worse despite her attempts to give him whatever he wants when he becomes upset. What should this mother do to decrease the temper tantrums?

Temper tantrums are common in a developing child, and often occur when children become frustrated while trying to master new skills. The parent should consider the precipitants and avoid or address them if possible. For example, the child may become upset because he is actually tired or hungry. The best advice for the parents is to focus on consistency and not giving in because of a tantrum.

When does separation anxiety become abnormal?

Developmentally appropriate separation anxiety is expected and normal starting at around 10 months and extending into preschool age. However, when anxiety related to separation becomes extreme or persists into school age, a diagnosis of separation anxiety disorder should be considered.

What are the diagnostic criteria for separation anxiety disorder?

The diagnostic criteria include three or more of the following for at least 4 weeks:

Recurrent excessive distress when separation from home or major attachment figures occurs or is anticipated

Persistent and excessive worry about losing, or about possible harm befalling, major attachment figures

Persistent and excessive worry that an untoward event will lead to separation from a major attachment figure (eg, getting lost or being kidnapped)

Persistent reluctance or refusal to go to school or elsewhere because of fearing separation

Persistent and excessive fear or reluctance to be alone or without major attachment figures at home or without significant adults in other settings

Persistent reluctance or refusal to go to sleep without being near a major attachment figure or to sleep away from home

Repeated nightmares involving the theme of separation

Repeat complaints of physical symptoms (such as headaches, stomachaches, nausea, or vomiting) when separation from major attachment figures occurs or is anticipated

A second grader who is developing normally begins to become anxious and complains of a stomach pain or headache every day prior to school. These symptoms resolve almost immediately after her mother agrees to keep her at home. On the days when she is forced to go to school she does fairly well, but the next morning she again complains of physical symptoms. How can this behavior be changed?

A phobia is a type of anxiety disorder and is characterized by excessive worry or anxiety that occurs more days than not for a period of at least 6 months and are associated with physical symptoms. These can be further classified by the specific anxiety. In this case, it is important to determine the underlying fear that has resulted in this child's school avoidance (ie, separation anxiety, fear of crowded areas, social anxiety, etc). Relaxation techniques and not allowing the child to avoid the fearful stimulus are important first steps. However, when phobias affect normal functioning or do not remit with basic behavioral interventions, referral to a mental health specialist is warranted.

An 8-year-old boy who survived a car accident, in which his father was killed, is brought in by his mother. She tells you that although the accident happened 3 months ago, he still seems withdrawn. He is having trouble sleeping and has started to wet the bed. As well, he throws a fit every time they get in a vehicle, and he has thrown away all of his toy cars. What is the most likely diagnosis?

This child is suffering from posttraumatic stress disorder (PTSD). PTSD results from a child's exposure to a traumatic event. Children with PTSD often have recurrent nightmares, act or feel as if the event is recurring, and have intense psychological stress when exposed to something that reminds them of the event and thus develop avoidance of these cues.

What is the most appropriate treatment for PTSD?

He should be referred to a mental health specialist and cognitive behavioral therapy should be initiated. Combined parent-child sessions are often helpful in the recovery of this disorder.

An 8-year-old boy frequently makes barking sounds and sometimes repeats phrases over and over again. His parents also report he jerks his head frequently when he is frustrated. The boy is very embarrassed by these behaviors. Could this patient have Tourette syndrome?

Tics are classified as either motor tics or vocal tics. A tic can be simple (such as eye blinking, opening the mouth, barking, or clearing the throat) or complex (head shaking, imitative speech). Tics are considered transient if they last for 1 to 12 months. Tics that last for a period of greater than 12 months are considered chronic. The diagnosis of Tourette syndrome requires both motor and vocal tics that are chronic.

How does Munchausen syndrome differ from malingering?

Munchausen syndrome involves a conscious production or feigning of symptoms in order to play the sick role. The gain is primary and the reason behind the disorder is an unconscious desire to seek attention. Malingering is done consciously for secondary gain, such as missing school or family functions.

Is Munchausen by proxy considered a form of child abuse?

Yes. This syndrome, which is now often referred to as factitious disorder by proxy, is characterized by a caregiver who intentionally fabricates or produces symptoms in a child in order to get medical attention. When separated from this caregiver, the acute signs or symptoms of the child's illness disappear.

A 6-year-old girl will speak freely at home, but in school she refuses to speak if called on by the teacher. Her best friend will often speak for her. What is the diagnosis?

This child has selective mutism. Behavioral therapy and psychotherapy may be required to empower her to speak in school.

ADOLESCENT AND ADULT PSYCHOLOGY

A 14-year-old adolescent girl who comes to her yearly doctor's appointment is having difficulty concentrating, irritability, and diminished interest in her usual activities for the past 2 months. She denies thoughts of suicide or wanting to harm herself. What is the likely diagnosis?

The patient is likely suffering from depression. Depression can interfere with normal growth and development and impair one's ability to function in daily activities. Because depression is a significant risk factor for suicide, it is important to always ask a depressed patient about risk of harm to self or others. Depression affects 3% to 8% of adolescents, and is three times more likely in girls than in boys. Depression manifests in a variety of physical and behavioral changes, and also varies in severity and duration.

What are the typical treatments for adolescent depression?

Three types of modalities are used to treat adolescent depression. Pharmacotherapy with antidepressant medication alone or in conjunction with psychotherapy, cognitive behavioral therapy, and interpersonal therapy have all been shown to decrease depressive symptoms in teens. Treatment choice should be based on the individual and the resources available.

A 16-year-old adolescent boy is brought into the emergency room after being found holding a gun to his head. He tells you that his girlfriend broke up with him and he no longer wants to live. What are the risk factors for suicide in adolescents?

Suicide is the third leading cause of death in adolescents. Certain factors have been shown to increase risk of suicide in adolescents: mood and anxiety disorders, death of a loved one, family discord, social isolation, family history of suicidal behavior, previous suicide attempt, availability of firearms, and substance abuse.

The mother of an 18-year-old man reports that she is very worried about him. He was a normal adolescent boy up until 6 months ago when he began to withdraw from sports and social activities. He has become increasingly angry and she has even witnessed him speaking to people who were not there. She found articles that he had printed about mind control and government implantation of microchips. She wants to know what is wrong with her son.

Schizophrenia is a severe and debilitating psychiatric disorder characterized by disturbances in thoughts, mood, perceptions, and relationships. It is frequently accompanied by hallucinations and delusions. The onset of the disorder is usually in late adolescence. The cause of schizophrenia is not known, but is thought to have both genetic and perinatal risk factors.

The parents of a 14-year-old adolescent girl bring her in for evaluation for depression. They report that she has been extremely moody and irritable lately. Further questioning reveals that last month she was quite happy and active. However, her parents did notice that she did not sleep much, completely rearranged her room, and got in trouble for using her parents' credit card during a shopping spree at the mall. What disease should you be most concerned about?

This child is exhibiting features of bipolar disorder. Bipolar disorder is a mood disorder in which periods of mania are followed by periods of dysphoria or depression. Manic episodes last for greater than 1 week and often include expansive mood, decreased need for sleep, racing thoughts, increased goal-directed activities, and sometimes reckless and delusional behavior.

What is the main difference between anorexia nervosa and bulimia nervosa?

The diagnostic criterion for anorexia nervosa includes the refusal to maintain normal body weight, a disturbed body image, and a fear of gaining weight. There are two subtypes of anorexia nervosa: binge eating/purging and restricting.

Bulimia nervosa is characterized by self-evaluation unduly influenced by weight and binging behavior along with compensatory behaviors in order to avoid weight gain. Bulimia nervosa is divided into purging and non-purging subtypes.

An 18-year-old woman is brought to the doctor by her mother, who is concerned by her daughter's drastic weight loss. The mother reports that she has heard her daughter vomit after meals and found laxatives in her bedroom. The daughter's body mass index (BMI) is 16. What is the appropriate diagnosis?

This patient has anorexia nervosa, binge-eating/purging type. Although binging and purging are commonly thought of as defining characteristics of bulimia, this patient's BMI classifies her as underweight, which is more consistent with this subtype of anorexia. The Centers for Disease Control and Prevention (CDC) provide BMI classifications by age and gender.

In anorexia nervosa, restricting type, the weight loss is primarily through dieting, fasting, or excessive exercise.

A 17-year-old adolescent girl presents with sudden loss of vision. However, on examination she reacts to visual stimuli. Past history reveals that she was sexually assaulted 3 months ago. What disorder is she likely suffering from?

She has a conversion disorder, which is type of somatoform disorder that typically develops after a traumatic event and has no medical explanation. Conversion disorders are usually self-limited but in most cases, counseling should be provided.

What is the difference between a somatization disorder and hypochondriasis?

Somatization disorders involve experiencing or communicating symptoms that do not correlate with actual medical pathology, such as the patient described with the conversion disorder. Hypochondriasis is a type of somatization in which the patient is preoccupied with having a serious disease, and thus misinterprets normal physiology. Both are somatoform disorders.

What are the three types of attention deficit/hyperactivity disorder (ADHD)?

ADHD is one of the most common behavioral disorders of childhood. It is characterized by a persistent pattern of inattention and/or hyperactivity-impulsivity. The three subtypes are predominantly inattentive, predominantly hyperactive/impulsive, or combined type.

A 14-year-old adolescent boy was diagnosed with ADHD at age 7. How does ADHD in adolescents differ from that in young children?

In adolescence, hyperactivity is usually less of an issue, whereas difficulty with attention and focus become more apparent. This can lead to poor motivation and delinquent activities, and can create social difficulties. Many adolescents who were not diagnosed at a younger age can be difficult to diagnose in adolescence, because the symptoms may be confused with "normal adolescence."

Why is it important to recognize ADHD in an adolescent?

Adolescents tend to respond well to pharmacologic and behavior therapy. When missed, the adolescent can become an underachiever, and is more likely to engage in risky behavior.

What is the treatment for ADHD?

Stimulants are considered the first-line therapy for treatment of ADHD and treatment should be undertaken after clearly establishing the diagnosis. Second-line therapy includes non-stimulants and other medications that are not FDA-approved for treatment of ADHD (antidepressants and alpha-2-adrenergic agonists). Behavior therapy is used when symptoms are mild, or when medication therapy is undesired or inappropriate.

A father presents to your office with his 11-year-old son. He is concerned because his son's teachers report that he is constantly argumentative and refuses to follow the rules. Father also reports that his son always seems angry and spiteful at home. What disorder may this child be at risk for in the future?

Although a thorough history and investigation of social stressors is warranted, this child most likely has oppositional defiant disorder (ODD). ODD is a pattern of disobedient, hostile, and defiant behavior directed toward authority figures lasting for greater than 6 months and leading to significant impairment in normal age-related activities. It is more common in males and associated with other comorbid behavioral disorders like ADHD and anxiety. Children with ODD are at increased risk of developing a conduct disorder later in life.

How does ODD differ from conduct disorder?

ODD does not typically encompass actions that violate the rights of others. In conduct disorder, the child often commits acts of aggression toward people and animals, destroys property, or other serious violation of rules and laws.

A 16-year-old adolescent girl is known as a "perfectionist" by her classmates at school. However, she is often frustrated that she is unable to complete her list of things to do because she becomes so preoccupied with certain aspects of each task that it consumes all of her time. She has recently gotten into the habit of locking and unlocking the door of her bedroom five times every night before she goes to sleep. What disorder is she suffering from and what are her treatment options?

This young woman likely has obsessive compulsive disorder (OCD). OCD is a type of anxiety disorder characterized by unwanted thoughts (obsessions) and the need to repeat certain behaviors (compulsions) over and over. Treatment includes behavioral therapy as well as antidepressants such as selective serotonin reuptake inhibitors (SSRIs).

AUTISTIC SPECTRUM DISORDERS

A child presents for his 15-month-old visit and you notice he does not make eye contact with you. Mother says he has not spoken his first word yet and she has never seen him point to an object. She is concerned he may be deaf, as he rarely turns his head when she speaks to him. He does not like to be hugged, but does enjoy repetitively spinning the wheels on his toy truck. Hearing test results come back normal. What is the most likely diagnosis?

This child likely has autism. He is displaying signs of impaired social skills and communication, as well as stereotyped, repetitive behaviors.

Mother asks what type of treatment is available to cure her son?

Although there is no cure for autism, early initiation of behavioral and developmental therapies have been shown to improve outcomes and increase an autistic child's ability to become an independent adult.

The parents of this child are hoping to have more children. What should you tell them about their risk of having another child with autism?

Parents of a child with an autism spectrum disorder should be counseled that there is a 10 times increased risk that subsequent siblings will also have an autism spectrum disorder.

How does Asperger syndrome differ from autism?

Asperger syndrome is also a developmental disorder that involves many of the same deficits in social skills. However, patients with Asperger syndrome are typically diagnosed at a later age, are more high functioning and do not have the same language or cognitive impairment.

A new female patient presents for an 18-month-old well-child appointment. Mother reports that she was a normal infant, but that she seems to have started to forget how to do certain skills over the past couple of months. You observe that the child is constantly wringing her hands. She is hypotonic on examination and is not interested in play activities and does not meet the age-appropriate requirements on her Denver assessment for motor skills. What disorder should you consider?

A female child who starts to have developmental regression, loss of language and social skills, and is demonstrating stereotyped hand movements most likely has Rett syndrome. Rett syndrome is an X-linked dominant neurodegenerative disorder characterized by normal psychomotor development in the first 5 months of life, followed by deceleration of head growth, developmental regression, and eventual psychomotor retardation. The specific defect appears to be a mutation in the methyl-CpG-binding protein 2 or so-called "*MeCP2*" gene.

What is the expected course of Rett syndrome?

There are four stages of Rett syndrome that are described. In the first stage, vague symptoms including loss of interest in toys and decreased eye contact are noted. Children with Rett syndrome in stage 2 typically start a period of global regression usually between 1 and 4 years of age. During stage 3, known as the pseudostationary phase, some motor skills and behavior may improve although oral motor function declines and seizures are frequently noted. After the age of 10, stage 4 is described as a second period of decline with additional loss of motor skills.

CLINICAL VIGNETTES

A 13-year-old adolescent girl tells her pediatrician that she does not take any "hard drugs" but that she and her friends often sniff things such as spray paint cans and glue. She states that she thinks this is a safe way of getting high. What should the pediatrician make her aware of?

Huffing, or inhaling volatile solvents, is one of the most serious and most common forms of illicit substance use in teens. Careful questioning is warranted, as detection is difficult due to the rapid disappearance of the inhalant from the body. Huffing can induce hallucinations, anoxia, and sudden sniffing death syndrome, which is thought to be caused by ventricular fibrillation.

What are the most commonly abused substances among teenagers?

Alcohol is the most commonly abused substance in adolescents. As well, marijuana is the most common illicit drug of abuse. Substance abuse increases the risk of motor vehicle crashes, suicide, and homicide in teenagers. Screening for these high-risk behaviors is essential during an adolescent health examination.

What is the CAGE mnemonic?

The CAGE mnemonic is helpful in screening for alcohol or substance abuse. The practitioner should ask if the patient has ever had the following symptoms:

Felt the need to "Cut back" on the use of alcohol or substances?

Felt Annoyed when others mention their use?

Felt Guilty about things they have said or done while using?

Had a drink or used drugs in the morning to get started or treat a hangover (the so-called Eye opener)?

If any of these questions elicit positive responses, the practitioner should delve into a more detailed assessment of the substance use.

CHAPTER 20

Pediatric Emergencies and Trauma

INITIAL EVALUATION AND TRIAGE

What are the five components of the primary survey?

The primary survey is the initial assessment of life-threatening conditions when a patient enters the emergency department (ED). The five components are:

1. Airway
2. Breathing
3. Circulation
4. Disability
5. Exposure

After the airway, breathing, and circulation of a patient are surveyed and established, what assessments are made of *disability* and *exposure*?

Assessing disability involves performing a rapid neurological examination, focusing on basic findings such as level of consciousness and pupillary response. Exposure refers to completely undressing the patient and exposing the body to observe for injury.

What does the Glasgow Coma Scale (GCS) assess?

The GCS is a 15-point scale used to assess a patient's state of responsiveness according to three categories: eye opening, motor, and verbal responses. (See Table 20-1.) A modified version is used for infants and children less than 5 years old.

What is a normal GCS score?

A normal, healthy individual has a GCS of 15. The lowest score is 3.

Table 20-1 Glasgow Coma Scale

Response	Adults and Children	Infants	Score
Eye Opening	No response	No response	1
	To pain only	To pain only	2
	To voice	To voice	3
	Spontaneous	Spontaneous	4
Verbal Response	None	None	1
	Incomprehensible sounds	Moans to pain	2
	Inappropriate words	Cries to pain	3
	Confused	Irritable cries	4
	Oriented, appropriate	Coos and babbles	5
Motor Response	None	None	1
	Extension to pain (decerebrate posturing)	Abnormal extension posture	2
	Flexion to pain (decorticate posturing)	Abnormal flexion posture	3
	Withdraws to pain	Withdraws to pain	4
	Localizes pain	Withdraws to tough	5
	Obeys commands	Normal spontaneous movement	6

Below what GCS score is indicative of severe brain injury?

A score of 8 or less suggests severe brain injury.

AIRWAY MANAGEMENT

An 8-year-old girl is wheeled into the emergency room (ER) after suffering head injuries. She is having difficulty breathing and is vomiting upon arrival. What is the first step in management?

Addressing the ABCs always comes first. The patient's airway must be secured. The oropharynx should be suctioned, and the airway should be opened with a chin-lift or jaw-thrust. FiO_2 (100%) can then be administered with a facemask, and if necessary an advanced airway can be placed.

The 8-year-old patient does not have adequate chest wall excursion despite her secure airway. What size endotracheal tube (ETT) should be placed?

The size of an uncuffed ETT is calculated as:

(age in years/4) + 4

Using this equation, the correct ETT size in this patient is 6.

How does one confirm successful ETT placement in the trachea?

End-tidal CO_2 determination is the most accurate way to confirm ETT placement. Clinical indicators such as visualization of the ETT passing through the vocal cords, misting of the tube with ventilation, and auscultation of breath sounds in bilateral lung fields may also be used.

HEMODYNAMIC INSTABILITY

What is a more sensitive assessment of circulation in a child: blood pressure or heart rate?

An elevated heart rate in a child is a much more sensitive indicator of depleted intravascular volume than blood pressure.

A 5-year-old child who has suffered significant blood loss enters the ED and has a very weak femoral pulse. The child was intubated in the field and a secure airway was verified upon arrival. What is the next step in management?

Vascular access needs to be established and fluids given as the patient has had significant volume depletion. A bolus of 20 mL/kg of isotonic crystalloid (normal saline or lactated Ringer solution) should be administered as rapidly as possible, and then repeated as needed.

If a patient is being resuscitated and continues to require repeated fluid boluses, what additional fluids may be administered?

Type O-negative whole blood or albumin may be administered during resuscitation if a patient does not respond to boluses of normal saline or lactated Ringer.

If vascular access is difficult to establish via the peripheral veins and a critically ill patient needs fluids for resuscitation as soon as possible, how can fluid, blood products, and drugs be administered?

An intraosseous (IO) line can be placed in the anteromedial tibia. A needle is inserted 1 to 3 cm below the tibial tuberosity using manual pressure or a battery-powered handheld drill. Fluids, medications, and blood products can then be infused safely using this route.

What are the three stages of shock?

1. **Compensated shock** occurs when organ perfusion is maintained via homeostatic mechanisms. Heart rate is increased, while blood pressure remains in the normal range.
2. **Hypotensive (uncompensated) shock** occurs when these homeostatic mechanisms are overwhelmed. Signs and symptoms of multiorgan system dysfunction appear.
3. **Irreversible shock** is the stage in which continued hypoperfusion leads to irreparable organ damage and death.

Examples of different categories of shock are seen in Table 20-2.

Table 20-2 Characteristics of the Different Shock States

Type of Shock	Common Pediatric Causes	Preload	CO	SVR
Hypovolemic	Hemorrhage Vomiting/diarrhea Dehydration	↓	↓	↑
Cardiogenic	Congenital heart disease Arrhythmias Cardiac tamponade Cardiomyopathies Tension pneumothorax	↑	↓	↑
Distributive	Sepsis Anaphylaxis	↓	↑	↓

A 10-year-old boy is hit by a car while riding his bicycle and receives multiple lacerations and broken bones. When he arrives in the ER his blood pressure is decreased. What type of shock is this patient likely experiencing?

This patient is in hypovolemic shock due to blood loss. The cardiac output (CO) is a result of both heart rate (HR) and stroke volume (SV) (CO = HR × SV) and is decreased in the case of hypovolemia due to decreased venous return and preload. Systemic vascular resistance (SVR) subsequently increases in an attempt to shunt blood away from the periphery to the heart and brain.

An 18-year-old man with an allergy to tree nuts mistakenly ingests a chocolate-covered brazil nut and begins to break out in hives and have difficulty breathing. He is brought to the ED and is found to be hypotensive. What type of shock is this patient experiencing?

This patient has distributive shock due to an anaphylactic reaction to the tree nut. His systemic vascular resistance dropped and peripheral pooling of blood occurred, causing decreased preload and therefore decreased cardiac output. The relative hypovolemia causes hypotension.

A 4-year-old boy with pneumonia develops a high fever with warm extremities and tachycardia. His condition worsens as his extremities become cold and he becomes pale and diaphoretic. He is oliguric and goes in and out of consciousness. What type of shock is this and what are the next steps in management?

This patient likely has septic shock due to the spread of bacterial pathogens into his blood and subsequent release of inflammatory cytokines. His initial warm sepsis evolved into cold sepsis as his shock went from compensated to uncompensated. After first assessing the ABCs, immediate treatment includes broad-spectrum IV antibiotics, fluid boluses, and vasopressors.

A cyanotic newborn has hypotension with poor stroke volume and cardiac output. She does not respond to oxygen administration. What type of shock does this patient most likely have?

This baby is in cardiogenic shock as a result of pump failure. This is likely due to congenital heart disease as indicated by her cyanotic presentation.

A 6-year-old patient enters the ED in supraventricular tachycardia (SVT). (See Fig. 20-1.) An IV is placed and oxygen is administered. What can be done to convert his heart back to sinus rhythm?

If the patient's vital signs are stable and the patient is awake and alert, vagal maneuvers may be performed first such as bearing down (Valsalva maneuver) and the application of ice to the face. If this does not convert the rhythm, 0.1 mg/kg of adenosine IV may be pushed followed by a rapid normal saline flush. The rhythm will need to be converted using synchronized cardioversion if the patient becomes hemodynamically unstable or has alterations in his mental status.

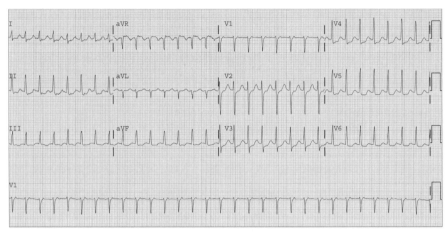

Figure 20-1 ECG tracing demonstrating supraventricular tachycardia. (Reproduced, with permission, from Knoop KJ, Stack LB, Storrow AS, et al. *Atlas of Emergency Medicine*. 3rd ed. New York: McGraw-Hill; 2010: Fig. 23.30A. Photo contributor: Lawrence B. Stack, MD.)

An infant is rushed to the ED with a heart rate of 55 and poor perfusion. ABCs are assessed and IV access is obtained. He is intubated and given oxygen, and cardiopulmonary resuscitation is begun. What medications should be administered if the patient continues to be bradycardic?

Epinephrine can be given every 3 to 5 minutes. Atropine may also be given to aid in the resuscitation.

A 10-year-old patient with known hypertrophic cardiomyopathy collapses at school while playing basketball and a carotid pulse is not palpated. What treatment gives him the best chance at survival?

Defibrillation with an automated external defibrillator (AED) as soon as possible gives this child the best chance of survival. Cardiopulmonary resuscitation with adequate chest compressions must be performed until the AED arrives.

What are some of the major causes of asystole, ventricular fibrillation, pulseless electrical activity (PEA), and ventricular tachycardia?

Use the Hs and Ts as a guide to evaluation:

Hypoxia	Trauma
Hypothermia	Cardiac Tamponade
Hyper/ Hypokalemia	Tension pneumothorax
Hypovolemia	
H$^+$ (acidosis)	Toxins
Hypoglycemia	Thrombosis (coronary or pulmonary)

TOXIC INGESTIONS AND EXPOSURES

A 2-year-old boy is being resuscitated in the ED and is suspected of ingesting a toxic substance. Which tests should be obtained in addition to a complete blood cell count (CBC), venous blood gas, and basic metabolic panel (BMP)?

In the case of any suspected toxic ingestion in children, acetaminophen and salicylate levels should be obtained, in addition to urine toxicology (see Table 20-3).

Table 20-3 Toxicology Reference

Drug	Signs and Symptoms	Antidote/Therapy
Acetaminophen	Nausea and vomiting, malaise, diaphoresis initially, possible progression to liver failure with encephalopathy, metabolic acidosis, coma	N-acetylcysteine
Anticholinergics (ie, atropine, antihistamines, jimson weed)	Dry skin, mydriasis, delirium, flushing, fever, sinus tachycardia, urinary retention	Physostigmine
Cholinesterase inhibitors (ie, organophosphates, insecticides)	Salivation, lacrimation, bradycardia, miosis, urination, defecation, vomiting, confusion, coma	Pralidoxime, atropine
Ethylene glycol	Metabolic acidosis, renal failure, hypocalcemia, cranial nerve abnormalities	Fomepizole, ethanol
Iron	Nausea, vomiting, abdominal pain, diarrhea, metabolic acidosis, GI bleeding, hepatic failure	Deferoxamine
Isoniazid	Seizures, severe metabolic acidosis, coma	Pyridoxine
Lead	Abdominal pain, vomiting, constipation, pallor (anemia), peripheral neuropathy, encephalopathy	Succimer, Dimercaprol (BAL), $CaNa_2EDTA$
Methanol	Disinhibition and ataxia, metabolic acidosis, visual impairment, damage to basal ganglia	Fomepizole, ethanol
Opiates	Respiratory depression, stupor, pinpoint pupils	Naloxone
Tricyclic antidepressants (TCAs)	Sinus tachycardia, QRS prolongation, ventricular tachycardia, seizures, delirium, disorientation, agitation, anticholinergic effects (see above)	Sodium bicarbonate

A 17-year-old adolescent boy with depression presents with diaphoresis, vomiting, and abdominal pain. He tells you that he took "a bunch of pills" about 5 hours ago. You send off the necessary laboratory values, and his acetaminophen level returns as 250 µg/mL. What is the next step in management?

Acetaminophen overdose can lead to significant liver damage and failure due to the metabolism to a hepatoxic metabolite, N-acetyl-p-benzoquinone imine (NAPQI). Administration of N-acetylcysteine for the next 72 hours is indicated, and prevents the formation of NAPQI. His liver function tests also need to be closely followed. (See Fig. 20-2.)

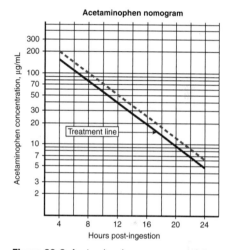

Figure 20-2 Acetaminophen nomogram plotting the threshold for treatment for acetaminophen toxicity based on acetaminophen levels and timing from ingestion. (Reproduced, with permission, from Nelson LS, Lewin NA, Howland MA, et al. *Goldfrank's Toxicologic Emergencies*. 9th ed. New York: McGraw-Hill; 2011: Fig. 34.2.)

If this patient had presented to the ED less than 2 hours after this ingestion, what additional treatment may have been provided?

Activated charcoal may also be given in awake and alert patients, and is ideally given within 1 to 2 hours after ingestion give the rapid absorption of acetaminophen from the gastrointestinal (GI) tract.

By what mechanism does activated charcoal act as a decontaminant?

Charcoal works by binding to harmful chemicals within the GI tract, thereby decreasing their absorption and increasing their elimination.

What substances are not bound by activated charcoal?

The alcohols, acids and alkalis, iron, lithium, magnesium, potassium, and sodium salts are all unable to be bound by activated charcoal.

When is syrup of ipecac contraindicated in a patient with a toxic ingestion?

The use of syrup of ipecac for decontamination is controversial. Its use is contraindicated in patients younger than 6 months, if hydrocarbons and caustic acids or bases were ingested, if the patient has a depressed mental status or gag reflex, or if repeated vomiting poses a health danger. The American Academy of Pediatrics (AAP) no longer recommends ipecac for home use.

A 2-year-old girl who was at her grandmother's house develops a fever, flushed and dry skin, dilated pupils, tachycardia, mydriasis, and seizures. Her grandmother reports taking an antidepressant. What is the appropriate treatment for this child?

This is likely TCA poisoning, which causes central nervous system and cardiac toxicity, as well as anticholinergic effects. Sodium bicarbonate should be administered to potentiate the effects the TCA may have on cardiac conduction.

An ECG should always be performed when a TCA overdose is suspected because of the known cardiac toxicity. What would you expect to see?

An ECG may show sinus tachycardia, a widened QRS complex, atrioventricular (AV) nodal block, and flattened T waves. Sinus tachycardia is the most common cardiac abnormality seen following TCA overdose.

A 3-year-old girl enters the ED with abdominal pain, anorexia, occasional vomiting, and constipation. The patient has a developmental delay and behavior problems in school. She lives in a housing project built in the 1940s and her lead level is found to be 65 µg/dL. What is the appropriate course of action?

This patient has lead poisoning and should be treated with chelating agents—oral succimer (DMSA) or IV EDTA (ethylenediamine tetraacetic acid). Most importantly, the child needs to be removed from the source of lead exposure.

A 3-year-old boy found some pills in his mother's purse and ate them thinking they were candy. He presents to the ED with tachypnea, vomiting, and mental status changes. Metabolic acidosis is found on an arterial blood gas. What did this child likely ingest? What should he be given?

These symptoms may be due to aspirin ingestion. Salicylate toxicity results in both a respiratory alkalosis and metabolic acidosis. Intravenous sodium bicarbonate can prevent salicylates from entering the brain and enhances excretion of salicylates in the urine. Hemodialysis may also be used.

A 10-year-old boy presents with convulsions, muscle fasciculations, weakness, respiratory distress, bradycardia, miosis, diaphoresis, and profound drooling after helping his father on the farm. What do you suspect as the cause of these symptoms?

The patient most likely has cholinergic poisoning secondary to organophosphates often found in pesticides. These pesticides can be ingested, inhaled, or absorbed through skin. They inhibit acetylcholinesterase, leading to high levels of acetylcholine.

How would you treat organophosphate poisoning?

After decontamination and supportive care, treatment consists of atropine, a competitive antagonist of acetylcholine at the muscarinic receptor, followed by pralidoxime, which acts to regenerate acetylcholinesterase.

A previously healthy 10-month-old infant is brought to the ED with blue lips and lethargy. She is teething, and her parents have been applying topical benzocaine to her gums. Her oxygen saturation is 86%. When her blood is drawn it appears chocolate brown. What is the cause of her cyanosis? What is the treatment?

Methemoglobinemia is the likely cause. The iron in hemoglobin (ferrous, Fe^{2+}) is oxidized to its ferric state (Fe^{3+}), which has a higher affinity for oxygen. In this case the responsible oxidant is the benzocaine. The oxyhemoglobin dissociation curve is shifted to the left, resulting in less oxygen delivery to the tissues. The blood should be sent for cooximetry, and the treatment is the administration of methylene blue.

On a snowy, February evening, a 9-year-old girl presents with headache, lightheadedness, and nausea for the past several days. Her mother and her older brother with whom she lives have also had similar symptoms recently. What should you suspect?

Carbon monoxide (CO) poisoning should be suspected based on her symptoms and the presence of symptoms in other household members. CO is formed when organic compounds are burned and is emitted by stoves, portable heaters, and automobiles, among other sources.

What is the treatment for carbon monoxide poisoning?

Treatment is 100% oxygen via a nonrebreathing facemask, or hyperbaric oxygen in more severe cases.

What is the pathophysiology of carbon monoxide poisoning? Why does increasing the amount of respired oxygen help?

CO has a 200 to 250 times greater affinity for hemoglobin than that of oxygen. It also shifts the oxyhemoglobin dissociation curve to the left. Administration of supplemental oxygen will increase the dissolved oxygen content of the blood and decrease the half-life of carboxyhemoglobin.

A 16-year-old adolescent boy is brought to the ED by emergency medical services (EMS), yelling that he feels as though ants are crawling on his skin. On examination he is noted to be tachycardic, hypertensive, and have mydriasis. What drugs of abuse would you suspect?

Intoxication with a sympathomimetic drug such as cocaine or amphetamines can cause these symptoms. Formication is the medical term for the sensation that insects are crawling on or under the skin.

An 18-year-old woman is brought to the ED by her friends. After smoking marijuana, she became agitated and combative, and now on examination is confused, has disorganized speech, and both vertical and horizontal nystagmus. The marijuana she smoked was likely laced with what drug?

Phencyclidine (PCP) intoxication will present in this manner. This patient was inadvertently exposed to PCP as it is often used as an additive to marijuana, lysergic acid diethylamide (LSD), and methamphetamine.

TRAUMA

An 18-lb, 8-month-old infant is involved in a motor vehicle accident. What position should his car seat have been in for ideal protection from injury?

Babies less than 1 year of age and less than 20 lb should be placed in a rear-facing car seat to prevent spinal injuries. The child may face forward in an appropriate car seat once he is over 20 lb and older than 1 year of age.

CLINICAL VIGNETTES

A 4-year-old boy accidentally falls onto a fire while camping with his family. He suffers severe burns on both his arms. The majority of the burns on his right arm are exquisitely painful. While some areas are erythematous, others are blistering. What degree burns does this patient have?

The erythematous, painful burns are superficial, first-degree burns that only affect the epidermis. The blistering, painful burn areas are likely second-degree burns (also known deep partial thickness burns) that affect the dermis but leave sensory nerves, hair follicles, and sweat glands intact.

The patient has third-degree burns on his left hand. How do these burns differ from the first- and second-degree burns on his right hand?

Third-degree burns (full-thickness burns) extend through the dermis and into the subcutaneous tissue, including the sensory nerve fibers. As a result, these burns are blistering but nontender. Fourth-degree burns are also nontender and involve muscle, bone, and/or connective tissue.

The burn patient is brought to the pediatric ED. How are intravenous fluids calculated in this case?

Fluid resuscitation in thermal injury is calculated using the Parkland formula:

percentage of body surface area burned (second- and third-degree burns only) × weight (kg) × 4 mL of lactated ringer (LR).

The first half of this total is given in the first 8 hours after the injury, and the second half is given during the next 16 hours.

What is the proper method to clean and manage the wounds?

Cold compresses may be placed on the wound initially. Analgesia should be provided and the wound should be gently cleansed with sterile water. Blisters should be debrided and silver sulfadiazine or bacitracin applied to prevent infection. Dressings may be applied to the wounds.

Index

Page numbers followed by *f* indicate figures; page numbers followed by *t* indicate tables.